Memoirs of a Middle-aged Hummingbird

Suellen Zima

iUniverse, Inc.
New York Lincoln Shanghai

Memoirs of a Middle-aged Hummingbird

iUniverse books may be ordered through booksellers or by contacting:

iUniverse
2021 Pine Lake Road, Suite 100
Lincoln, NE 68512
www.iuniverse.com
1-800-Authors (1-800-288-4677)

ISBN-13: 978-0-595-39460-9 (pbk)
ISBN-13: 978-0-595-83858-5 (ebk)
ISBN-10: 0-595-39460-4 (pbk)
ISBN-10: 0-595-83858-8 (ebk)

Printed in the United States of America

Memoirs of a Middle-aged Hummingbird

To Julia,
Enjoy the journey!
Suellen Zima
July, 2007

To my friend, Carolyn, who always welcomed me to her nest and listened to my stories.

To my former husband, Les, and my son, Sebastian, whom I hurt by my choices.

To Stan, who started me on my inner journeys.

To my mother, who loved books.

Contents

INTRODUCTION

The hummingbird and I share several characteristics. We both plant our feet firmly in mid-air, hover, drink deeply, and then flit away. We are very independent creatures who live life quickly and intensely. If someone tries to hold us, we will die. But we can fly backwards as well as forwards at will.

In middle age, my strong desire to travel and live outside the United States catapulted me outside the cozy confines of a traditional life as wife and mother. In 1983, I went to Israel as an immigrant social worker. That was the beginning of new adventures that I had never even imagined. In 1988, my curiosity led me to China where I discovered I was a much better teacher than a social worker. It also resulted in a love affair with China that has brought me back 14 times to continuing and deepening relationships with former students turned friends. Bali, Taiwan, Macau, and Korea also became "home" to me. I found what I was good at. I had a talent for adjusting to other cultures and flourishing in them. I intuitively became a bridge builder in whichever culture I ventured.

I was content and, indeed, often elated living as a hummingbird throughout much of the world. I discovered that the hummingbird lifestyle was not just a brief aberration from "normal" life. Meeting other young and middle-aged hummingbirds along the way made me feel I had joined another society instead of leaving society. The intensive gathering of new experiences challenged me and kept me awake and alert. Although there were many discomforts and inconveniences, I knew I tired of the "known" much more than the "unknown."

Although my journeys were geographical, they were also explorations into deeply personal, emotional, and cultural realms. My overflowing cornucopia of memories constantly triggers recall of similar places I've seen, other times I've lived in, and people I've met. Along the way, I kept journals as well as wrote articles to help explain my experiences to friends. My mother kept every letter I wrote to her and my father along the way. It is mostly from my journal jottings and letters that this book is composed. Except for notations and some attempts to clarify, the writing is as it was written at the time. This is important because the times and places and people have changed greatly. The people in the book are real, but their names have been changed to protect their privacy. It is arranged loosely chronologically, flitting back and forth from in-depth descriptions to what are more like quick snapshots catching a fleeting moment in time.

I had not read the journals or letters since I wrote them. In reading them again, what impressed me was how passion and intensity became my traveling companions. There were many truly magical moments of serendipity along the way as well as pure luck. Although I certainly met and heard of people who got ugly fevers, diseases, parasites and were injured or worse in dangerous situations, I only had times of dirt and discomfort which receded in my memory. Like the plant of the same name, the wandering Jew is a hardy species that needs little encouragement to spread itself into new terrain.

So, come back in time and follow me.

1

ISRAEL 1983–1985

Sept. 24, 1983

"How did you get a name like that?" he asked me with a look on his face of having eaten something distasteful.

"I made it up from Swahili," I answered helpfully although taken aback by this strange beginning to our conversation.

"It's a very bad word in Hebrew."

"What does it mean?"

"I can't tell you," he said with a faint blush.

And so went the beginning of signing up for immigration to Israel. I explained to the *sheliach*, the person in the U.S. who would handle the paperwork and arrangements, how I had taken the name of Zima after I divorced. The name was not a Swahili name, but taken from a Swahili word that held symbolic meanings for me following a long-awaited trip to Kenya, which ended up being the last trip my husband, son and I took together.

I took his suggestions to minimize the effect of my name being a dirty word in Hebrew. I used a different Hebrew letter at the end of Zima that was not the same as the offensive word and practiced putting a much stronger emphasis on the first syllable than on the last syllable.

My seatmate on the plane to Israel was a Canadian born again Christian on a visit to the Holy Land. I knew I was in trouble when she said that the others on her tour were seated way up front and that she must have been seated next to me for a special purpose, whereupon she attempted to convert me. I promptly fell asleep, and except for waking up to eat, I slept quite deeply for eight of the nine hours of the flight.

I wouldn't exactly say there was a band to welcome our small group of new immigrants at the airport, but someone was there to greet us and bring us to our first home in Israel. I feel quite comfortable at our immigration center called *Beit Milman*. I wasn't expecting much, so I wasn't disappointed with the accommodations. They actually gave me one bowl, one plate, one fork, etc. They also gave me only one hanger, but that's okay because the closet only holds about five hangers. It's adequate, and I have a beautiful view of Tel Aviv out my window, and a park right next door to jog through. I also have a 26 year-old roommate to share our one room with a small kitchen and bathroom. I'm very happy to be here and wondering what will happen next.

Oct. 10, 1983

I've been in Israel about a month. My adjustment has been surprisingly non-traumatic. I find my days filled with the challenges of living outside my familiar environment. I now go to Hebrew class six days a week, five hours a day. This, plus two hours of homework a night, swimming, aerobics, Israeli folk dancing, running, and spending a couple of hours a week in the Diaspora Museum to learn more about Jews of the world easily fills a week. I appreciate the calm that settles over the country for 24 hours from Friday at sunset until Saturday at sunset for *Shabbat*. Even the buses don't run.

I have been told, and can easily believe, that change is the only constant here. Knowing that, I'm able to flow with it a lot better. In many ways, it is remarkable that this tiny country functions at all. On the other hand, it does function, and sometimes surprisingly well. Another "truth" here seems to be that Israel has the façade of a western country, but is really much more oriental—which means eastern here rather than Chinese or Japanese. I find this eastern mixture fascinating and hope to understand it better as I live here longer. I have never before had contact with people from eastern countries, including Sephardic Jews from places like Morocco and Yemen, as well as Arabs.

How and why immigrants come here is also intriguing. In my Hebrew class, an elderly Iranian man explained how he had to pay $40,000 as bribes to guards so he and his wife could walk almost two days without food or water while eluding patrols in order to get a plane to Spain, then to Switzerland, then to Israel. My Hebrew teacher explained how she and a brother and sister came by boat to Haifa many years ago from Syria. They kissed the ground when they arrived. A Hungarian man went on a trip to London and from there contacted a Zionist agency that sent him to Israel. In my Hebrew class there are people from Uruguay, Romania, Mexico, Russia, England, Iran, France, Belgium, Canada, New Zealand, Australia, and Scotland. Because we all speak such baby Hebrew, it's easy to forget that among the students are an engineer, a psychologist, a millionaire, a boss of a big company. I'm sorry to say that the English speakers are by far the slowest students to catch on to Hebrew with the worst pronunciation. On

Fridays, we all listen eagerly when our teacher tells us stories from the Bible in Hebrew. It is amazing that she can do it so that we beginners can understand. What is even more amazing is realizing that these stories are history here in Israel.

By the way, my last name isn't causing any problems so far. Only native Israelis know my name as a dirty word in Hebrew because they never teach sexual words to new immigrants. Besides, just about everyone in this country watches re-runs of an American drama called "Dallas." Apparently, there is a character in the program named Suellen. So, when people ask my name and I say "Suellen," I never get to the Zima part because they are so excited to meet someone named Suellen. Even my name is an adventure in Israel. And I absolutely love the diversity all around me!

Nov. 26, 1983

I went to a performance of "A Moroccan Wedding." Not only the dance, but the audience was mainly Moroccan. They talked all through the performance and clapped and ululated throughout the wedding scene. The audience definitely enhanced the performance. The music and movements of the dance were very different from western music and dance and gave me more appreciation of my belly dancing days of years ago.

I am also learning more about the Arabs from two of my roommate's friends who are Arab. One talks of the discrimination he feels as a second class Israeli citizen, and the other one feels caught somewhere between two cultures—Arab and Jewish. Even though I think some of his confusion and conflict is part of the normal "Who am I?" questions of those in their 20's, I feel connected to the broader and more universal problem of how to make personal peace with the world around us. Even though he and I are worlds apart in background, I, too, have had to face bucking the tide and tradition, and I also know what it's like to be out of my culture. I am a 40-year-old American, and so can never be totally Israeli. For some of us, there is no choice but to be somewhere in between personal needs and societal and cultural realities.

Keeping a sense of humor about the slumping economy here helps, but the situation is very serious and getting worse. The government continues to talk about cutbacks in just about everything. The value of the Israeli currency called *shekel* changes daily.

We had an air raid alert for practice this week. We were forewarned, but it was still strange to hear it. I vaguely remember them from the U.S. in the 1950's, but they seemed very unreal. There was much more of a real quality about it here. If it sounds monotonous, then it's a drill. If it wails with an up and down sound, it means to go to shelters. Every building has a shelter. In this, and many other ways, life here seems very real.

Some good news is that those squiggles called Hebrew are making more sense although being an illiterate deaf mute continually humbles me. There are many funny and frustrating moments such as when I said I did not want to eat too much and become sour cream (I meant "fat.") Later, I told someone we had been invited for wine and ice cream and tomatoes (instead of "cake").

Dec. 31, 1983

The Jewish New Year comes in the fall, so only new immigrants from western countries and Israelis who like parties observe Dec. 31st. They call it "Sylvester" here which is its European name. Catholics celebrate it as a religious holiday because it was the circumcision day of Jesus. We had a good discussion in Hebrew class about why Israelis don't observe Dec. 31st as the New Year. It led to one of Israel's burning questions—"What is a Jew?"

Before Israel became a country, religious Jews thought and prayed about Israel. The new pioneers who came to the land of Israel discarded the passive prayers of those Jews and decided to actively return to the farm and hack out settlements in deserts and swamps. They also discarded the traditions of the elders and became non-religious. Now, not only the *kibbutzim*, collective farms, but Israel in general has some regrets about its wholesale discarding of traditions along with religion. Jews in the rest of the world, whether religious or not, observe certain religious traditions as their only link with Judaism and other Jews. In Israel, though, one does not need to do artificial things to feel Jewish. But yet, there is a certain sense of loss for traditions in Israel. This loss has created a vacuum which adoration of western materialistic values seems to be filling. With the Jews from eastern cultures like Morocco, Yemen, Tunisia, there is also a vacuum, but for different reasons. They lost their culture when faced with the western level of Israeli society and the reality of life here in Israel. For example, how could the father still be revered as the family king when he couldn't find work and was illiterate and poor in Israeli society?

Not only is this now the 1984 that Orwell wrote about, but, according to the Jewish calendar, it is the year of total annihilation. Perhaps it is not coincidence that the Israeli economy is collapsing. In spite of all that, I wish you a Happy New Year!

Feb. 11, 1984

What a thrill it was to go to my first *Bar Mitzvah* in Israel. One of my classmates invited the whole class, and some of us took him up on it. In the row where I sat, I was the only American. I was with a woman and her daughter from Sweden, Sarah from Scotland, Diane from Montreal, Yvette from Belgium, Yolanda from Mexico and a woman from Argentina. There were also religious Israelis, and the relatives of the two 13-year-old boys who were earning their rite of passage to Jewish manhood. This was my first Jewish Orthodox service, and it was a good example of what the ingathering of the exiles really means. All of us were Jews. We made comments about which ways were similar or different from services in our own countries. At a certain point, the women, who must sit in a balcony away from the men, threw candy down upon the *Bar Mitzvah* boys to wish them a sweet life. There, in that rather formal, austere setting, the *Bar Mitzvah* boys and the other men looked up happily and expectantly as the women threw the candy upon them.

The contrast between the two boys was striking. Maurice's son from France was neatly and carefully dressed. The other boy was Israeli. He was dressed in white jeans, blue sneakers, a white t-shirt, and a brown jacket with a blue *kipa* askew on his head. The temple's décor resembled the Israeli boy's relaxed, plain style so unlike the adornment of most temples in the U.S.

We went back to Maurice's apartment after the service. What seemed like hundreds of people crowded into the living room. Champagne flowed. Delicious food was passed around. People sang Hebrew songs with a stunning backdrop of a blue sky, sand dunes, and the Mediterranean ocean in the distance. French, English, and Hebrew filled the air. Someone trying to pass would say, "excuse me" in three languages, figuring that one of them would work. It was great fun.

June 4, 1984

Jerusalem must be the most beautiful city in the world. Our class took a trip there for a special holiday called Jerusalem Day. We visited some parts of Jerusalem that I hadn't seen before, as well as some areas by the Western Wall and other parts of the Old City that I had visited on another trip. Jerusalem has an ambiance all its own, but its fragility is a fact of life. The guide showed us how all the neighborhoods around and in Jerusalem are now strategically placed so that Jerusalem can never be cut off again as it was in 1948. It is a very, very special place and I often feel a rush of excitement go through me when I realize I am really there.

Our day ended with a special ceremony for new immigrants in a Greek amphitheatre on Mt. Scopus looking out over an incredible landscape. The hills and mountains stretched out to the Dead Sea and Jordan beyond. A shepherd and his sheep completed a picture perfect peek into the closest I can imagine what heaven looks like. The ceremony was filled with happy music and dancing. All of us were recent immigrants from all over Israel. It was exciting to see that over half of the immigrants there were Ethiopian Jews. They are now coming to Israel in record numbers because of the political problems in Ethiopia.

I've heard that their adjustment to life in Israel is quite traumatic, but I'm glad they are here. I wish Israel could do better helping them feel comfortable. Looking at their strikingly handsome faces and gleaming white robes, I had the thought that I'd like to work with them when my Hebrew is good enough to get a job.

June 23, 1984

If the economy crashing, the elections coming in July, and the dissension over the Jewish terrorists who are now being sentenced for their crimes is not enough to tear this tiny country apart, there is yet another issue that is going to shake this country mightily. Ethiopian Jews have been escaping from Ethiopia in small numbers, but there is soon to be a wave of *aliyah*, immigration, from Ethiopia of a majority of the 25,000 left there. I have the chance to be in on that event.

The agency called Youth Aliyah is opening a children's village near Akko for Ethiopian children aged 11 to 18 this summer. I do not yet have the fluency in Hebrew to work as a social worker, but there is a chance for me to be a housemother there. Being a housemother is a very hard job under any circumstances, but these 25 children will be in culture shock and there will be no common language. Added to this is the fact that the Ethiopian Jews are extremely religious. I would have to be an observant Jew by Orthodox standards to live with them.

I am very drawn to the idea of being in on this from the beginning. I have always had an idea in the back of my head to live in Africa. And now they are coming here. Even before we adopted our mixed-racial son, I have felt drawn to blacks. Israeli society has, at best, mixed feelings about them coming here, and at worst, outright prejudice against blacks of any religion. I believe I could feel a sense of purpose in helping with a new wave of *aliyah* that requires a pioneering spirit. Having to live like an Orthodox Jew holds me back. On the other hand, the thought excites me because I am also somewhat curious about religious Jews. The religious—non-religious split here is raw and wide, a big problem in Israeli society.

I thought my life couldn't change more than it has already, but I can see I can go in even further directions from where I used to be.

August 26, 1984

Someone I met recently said that his impression of Americans is that we have a childish quality and always seem to play at living. I think that is accurate. We have a childish way about us that I feel is quite charming in some circumstances, but quite strange in other circumstances. I am now able to see the American in me a bit more objectively through the eyes of others.

Whatever our faults, however, we do know how to make some aspects of daily living, like going to a bank or a post office, efficient. For example, I went to the post office today to send off a letter. There were two employees there to hand out packages that had come for people, but no other services were available. Why? All the other employees had gone on a two-week vacation. For these two weeks, we are supposed to go to a post office that's further away. Then the situation will reverse.

My American mentality really has a tough time accepting such a system. So, not only are there surly employees, general inefficiency, changes in the hours they are open, an economy that requires us to constantly go to the post office because the price of stamps rises with the currency's downfall, slowdowns, strikes—but also communal vacation schedules.

Oct. 27, 1984

One of the most heart-wrenching experiences I've had was watching 120 Ethiopian kids saying good-bye to each other as they were being transferred in small groups to different Israeli boarding schools. They had been together for four or five months at the same location where I have been going daily for my present Hebrew class. Because we were in the same location, I got to know several of them.

Everyone was sobbing—boys, girls, and the staff. It was like a mass funeral because they never expected to see one another again. When each bus pulled away, the sobbing became hysteria. These teenagers have had so much separation to deal with in their short lives. They came to Israel without their parents and siblings, not knowing if they would ever be reunited. I like them a lot. They are generally strikingly beautiful, friendly, intelligent, and extremely eager to study and learn.

Yesterday I visited the children's village that was set up in July for Ethiopian children that I had thought about working in. The American rabbi in charge let me know my chances of working there are nil, but does that deter me? No. I just became surer that I intend to find a niche for myself working with these children in any way I can. I have been pleased with the contact I was able to make with the kids while I was at that language class in the brief opportunities we had to be together. In a few years at the most, this *aliyah* from Ethiopia will be over. I'm very glad to be here at the same time. Jews certainly cross all barriers—racially and culturally.

AMONG THE ETHIOPIANS

I arrived at the boarding school ten days after they did. The 25 mostly mid-teenage Ethiopian Jewish boys had come to Israel by plane from refugee camps in Sudan. I was a 41-year-old American Jewish social worker who had been in Israel 14 months. They came without parents, and without personal possessions. Some came from cities, but most came from small extended family villages with no knowledge of "modern" life. I came from a modern, extended world that had not included most of everything that had filled their lives. They came with no Hebrew, but a solid Jewish religious tradition. I came with an inexperienced, limited Hebrew, and with no religious beliefs or convictions. I came white from a middle-class liberal culture. They came black from the all-black world of Ethiopia. They came to Israel because they had no other good options. I came to Israel voluntarily in the spirit of adventure. They had stared at starvation and death. I had only read about it and studied how such experiences might affect children. They came to Israel filled with expectations and dreams for their future. I came to Israel with few expectations and no dreams.

We lived together in a small all-male Orthodox religious school with a view on one side overlooking the mountains of northern Israel extending into Lebanon. On the other side were white non-descript buildings of the small development town called Maalot. The nature there, including the howls of the nearby jackals at night, reminded the boys of their mountain villages. It reminded me of nothing I had ever lived in before, but had only visited occasionally on camping trips.

Along with us in the school were about 15 religious families, mostly all Israeli-born and raised, who were the teaching staff, 120 Israeli high school boys, and 17 Ethiopian boys who had been in Israel less than half a year. They had been transferred from a transitional place in the Tel Aviv area. I was to live in that boarding school for eight difficult, very intense months. It was to be one of the most fascinating times of my life.

Over the months, I would come to know each child as a separate personality, his strengths, weaknesses, and quirks that one learns from the daily familiarity of living together. However, in the very beginning, their Ethiopian names defied my tongue, and the absolute lack of verbal communication rendered them harder to differentiate as individuals. Their behavior was also more or less "communal" since they were not relaxed enough in their new situation to assert their individuality. Even so, one child obviously had artistic talent judging by a large lion he drew on the dormitory wall. One had a tendency to fight. Another promised to be an excellent student because he used every moment to study the simple Hebrew letters an Ethiopian counselor was trying to teach in the time before an experienced Hebrew teacher arrived.

Some communication was possible with the 17 Ethiopian boys who had been in the country for some months. In the six weeks they had been at this boarding school, these 17 already had a reputation as troublemakers and tough kids who had no respect for authority. They were known for complaining loudly about everything, accentuating their demands by striking—food strikes, study strikes, whatever they felt worked.

I immediately saw there were definitely reasons to complain. A "mother's" job is to make everything all right. As their housemother, the children saw me as the appropriate person to complain to. There were their reasonable and unreasonable complaints to deal with, as well as my own interpretation of how things "should" be. The habit of complaining spread like a virus from the 17 *vatikim*, old students, to the 25 *hadashim*, new students, until they plagued both my waking hours in which I tried out possible ways to solve the problems, and my sleeping hours in which I tried to dream up solutions. For a variety of complex reasons, not the least of which was my newness in a foreign work environment that followed unwritten rules which were unknown to me, my powerlessness to make changes left me frustrated, ineffective, and sometimes ridiculous. It often made me feel that I had joined Alice at the Mad Hatter's Tea Party. A discordant theme ran through our time together.

My very first hour of work was to aid the staff nurse and an additional nurse from the local clinic who were giving the newcomers TB tests. A substance was injected just under the skin on the forearm that would have to be "read" a few days later. It was complicated to listen to the child's version of his name, and then try to find the Hebrew transliteration on a list.

I wondered what the children understood about this medical procedure and later learned that they subjected themselves to many forms of medical care on faith without often being offered an understandable explanation. This was partially inherent in the situation of having an Ethiopian interpreter who only partially understood Hebrew and who also had no cultural background for understanding the medical procedures. The children approached one by one with arm outstretched, either grimacing, nervously smiling self-consciously, or with tightly closed eyes.

"Don't get too close to his head. He probably has lice," the nurse said to me as I cradled a smaller child protectively while he received his TB test. Strangely, I came to accept lice as the most positive part of the continuous medical morass I sloshed through daily as a housemother. Lice were a problem I could do something about—at least temporarily. The first de-lousing was done en masse, with eager, wet, curly heads being thrust forward for the special shampoo. Ten minutes later came the special combing which was often painful for them because of their tight curls. We joked about the lice, calling the little ones "babies" and the larger ones "fathers." This grooming procedure was readily accepted. They would often come to me and pantomime that their heads were itchy.

Other aspects of their medical care were much more elusive. The Ethiopians came with diseases that generally were outside Israel's modern medical knowledge—active tuberculosis, stomach parasites, abscesses that erupted all over the body, and malaria which had been eradicated in Israel by its intrepid pioneers. The scariest of these for me was malaria that would rather suddenly turn a happy, active, teenage boy into a sweating, listless, shaking and shivering mass.

Amara, one of the children who succumbed often in the beginning months to a high fever, had a particularly beautiful face with finely chiseled features. His personality was generally friendly and happy. He was the joker of the group—the one who could lovingly drive me crazy.

One time, his fever would not break. I took him to the emergency room of a hospital a half hour away. At that time, we had just about no common language, but had developed a certain trust and rapport through smiling widely at each other. I had had gratefully little acquaintance with hospitals, especially in Israel, and felt at a distinct disadvantage with my puny Hebrew.

The doctor was a bizarre middle-aged man who seemed much more interested in me than in the patient. Seeing that the patient was an Ethiopian, he launched into a broken-English historical account of how the Ethiopian Jews were descended from Menelik, son of Solomon and the Queen of Sheba. Interesting though this was, I was more worried about Amara than in his ancestry.

A more pleasant encounter during that hospital examination was with a man who had the face and body of a young man, but the wrinkled neck of a much older man. His skin was whiter than mine, and quite freckled. His hair was not as dark as my Ethiopian children, but equally curly, even kinky. He spoke soft

Amharic, the language of Ethiopians, to Amara and told me simply that he had been born in Ethiopia.

Amara's blood test indicated he needed to be hospitalized. I explained to him as best I could that he would have to stay there for awhile. As we walked to his ward, the halls were lined with beds. Many were filled with Ethiopians, their faces and bodies dripping with sweat from malarial fevers. At least he did not have to be in a hallway, but his ward was with old men rather than children.

I left some small toys, pens, and crayons to use when he hopefully would have more energy. And I introduced him to those in nearby beds. As I prepared to leave, he looked at me somewhat fearfully and tearfully. I looked at his brown body against the white sheets of his bed, his smallness compared to the men around him. The hospital smell surrounded all of us; the man in the next bed was throwing up his supper. With a heavy heart and a large effort, I smiled widely at Amara. He responded with a broad grin—our way of assuring each other that things were okay. I turned and left. That was the first time I had to leave a child in the hospital. I was to return to that hospital several times more.

A ROUGH BEGINNING

Waves of immigration are not new to Israel, but each wave of people from a different country and culture brings with it unique complications. Before it became world knowledge, Israel had been bringing in Ethiopian Jews from refugee camps in Sudan. In 1984, almost all the Ethiopian teenagers arrived initially without their parents. With or without their parents' permission, they had left a traditional, close, extended family of loving parents, grandparents, siblings and cousins, and trekked in groups for two weeks or so into Sudan. It was a perilous escape in which both wild animals and Ethiopian patrols had to be avoided or outwitted. A refugee camp in Sudan was a waystation in which thousands crowded into tents. Death and dying from starvation and disease was a daily sight. Jewish Ethiopians, in fear of death or injury, lived in the delicate balance of hiding their Jewishness, and, at the same time, revealing it to the proper sources in order to make it to Israel. In this environment, most of the children waited three to six months, but some remained two to three years.

Arriving with literally nothing but the paper-thin, worn, and mended clothing from Sudan, they came to the land of their dreams. As Jews, they had heard all their lives about the "promised land." While still loving their birthland, the political climate in Ethiopia, harassment as a religious minority, the chance of being drafted indefinitely in Ethiopia's war, and the spreading famine gave them the incentive to pursue their Biblical homeland.

The boarding school concept of education is a time-tested, well-developed, and popular manner in which to educate large numbers of its youth. Education in these live-in institutional settings is usually for Israeli children with parents. However, when necessary, they have become destinations for new immigrant teenage children who need to learn Hebrew and the Israeli way of life. The Ethiopian teenagers were purposely sent to strongly religious boarding schools. Although having been isolated from other Jews for a very long time, most had been raised with a firm set of beliefs based on the Old Testament. Newer rituals as practiced by the Orthodox of Israel had to be taught to them.

Their flights to Israel on giant planes also transported them in mere hours into an expanded, highly developed technological world, as well as a different social structure and culture. Many, having come from remote mountain villages, were amazed by the gadgets of our lives. My alarm clock, hair dryer, and pocket calculator were sources of wonderment. The tape recorder soothed their homesickness as they recorded their chants and listened, alone or in small groups, for hours every night. For several months, this activity became a very important link for them with their birthland.

There were humorous first experiences—such as trying to open a pop top can, blowing up a balloon, or a child looking blankly at a photo of himself until a wide smile crossed his face at the realization that it was a picture of him! One child, seated next to me in my car, kept holding his arms out, looking frightened, and telling me over and over again to be careful. I finally understood that this was his first time in a car rather than a bus, and he felt very insecure being so close to the road.

They showed unusual spatial concepts in their artwork, and in their body movements. In their first original drawings, they placed huts with the Star of David (their Ethiopian synagogues) alongside wild and domestic animals, next to buses, planes, watches, and guns—a general impression of both familiar and new items. While showing impressive skill and easy movement in scampering up trees and mountains, they were uncoordinated for certain movements and sports unfamiliar to them. They quickly filled in gaps such as how to ride a bicycle, play basketball, and propel themselves on a swing. They took to chewing bubblegum, but never did quite master blowing bubbles. They were curious and fast to learn modern tools such as faucets, forks, and toilets.

Technical knowhow came faster than adjustment to the Israeli culture. The translation for the Hebrew word *klitah* is "absorption." Absorption requires acculturation into the Israeli culture. It begins immediately upon entry into Israel. Each Ethiopian was given an Israeli name at the airport. Thus, Gwadye,

Malafia, Warku, became Eli, Uri, Asher. We began to use their Israeli names a few weeks after their arrival at the boarding school, to which they responded proudly.

One as yet unsatisfactorily answered question is how, and at what pace, to achieve the "right" balance between integrating a minority culture into a majority culture without destroying the integrity and special characteristics of the minority culture. The method preferred at the boarding schools was to put all possible energy into converting the youth as totally and as quickly as possible into Israelis. Other theories claim that this approach to absorption has been disastrous in other large immigrations, leaving in its wake a cultural void for the immigrant. At the very least, each immigrant faces some degree of individual and group identity crisis.

These Ethiopian teenagers arrived young enough to learn new ways and adapt, yet old enough to remember their culture and feel a strong identity with it. Those in the boarding schools had to learn how to cope with balancing two worlds—the all-Israeli environment in which they functioned daily, and the transplanted Ethiopian traditional culture in which they visited parents and relatives newly arrived in Israel. All must cope with the ramifications of a much greater generation gap than in normal parent-child relationships because the parents, much slower to learn Hebrew and the Israeli lifestyle, relied heavily on their children to make decisions for the family.

In the push toward rapid acculturation, it was often easy to concentrate on the dramatic aspects of their rescue, and to expect gratitude for the health and safety Israel offered, without adequately remembering the shock and trauma that had preceded each Ethiopian's arrival. They were "saved," but from a birthland they loved, and at the cost of many personal and cultural losses. For many, parents and relatives would never arrive in Israel. Every child was in mourning for someone, and in a state of continuing worry over the worsening plight of those still in Ethiopia.

In this state of trauma and grief, health was a major subject. Health problems of the children were connected to actual physical ailments, but also to cultural differences in perceptions of sickness. These teenagers were thin, but had not been victims of severe malnutrition. They were generally healthy since severely physically or mentally limited children would not have been able to make the long trek by foot out of Ethiopia.

In addition to serious ailments like malaria and stomach parasites, there were many daily complaints of headaches and stomachaches. It was usually quite difficult to diagnose and treat these since the origins of the problem had numerous possibilities. Sometimes they simply didn't drink enough water and had to be encouraged to drink more frequently. Some aches were reactions to strange, new foods, or were side effects of the trauma they had been through. Of course, there was homesickness as well as worry over parents and relatives who had not arrived in Israel. Sometimes they simply wanted to sleep longer, or give themselves a plausible excuse to stay huddled under blankets in a winter climate more cold and harsh than any they had ever experienced in Africa. Being sick was also a way of avoiding a long, rigorous day of studying Hebrew, especially since many had had little or no formal education in Ethiopia. Some suffered from learning disabilities that could not be properly diagnosed or given specialized, professional attention in the first several months.

Some aches and pains were responses to stress, or to gain attention. In the Ethiopian culture, someone who is ill is put to rest, relieved of all responsibilities, and has food brought to him. The Ethiopian boys interpreted the Israelis' casual attitude toward minor illnesses as a lack of warmth or caring for them.

The expectations that doctors and modern technology could solve all medical problems instantly and completely also led to disillusionment and an unloved, uncared for feeling. The high level of expectation that all could be cured in Israel was particularly problematic in children with psychosomatic ailments. They complained often and loudly, and wanted to be constantly taken to outpatient clinics, or even for hospitalization. The other Ethiopian children exhibited endless patience and sympathy for those who regularly complained of illness.

At our boarding school, out of 42 children, we had four fairly serious cases of depression. Their depression was expressed through apathy, psychosomatic illness, extreme anger focused on some relatively minor complaint, rebellious behavior, or talk of suicide. The staff was warned to take all talk of suicide seriously. While not a part of their culture in Ethiopia, suicide was a reaction to the stresses of absorption by teenagers as well as adults. There had in fact been several suicides around the country.

Talk of hanging began at our boarding school shortly after the celebration of *Purim*, a Jewish holiday in which the hanging of the villain is part of the history. This holiday, and the beginning of talk of suicide, came about three months after the children's arrival. In those three months, much of the newness of their experiences had become more commonplace, and the homesickness had had a chance to set in. By this time, their dream-like expectations of Israel had confronted reality and turned into impatience and disappointment. This was also a fertile time for depression because the mass of Ethiopian Jews had already arrived, and little hope was offered for others still in Ethiopia. Israel is itself an extremely family-centered society, and these children had come from even closer extended family ties. Being without at least one parent was a terrible deprivation even though other relatives may have arrived in Israel. Death was also prominent in their minds because they were receiving word of the deaths of parents, grandparents, brothers and sisters, uncles, aunts, cousins. Whereas lack of a common language for communication sometimes led to hilarious pantomiming and guessing, or was an annoying inconvenience, it was a definite liability in trying to respond to deep depression or suicide attempts.

Along with knowledge of an expanded world came the desire to acquire material goods. This led to much complaining, and in some cases, actual stealing. Clothing became a highly emotionally charged issue, taking on the burden of generalized frustrations with their new world. Exacerbated by staff problems with purchasing and distribution, items of clothing became significant symbols to the children of whether or not they would be properly loved and cared for in Israel. Having come with only a few tattered clothes, they were at first extremely grateful for everything they received. However, after a few weeks, they complained endlessly about every item of clothing. To add fuel to their discontent, the wide, baggy style of Israeli clothing insulted their concept of tight fitting clothes as what looked best on them. Not being used to shoes, they were sensitive to the smell inside the shoes after being worn. Thus, they continually subjected all shoes, including leather, to vigorous and frequent washing in spite of being repeatedly told that it made the shoes fall apart.

The Israeli students at the boarding school watched the Ethiopians receiving free clothing and called them "spoiled" in Hebrew. The Ethiopians openly called the Israelis "jealous" in Hebrew. Thus began the conflict between the Israeli and Ethiopian students. Compared to the parents and grandparents of the mainly Sephardic Israelis at our boarding school who had come to Israel in the earlier North African waves of immigration, the Ethiopians were received in grand style. Not only did these Ethiopian newcomers share the same school, rights and privileges as the Israeli boys, but they also received special consideration, free clothing and supplies, plus a lot of attention.

Cultural differences in temperament and fighting techniques compounded the initial jealousy of the Israeli teens who perceived the Ethiopians as imposing on "their" school territory. Ethiopians, as a rule, are quiet and dignified, reserved and sensitive individuals. In contrast, Israelis are apt to threaten loudly and grandiosely, backing up their macho stance with heavy-handed fists. The Ethiopian children, unused to idle threats and hero talk, and inexperienced in fist fighting, became genuinely frightened for their safety.

Ethiopian children learn the art of stone throwing as sport, and as self-defense. Not only aren't the Israeli boys particularly adept at throwing rocks, but there is, of course, a real danger of serious injury. The pattern became one of an Israeli insulting an Ethiopian or threatening him physically until the Ethiopian picked up a rock. A threat to one became a rallying cry to all. The Israeli boys would then goad the rock-holding Ethiopians into throwing. That then gave the Israelis, they felt, justification to attack the Ethiopians.

There were many repercussions to such interactions, including smashing the Ethiopians' expectation of being accepted as an equal in Israel, a first realization of being black in a white world, and a punitive reaction against the Ethiopians by the staff of the school. At first, the Ethiopians asked me, "Why don't they want us here?" They later expanded the question to "Why don't the Israelis want us?" And, after some Israelis made an issue of their being black, the Ethiopians asked me, "Why don't the whites want us?" Thus, it went through the stages of we—they, Israeli—Ethiopian, to white—black.

No doubt one of the most confusing and distressing aspects of the entry of the Ethiopian Jews into the modern world was not the realization that they were black, but that, to some people, color mattered. They had come from an all-black society unique even in Africa because whites had never dominated Ethiopia. All friends as well as foes had been black. With limited or no knowledge of blacks in the rest of the world, they knew no color line experientially or intellectually. Ethiopian Jews had suffered persecution in Ethiopia and Sudan because of being Jewish, but never because of their color. They came to Israel with a deeper feeling of connection to other Jews than to non-Jewish Ethiopians.

I, as a white American, had grown up aware of a white/black boundary in relationships, even if very subtle. I felt a definite difference with these children to whom there was no color line. I rejoiced in their open and easy acceptance of me. More than once I could see the confusion and hurt pride in their eyes after an Israeli-Ethiopian confrontation. Some began to make comments about wishing they were white, or comparing their shade of brown to each other. They had had no reason in their all-black world to develop a protective shield. Such a consciousness began to develop.

While censoring the actions and words of the Israeli boys, the staff reacted punitively to the Ethiopians because of the danger in rock throwing. The Ethiopians took criticism of their form of self-defense as a further sign of being unwanted and unprotected. The Israeli staff knew how to use disciplinary action on Israelis who are guided from a very early age into a group consciousness and a deep feeling of responsibility for others in the group. When one Israeli in a group is disciplined, it serves as a warning and deterrent to the others. These same assumptions did not hold true of the group consciousness of the Ethiopian teenagers. Although they responded protectively as a group if one of their members were attacked by an Israeli, they were much more self-centered. Making an example of one child did not have the same impact. While they had very close ties to their many blood kin, they did not necessarily extend this social responsibility far beyond bloodlines.

In conjunction with a self-centered view that had been stretched to an even greater extreme because of having had to survive under hostile conditions in Ethiopia and Sudan, they did not see, or care, that their individual actions could somehow affect the group. This was evident in survival issues, such as stealing clothing and food, as well as in play. Never having developed a sense of team competition in Ethiopia, they often spoiled competitive games by, for example, dropping out of relay races if they became bored or uninterested, or simply ruining the goal if they became frustrated with a game. Other members of the group tolerated such tactics.

They did not accept consequences of their own actions. Wanting to emphasize the positive and improve classroom behavior, I set up a system with their teachers giving out points to each student according to effort and progress. These points could later be redeemed for items of their choosing that they would not ordinarily receive. The system eventually broke down completely because they blamed the teachers for not giving them enough points, and me for not giving each of them equal rewards, regardless of the number of points they had earned.

They could also exhibit an amazing capacity for group behavior that could escalate to spontaneous and contagious group hysteria well beyond normal teenage peer group influence. This phenomenon was potentially always present whether in what might be considered important issues as well as fairly trivial ones. One had to be very cautious in extending permission to one child for something as simple, for example, as ironing a pair of pants because almost immediately many of the other children appeared with items to iron.

Another baffling challenge of working with these children was how to deal with young teenagers who had developed a premature independence and general mistrust of everyone but himself. While most of the children had faced the trauma of separation from family and familiar surroundings for some months, a couple of the children had left home at about age 11 and had spent three years on their own as refugees in Sudan. Such children did not fall back into dependency and malleability. The self-centeredness that had kept them alive did not disappear with inclusion in a warm, protected group. Reunion with their parents did not turn them back into compliant children. This type of child was more isolated from the other children. They possessed a confusing configuration of child, adult, and teenage qualities that made dealing with their needs in a group situation more complicated.

A major shock to Ethiopians upon arrival to Israel was the discovery that the majority of Israelis were certainly Jewish, but not religious. They had expected all Israelis to be observant Jews. The Orthodox Jews in Israel, to whom the Ethiopians felt the closest religiously, followed many different customs in their religious observance to which the Ethiopians had to adjust. The children in the boarding school spent hours daily learning and praying by Orthodox Jewish standards. The demand of the Orthodox Israeli leaders that Ethiopians had to undergo symbolic conversion before receiving permission to marry in Israel horrified and humiliated the proud Ethiopian Jews. Having been persecuted for centuries as Jews by non-Jews, they came to Israel expecting non-conditional acceptance as Jews by Jews.

Jan. 4, 1985

The boarding school has become their home, and I have temporarily become their mother. They call me "my mother" in Hebrew with all the sweetness of homesick children missing their mothers. There is added poignancy because most aren't sure they will ever see their mothers again.

One child just left to visit relatives today. He didn't know until he arrived that it was because his mother had died in Ethiopia. There seem to be several now without one or both parents.

Although their Hebrew is coming along well, I wish there were more words between us. When I think of the hours I sat in social work classes discussing nuances of words and how important it is to use just the right words in therapy, I wonder how I can ever do an adequate job here in my childish Hebrew along with their baby Hebrew.

They are basically eating well, but generally avoid cucumbers and don't like hard cheese, figs, and dates. They'll try some new foods, but they all refuse to eat olives and small fish.

Clothing remains a constant source of friction. I think wanting more and more regardless of need is a desire for attention and something tangible to make them feel cared for. But, in spite of the draining battles over clothing, I looked around at the handsome, freshly scrubbed faces of my kids at a recent group meeting with the director, and I felt very proud of them and proud to have become so closely connected to them.

I'm learning not to get alarmed when I hear their sharp intake of breath when they're listening to me. It is apparently the Ethiopian equivalent of "uh-huh" to show they're listening.

Jan. 5, 1985

The Orthodox reverence for the sanctity of *Shabbat* is one of the ways I have felt the strength of the Orthodox believers I'm living among at the school. Unfortunately, on this particular Saturday, after I enjoyed a very quiet *Shabbat* sleeping and writing some letters, the place exploded. It was the Ethiopians against the Israelis. I took away a handcrafted wooden weapon from one boy just as he was about to clobber two Israelis who had come up to the Ethiopians' floor. Both sides know how to goad one another, and then there are the wild ones who are very hard to control when they get angry. When the rocks started flying, I retreated with two confiscated weapons to a high rock. Yosef came up to me to ask if I was afraid and to make sure no Israeli had hurt me. In the middle of all this, my friend and her boyfriend arrived with a trunkful of games and clothes for the Ethiopians.

Dov, the director of the boarding school, came by and I told him the children were collecting weapons to fight at night and that we definitely needed an Amharic-speaking counselor there. They gathered all the Ethiopian kids together. The rabbi told them that there had never been a problem of rock throwing here, or of groups against groups. He raised his voice gruffly and said that children who did not behave would be sent away. Some of the kids wanted to talk, but they weren't allowed to speak. A couple of the boys began to cry. They were feeling unloved, unwanted, and unlistened to. I could take it no longer and left the room when I, too, started to cry.

Jan. 8, 1985

This schedule is crazy. It is now 2:30 a.m. Today had definite extremes of positive and negative. Yosef was at my door promptly after breakfast when I didn't appear and asked, "What happened to you?" He and Gadi came in and spent some time listening to the tapes and then went off to class. Uri woke me up a little later on the pretext of needing more pills. I gave him some attention instead. I brought Moshe to my room and showed him how to do watercolors. I then gave him a little paint set and more paper. Later on, he excitedly brought me some drawings and paintings he had done after he saw me. One piece was particularly good, I thought. He was genuinely pleased and it was really good to see him smiling.

I spent some time talking to another boy who had been disciplined under the watchful scrutiny of one of the staff. I once again put Vaseline on his perpetually drippy nose and gave him some soft tissues. Fortunately, the donations I've received from organizations through my Israeli friends and even stateside organizations with mom and dad's help has allowed me to buy some "extra comfort" items like Vaseline, soft tissue, cream to minimize their dry skin, gloves and scarves to ease the cold they feel so keenly in this climate, as well as games, toys, paper and paint to occupy their minds.

I had fun making Svika happy in a quiet, after dark jaunt to some of the used clothing. Another boy finally gave me back the sweater he had stolen. David came by to demand I get him a watch now that I'm his mother. He expressed his anger with a smile and a bang on the furniture when he told me his mother and father hadn't yet arrived in Israel.

On the negative side, I once again witnessed the degrading and humiliating way a member of the staff treats the boys. He calls it discipline. I can't figure out any way I can really work with that guy. The kids just seem to accept that he's not a nice guy and don't blame me for his behavior. Even more troubling is the fighting. I saw one brawl actually start between two Israelis and eventually turned into an Ethiopian vs. Israeli fight with me dashing to intercede. The Ethiopians are also fighting amongst themselves. Tonight I even had to run to get help from some other staff to break it up.

Jan. 15, 1985

I learned a lot today that I hope will help. One of the staff members, also an American immigrant to Israel, gave me what I think is very good advice. He said that I must remember that there is a very different mentality here that cannot understand my way of thinking. He suggested that I become an expert in learning and creating bypasses around conflicts with staff members.

Jan. 16, 1985

Today was like a whole week. I went through a variety of feelings about the *Bar Mitzvah* and the official opening of our *Mercaz Klitah*, Immigration Center, of the boarding school. All in all, I enjoyed the festivities immensely. It was like I had thirty sons going through their *Bar'Mitzvah*. I understand now why we had to rush to move into the new trailers even before they were ready. There was an official ribbon cutting ceremony for the new housing today along with the group *Bar Mitzvah*. Up until the last second, the workers were putting on closet doors and adding furniture to the rooms. The supervisor from *Aliyat Ha Noar*, Israel's organization that oversees the young Ethiopian immigrants, did her best to make the rooms look neat and clean, to the point of looking unlived in. At times I resented all the slapdash, rush, rush attempts at putting on a good show.

Of course, at the last possible minute, each child insisted he had no suitable clothes to wear. I pulled out many used sweaters that came in handy. Some of the boys even went so far as to steal a few coats that I took back from their rooms when they were gone.

When three rooms were ready for visitors, there was a big crush of people, including Ethiopian representatives, and relatives of the children. The television cameras and microphones were rolling and clicking away. At first, the kids were quite intimidated by the numbers of people as well as constantly being photographed both by amateurs and professionals, but some of the kids basked in the attention and excitement of the moment.

Even though it was for publicity's sake, everything really was special. The dining room was decorated festively, and the food—what little I got of it—was scrumptious. And the boys actually put on a decent performance considering their general lack of organization, inability to focus on anything for very long, and the fact that they had to speak into a microphone before so many people. I have a nice memory of one child whose very scared look transformed into a big, beautiful smile when I caught his eye. Afterward, the children sang a couple of songs in *Amharic*, their native language, and showed Ethiopian dancing they love to do in which they rapidly move their chests. There was also a live Israeli band and some of the male staff taught the kids the *hora* and even danced around with a few of the boys riding on their shoulders.

At night, the kids were revved up and sang and danced Ethiopian style. I saw smiles on some faces that I hadn't seen smile before. Sorry we don't have a television to watch any of the television coverage. With all the pictures that were taken, I hope someone will think to give pictures to the boys. But now the television cameras are gone and the fanfare has ended. I am once again alone with them, trying to hurdle many obstacles.

Jan. 26, 1985

Staying up all night to do their laundry and leaving it by their beds didn't please them. I was greeted with variations of "How will I look for *Shabbat*?" I tried to help a few by giving them something used, but again, nothing seemed to please them. "Where's my shirt?" "Where are my pants?" Some pants returned from the laundry had three numbers in them, so it was really impossible to tell whose was whose. I would say that the situation with the clothes has heightened to hysteria.

And nothing is clean enough to their eyes. Every method we've tried to improve the laundry problems has failed miserably.

Jan. 28, 1985

It's so terribly hard to watch these children realize what it's like to be black in a white world. I look at the expression on Danny's beautiful face, the hurt in Avi's eyes, and the tears on little Benyamin's face. I can see the hurt pride in Gabi who doesn't understand why the Israeli students taunt him by calling him nasty names. The Israeli students at the school tell me outright that they don't want the Ethiopian kids here. They ask why the Ethiopians don't have to work for their clothes and education like they do. And the fights between them go on.

The winter here is harsh and my bronchitis is going deeper and deeper. I had a coughing fit today that was uncontrollable. Exhaustion and worry are making me even sicker.

Feb. 4, 1985

I made a tape today of their music making. Making their own music brings joy to every face every time. Although some of them are shy about it, many of them can sing quite well. Aaron has a particularly lilting voice. Even when they sing Hebrew songs, the music takes on an Ethiopian chant. It was a beautiful moment and I felt I had been able to contribute to bringing them joy.

Feb. 7, 1985

I entered another time and place warp tonight. They showed a video film at the school tonight. It was a grade D western, supposedly in Mexico, with a very predictable plot. The Israeli kids ate up all the violence, guns, and fist fights. The Ethiopian kids sat quietly through the movie, not understanding the Hebrew subtitles or the English of the stupid plot. A few of my kids asked me whether it is like that in America now. They also asked if the people in the film were Jews or non-Jews. So, there I was—watching a ridiculous American/Mexican western surrounded by Israeli and Ethiopian Jewish teenagers in a small development town not far from the border of Lebanon. What a strange world and what barriers I have crossed within this strange world!

March 6, 1985

Purim, one of the few happy Jewish holidays, is a much-loved holiday in Israel. I helped the children make masks for the evening celebration. I added make-up and stars on the faces of those who wanted it. After mask making and face painting, the kids went to prayers and I dressed up in my authentic Japanese kimono and a mask. I was already in the dining room when they arrived. Most paid me some curious attention, probably because I had whitened my face. Eitan was afraid to sit next to me until he realized that I was behind the mask. Several others kept staring at me, trying to figure out who I was. It was fun to watch the flicker of acknowledgement when they realized who I was. But they probably had no idea of Japan, so I may as well have been a stranger from another planet—which I do sometimes feel like.

Since there was some time before the party, the Ethiopians went with their teacher for their own little party with Ethiopian music and dancing. Feeling mischievous, I changed into my long African cape dress and a new mask. Once again, they had to identify me as someone they knew. *Purim* wasn't known to the Jews in Ethiopia, so they didn't know quite what to make of the general atmosphere of dancing and clowning around. It was a good first *Purim* for them.

March 11, 1985

I was so glad to be able to give them pictures of themselves. But, to my surprise, one boy ripped his up spitting out the Hebrew word for "black" like a curse. Another child refused to take his picture uttering the same word. Yet another said he wanted to be white like the Israelis. Then one boy told me that the Israelis had called them black and told them to go back to Ethiopia. So, the issue of black and white, and internalization of inferiority is alive and cruel. So sad, so very sad.

March 13, 1985

When I went to say goodnight to the boys, I found them all in one room listening to the Ethiopian music tapes. I'm grateful I was able to provide them with a tape recorder to soothe their homesickness. I left them in their beds pouring over their first Hebrew-Amharic dictionaries, which, while quite basic, are very dear to them. At last they have something in their hands that connects Hebrew and Amharic, Israel and Ethiopia.

March 16, 1985

Late into the night, I dreamed I was tearfully screaming at the Israeli students, "He is a Jew. You are a Jew. This is skin just like yours, only it is black." Sometimes I feel ashamed to live in a world where Israeli Jews cannot accept Ethiopian Jews, Semitic Jews cannot accept their Semitic Arab cousins. Why do those who have suffered the cruelty of others only learn how to dispense cruelty when given the chance?

March 17, 1985

I was told at the last minute that we were going on a short trip today. The boys usually run in the other direction when we tell them they will have to ride on a bus. They still throw up a lot on buses. However, we gave out anti-nausea pills and coaxed them onto the bus. We were given no food except some oranges because we were supposed to return by 1:00 p.m.

In a short time, we were on a beautiful, green mountaintop. It turned out to be a walking trip. I was with three or four kids when we realized that we had lost the group. Eventually, another counselor and several boys caught up with us. We had no idea where the others were, or where we were supposed to go. So, we stopped by a pool of water made by a lovely little stream and started splashing each other. It was quite deep. One of the boys jumped in, and then Miriam, one of the counselors, fell in. Getting into the spirit of the moment, I went in fully clothed. Several other boys followed and splashed around happily.

Asaf did a somersault into the water with amazing agility. All the boys seemed to take to the water as naturally and fearlessly as they do to running down mountainsides. We were a jolly group indeed.

Uri and Moshe came running down the slope yelling their relief at finding us. They yelled something behind them and then leapt into the pool. When we started back on the trail, we found the other part of the group. They were angry and worried that we had disappeared like that. When we were properly chastised, they noticed my clothes were wet. They saw the natural pool and jumped in. Soon the pool was full once again of happy, splashing, brown bodies.

When we were all ready to leave again, Uri took Miriam with one hand, and me with the other in order to keep track of us and make us keep up with the others. Then came a very long, hot, thirsty upward climb scrambling over rocks. My three months of bronchitis definitely made it harder. And, since I had not been told it was a hiking trip, I wasn't dressed the best for it. The boys were very solicitous and helped us all they could.

At 3:30, having had no food but oranges, we got back to the road. However, the bus driver had tired of waiting for us and left. We flagged down a car to go make a call to the school. Somewhat the worse for wear, we eventually got back to the school. We were lucky there weren't serious consequences to the lack of planning and coordination. I have found that so much of life in Israel is spontaneous, ad-libbing as we go. Sometimes that's nerve-wracking. But sometimes the unpredictability works out to be rather magical, as it was today.

March 19, 1985

Moods ebb and flow here, changing constantly. The kids can be so angry and grouchy with me, and soon afterward, laughing and playing and enjoying being together. After being very angry with me, Zion came to me while I was upset about the laundry. He gave me a caring look and said, "Why are you always yelling now? You're making yourself sick." A few minutes later, when Chaim talked about wanting to go to a different boarding school, Zion assured me he would stay here with me even if he had the chance to leave.

March 26, 1985

I've been worried that Saul would crack for some time now. Tonight, he started walking aimlessly, chanting the same words over and over again, and crying. His behavior is becoming stranger and stranger. Often, he sleeps in and refuses to go to school. Either he's silently depressed and uncommunicative, or he's furiously angry over little things. I've tried to bring him to the attention of the director to get psychiatric help, but it's hard to know what a psychiatrist could do because Saul hasn't been able to learn Hebrew. I know that he is terribly worried about his family in Ethiopia. Perhaps even more effective than a psychiatrist would be an adult who could speak to him in Amharic because I have also seen a gentle side to Saul. More and more, however, what I see in him is severe mental pain.

April 4, 1985

Mom and Dad were a big hit with the Ethiopian boys when they came to visit me in Israel for the holiday, *Pesach*. Dad brought his Polaroid camera, which, of course, amazed the kids as they watched their faces magically appear. At first pleased with their own photo, they then announced their picture to be *"lo tov,"* no good, and wanted Dad to take another one. He quickly ran through ten rolls of film.

The boys are really into group behavior now. If one irons a shirt, ten, twenty, thirty or more suddenly appear with every pair of pants, shirts—practically their underpants—that they want to iron. They didn't like the socks that the director's assistant had bought for them and rudely and angrily refused to take them. Between buying clothes they like, keeping the clothes clean to their satisfaction, not losing clothes, in the laundry, and their insatiable need for more, I'd like to dress them all like 42 identical twins!

I have started to look for a small apartment in Maalot that I can escape to. Living at the boarding school means that I end up working endless days and nights. Dov, the director, told me I'm expected to work 46 hours a week. Beyond that, I'm a volunteer. And that's that!

May 1, 1985

Saul attacked another Ethiopian boy today. I hurt my hand trying to take Saul's hand off the boy's neck. I guess I was lucky he didn't hit me. The situation is very critical now because his moods shift so quickly and erratically. Now, all the children are afraid of him. The director has brought an Ethiopian in occasionally to speak to Saul. That seems to help, but only for the moment.

Saul came to my door tonight for some company and comfort. He sat down at my invitation. I simply held his hand and we talked calmly and quietly about his family. Then, he asked me for the rope the boy he attacked had taken from him and given me yesterday. I told him I had thrown it away. He said it was not for killing himself. He just wanted to have it.

On a lighter note, I brought in some Ebony magazines which someone had sent me. They poured over the pictures and really seemed to enjoy seeing a basically all-black magazine.

May 3, 1985

A few hours on Friday afternoon before *Shabbat* began at sundown, Reuven came to my room to get help writing letters to some of the Americans who had visited our school. My radio was on and a report came on from BBC about the Ethiopian government closing a refugee camp in the Gondar region and sending everyone back home even though there was no food. He asked me for some details his minimal English couldn't pick out.

As I spoke, his brown eyes began to deepen. It was as though the covering over a well had opened and I was being drawn inward and downward into the depth of his private pain and suffering. He told me that his grandparents were still there, and said simply and practically, "But, what can I do?"

I had to go off to do an errand and told him he could stay there and listen to the radio while I was gone. When I returned, he was sprawled across the bed sideways holding the small radio and looking like a very sad old man-child. Although Reuven was a child to whom tears often came quickly, I saw that this pain was both familiar and deeper than tears. I knew he had also lost a young brother who hadn't survived the refugee camps.

I was awed by the depth of pain in his eyes, and I felt admiration and respect for the internal resources for physical and psychic survival that he had developed over three years in the Sudan before getting to Israel. I also felt guilty for having brought the news to his attention. I suggested that, in the time remaining before dinner, we take a ride in my car. My car, new and shiny, had been a source of wonderment, curiosity, and delight to all the children, and especially to Reuven. He readily agreed, and I turned my car toward the mountains leading to the nearby Lebanese border. I suppose I symbolically chose the mountain route because I wanted to lift his spirits. And it worked. As the car climbed higher, he climbed out of the well of pain. I knew, as I'm sure he knew, that the pain would remain unchanged deep within him. But he wanted to let go of the pain for now and just soar up there with the mountain and rocks.

He and I shared a common trait. He, a child of the mountains, and I, a product of city life, loved nature and went to it for comfort and revitalization. We both exclaimed over and over again at the breathtaking views. I put on a Stevie Wonder tape and we sang, "I just called to say I love you. I just called to say I care,"—I in my not-so-in-tune American accent, and he in his Ethiopian approximation of the sounds.

Well before the border, we stopped and walked a bit in the quiet and stately beauty of the place. We investigated the rocks and small vegetation, and he found an old, rusty knife blade. He spoke of how he had watched his father forge knife blades in Ethiopia, and how he had learned to help him. I was glad to see that he could feel the happiness of this memory, and with some shock, I realized that all the good and happy memories of his childhood came before he was 11 years old. I was glad that, at least for this moment, he could enjoy his childhood memories in a happiness uncontaminated by ugly memories or of missing and longing for what once was.

We drove back to welcome *Shabbat.*

May 4, 1985

My little apartment in Maalot has become my hideaway from the boarding school. It isn't anything special to look at, but it gives me a chance to grab some peace and quiet without the long drive to the shared room I still have in Tel Aviv. No one knows where I am, and there's no phone to wake me up when I try to catch up on much-needed sleep. For example, today I slept late, leisurely ate exactly what I wanted to eat, and then read the entire Jerusalem Post newspaper in English. Once again I was able to enter the worlds of English, drama, movies, and politics without knocks on my door. For brief moments, my mind was able to wander away from the Ethiopian boys and the barrage of everyday hassles and problems at the school. The worsening situation in Ethiopia has heightened the tension the kids are under. And their illusions about what life in Israel would be like have had time to shatter.

I even watched some television today since I rented this furnished apartment quite cheaply from a young Israeli man who has gone off traveling. How I laughed at myself when I started watching a movie called something like "Garage Girls." At first I had thought, "How nice that they are showing females in non-traditional roles." I then began to notice some peculiarities of this movie. For example, the female mechanics were uncommonly pretty and wore extremely short overalls. All too slowly, I caught on that this was a porn film. Knowing that Israel did not put porn on television stations, I eventually found out that it was done illegally with some connection up on the roof for which the subscribers paid regularly. I did not renew my young landlord's subscription.

May 10, 1985

With all that hatred in him, I expected Meir Kahane to be a big, strong man with fiery eyes and a tongue that lashed out like a whip. So, I wasn't prepared for the short, ordinary-looking man who spoke quietly and logically about his solution to Israel's "Arab problem." I had never really expected to see this man at all, but the Israeli students, with the consent of the rabbi at school, invited him to come and speak. I listened to his talk with a sour expression on my face, imagining all the awful things he must be saying because my Hebrew was not yet good enough to understand a formal lecture.

Some of the Ethiopian boys were there too. Ethiopians are predisposed to fearing Arabs because of some bad experiences with Arabs in Sudan. The mainly Sephardic Israelis at our school had parents who had come from several of the countries controlled harshly by Arabs.

My Ethiopian boys knew my feelings about the anti-Arab views of Kahane and his following.

"She has something to say to you," one of the Ethiopian boys told Kahane as we all exited the meeting together.

Shocked into having to say something to him, I said simply, but emphatically, "I'm ashamed you're an American."

"That's your opinion," he said simply, also not seeing any sense in a real dialogue.

The rabbi was obviously not pleased that I had said something non-complimentary to his guest. Later, the Israeli boys yelled at me and wanted to convince me that Kahane was right. When I asked them if they had any Arab friends, they were shocked at the idea and stupefied when I said I had made friends with a few Arabs in my first year in Israel. There was no hope of getting the Israeli boys to change their minds, but at least I was a voice counterbalancing Kahane. My Ethiopian boys knew I was upset and at least listened when I tried to explain how the hatred of group against group works against them as blacks.

I expected Dov, the director, to chew me out too. But it turned out that he was furious that Kahane had been invited without his knowledge. I don't know how he personally felt about Kahane, but the Maalot officials were quite upset with Dov because Kahane took the opportunity of being in Maalot to go into town and rabble rouse among the residents.

May 14, 1985

Saul tried to kill himself tonight by hanging, but was not physically hurt. I wasn't there at the time it happened, but returned at around midnight and learned that the school nurse had summoned a doctor. They had to find Saul first, and then tried to give him a tranquilizer. He reluctantly took one pill, but refused the second pill. The doctor talked about forcibly giving him a shot, but I didn't want the children to have to hold him down. While we talked, Saul went out through the window.

By 1:00 a.m., I didn't hesitate to call the person overseeing the Ethiopians at our school and wake him up. Just that afternoon, he had come by and whizzed through my concerns about Saul's deteriorating mental condition. I wasn't going to stay up all night alone wondering where Saul was roaming and what he was doing.

May 15, 1985

Dov was not pleased that I had awakened the authorities last night to alert them to Saul's attempted suicide. But I don't regret it because they are at least finally willing to accept the serious nature of his mental condition. He will be hospitalized in a children's unit of a psychiatric hospital. Except for sending him to relatives, I guess there isn't much alternative. I do hope his treatment extends beyond drugs. At first Saul said he would not go, but we talked a bit and he said "maybe."

On an upbeat note, the director said that we needed to do something to make the rooms look nicer. So, tonight I had the kids do artwork and many of the walls are now artistically covered. Their artwork has changed from what they drew when they first arrived. Interestingly, they are now writing Hebrew sentences to go with their artwork. I also talked to them about making the rooms look nicer with flowers. Soon, I found three glasses of flowers on the table in one of the rooms. And I'm amazed at how well everything is folded in their closets. Sometimes they do listen to me!

May 18, 1985

As we drove Saul to the mental hospital tonight, I was thinking how sad "absorption" really is. As an immigrant, one has to re-adapt one's heritage and culture to cope with becoming an Israeli. And, Saul is most likely one who will never cope well with being transplanted. But, the alternative for him could have been an early death. There he sat at the hospital, amongst the strange-eyed Israeli "crazies" who share the same mental illnesses with humans all over the world. How he will fare there, without other Ethiopians and only an occasional translator, indeed worries me.

May 21, 1985

I'm so exhausted, I can't be sure what my level of coherence is now, but I'm anxious to set down some memories of today before I sleep. We went to Jerusalem to celebrate Jerusalem Day together with all the Ethiopian kids in all the boarding schools throughout Israel. What a grand reunion it was!

We left on a special train from the city of Nahariya that stopped to pick up hundreds of Ethiopian teenagers all along the way. The following brief descriptions are of pictures I took, or wished I had taken.

The flag of Israel was flapping across the train window as the sights of Israel passed through the white and blue of the flag. A brown hand and my white hand reached out to touch the flag.

Lines of Ethiopian teenagers with different color hats according to their boarding schools walked against the backdrop of the magnificent, ancient walls of Jerusalem's Old City.

Rows of Ethiopian girls lined up praying against the women's section of the Wailing Wall.

Kids I had known at other boarding schools remembered me and greeted me warmly.

The Ethiopian children stood with arms intertwined and shoulders touching in friendship, inadvertently forming a poignant human sculpture.

The colorful dots of the *kipot* perched on the Afros of the boys as they stood by the open window of the train made an unusual kinetic art piece.

I opened my train window wide to be closer to the darkness and stars rolling by and greeted the trees, the fields, and Israel itself in a rush of glee and bewilderment that I am here and part of it all.

My happiness stirred my American roots and I let out a cowboy yelp into the darkness. A second resounding Ethiopian version of "Yahoooooo" quickly followed.

The kids fell asleep draped over and around each other. Some crawled on the luggage racks to stretch out.

Sadly, our trip ended on a sour note. We arrived back at our school at about 1:00 a.m. to find that the Israeli students had stolen money, shoes, notebooks, etc. from the rooms of the Ethiopians.

June 6, 1985

Fiasco! And I brought it on myself believing that it was a wonderful idea. To help encourage their studying and reward their individual progress in their lessons, I used money I had raised from donations to buy useful, various "treats" that the students could "buy" with coupons they had been given by their teachers. Today we tried to open a mock store to exchange the coupons they have earned for prizes.

Everyone wanted a calculator, regardless of whether or not they had accumulated enough coupons. They started trading coupons with each other, or just plain pleaded for a calculator. Absolutely everyone was angry that he had not received what he considered he deserved. Even the children who legitimately exchanged coupons for calculators were not pleased with what they got. One of the boys even staged a royal tantrum. Of course, they refused to wait in line, so stealing became hard to control.

I was close to tears, but the boys had a great time and couldn't quite figure out why I was upset. Social responsibility and a sense of pride in earning what you get were totally missing in these boys.

I left in disgust and went to town to see a movie. In that movie, they made the point that discipline helps people to discover their true selves, and we can love the one who dispenses the discipline. That hit home because I don't know how to be an authority figure. I hate discipline and I can't seem to impose it on others. The boys may not like the counselors who yell at them and hit them, but those counselors command a respect from the boys that I don't.

So, there are several issues here—discipline, the impact of materialism, social conscience, and what can I do with the rest of the donated money I have raised on their behalf? It was great fun in buying, pricing, and most of all, imagining their pleasure and pride in what they earned by their effort. The reality, however, was a nightmare.

June 24, 1985

More confusion and bad feelings today. The staff found out that many of the Ethiopian students are lying about where they're going for *Shabbat.* They have been accepting money for bus rides to faraway places and only going a short distance, pocketing the difference. This has caused bad feelings all around. The staff feels used and angry. They are also disappointed that their invitations to some of the boys to come to their homes to spend *Shabbat* with their families have been turned down. On their side, the boys are angry that they are being accused of lying and are refusing to leave the school and go anywhere for *Shabbat.*

June 28, 1985

I didn't feel too great after lunch. About four hours later, I knew I would soon be throwing up. I did—one, two, three times, with about one hour in between. The last time, I felt really faint. I heard the school nurse's voice through the door while I was gasping and spewing. Apparently, one of the Ethiopian boys was also sick and we were being sent to the hospital in Nahariya.

I couldn't imagine being without a bathroom for any length of time. But, she insisted we go. So, in the dark of night, I could just about make out the concerned faces of my students who had gathered around to wish me well as I got into the ambulance with the student who was sick and one of the counselors sent to accompany us. This was my first time ever in an ambulance and I was surprised at how uncomfortable it was to lay down as we bounced over the rutted road for the thirty-minute ride.

Out of the ambulance, I headed for a bed in the emergency room and hoped they would do me no harm. I gasped when the doctor came over. I had seen her before on one of my visits to the hospital with a sick child. She was Russian and had been smoking in the emergency room. In another setting, she would be taken for a streetwalker. In her dyed hair were two pink flower barrettes. Gaudy make-up covered her face. Her pants fit her like tights, ending in high-heeled boots. She put her long, bright red nail polished fingers on my stomach, gave me a pill and a shot, and strutted off to do the same with my sick student, Gadi.

We had arrived in an ambulance, but had to fend for ourselves to get back to the school. There we stood in the cold night while the counselor haggled for a good price with several taxi drivers. When we finally arrived back at the school, I headed to my room just in time for one more bout with the bugs in my body.

I awoke early in the morning after a few fitful awakenings and went outside to turn on my electricity that still maddeningly snaps off every night for some reason. I decided to escape to my little apartment because I couldn't face the daily demands, room inspections, and the weekly laundry battle. I left a note and, with the little strength I could muster, I bought some simple food supplies for my wobbly stomach and intestines and slept for the entire day.

July 6, 1985

I returned from our day out hiking and crawling through a cave with a definite need to take a shower. Several of the children were angry with me for a variety of offenses they think I've committed against them, and one of them must have turned off the electricity to my trailer to annoy me. So, after showering, I laid down on the bed to muster up some fortitude for what I figured would be a long, hard evening as the subject of laundry always is.

Gabriel kept coming to my door and then to the window yelling for me because he wanted his laundry. I didn't answer, and he refused to believe I wasn't there. Finally, I heard him trying to break his way in. He actually went so far as to take off the two screws holding the screen. I wondered how far he would go, and quietly waited. I wasn't sure what I would do. I wanted to scare him, but didn't want to yell and scare others. I waited while he got the screen off and stuck his head in—whereupon I screamed. He ran like the wind. I needn't have worried about disturbing others. He was the only one who noticed my scream.

He came back almost immediately and knocked politely. I told him something not nice had happened and I was scared. When I was dressed, he was waiting at my door.

"Someone tried to break into my room while I was sleeping," I told him. I awoke with a start when I saw a head coming through my window."

"Did you see who it was?" he asked nervously.

"No, I didn't see a face, only a head."

Relief spread over his face, which he quickly covered over with a look of fear. "How horrible! I'm afraid to sleep here anymore."

It was hard to keep myself from laughing.

July 11, 1985

There was such a sparkle in Asaf's eyes when he told me what he's learning with his sports tutor. It is opening up another world for him. It was obvious that he has real athletic talent, so I found the tutor for him and am paying for his lessons with some of the donated money. It's been wonderful to have a pool of money to be able to dispense as I see fit because these donations have been sent directly to me rather than the school. I wish the people who have given the money to me could see the happiness on Asaf's face.

July 17, 1985

The Ethiopians in the town of Sfat are demonstrating against forced conversion. When the Ethiopians came to Israel in smaller numbers, they went along with the requirement of the Orthodox to symbolically convert. No rabbi in Israel is allowed to marry Ethiopians who have not gone along with conversion. But, now that Ethiopians are here in large numbers, they no longer accept what they consider the humiliation of "converting" to Jewish when they have been Jewish for centuries. I understand how the Ethiopians feel about it, but most of the Orthodox staff at the school absolutely agree that conversion is necessary. So sad to have another issue that divides the Orthodox Jews of Israel from the Ethiopian Jews.

July 25, 1985

What a day! The group of American Orthodox young volunteers had their last day at our school to play with the Ethiopians. They have been such a help organizing activities during the summer break. Their parting activity was a rousing color war. The Ethiopian boys were wild and crazy—some of which was in the spirit of the event, and some of which showed their lack of understanding of competition and team play. Some simply stopped when they felt like it during a relay race, or intentionally dumped over a bucket of water that was a goal when they weren't allowed to cheat. But there was also genuine fun. The director couldn't quite believe religious Jewish young women who enthusiastically cheered on the students or stood on chairs to belt out songs with the kids.

As I sat there watching it all, I was alternately feeling very fond of the children, and also very irritated with their bad behavior. The goodbye to the Americans was noisy, and heavy with the air of all goodbyes that are, most likely, permanent. Some of the children who had grown close to certain volunteers were quite sad. And the Americans had also been affected by their time with the kids. One had even cancelled a trip to Rome in order to stay another week at our school. What worried the Americans the most, they said, was the lack of acceptance of the Ethiopians by the Israeli students.

July 26, 1985

Goodbye was also the main theme for today. I have been fired! Dov, the director, arranged to meet me at my trailer this morning. He started out by saying that what he had to say wasn't pleasant, and that he thought my work was wonderful, but *Aliyat Na Noar,* which was in effect his boss concerning the Ethiopians, didn't want me to continue as housemother. He was apparently expecting a scene, and said, quite surprised, "Aren't you angry?" I told him that I had been expecting it and we discussed details like receiving unemployment benefits, and getting a letter from him about my work. Miriam told me later that Dov had explained to her that my not being religious enough was the reason.

I can speculate about many possible reasons, some circumstantial, and some that undoubtedly have to do with my strong personality. What I didn't tell Dov was that I was planning to quit before the cold weather set in again because my health had suffered just about the whole time I'd been there. I knew that, with my tendency for bronchitis, I couldn't handle another winter there. For me, that was more of an issue than the enormous difficulties of the job.

My many and constant frustrations with the job will not be missed. Much of the warmth, caring, and even love between the children and me will be sorely missed. So much went wrong during my seven months here. But, so much has gone right.

August 10, 1985

My leave-taking has been a long one. The Ethiopian boys had their first *Gadna,* army training, in the sands of Sde Boker. The Israeli army, itself a tough group, found the Ethiopians a tough group to handle, but said they are great kids. Being with the Israeli soldiers for even a couple of days gave me more respect and admiration for these Israeli young adults who all defend Israel with such dedication. I did something I never expected I'd do—I learned how to shoot a rifle and even hit the target. I also saw where the Israeli habit of gulping down food at mealtimes beat all records. I was barely starting to eat when everyone else was getting up to leave the dining room.

While technically on vacation, I returned to the boarding school with an artist friend who painted wall murals of Biblical stories on the sides of some of the school buildings. The kids were rather intrigued, especially since he drew some of their faces as part of the artwork.

Dov had planned to tell the children in a group meeting that I was leaving, but I wanted to tell them myself. It was hot in the room, and they didn't particularly want to be quiet and listen. I didn't use the word, "fired." Instead, I told them that I was not being allowed to return after my vacation and wanted to wish them goodbye and good luck. I explained that it had been mostly a happy time for me to be with them, and that we had shared happy times, sad times, good times, and bad times. I then individually gave each boy an envelope with an equal portion of the donated money that was left. It was about $5 apiece.

Some of the younger children cried. Reuven did not know what to say, but wrote me a note in which he said he now was alone and had no mother at school. Many said nice things to me and looked genuinely sad.

I requested that they decorate the cover of my car that they had loved so much. With the special markers I brought, they did a wonderful job covering the cover with pictures and loving messages.

Before leaving, I finished the last mural as they watched. They looked at me wistfully, and I at them wistfully, each of us feeling that I had already left.

2

ISRAEL 1985–1988

Sept. 28, 1985

I am back in my shared room near Tel Aviv, once again awed by the purple sunsets out my window. When they aren't purple, the sunsets are variegated shades of gray. I've never seen such sunset colors anywhere else. I'm not yet working or studying Hebrew again. I'm mostly just resting to regain my energy.

What's next? I definitely have to return to Hebrew class to improve my level. And I've decided to apply for Interns for Peace. If I qualify, I will begin training next summer or fall. They require a two-year commitment during which I would live in an Arab village inside Israel. That aspect of the program intrigues me because I really want to learn first-hand about Israeli Arabs and their culture. The other interns would be Jews, some American, some Israeli, and Israeli Arabs who speak Hebrew much better than I. Our job is to be community workers where we live. Arabs, even Israeli Arabs, live mostly in towns and villages without contact with Jews. They study in Arabic, but learn Hebrew intensively after age 12. That's good for me, because I don't have much hope I'll be able to learn Arabic. Hebrew is more than enough challenge for me. With the local elementary schools, the interns arrange meetings between Israeli Arab, and Israeli Jewish children in the same geographical areas.

The underlying goal is to encourage an attitude of coexistence between the Jews and Arabs living inside Israel through face-to-face experiences. I seem to always link my work to causes I believe in. The tolerance/intolerance between Arabs and Jews, especially the Arabs who are Israeli citizens and live inside Israel, seems crucial to the future of Israel. The chance for making a large impact through Interns for Peace is small, but I think it's something I can feel good doing. And it should be fascinating to live in an Arab village. I came here to do things I couldn't do in the U.S., and this fits that description well. I just hope I'll be flexible enough at age 43 for such a lifestyle. It will mean living with a roommate and having a lot of contact with people. The program is based on the Peace

Corps, including the lack of salary. Instead, I'll get living accommodations for free and a small monthly stipend. At the end of the two years, I'll get a small lump sum. I should be able to manage financially.

My time in Israel has definitely strengthened my ties to my Jewishness. I have come to appreciate the Sephardic side of Jews that I was never exposed to in the U.S. The Arabs also come from the Semitic race—our cousins with many physical and cultural similarities to Jews. And now we have no choice but to live together in Israel.

Dec. 8, 1985

Before my surgery, I never truly appreciated the miracle and joy of waking up! I was shocked when I awoke instead of died. I have now experienced the good and bad parts of socialized medicine in Israel. Concerned about two breast lumps in my left breast, a doctor arranged for me to have the lumps removed and biopsied. Very little is done here outpatient, so I actually spent three days in the hospital. The first day was just to check in, and talk with the anesthesiologist. Another advantage was to get to know the other patients in my room. That turned out to be quite important because most Israelis always have a family member who stays with them after surgery.

My poor Hebrew is always a liability living in Israel, but made me feel even more vulnerable in a hospital. Since this was a teaching hospital, many rounds of medical students came by to see the "American breast lumps" which I was introduced by rather than my name. I was really annoyed by the smoking of the doctors and nurses.

The second morning, the day of the surgery, a man came by and muttered something to me in Hebrew and indicated I should follow him. I was elegantly dressed in my hospital attire as we walked through several clinics with people dressed in street clothes. The Israelis are used to reality, but I was not quite prepared to go on elevators along with dead people being transported here and there.

Several times, I came close to losing the man I was supposed to be following through the crowds. At last, we got to a room where he indicated I should sit down and a manila folder was put in my lap. I looked down at the Hebrew writing and gasped. <u>It wasn't my name!</u> That can be very serious when the surgeon on duty follows whatever instructions are in the manila folder that comes in with the patient he has never seen before that moment. I excitedly explained that the name on the folder wasn't my name. Someone gave me another folder that, thankfully, had my name on it.

I was eventually given a place to lie down and was wheeled into the operating room. I hadn't yet been given the anesthesia. The unknown surgeon looked over his mask and calmly asked in decent English, "Which breast is it?" As the anesthesia was being administered, I yelled in a panic, "Left!"

My first feeling upon waking up was shock at being alive. A nice young woman in my room who wasn't having surgery until the next day tended to my needs for that night and the following day. It was this stranger who brought me a bedpan and called the nurse when the bag draining into me needed to be replaced. One of my friends tried to visit me a few times, but she always came when a doctor, for some unexplained reason, saw her and asked her to leave.

Three days later, I saw the face of the surgeon who had operated on me. I had been told to return at that time to have my stitches removed. I said I thought it was too early to remove them. "Nonsense," he said, and ripped them out. "Oh," he said, "you were right." Later, the doctor who had ordered the surgery checked me again. "How did you let them do such a bad job?" was his comment. But my entire surgery didn't cost me even a dime.

Dec. 21, 1985

I continue to correspond with several of the Ethiopian kids in the boarding school. I went up to visit once, and I plan to go up again in January. I still miss them terribly, but through letters between us, am managing to keep in touch and even strengthen some of the relationships. One of them, Reuven, came to visit me in October, and then we spent a wonderful week together during his *Chanukah* vacation.

His visit roused me out of the depression I had gone into after my surgery even though the lumps had been declared benign. I introduced him to new things like video games and he, in turn, taught me new things. For example, we went to a museum that had agricultural tools from 1,000 years ago. He explained the uses of each one to me because he had used most of them himself in Ethiopia! We went camping at the Dead Sea and Ein Gedi where he showed me how he can literally run up and down mountains at great speed. He explained how he plans his strategy to make sure where each step will go without slipping or falling down.

I drove him back to his family before the end of vacation. They invited me to sleep over for *Shabbat.* That was quite a treat for me. While being treated as a guest of honor, I got to see daily family life among the Ethiopians. That helped to round out my knowledge of the Ethiopian boys I had cared for at the boarding school. I got along very well with the many young children at the immigration center because they have learned Hebrew. Besides, the language of play is international. The parents can't speak Hebrew well, so the children had to be my translators.

Reuven's mother prepared food especially for me because I can't eat very spicy food. Other than that, I was just one of the crowd. And what a crowd! The large families spend a lot of time visiting from one apartment to another. The food, *injera*, was different from anything I've eaten before. It's a type of flat bread with different toppings, sometimes meat and sometimes vegetables or beans, ladled on top of it. I liked it a lot. It's eaten with the right hand instead of using utensils. There are endless quantities of everything to drink—cola, tea, wine, brandy. Here, they don't have the exact type of drink they used in Ethiopia that is apparently less sugary than our carbonated beverages. It's the children's job to be sure every guest has a glass of something to drink filled up to the top at all times. They have a wonderful ritual for making very, very strong coffee. The smell of the coffee must be strong to pique the tastebuds, and involves cooking the coffee beans to release the smell.

There's a new baby boy in the family and Reuven's father has invited me to a special ceremony for the baby forty days after his birth. He explained that it's eighty days after a baby girl's birth. It was obvious I wasn't used to their customs, but Reuven helped by explaining what was happening. They were all so gracious to me and hope I will come back often. I'm looking forward to it.

ONE YEAR AFTER OPERATION MOSES

Judging from the Ethiopian teenagers I personally know, their adjustment has been difficult, but dramatic in their first year in Israel. There are scars from the trauma before arriving in Israel, and the trauma of rapid acculturation after arrival. However, they are physically blooming, their Hebrew is improving rapidly, and their self-confidence is growing. During this year, they have passed through the initiation rites of entering a previously all-Israeli domain, and they have established a basis for tolerance, coexistence, and even fledgling friendships with Israeli boys. Many of the basic differences in character and mentality between Israeli youth and Ethiopian youth remain, but without the open conflict. The Ethiopians retain the underlying softness and sensitivity that made them so appealing a year ago.

It is long past the time when forks, faucets, and pajamas were strange, foreign objects. There is a lot less frantic pantomime to convey what they can now express in Hebrew. They still scamper up hills and trees quickly and gracefully, and have become much more adept at soccer and basketball. They still can't blow bubbles with bubblegum very well, but can now do a much better job blowing up balloons.

It is rarer now to hear a child walking along chanting to himself in a distinctive Ethiopian melody. They are more apt to spontaneously break into a Hebrew song. To each other, they still speak in their native tongue, but Hebrew words are often interspersed.

They remain thin, but have sprouted up substantially since their arrival. Shirts and pants tell the story as arms extend beyond the sleeves, and legs strain their pants. Still in their closets are the paper-thin, worn, patched, outgrown clothing they brought from Sudan. Although no longer useful articles of clothing, they remain as symbols and mementos of their dangerous and dramatic escape to Israel when giant planes whisked them away in the blackness of night.

Their palates have now adjusted to foods that were unfamiliar and bad tasting to them, but they still generally reject cucumbers, beets, and small fish. They continue to eat large quantities of bread at each meal. More foods fall into the "I don't really like it, but it's beginning to taste better to me" phase. But, if given a choice, each would still choose Ethiopian food.

They have learned how to adapt to customs that were unknown to them in their Jewish religious practices in Ethiopia. They will eat warm food on *Shabbat* that is prepared and served by non-Jews. After intensive hours of religious study, they have learned the ways of the Orthodox. They pray according to Orthodox traditions but they remain hurt and humiliated at the Orthodox demand that they undergo a symbolic conversion. It still surprises them, but no longer shocks them, that Israel is a country of Jews, but not religious, observant Jews.

These children loved their birthland, and have missed it very much. For those whose parents have not made it to Israel, the burden and worry and grief has been very heavy this past year. Although sometimes letters or a few precious moments on the phone have temporarily lifted the burden of separation, the pain of not belonging to their own family unit remains acute.

A different problem has emerged for those whose parents have arrived in Israel. Generally, the parents who are living in absorption centers around Israel are adjusting more slowly than their children to the changes in their lives. They have transplanted their traditional Ethiopian lives to Israel as best they can. Added to the normal generation gap is a greater gap between the teenager's daily life in an all-Israeli environment at the boarding school, and the twice monthly visit to a transplanted all-Ethiopian environment. Therefore, they struggle to find a balance between these two worlds that sometimes seem in opposition to one another.

One year later, many of them have discovered that their expectations of life in Israel bear little resemblance to what they have found here. Some are still homesick, and most are somewhere in between worlds. But they are coping, growing, maturing, learning, and progressing.

May 31, 1986

This is my first time visiting in the U.S. since I moved to Israel in 1983. Like my suitcase, there is so much packed, squeezed, and compressed into a short time. And the words, so and too definitely describe my reaction to being back. Everything is so big, so green, so rich, so delicious, and also too big, too grand, too delicious, too easy. It's too difficult to find the purpose of it all. If I am so bemused and bewildered, I wonder how it would all seem to my Ethiopian boys.

In this land of more-than-plenty, I feel like an alien from another planet. I walked into a giant-sized mall, looked around at the overchoice, froze, and then fled. The size and variety of supermarkets paralyzes me. Just how many different kinds of cereal can there be? I feel out of breath when totally surrounded by things, things, things—mine, theirs, everyone else's. My friends and relatives all seem to be living "the good life," defined by money—making it, saving it, spending it, living submersed in it. I seem closer to my brother, Bennett's style—a few passions on which to spend money amid contentment in a one room cabin in the redwoods.

Does Israel exist? Does my life there exist? I feel disjointed and unconnected.

July 4, 1986

As I sat among relatives in New York watching the televised fireworks display, I felt the twinge of being a part of two countries and belonging in total to neither one. I felt a lump in my throat as the super patriotism of this Independence Day was expressed with spectacular hype as only the U.S. has the money, arrogance, technical know-how, and fun-loving nature to do.

I've spent time with many friends and relatives and was able to buy some books in *Amharic* and other items some of the Ethiopian boys requested. I will soon return to my other country where this easy life will abruptly come to an end.

July 14, 1986

Sitting among the other interns in the Interns for Peace program I am now working for, my first thoughts are that I won't be able to cut the mustard, but that really remains to be seen. I am, and have been, capable of many things I never believed possible.

There are ten new members in training—two Israeli Arabs, two Jewish Israelis, five Americans, and one Australian. I feel comfortable with them, but am constantly reminded of how different our stages of life are even if we are living and working together. They range in age from 21 to 28. I admire their boundless energy and enthusiasm, but I can honestly say I prefer to be turning 43. They are so unsure of themselves in so many ways, so serious, so emotional, so intense, and searching so hard for directions to go in their lives. Four are heavy smokers, and that, of course, means that I can't socialize with them because of the smoke. Even though we live together, I do jealously guard any time I can have alone. I really need and love my time alone. So, I'm feeling tired, but good, and getting caught up with what still promises to be as fascinating and difficult a job as I thought it would be.

August 17, 1986

Our training course continues to be very intensive indeed. Since we are living on a *kibbutz*, collective farm, during training, we also need to work half a day for the *kibbutz*. My job is to sort eggs into similar sizes as they come off a conveyor belt. Although the work is mundane, I really love being back on a *kibbutz*. It brings back fond memories of my summer of 1982 as a volunteer on a different *kibbutz* in Israel. Ever since that wonderful summer of my first visit to Israel, I always feel a sense of quiet and peacefulness on any *kibbutz*.

During egg-sorting today, I had to confront some conflicts about working for coexistence between Arabs and Jews. Over packing eggs in cartons, an Israeli who lives on the *kibbutz* tried to convince me that I was making a mistake trying to make peace with the Arabs. This wasn't the first person to say that to me, but he didn't say it antagonistically like others have done. There was something deep, sure, and sincere about his warning. I asked him why he felt that way.

He told me, "In 1948, I was a very young child. My mother sent my 14 year-old sister to buy milk from the Arab milkman we had been buying milk from. When she didn't return, my mother sent me out to look for her. I found her—her head in one place and her body in another. You can't turn your back on the Arabs. Today, I have some Arab friends, but there is a border to our relationship that must always be there."

Listening to his sad story, I had the sudden flash of seeing myself like a German Jew in 1939 trying to convince my Jewish friends that the Nazis would be friendly if we treated them well and got to know them better. I have never suffered at the hands of the Arabs. Many Israelis have, and they must continue to live here while I could leave at any time.

When I think of Arabs, I think of my roommate's classmates that I know. They are college-educated and ambitious, but limited by being second-class citizens in their own homeland. I also think of Jamal who comes every day to clean the immigration center where I live in Tel Aviv. Jamal lives outside the borders of Israel, so he is not an Israeli citizen, which makes life even harder. Politically, he lives in no-man's land, neither Israel nor anyplace else. Knowing him, and even going to visit his family in the small village where they live, has shown me how hard life is for the Arabs in the "territories." This is the exact land his ancestors lived on and passed down through the generations. Though poor, they have a "sense of place" there that they can feel nowhere else.

I've been thinking about rootedness and its importance. When some Israelis say that Arabs should go to live in other Arab countries like Jordan or Egypt, I remember an Israeli-Arab friend telling me that he feels Arab in Israel, but Israeli when he's in Egypt. Many American blacks traveled to Africa expecting to go "home" and found instead a strange land and culture. How often have I not felt "home" in the U.S.? How often have I been aware of the gap between me and native Israelis? It seems rootedness is a strange phenomenon that is based more on feeling and intuition than logic.

Sept. 1, 1986

Only someone who has lived in Israel can believe what my day was like. I was expecting a day of frustration because it was the day to free from Customs the small cartons I had shipped from the U.S. during my visit. Dread mixed with relief knowing that I would be reunited with this "stuff" which I never really doubted was not worth the price and aggravation of sending.

My car took a long time to start, which presaged things to come—fortunately, not in connection to the car, which behaved gallantly and ended up a true friend. I arrived at approximately the place of the handlers who had notified me all was ready. I temporarily parked near a restaurant, sure I would be blocked in soon because the port area in Haifa is a jungle of cars. I discovered, once again, that numbers on one side of a street bear no relationship to numbers on the other side of a street (25 across from 60). A clerk presented me with some papers, and a bill for 37.50 *shekels* for removing seven puny packages from the massive crate. He then pointed me over to Customs.

I just managed to extricate the car before two cars came to block it in. I drove to Customs and parked. I was greeted by a young Israeli who wanted to "help" me. And, as it later became clear, wanted me to hire him to take all my stuff wherever I wished. He identified himself as somehow connected to the shipping company I had just paid. When I said I planned to send my things through a service offered by the Jewish Agency that helped immigrants, he sweetly lied that the Jewish Agency office was closed today.

I eventually got rid of him and proceeded to a window. There were not a lot of people waiting, but that's immaterial since the clerks move agonizingly slow no matter how many people are in line. I got through that window and was told to wait at another window. I stood next in line, but someone seated informed me that he was next and he'd been told that it would take 90 minutes to get to him. I read my book standing in line until one of the unbusy clerks decided to help out.

He was rather a pleasant chap who appreciated my glowing description of National Geographic magazines I had written in my inventory of shipped items. He carefully documented in my Israeli identification papers the many requested items I was bringing back to the Ethiopian boys. He agreed that I did not owe Customs duty, but there was the matter of a Port tax. Back I went to window #1 and got a bill for 44 *shekels*.

This was a problem because, after paying the 44 *shekels*, I would have only 15 *shekels* left to pay the Jewish Agency to transport my cartons from Haifa to Tel Aviv. I worked that out by offering some *shekels* plus a check that I hoped would not bounce. In this way, I paid the 44 *shekels* and returned to the little, not closed Jewish agency office. The price was reasonable, but they said their truck was too big to go down Geula Street where the Interns for Peace office is and from which I had a letter of permission to deliver my cartons.

Now, what to do? I called the immigration center where I still had my shared room and asked permission over the phone to bring my cartons there. Permission was definitely and rudely NOT given. When is a home not a home? When you are made to know you exist there only at someone else's good graces.

Would all this stuff fit into my car? All of it would have to fit because I couldn't take only part of my shipment. And I wasn't allowed to unpack anything at the warehouse before driving out.

A seemingly nice man wanted to "help" me out, but knowing help costs $, I told him I could give him only what little cash I had left. I gave it to him and told him it was useless to ask for more. He got his truck and picked up my stuff huddled obscurely among huge trunks. We returned to my car, opened the cartons, and the blessed man found room in my car to stash everything.

There was even enough space left for the parking ticket I found waiting on my windshield!

Sept. 14, 1986

As I came to the Arab town of Shefaram for the first time, there was music and dancing in the streets. It was not for my arrival, but for a wedding. Since they were going in my direction, I marched along not really knowing if I should participate or not. I got some strange, even not so friendly stares, but there were friendly children who helped me find my way to my new home.

Now, when I look out the windows of our amazingly airy, spacious apartment and see the town and the truly lovely surrounding mountains, I hear the call to prayer and marvel that I am in the midst of it all.

Sept. 16, 1986

Our reception in Shefaram has been quite good. I feel more comfortable here than I expected to. One of the second-year interns has given me some pointers to help me conform to the Arab culture. One is that women should not start eating before the men. Arab women are used to feeding guests without first asking if they would like some food. According to American courtesy, I was trying to empty my plate at someone's house, but as I was finishing what was on my plate, they kept putting more food on. The intern explained that I must finish by leaving some food on my plate so that the hostess will not add more food. The Arabs are so generous with their hospitality, I will really have to watch my weight here. My American partner in Shefaram is a vegetarian. That really makes the Arab families uncomfortable since they never feel they can fill her up without meat.

Sometimes I feel so comfortable here, the reality of the pain between Arabs and Jews is even sharper when it surfaces. Last night, we met with several of the Arab school principals whose schools will participate in meetings with Jewish school children. Their faces showed their feelings when they talked about Jewish principals who didn't return their phone calls, or the school that didn't come at the last minute because they had to bring an armed guard. There was restrained anger on all of their faces when they spoke of not being accepted, and "having to get along together" with their Jewish counterparts. I can still see the pained smile on the principal who was Druse and said he had served in the Israeli Army and his son had fought in Lebanon.

Sept. 18, 1986

Shefaram is an unusual Arab town because its population of 25,000 is over 50% Moslem, 30% Druse, about 20% Arab Christians, and now two American Jews. I will need to learn more about their similarities and differences.

A Druse young man (thankfully, the Druse don't smoke) treated me to a visit in his home, and then to the ruins of an old castle on a hill. From atop the castle, I could see the eight mountain tops encircling Shefaram—a breathtaking view! From that vantage point, Shefaram is a picturesque maze of houses and rooms and backyards and horses. The Arab homes are so spacious and airy, it is a welcome relief from the stuffy overcrowded feeling in most Jewish apartments.

Sept. 21, 1986

My third year in Israel ended yesterday, and my fourth year is about to begin with me sitting in one of the largest Arab towns in Israel. I have lived in Shefaram for one week now. Sometimes I still can't believe I am here until I hear the loud call to prayer or look out my window and see an old man and his donkey climbing the hill. I can see the differences between this and a Jewish town. Here, the narrow streets resemble the Old City in Jerusalem. Unlike the Jewish communities in Israel, the Arab homes have large rooms with many airy windows. It is comical to think of how hard I am trying to get a tiny, permanent, truly closet-sized room in Kfar Saba from the Jewish Agency for my very own permanent spot in Israel. I even have a phone here, which I haven't been able to get in Tel Aviv. However, also typical of Arab towns in Israel are rutted streets, frequent electricity blackouts, and badly overcrowded classrooms that are not as common in Jewish towns.

So far, the atmosphere has been friendly and curious. Of course, I get along well with the young children even though they haven't yet learned to speak Hebrew. I have even joined a women's exercise class in the basement of someone's home across the street. There are weight machines there. It's an energetic workout that I badly need to fend off weight gain from the continuous glut of good food people are feeding me.

Sept. 27, 1986

I went to visit my Ethiopian boys at the boarding school. I had great fun with the ones still studying there. I felt high and happy in their company. Gabriel seemed like he really wanted to talk with me. How sour, dour and serious he has become the last few times I saw him. Such a contrast from the bubbly, mischievous, smiling child he used to be.

A chubby, unsmiling man walked into the room. "Which car is yours?" he asked me directly. "You are to leave this school within ten minutes or I'll call the police. I'm the boss, you are a stranger, and you are not good for the kids."

That line—that I was not good for the kids—was too much for me. He gave me no other reason why I should leave, but I figured out it was because I was living in an Arab town and holding meetings between Arabs and Jews. On previous visits, some Israeli students who remembered me as a housemother there had asked me where I lived and what I was doing. I told them about Interns for Peace.

Indignantly, I replied to this man who called himself the boss, "This is racism."

"So what?" he countered. "Get off this property and don't come back unless you have a note from the director giving permission."

I toyed with the idea of making a scene by forcing him to call the police, but he stayed out of my way and didn't check back in ten minutes to see if I had left.

My welcome at Reuven's family for *Shabbat* was a sharp contrast to that miserable encounter at the school. After so many visits, I feel quite at home there and have come to love each of his brothers and sisters. Even though verbal communication with his parents is still quite limited, their love and warmth comes through clearly. I especially enjoy playing with the children and watching how quickly their eager, agile minds catch on to the many new games and toys I brought back from the U.S.

Oct. 1,1986

When I called Dov, the director of the school, to complain about how I was treated when I went to visit, he replied in his usual wishy-washy way. On the one hand, he agreed with the new rabbi of education that all visitors should have prior approval. When I pressed him, he agreed to talk to this new rabbi again.

Yom Kippur, 1986

I have a home in the city of Tel Aviv. It is one half a room that I share with another immigrant like me. I have Jewish Agency furniture and a wonderful window that looks out toward the city. From my one window, I can see unusual purple sunsets and variegated gray nights.

I feel at home in the bustle and noise of the big city, with the comings and goings, buying and selling, frenzy and hurry, street food and street people. The impersonal and the cold side of Tel Aviv is there too, but I have my friends and the ocean to warm me.

I have a home in the city of Shefaram. It is a two room apartment among 25,000 Arab neighbors. I share it with one roommate, and, upon occasion, many colleagues. The rooms are big, the air is plentiful, and the views from the windows look out upon the rolling hills and white rocks of the countryside, and upon a Jerusalem Old City look-alike.

I feel surprisingly at home here too, wandering the narrow alleyways that hide multitudinous little shops, or watching a multi-colored pink sunset over the hills from my porch. The sounds of Shefaram are close and personal—the children coming home from school, the Christian church bells, the monotonous Moslem call to prayer, and the frequent splash of the washing water from my neighbors' daily housecleaning.

Oct. 14, 1986

Today was a happy high and a surprise! I tried my hand at being an English teacher at the request of Shefaram's community center that pays for our housing. I started an English Club with 15 girls—all bright, all enthusiastic, with a higher than I expected level of English. Even though I was flying by the seat of my pants, I didn't have a moment of discomfort. Teaching them just seemed to flow naturally. We all enjoyed ourselves. I think we can have a really good club, and actually make it into something worthwhile. My mind keeps working on new ideas and I get energized from my contact with these bright high-school girls. It seems I can always find a niche with children. We make a bridge, and it is a fun bridge to cross over from culture to culture.

Oct. 28,1986

What a variety of activities today! First, I was able to see our group meetings in action. It was good to feel that I am capable of handling these meetings between Arab and Jewish sixth graders, although it is a definite challenge for me to understand the Jewish children's Hebrew, which is much more advanced than mine. It was encouraging to see that the children who had been to prior meetings had a definite difference in their attitude toward the Arab children. The Hebrew level of the Arab children is much lower than the Jewish children because, by sixth grade, they haven't been studying Hebrew in school for very long. Fortunately, play is a universal language for children.

And then I went to see my Ethiopian boy, Yacov, who has finally been able to move to a different boarding school. It was so good to see him so much happier at his new school. He is growing into a young man now, complete with pimples. I gave him the radio I had brought back from the U.S. for him. And he gave me back his tape recorder to fix. I may no longer be his housemother, but it seems I will never stop being responsible for his things. He is doing well in school there, and his counselor told me he is adjusting well.

I raced back to Shefaram in time for my English Club. What fun I have with those girls. One asked me about Interns for Peace—she had heard that it was not good. I spoke about stereotypes and the privilege of being a Jew living in Shefaram.

When I came home, a neighbor asked me to drive his wife somewhere. In return, he invited me in and gave me coffee and then offered me dinner. Most of the family spoke good English, especially the old man and his sister who had been educated in British schools.

It was again a day of contrasts and unlikely situations to find myself in. And I loved it!

Nov. 2, 1986

Identity is a strange bird. It hovers around and then flies away, quite incapable of being tied down. I thought about the complexities of Arab identity in Shefaram. The Druse are Arabs, but, unlike other Arabs, they serve in the Israeli Army. How can a Druse put together his Arab identity and his Israeli soldier's uniform? What does he strip off of his Arab identity before he puts on his Israeli soldier's uniform and shoulders his gun?

The Christian Arab must feel the confusion of loving Jesus who was born a Jew, and living in a Jewish state which both houses him and oppresses him. The Moslem Arab is tied to many brothers in many countries while he claims citizenship to Israel, the land of his birth and also the Jewish homeland as declared by the United Nations.

Then, there is my own identity. I sit quite comfortably in my little home in Shefaram and look through slides of me as a typical upper-middle-class Jewish American liberal, wife and mother. Now, I am one of two Jews among 25,000 Arabs, and yet I feel quite okay, quite intact, and quite excited to challenge my identity to so many variations.

My identity must not be a simple thing. It has developed a resiliency and flexibility that travels from Ethiopian homes, to Arab homes, to Israeli Jewish homes, to American Black homes and to American White homes. Who knows where else it will go to in the years to come? My identity is such that I will, no doubt, always become excited by M & M peanuts, hugging black children, and teaching English to those who speak it with an Arab accent. My identity is like a rich and interesting compote.

Dec. 15, 1986

Work has been going well. I've been part of several meetings between the school children and they have generally gone okay. I think the hardest part is the lunch-time visit when a Jewish child takes an Arab partner home for lunch, and then vice versa at the next meeting. The Jewish children complain that the Arab children look around and touch things in their rooms, even in closets and drawers. The Arab children have a difficult time eating at Jewish homes because they are not used to being asked if they are hungry or want more food. They are used to being served food and automatically say "no" when asked if they're hungry or want more to eat. And neither group particularly likes the food at their partner's home. Guess this is all part of cultural exchange. Although I must say I despair more and more about the "big picture," it is good to be the catalyst that brings Jews to visit Arabs and vice versa. That is their reality. They can't run away from it.

I have started two more after school English clubs in Shefaram that are pure joy. These clubs are mixed with junior high students and even a good number of adults who have joined. Somehow, I keep coming up with activities they enjoy. I like teaching.

On the health front, although I was worried about it, I've been able to keep myself warm enough during the cool winter here, and happily counted seven months without a cold.

ARAB WEDDINGS

The bride sat sadly on a dais decorated with palm fronds in a very large room in her home. I sat among the women in the room who chatted and ate the variety of fruits, nuts, and drinks continuously served to us. It was a Druse wedding in Shefaram.

Druse, who share Arab culture and language, have a very separate religion with its own traditions. Men and women are separated at celebrations, and often there is neither music nor dancing. Feasting is a major part of the wedding with huge quantities of meat, rice, and vegetables heaped on hundreds of plates. I was taken into a side room to view the dowry—basically clothing and furniture that this bride would bring to her new husband's home.

The chatty, informal atmosphere changed abruptly when several women began to cry. The bride herself cried rather hysterically. I, who was used to only gaiety at weddings, was confused. I was told it was sad because the girl was leaving her family even though she would actually be living quite close by.

The bride's father and brothers, who had been together at the groom's home next door, entered the room and came up to the bride. They placed a cloth over her head and led her out of the room, down the steps, and over to the next house. Young girls threw flower petals along the way and we women followed her. Once she was settled in a chair in a room in the groom's home, a very nervous young man approached apprehensively, threw the cloth off her head, and immediately ran out. This was the ceremony that marked their union forever. The women and the bride intensified their crying as each woman came up to wish her well. Then we were given extremely bitter, unsweetened coffee. When I commented to a woman I knew how strange it was to see so much crying at a wedding, she said, "I cried much harder at my wedding."

Since that time I have also been to a Druse wedding without the bride who was in her own village having a wedding celebration at the same time as the one in her groom's village. A Christian Arab wedding has quite a different tone. There I ate excessively and danced too wildly—the woman is supposed to restrain her exuberance while the man is the showy, more active dancer.

It is still common in the Arab culture to have an arranged marriage, sometimes putting together people who have never met, or are actually first cousins. Unfortunately, as evident in Shefaram, deformed children are often the result of first cousins marrying. When I asked a young Arab co-worker if he wanted his parents to choose his bride, he surprised me by saying, "Yes, because my parents can choose better than I can." While I, from a Western tradition, worried that a loveless marriage would be an unhappy marriage, I discovered instead a solidarity among the women in an extended Arab family that was a strong, secure, support system. Unlike the Western tradition, the husband was not expected to be the "best friend" in the woman's life. While it is also true that Arab women suffer from gross inequality and the subservience expected of them, I was impressed that the marriages I saw worked as well as they did.

Dec. 21, 1986

This evening began with a 16th birthday party for Reuven and ended with my being arrested. I reacted with the bravado of a cowboy showdown and a hint of Sarah Bernhardt.

My intention was to have an American style birthday celebration for Reuven's 16th with candles, cake, wishes, and the wonderful sound of the Ethiopian boys trying to sing Happy Birthday in English. Ethiopians acknowledge age more by group than individually. But, I knew his own birthday was important to Reuven. And, birthday parties were also part of the Israeli culture. Although many of the

Ethiopians had already been transferred to other, and I believe better, boarding schools, there were still several there from our original group. The Ethiopians and Israelis were now mixed in the bedrooms, but the boys told me there were still problems between them.

Miriam, the counselor, came into the room looking worried. She said the rabbi wanted to talk to Reuven. When Reuven returned, he told me in Hebrew that everything would be okay, but he spoke a lot of *Amharic* to the other boys. We tried to continue the party when the rabbi came in.

"Did you bake this cake?" he asked as if thrusting a sword in a duel.

"It's an absolutely *kosher* cake bought in a store. Here, you can look at the wrapper yourself," I parried. "Have a piece. Why do you want to spoil the party?"

"I want to talk to you outside."

"Say whatever you want in front of the kids."

He walked out. Seeing little choice, I packed up my things, gave Reuven his present, said goodbye to the boys and walked out. Miriam sadly told me in English that the rabbi wouldn't change and would only make it harder on the Ethiopians. She was afraid she would lose her job for not reporting that I was there and asked me earnestly to leave right away and not come back. She even told me that the rabbi had considered letting the air out of my tires, but discarded that idea because then I would be stuck there.

The rabbi and two older Israeli students stood by the door of my car. We really had nothing to say to each other, but they wanted to keep arguing. Eventually, I realized they wanted to keep me there until the police could arrive.

I spoke loudly and angrily, finding it difficult to come up with the right Hebrew words in the heat of the moment. My boys hovered nearby, offering me moral support. I wanted them to see a woman standing up for herself. I choked back some unkind words I wanted to say about the rigidity of the Orthodox, and settled instead on calling the rabbi "*tipesh*," stupid. That shocked everyone except me.

The rabbi said the children would be punished. Ridiculous! Punish the boys for my coming? I decided then and there I would have to call Dov, the director. I got in my car and started down the path to the street. Reuven ran after the car. He silently said his thank you and goodbye to me by putting his hand on the outside of the car window. I put my hand up against his on the inside of the window and then continued down the road.

A police car came by and flagged me down. He asked for my license and then my identity papers, took them into the boarding school office, and told me to come up to the office. My boys all tried to explain to him that I had been their housemother, but he brushed them aside. Reuven yelled to me in English, "Don't be afraid." I really wasn't afraid at all because I felt "right" and "justice" were on my side.

While one policeman spoke with the rabbi, I spoke with the cute, friendly one and explained what had happened. The other policeman called me, grumbled something in Hebrew which I didn't understand, and then ridiculed my inability to understand Hebrew. Then he told the cute policeman to take me down to the police station in Maalot.

The kids had gathered outside in the rain—their dark faces hooded in their dark jackets in the dark of night. They all looked so terribly concerned. Most likely, being taken away by police in Ethiopia had meant torture and mistreatment. I had no such fear, but the bond between these boys and me strengthened in that moment.

The police only wrote up some report and let me go. After I got out of the police station, I went straight to a pay phone and called Dov, the director, even though it was 11:30 at night. I told him I was standing in the rain in Maalot, briefly explained what had happened, said I wouldn't come again, but I wanted his promise that the children would not be punished because of me. I added that I believed the rabbi had lost a lot of respect from the Ethiopians tonight. He said very little, probably because he was angry. But I'm not really sure whom he was angriest at. He said the children would not be punished and finished with the familiar Hebrew palliative that ends discussion, *Yihiay tov*, "it will be okay."

Somehow, I felt like a rather wet, bedraggled heroine as I headed home to Shefaram.

Dec. 25, 1986

Merry Christmas! They came to church dressed in all new clothes. The weather was deceptively springlike, and there were far more than just one "real" Santa Claus parading down the street. Unlike the American Santa Claus, the Arab Santa Claus wasn't fat and chain-smoked. In the crèche in the church, Jesus was born in a cave instead of a stable. While the themes were familiar, the words were in Arabic. The food was in abundant supply, but there was no turkey bulging with stuffing. It was the first and only time I saw two beggars on the street. I accompanied my Arab Christian neighbors to mass where these Catholics don't kneel and have an 80-year-old Roman priest who has parapsychological powers.

Gifts are not emphasized for Arab Christmas, but the children's faces lit up like kids anywhere when they saw several Santas ride by in a horse-drawn wagon rather than a sleigh. The wealthier families pre-arranged for a Santa to come to their home to personally hand a gift to each child in the family.

Jan. 18, 1987

I've got it—my very own permanent, subsidized, tiny one-room apartment in Kfar Saba with no roommate! Because it's subsidized by the Jewish Agency, it will only cost me about $35 a month. Part of me wants to furnish it first class, but the practical, poor side of me warns not to go overboard. Its tiny size will be a natural curb to how much I spend on furniture. The best part of the room is the one window that looks out over fields where they grow strawberries. Israel is so narrow, I actually look out onto the no-man's land of the "territories." I love the view, but I really regret there is no balcony to sit out and enjoy the view. Kfar Saba is a nice suburban community, not all that far from Tel Aviv. So, now I'll have a place to live after I finish my two years in Interns for Peace. In the meantime, it will be a welcome occasional break from my fish-bowl life in Shefaram.

Feb. 3, 1987

I continue to marvel at the variety of my life as I sat yesterday tickling the toes of an absolutely perfect doll of a three-year-old Arab girl while listening to her great-grandfather reciting by memory the poems by Lord Byron that he had learned during the British Mandate period. He had been a customs inspector at the port of Haifa and even showed me the uniform he had saved when he retired. This is the same old man who appeared at my door one day with a freshly picked flower and an invitation to accompany him to the Pensioners' Recognition Day celebration run by the Shefaram community.

March 4, 1987

The words of a sweet, friendly 17-year-old student in my English class have had a profound, depressing impact upon me. It was a simple assignment to get them to talk. I told them a modified version of Rip Van Winkle where a man fell asleep for 100 years and then woke up. I told them to put themselves in Rip Van Winkle's situation and tell us what they saw when they awoke.

Most of the girls had fairy tale endings that somehow involved a Prince Charming. But, almost spontaneously, one very quickly put a story together that went like this—

"I woke up and got in my car. While driving to Haifa, I noticed that all the signs were only in Arabic. The land was returned to the Arabs and all the Jews had left, going to America, Europe, and Ethiopia."

The rest of the class gasped audibly. I was speechless. This was not a radical Fundamentalist that I knew existed in every Arab town and village. No, this was one of my non-political, gentle, friendly, intelligent female students who voluntarily came to my class once a week.

If she, having been raised in the protected life of a Shefaram high school girl, feels this way about Jews, and can say this directly to me and feel it, I cannot find any hope. My non-Jewish artist friend, who has been painting murals on the walls of the school buildings in Shefaram, has told me that the Arabs talk to him differently about Jews when I'm not around. But I had never kidded myself that I was wanted and liked by everyone in the village. Now I wonder just how much I, simply because of being a Jew, am hated here.

Some have told me not to take my student's words to heart, but, for me, she was the child who changed everything by exclaiming aloud that the Emperor wasn't wearing any clothes. The subtle currents of tension between Arab and Jew flow deep, and sometimes are hidden so well that they seem not to exist at all, but they are there nonetheless even after all these years. Being surrounded by Interns for Peace and like-minded Arabs has given me a skewed view of what I'm doing here. I am now much more aware of the every day, routine tensions my Arab and Israeli friends have grown up in. But understanding that it exists doesn't lead me to any answers.

March 10, 1987

I have just returned from a painful confrontation with some visiting Germans, which, in turn, was a painful confrontation with myself. They were young and idealistic, wanting to "help" Arabs and Jews get along better. I had no particular reason for hating them, but I did—almost instinctively. Why? Without the Germans, there would have been no Holocaust. Without the Holocaust, there would be no Jewish/Arab conflict in Israel because there would be no country of Israel. There would be no need to force Jews and Arabs together onto the same ground. I also hate them because they invalidate my work. How? They make me confront what I know and don't want to face. How I feel toward Germans is just like the deep distrust Jewish Israelis feel for the Arabs.

When one of the Arab men said tonight that what we did in Interns for Peace—helping Jews and Arabs know each other as human beings—would also break down the barriers between Germans and Jews, I winced at the comparison.

And when my intern partner said she wanted to work on breaking down her hatred of Germans and accept them as people, I screamed inside, "NO!" While it may be true that my Arab friends would not shoot me, or I them, I don't for one second believe that the Arabs wouldn't wipe out the Jews if they could. If you take away the rabid hatred of people like Kahane, I'm not so far from the opinion of some of my Israeli friends that I'm working for a useless cause.

I don't want to believe that Jews and Arabs are a threat to each other. I want to be wrong. Because of wanting to be proved wrong in believing there is no solution, and because I don't have any hatred toward Arabs, I can live in Shefaram and work in Interns for Peace and consider the possibility of really coexisting in the same country. I can lie to myself until someone suggests that the Interns for Peace approach be put to the Jewish/German hatred.

March 24, 1987

Today ended one of my first successful and satisfying parts of my work here. I ended the English Club for the high school girls because they must study for some compulsory exams very seriously now. I will miss them. I learned from them what it means to be a teenage Israeli Arab girl with brains and potential.

They said they had also learned a lot from me because they feel more confidence in speaking English. They asked me why I had chosen an all-girls club, and what I thought about them. I told them that it was harder for women to succeed than men, and that they were bright and could go on to college and professions. I had hoped to give them a bit of an edge to succeed, and apparently they appreciated that.

March 28, 1987

I may not be progressing much in learning Arabic, but through the lessons and my contact with my Arab teacher, I am learning more about the culture. He clarified something that I've suspected, but haven't really thought about. It's about trust.

Americans are taught to trust; other cultures, less so; Arabs, not at all. It is not a matter of lying, but more a matter of simply not believing what the other says. I believe this is an important clue for me in understanding more about why the Arab/Jewish problem seems so insoluble, and why the different Arab nations are in so much conflict with each other. It is a deeply ingrained trait not to believe, not to trust. My teacher, with his boyish round face, said it so matter of factly because it is taught matter of factly to each Arab child.

I know that we Americans are at an extreme in teaching, if not practicing, honesty and trust, but I hadn't given enough weight to the impact of being taught the other extreme.

April 20, 1987

Today was a day when fried *matzoh* and Arab Easter crown of thorns cookies came together. I celebrated Easter in church with my Christian Arab friends while my mind wandered from Shefaram to China to Tahiti, from musings of the future to past meanderings, to friends and relatives in faraway places, to comparisons of similarities and differences. I returned home longing for fried *matzo* like my grandfather used to make for the Jewish holiday of *Pesach* when my cousin and I stayed at the broken down hotel my grandparents owned for awhile. It is strange, but necessary—these traditions, rituals, memories.

How dear was Yacov's aunt who ran after me yesterday after I visited to reiterate that she and I are sisters, and hugged me to seal it. I have so many homes, and so many families. My future is just a haze now. I wonder where it will lead me. Where will I die? Who will care? What families and children have I not yet met?

August 3, 1987

I am reading about the war against the Arabs in the city of Jerusalem back in the late 1960's while all around me in Shefaram I hear guns. They are probably celebrating a wedding, but it scares me. It is too real and too violent. I think of how violent it is here, and then I read that there are actually random shootings on the freeways of Los Angeles—another form of insanity.

My roommate has quit her job without any explanation to me. We weren't close, but I'm not sure if I'll have to leave Shefaram and live in a Jewish community or will get another partner who is new to the program. I've also begun to think about what I'll do next June when my two years in Interns for Peace is up. After reading some Pearl Buck books about China, I'm curious about that place. I know nothing about China and have never really known a Chinese person.

Sept. 15, 1987

Sleep came and went. Somewhere in the middle of the night, I awoke to mosquitoes and never fell back to sleep. My mind wandered back to my visit to a different boarding school where several from my original group of Ethiopians are studying now. It is indeed a fine, fine place. There is so much right there that was wrong at the other boarding school. Most wonderful is that there is none of the

Israeli-Ethiopian feuding! I'm so happy these boys are finally in a good school where they can concentrate on their studies and are treated with respect.

Sept. 30, 1987

I'm able to stay in Shefaram because I have a new roommate. She's more congenial and somewhat older than the first one. She's a curious mixture of cultures. Her parents were German Jews who escaped from Hitler's grasp to Uruguay where she was born and grew up. She spent her last ten years living in Frankfurt, Germany, which she apparently loved. The mindsets and cultures of Germany and Uruguay couldn't be further apart and I can see both the spontaneous, emotional Uruguayan side of her and the picky, detail-oriented, conservative German side. We get along okay, but there's a big difference in our sleeping routines. She gets up literally at the crack of dawn and starts her day. Of course, she goes to bed just about the time I begin my evening. So, we are each doing our best to tiptoe around quietly while the other is asleep. Since we have rooms without doors, it's a bit tricky.

A FAMILY GATHERING

It was a family gathering. Whole families with babes in arms were there. Food was handed around. Radios blared music and people sang. Greetings were exchanged, and family news shared about who was well, who was sick, who had died, who had married.

The beauty of the nature surrounding the gathering was stark. Bold mountains dotted with gray and white rocks contrasted with the deep blue of the sky and the brown strip of road that wound its way up and over the mountaintop. Scrubs of plants dotted the mountainsides. Clumps of people stood or sat among the scrub. Mothers and fathers spoke to sons and daughters, children to grandparents, sisters to brothers, uncles, aunts, cousins.

But this ordinary family gathering was not ordinary in many ways. Instead of hugging and handshaking, towels and arms waved from the separate mountainsides. Instead of looking into each other's faces, they struggled to find one another through binoculars. Instead of quietly chatting and sharing family secrets, their strained voices shouted and broke the silence of the mountains, distorted and amplified through hand-held loudspeakers.

In between the children and their parents, grandparents and their grandchildren, brothers and their sisters, nephews and nieces, aunts and uncles, cousins—in between the mountains was a strip of land mined to explode at the pressure of a human foot. Two strong brown fences sandwiched a brown strip of road on which only an army jeep patrolled, with a soldier and a machine gun protruding from each side aimed at opposite mountainsides.

These were families like many others, but some lived now on Israel's side of the mountains, and the others on Syria's side. Their Druse Arab villages were divided by the ugliness of war. Letters and phone calls are forbidden. Being close is forbidden. But families are not easily divided, and so they continue to come to their country's side of the mountain for family reunions.

The talk of this day was a 12-year-old boy who had had a fight with his parents and had run away to his uncle, who happened to live on the Israeli side of the village. By sheer luck, he had somehow eluded the notice of soldiers and the land mines in between the two sides of the village. How complicated and dangerous a simple family fight could be in one village divided by two countries!

Yes, this was a big family gathering repeated with different families every weekend. It was one of the saddest things I saw in Israel.

Nov. 16, 1987

I'm caught in the clutches of another cultural conflict. Israelis and Arabs don't share the American view of "man's best friend." The first dog I remember seeing in Maalot was a handsome, medium-sized dog that lay writhing in agony in the street. I ran to find a policeman, yelling to get help for this poor animal. The policeman looked at me in disbelief and explained, "That's what's supposed to happen to stray dogs. We put out poison to kill them." I was dumbfounded. I went back to the dying animal and met the pain and panic in its eyes with the pain and sorrow in my eyes.

A few weeks later, when a soggy mop of a little dog hung around the boarding school looking for food scraps, I remembered the terrible death throes of the other dog and took this little one in. From childhood, I had taken in stray dogs who became beloved companions. I named this one Woosha, the *Amharic* word for dog. The Ethiopian boys weren't too kind to dogs, but I let them know very definitely that Woosha was my friend and needed to be treated like it.

The director, Dov, didn't want me to keep Woosha even though I licensed the dog and had him vaccinated. One day, while I was away, he ordered my moppish, very lovable companion banished. To where, I never found out. He lied about taking him to an animal shelter because no one remembered such a dog when I went there to find my Woosha.

A family near me in Shefaram had two dogs. One was a "useful" hunting dog as large as the other was small. Although they had owners, the dogs regularly had to fend for themselves by foraging for their food. And they were never allowed indoors.

It seemed natural to me to help the dogs out, so I began to buy and cook liver for them to eat. It was also natural for me to want to pet the dogs, but they were very dirty. So, I sometimes brought the little dog inside and gave him baths. Having grown up with the children's tv show, "The Cisco Kid," I named the little dog Pancho, Cisco's sidekick. He became my loyal sidekick. My back porch had an old couch on it, and I sometimes sat on the couch with the big dog lounging on one side of me, and Pancho on the other side. Arab neighbors who saw me sitting with the dogs and petting them looked surprised and disapproving.

The young children in the neighborhood usually kicked little Pancho or tormented him in any way they could. He loved to sunbathe on the wide windowsill and the children would close the shutters and imprison him between the shutters and the bars of the windows. Although in vain, I tried to model for the children how to treat a dog.

The dogs became a divisive issue between my roommate and me, and my Interns for Peace supervisor who was an Arab man. They felt I would damage our relationship with the Arab community because Arabs didn't accept my behavior with the dogs. It really became a big problem when Pancho started following me around regularly. I even started sneaking out of the house to avoid the dog and using my car instead of walking to my destination.

Yesterday, a neighbor invited me to come to her home for coffee. It was raining. Both dogs saw me walking and came up to me, jumping up on me with their wet paws. They insisted on following me to the lady's house even though she began whacking them with a big stick. They wouldn't leave, and I couldn't bear it. So, I just turned around and went back to my house so she wouldn't hit them anymore.

Nov. 29, 1987

My new roommate didn't last long. She has quit the program and will be leaving. It's really not acceptable for me to remain a woman alone here in Shefaram, so I'm not sure what will happen. Right now I'm looking forward to taking a vacation break in Europe in December. I've felt quite restless these last few months trying to decide what I want to do in June after I finish Interns for Peace. It's also become nerve-wracking with too many changes because some of the interns have quit early.

Jan. 31, 1988

What a shift! I returned so excited by my time in Spain's Granada, Toledo, and Cordoba—three wonderful cities where Arabs and Jews had lived for many years at the peak of each culture's development and in harmony. They were proof that Arabs and Jews can coexist in peace.

Sad to say, that is not the case in Israel now, perhaps never. While I was gone, all hell broke out in the "territories." Things are not a whole lot better now. Kahane's goons actually showed up in Shefaram to visit a long-forgotten ruin of what was once a synagogue. They came to intimidate, but stirred up the anger and frustration of the Shefaram residents. Before, the people I knew in Shefaram didn't want to talk politics with me, but now they often bring up politics.

Israel is taking a beating in the world press, and our program is falling apart. The jittery Jewish schools are now postponing and canceling the school meetings. Even though Shefaram is in Israel, the Arabs here have relatives and a lot of sympathy for what goes on in the territories.

While not in a declared war, this country is very much in an undeclared war. I saw this for myself when I went with a Druse family and a scout troop to visit the snow at Mt. Hermon. It's so amazing to actually be able to build a snowman and sled down the hills in only this part of Israel. Soldiers were as much a part of the scene as the snow was. They rode by in double-sided machine gun jeeps.

Feb. 14, 1988

It's Valentine's Day, but one can't feel it in Israel. I am becoming more and more aware of the tremendous pressure I live in daily. The Jewish/Arab "situation" has worsened. Instead of feeling the energy of having a firm direction, I absorb the pain from both the Jewish and the Arab side. The tension grows and grows. When I watch the news on television, I now place the faces of Arab boys and men I personally know on the Arabs shown on the news. I put the faces of my Ethiopian boys on the Israeli soldiers shown on the news. An added sorrow is that the relatives still in Ethiopia are pleading with their families in Israel for money, food, and getting them to Israel.

Feb. 18, 1988

<u>There was a murder tonight in Shefaram!</u> My wonderful car, dubbed Magic Carpet Leaf from the moment I bought it, was bombed. I slept through the time gas was poured over the front tires and ignited. I slept through the fire department putting out the fire. And then my neighbors came to wake me and tell me what

had happened. We saved some things from the trunk, somewhat the worse for wear and smelling terrible, but still useable.

Amidst the confusion of the policemen, the firemen, and neighbors telling me not to cry, little Pancho suddenly appeared. I ran and picked him up and held him close and didn't mind who saw me.

I walked outside in the early morning—too early for people to be around—so that I could grieve and have a funeral for Magic Carpet Leaf. The pretty green of the back of the car made such a sad contrast to the ugly blackened front of the car. As I've often done, I talked to it. In the misty early morning, I hugged as much of its wet, cold metal as I could get my hands and arms around. I cried over it, thanked it, apologized to it, and bid it farewell. Pancho was there too. He sensed that I was upset and stood loyally by my side for comfort.

Feb. 26, 1988

These last several days have been very difficult ones. The Shefaram police came to take details and make a report. However, when I asked them if they could patrol the area around where I live more frequently, especially since I was living alone, they said they couldn't do that. It was not unusual for the electricity to go out suddenly for awhile, but I became very nervous when it did. It was more unusual for the phone to go dead, so when it went dead one night, I checked all the locks and then put chairs against the doors like they do in bad scary movies. I kept Pancho inside with me at night. He would be useless as a protector, but his bark could alert me to trouble.

I received a hand-written letter on notebook paper from a Shefaram local official. The English was hard to understand, but he expressed his regret at what had happened, saying I should not be blamed for Israel "invading the West Bank." He hoped I would remain in Shefaram and not think badly of the Arabs there. The founder of Interns for Peace sent a letter to console me about this act "by an obvious social misfit," and said it had been a mistake in judgment for the program to allow me to have my own car in Shefaram. He encouraged me to finish out my four months in a nearby Jewish town.

I think my neighbors feel embarrassed, so they relate to me as usual except for a few saying they hope I won't leave. But tension is high because a bus was torched in Shefaram a few days after my car. The Egged bus service is Jewish-owned, but there are Arab drivers. As was usually the case, a Shefaram bus driver took his bus home after he finished work so it would be there to start his route again in the morning. But, someone torched the bus in the middle of the night, just like they did my car.

March 3, 1988

I've left Shefaram and am back in my Kfar Saba room. I began to worry too much about my personal safety after the Egged bus was burned and decided not to risk staying. My reasoning was that, if I were personally hurt or worse, it certainly would not be good for me, Shefaram, Interns for Peace, or Arab/Jewish relations. It was hard for me to leave Shefaram under these conditions after 18 good months there. It was sad to leave the people in Shefaram who had been so kind to me. They can't quite believe such violence is happening right in their quiet little corner.

I decided not to spend the next four months in the Jewish community not far from Shefaram. The place holds no interest for me, especially without a car. It is filled with Orthodox Jews who are becoming more and more active in this confrontation over the occupied territories. After my treatment by the boarding school because of working for peaceful coexistence with Arabs, I don't think I'd feel all that wanted among the Orthodox in that Jewish town either.

Getting the insurance money is also complicated. The insurance company won't talk to me because they claim I am not the sole owner of the car. That's because I bought the car with immigrant rights, which means I only paid 50% tax when I bought it compared to the 200% tax Israelis pay. The rule is that I don't owe any more taxes if I keep the car for five years. However, it has only been three years, so Israeli Customs says it is like I "sold" the car before my five years. By their logic, I owe them about $6600 so I can have clear title to the car. Then, I can make an insurance claim as sole owner.

I'm not sure what will happen to the plans I was making to travel in June because there is a work strike and no new Israeli passports are being written. They tell me that, when I accepted Israeli citizenship after three years of living here, I don't lose my American passport, but must use my Israeli passport to leave the country.

So, that's life in Israel. Surely Alice couldn't have found Wonderland any more confusing.

May 15, 1988

My restlessness for new adventures is a good, energizing feeling. At night, while lying in bed, I like to listen to Vivaldi's "Four Seasons." There is always one part where I feel my excitement rising and actually visualize myself dancing a ballet high on my toes. It feels so free, so wonderful. Occasionally I've actually gotten out of bed to dance, but the vision of perfection is more enjoyable than the reality of my clumsiness.

Israel finally began writing new passports, so I can leave. I looked closely at my finances. When I figured out I had only $15,000 left, I decided I'd better go around the world while I have enough money. So, I've purchased an Around the World ticket that is good for one year. I only had to set the itinerary, not the dates. I'll skip around to friends and relatives in the U.S., then Japan, then Hong Kong. From Hong Kong, I'll have to get another ticket into China. I didn't get any responses to letters I sent to China to find a teaching job, but I'll see what happens once I get there. Based on what happens in China, I'll decide later how much time to spend in Bali, Thailand, Singapore, Nepal, and finally back to Israel.

I want to try to teach in China as a tool to get to know the people without knowing the language. I surprised myself by doing so well as a teacher in my Shefaram English Clubs, so why not in China? However, since leaving Shefaram, I tried having an English Club at a Jewish boarding school not too far away from Kfar Saba. The Jewish students were totally different from the Arab children I taught. It seems Israeli Jews have an adversarial relationship with teachers. You have to show you're "tough enough" to be an authority to them. Even if I could be an authority figure, I don't think I would enjoy it. After just one half hour, I told the students they could leave because I couldn't teach them. They thought I was just being "tough," but I insisted I meant it. Then they said they really did want to learn English, so I arranged to tutor them in 2's or 4's, but not as a large group. That went reasonably well. I wonder if Chinese students are more like the Arabs or the Israeli Jews.

I've made some progress with my poor, deceased Magic Carpet Leaf. I must credit reading the surreal Waiting for Godot for preserving my sanity. I had to wait through several days, several lines, and several Customs clerks. I noticed that Israelis waiting with me were vigorously biting their fingernails and pacing the floor. I, instead, sat reading my book and laughing whole-heartedly. The insanity of the book was so much like the insanity I was going through with Customs.

Fortunately, one of the Israeli Interns for Peace administrators came with me. She could talk their language literally and culturally. Eventually we settled on my paying about $1000 tax on the parts of the cars that were not damaged in the fire—two back doors, two back tires, and the trunk. That satisfied Customs, and I could take my claim to my insurance company.

The insurance company has asked for more time since they believe the loss of my car was a terrorist act, and the state of Israel is responsible for compensation in terrorist acts. So, they've hired a lawyer to settle it while I'm away.

I can't predict now what a year of traveling will be like compared to the new challenges I've faced in my five years in Israel. But, I'm almost ready, and I'm very excited!

3

JAPAN HONG KONG CHINA 1988

Sept. 16, 1988

A typhoon literally blew our plane into Tokyo. Woozy from 11 hours on the plane, and particularly nauseous from the bumpy ride through the typhoon, I was greeted at the airport by members of an international organization I belong to. I had met them in Sweden at the last international meeting. Their chapter in Japan was going to host the next international meeting, so I was to be the guinea pig for a trial run of what they were planning when they hosted the next meeting.

Because the prices for hotels were so high in Tokyo, they offered the floor in their chapter's office for me to sleep during my stay. But, by a happy fluke, one of the members had to go on a business trip and he kindly offered me his apartment in Tokyo. I loved it. Tokyo is a mass of huge skyscrapers, but around a corner can be a small neighborhood with three or four-story buildings of apartments, lots of mom and pop grocery stores, street vendors, and most wonderful of wonderful—a public bath, surely one of the best parts of living in Japan. His apartment was in such a neighborhood.

Sept. 18, 1988

I woke up to an unfamiliar bird's squawk and gazed at the beautiful butterfly kite looking down on me from the ceiling in my little room. I tuned the radio to Far East Tokyo in English and heard an old Lana Turner radio play. It was followed by a talk about symptoms of malaise in women in their early 40's. I thought I fitted a lot of these symptoms that are supposedly aided and abetted by being pre-menopausal. Then came on an American Jewish disc jockey (I could tell from her name) playing Yardena Arazi singing gypsy music in Hebrew; whereupon, I began to cry, probably from a combination of being pre-menstrual and homesick for Israel.

My two delightful hostesses took me to the old Asakusa district where they have rows and rows of Pachinko machines and Las Vegas style gambling machines, which made a cacophony of clinking and clanging. There are shrines and temples all around. I took a picture of a statue to mothers of miscarried babies. There were little babies crawling on and around the mother, and each one had a carefully knitted red cap on its head.

Since the international organization is about children's right to play, and playground equipment is an important aspect of children playing, they took me to Hanegi Play Park to watch children playing. There, I met a father accompanying his child. He was an American married to a Japanese. He had left Palo Alto, California, and was missing that part of the world very much. He dislikes Japan and the Japanese people, finding them cruel, cutthroat and ruthless in business, ready to do anything for the sake of the group. He said television was filled with wanton cruelty, and everyone was obsessed with money. Japanese values disgust him. To him, this park was the only place in Japan where one could play freely, where dirt and disorder were allowed. I felt rather sad for this angry, out-of-place 1960's personal peace and freedom leftover flower child.

Sept. 21, 1988

I have now spent two nights staying in peoples' homes, one in the countryside near growing rice, and one right in the busy city. They are members of SERVAS, the travelers' organization I joined before I left Israel. Joining was a rather rigorous procedure, with two personal interviews plus personal references to insure that I would be a good guest in the homes of people throughout the world who also went through a rigorous screening to make sure they'd be good hosts and hostesses.

It seems it was well worth the trouble because being able to see life inside a family's home definitely adds an important dimension to understanding a country. The first woman I stayed with had recently married. Their small apartment had only one room that could be divided into two. At night, they laid mats in each room, and she slept in the room with me while her new husband slept in the other room. Hot baths are a daily ritual in Japan, and they had a great one right in their bathroom. My next SERVAS hostess lived in an even smaller apartment in the city. My luggage alone almost filled the room. To eat, she set up a small table in the room. To sleep, the small table was folded away and mats were laid on the floor. Japan has a lot of SERVAS hosts. That surprised me when I saw how small their living quarters are in Japan. The American concept of everyone with his or her own bedroom wouldn't work here at all. And the Japanese are even willing to add a guest or two.

By the way, Dunkin Donuts abound in this city. There is literally one on each corner. Why is it so appealing to Japanese?

Sept. 23, 1988

One of my goals in coming to Japan was to see a lot of Japanese gardens and try to understand them better. Japanese gardens combine a love of nature, plus careful arranging. A landscape garden combines six qualities—"spaciousness, seclusion, artificiality, antiquity, abundant water, and broad views." What an interesting, quite sensitive combination! Unlike western gardens, there are practically no flowers, and no grassy spots with people lounging and lying around.

There is a wonderful quality to the gardens in Kanazawa I've seen so far. The gardens are, to me, one of the few worthwhile achievements of mankind. They combine nature and man in a confluent way that fills me.

Sept. 24, 1988

Takayama is the charming town in the mountains I had hoped for. Unfortunately, it poured all day. I made quite a sight in my purple rain poncho and my Israeli blue and white umbrella. I'm staying in the Youth Hostel here which is actually an old, beautiful temple. It has a peaceful garden, and even a wonderful cemetery out back. I don't know if it will stop raining, but I'm warm and cozy for now. Soothing classical music is being piped in. I wouldn't expect the young Japanese clientele to enjoy it, but the ancient Japanese lady who runs the place and I appreciate this music.

To keep expenses down, I've been skimping on food. I can barely afford the grocery stores and steer clear of restaurants.

Sept. 25, 1989

Today I wandered wetly through the Hida Folk Village, an outside museum of historical old houses brought from all over Japan and reconstructed. I had to laugh at myself every time I went to another house because of the Japanese tradition of taking off your shoes in the house. Because of the rain, I wore my rainshoes that have laces up to my calf. On, off. On, off. On off. Annoying, but quite funny.

Sept. 26, 1988

How intimidating could a subway station in Tokyo be? But, even before I got there, I froze watching those thousands of lemmings coming from all directions in Shibuya station. Instead, I stood meekly waiting for a taxi, with my big brown pack strapped on my back, and the blue bag on my front. And then, I saw myself as the coward that I was.

"Go ahead," I encouraged myself, "You can do it!"

Gulping hard, I plunged into the madding and maddening crowd and did a real decent job of getting where I needed to go by subway during rush hour.

Sept. 27, 1988

I like staying in Youth Hostels because I am meeting so many kindred spirits. Instead of incredulous looks of, "You want to go where?" I find young girls who say, "When I was in China, Thailand, etc., etc. No, I'm not sure yet how many years I'll be on this trip."

They have much useful information to impart such as where to stay in which cities. One former Peace Corps girl's description of when she got sick with Japanese encephalitis and her strong recommendation to "get that vaccine" stopped my wavering on whether or not to get it. As we lay on our mats in a huge room with over 200 other young travelers, another young girl suggested I take a water bottle into China that can withstand hot water since all drinking water there must be boiled and they don't have water fountains around.

I feel a kinship with these young woman, and I'm very glad I am now in their ranks, albeit somewhat tardily. I still do not wish to be younger, but I realize I must constantly think of conserving energy and not expending too much too quickly. The energy level seems to be the only major difference between us.

Sept. 28,1988

My time in Japan has been short. Of course, there is much of Japan left unseen, but I'm satisfied. It was meant as an appetizer to whet my appetite for what awaits. I can tell I have a taste for culture contact even more than touring.

Oct. 2, 1988

If one wanted to get lost in a crowd, Hong Kong is the place to do it. Not that there weren't teeming masses in Japan, but there is a crowdedness about Hong Kong that can sometimes be frightening. On the other hand, I rather like the anonymity.

Hong Kong is quite a place, small in area, but a mass of contrasts. The bulging of the masses makes Brooklyn's tenements pale. There is sophistication and wealth as personified by silk-suited men walking on the street talking into hand-held telephones that travel. There are beggars and street people who make their homes on the sidewalks by putting up cardboard walls for privacy. There is a plenitude of every consumer article here, but it has a different feel from American style consumerism. Here, it just seems to belong. Money is king here too, but prices are so cheap compared to America. And, while I'm sure that profit-making is the goal, there doesn't seem to be the desperate cheating and gouging of trying to part people from their money.

The recreated Sung Dynasty Village with its magnificent hand-carved buildings stands alongside a crass, gaudy amusement center. And all is in a setting of huge, towering apartment buildings, and a green profusion of hillside and banana trees. But that's what this place is—a mixture in every way. You name it, and they seem to have it here.

There are some aspects to Hong Kong that remind me of home—Israeli rudeness and noise, brusqueness, jostling and pushing, dirt, and dilapidated buildings. Along with the dirt and dilapidation, there is the magnificent ocean harbor and the wonderful mountains.

I was right. The Far East was definitely a gap in my knowledge of the world. It definitely is its own culture and a place unlike anything I've seen before. And yet, there are differences between Japan and Hong Kong. And I assume I will see differences from the People's Republic of China, which I'm about to enter.

Oct. 5, 1988

Only one more day in Hong Kong. It has begun to feel somewhat familiar. I really love going from Kowloon to the Hong Kong side by the famous Star Ferry, crossing that picturesque, busy, unfortunately very polluted, harbor. To ease myself into China, I've signed up for a four-day tour, only I won't be coming back with the other tourists. After the tour, I'll be on my own. I have bought another book about China that has information my book doesn't have. I've spent some time reading it, and I alternated between being absolutely intrigued, and scared to death. Can I really manage? How much of my worldly money am I willing to put into this?

I know that this has been the easy part of the trip so far. I'm sure I'll wish I could bring my little YWCA room in Hong Kong with me. I will long for the simplicity in Hong Kong of brushing my teeth and eating food relatively unafraid of getting sick.

Oct. 7, 1988

Here I sit in the Canton airport in China. Yes, I actually made it to China. It definitely is a foreign country, and not too friendly at first glance. Inefficiency and cigarette smoke seem to be the major characteristics. While we wait for the plane, the tour guide has his eyes closed and is slightly rocking back and forth. He has been a tour guide for five years now, and having his tours torn to bits by the inefficiency, especially of the airlines, is nothing new for him.

Our guide told us that things were much different in China ten years ago. Life was simpler and people cared more for each other. Now, people are more and more worried about themselves, and terribly worried about money. Sounds very western to me.

People are sitting as Arabs might, men smoking up a storm, sitting, chatting, or doing nothing—endless doing nothing. When the guide found out I was from Israel, he said he thinks that Jews are very smart and clever.

As the guide quietly chants "oooohmm," my mind twitters from thought to thought. If Jews are so smart and clever, why is the Israeli army so efficient, while everything else is so inefficient? The smoke is stifling. Why do I choose to be here now and not in efficient and dull U.S.A.? Maybe efficiency brings a certain dullness. Why does there seem to be a correlation between boring and efficient? Sitting for hours waiting for a plane that doesn't come is boring. But our guide has said that sometimes planes in China leave <u>earlier</u> than their scheduled departure time. Why can the trains run on time in China, but the airplanes can't? Why does Japan work like clockwork with both extreme cleanliness and efficiency, and Hong Kong spins along at a dizzying pace?

At some unseen signal, our guide gathers us up and we board the plane.

Oct. 8, 1988

I have been charmed by the Li river and formations near Guilin, certainly one of the most unusually beautiful places in the world. This place is attempting to gear up for massive tourism. And, it really does have something to "sell." Its future is an interesting aspect of its time and place. How will it fare as it crashes into capitalism and commercialism, and short-term contact with hordes of outside world visitors?

As I watched the various Chinese I met, or at least brushed in contact, and those I stared at from above in the moving tour bus, I felt a curiosity to get to know them better—to somehow break through that tourist barrier.

Oct. 12, 1988

I'm on my own now. Here I sit in a park overlooking the river in Canton being stared at by locals as they stroll, bicycle, or sit by the water. Men carry around small bird cages with chirping occupants and hang them in the trees. I think about the wrinkled fruit vendor lady who smiled so when I gave her FEC's, Foreign Exchange Currency. It is a special currency foreigners must buy for twice the price of the regular currency called *renminbi.* Apparently, ripping off the tourist is also government policy. When I give a local vendor FEC's, they make double on it and give me any change in *renminbi.* So, one of my first tasks was to exchange money on the black market. I can use the local currency for some things because I'm on my own and not with a tour that goes only to expensive tourist hotels and souvenir shops. It felt familiar since I had been used to changing money on the black market in Israel. Same rather unsavory "dealers" leading me into small alleyways to transact "business."

My handy guidebook for independent travelers led me to a cheap, shared room that comes to about $3.77 a night. Actually, I'm really glad to be with roommates since they are two young women who are just coming out of China. I picked their brains mercilessly for information. But the most helpful part was just seeing them and knowing they had done it on their own.

With some difficulty, I managed to get a train ticket to Hangzhou. I'm looking forward to Hangzhou, but not the loooong 28 hours in hard sleeper.

HARD SLEEPER IN CHINA

How happy I was to see him hurrying over to the taxi dragging his worn-out small, hand-cart luggage carrier. He indicated he wanted to take my bags to the train. He was middle-aged, rather scruffy-looking, and by his smell at 7 a.m., also a drunk. He struggled to put all my bags on this tiny, very tired two-wheel carrier. Failing to get them all on, I took a couple of lighter bags.

My joy at seeing him was not only because I had no desire to lug all my bags alone, but because I also hoped he would help me find the right train and "hard sleeper." He did, and led me on in fine style, installing my luggage on the racks. I knew I was overpaying, but I gratefully handed him 10 FEC (about $2.50). He looked at it in surprised awe, and hurried out.

Chinese trains divide into hard seat, hard sleeper, soft seat, and soft sleeper. Buying a hard seat ticket had seemed to me to be entering the hardship of Chinese life too precipitously, especially for a 28-hour or more train ride. Soft seat, while less crowded and more comfortable, seemed less of a local Chinese experi-

ence. So, I had decided upon the middle approach for my first long train trip in China. Hard sleeper, I had been told, was usually the choice of hardy, individualist backpackers.

A hard sleeper isn't as hard as it sounds, being covered by a wafer thin pad. There are six to a cubbyhole—bottom, middle, and top, each with its own particular advantages and disadvantages. The bottom is convenient, but since there are only two small seats adjoining each window, the other people must either lie on their sleepers, or sit on the bottom sleepers together. The top sleepers, while providing some privacy, give a feeling of being wedged in, offer no view out the windows, and receive very little air since the windows don't open up that high. Middle, which I had been given, seemed the most convenient and comfortable since no one else sits on it, and it does afford a view that could be appreciated while prone.

Even before the train departed, people immediately made preparations for the long voyage. These included wetting towels for washing hands and face and hanging them carefully over the rungs of the luggage racks (which maintenance train personnel periodically come around to re-fold so that they do not hang below the upper window level), filling jars with hot water in which tea leaves float and seep their flavor, and arranging various food they have brought.

These tasks done, people sort of eyed one another to check out who would accompany them for the next 28 hours or more. Some Chinese carefully locked their luggage to the luggage racks to insure its safety. Apparently cash is often carried in this basically check-less, credit card-less economy. Theft is going up on trains.

I checked out my neighbors—a young married couple, the wife of which looked ill and who immediately lay down, and the husband who was a pleasant looking fellow, but a chain smoker. There was another woman traveling alone who smiled at me shyly, and a distinguished-looking older gentleman who somewhat timidly began to talk to me in fairly good English. He had a brother in Seattle, Washington, and he and his wife were going there to live in one month. He wasn't with us much because his wife was traveling in the more expensive and more comfortable soft sleeper section. So, he spent his awake hours there with her.

The other occupant of our cubicle was a young man who must have come from another part of China because he spoke a different dialect. Not that I could distinguish a difference, but eventually he and the other young man spent hours over a notebook on what seemed to be language lessons. He was a more occasional smoker, but I eyed him also as a problem to contend with. This young man said only one sentence to me, "Do you know what time the train will arrive?" but this sentence was said surprisingly clearly. I casually looked around at the rest of the car's occupants in other cubicles, and they stared at me. I was, as I later learned, one of only three foreigners out of all the train's travelers.

It was clear to me that my biggest problem would be how to contend with the smoke from hundreds of cigarettes—chain-smoking men who had nothing better to do for the next 28 hours. I decided to position myself on one of the two seats near the open window, and to rarely leave it except to go stand in between the railway cars.

I put off going to the toilet as long as possible, having been warned of its filth and stand-up style. While I can't claim it was pleasant, it wasn't as bad as I had expected. I rather enjoyed hanging on to the little railing and watching the scenery fly by.

Music drifted in and out of the car, our car's speaker either being broken or turned off. Sometimes I heard a distinctly Chinese melody while I looked out upon scenes of water buffalo, growing rice, and shouldered burdens. I felt amazement at being here. Sometimes the music was more like American Muzac style, Richard Cleyderman being very popular.

I watched the people peel off cigarette wrappers, food packaging, papers, and just about everything else that people throw away, and casually toss it out of the windows, or on the floor. I had looked in vain for a wastebasket. Finding something I thought was one, I threw in some trash, only later to watch the attendant simply take the bucket and dump its contents out the window. The floors and windows were indeed the wastebasket. Twice a day or so, the girl responsible for our car swept up all the junk and ran a filthy wet mop ceremoniously, but not very effectively, over the floor. The other grunge caked on the windowsills, etc. was never disturbed.

As haphazard as the mopping was, it was welcome because of the Chinese habit of spitting on the floor. I am not at all sure when this became a part of Chinese culture, and the government is trying to stop it through the media and fines, but it will be a long and tiring battle. Heavy smokers tend to spit more, but in places like Israel, the land of both Arab and Jewish chain smokers, spitting has not acquired such proportions and popularity. This abundant spittle is not a part of the Chinese culture that can endear them to foreigners, especially obsessively clean-conscious Americans.

So, amid the spitting, smoking masses, I, too, settled in for the duration. When the train neared a station, our car's assigned railway attendant rushed by, donned an official cap, locked the toilet door (one should not stink up already filthy railroad stations) as well as the door to the next railway car (to prevent people without proper tickets from entering), took a clip-on number 5 sign, and prepared for the stop. As soon as the train stopped, she opened the door, clipped on the number, and positioned herself outside the door.

People then poured out from the train and rushed over to some vendors selling a variety of things. They came back with plastic containers of food, skewered chicken feet, and other forms of food I could only guess at. However, having been to the Canton food market that sold many of the animals we would look for in a pet store, I did not allow my curiosity to wander much. Since I could not understand the loudspeaker announcements, and since one is only allowed to re-enter one's own car or not at all, I dared not stray too far from my unsmiling railroad attendant. Before leaving each station, a uniformed man came by and banged on some part of the mechanism underneath the train. This brought to my mind the question of just how safe the train really was. I did not linger long on that question.

Upon re-entry to the train, people intensely applied themselves to eating. Chinese, although all quite skinny, eat with great gusto, and in a hurry, with chopsticks flying. To a foreigner's eyes, it is much like shoveling food into the mouth. And then, of course, the plastic boxes flew empty (Chinese rarely leave leftover food) out all the windows.

The smoke cleared a bit between 2 and 4 p.m. when people tended to sleep. The noise level, always quite high, dulled down somewhat. At some point, I sleepily climbed the ladder to my sleeper. My neighbor was sitting on the lower sleeper and lit up another cigarette. As the smoke wafted upward, I donned a surgical mask that I had brought because I had been told it would help to keep me warm in winter. He looked up at me in great surprise, and then he began to laugh. He said something to his wife, who also looked up and laughed. I knew she was a silent sufferer of his smoke from watching her earlier. He tried to wave the smoke away, but knowing it was a useless gesture, he left the car to finish it elsewhere. I thanked him.

I watched the scenery from my sleeper and nodded off. Sleeping on a sleeper is actually a pleasant experience. The noise of the train blurs the noise of the people, and the movement is like a cradle, albeit with occasional lurches. There are straps to securely hold you in. And, all lights go out at 10 p.m.

Some people went to the trouble of changing into clothes for sleeping, but most did not. There was, however, much evening and morning movement to the sinks for face and handwashing, and toothbrushing. Eventually the washing water ran out, which I understand is usual, and then people relied on wet towels and the large boiled water containers for tea making. The Chinese seem to have excelled in the art of keeping hot water hot in thermos bottles for as much as 24 hours. Even advanced American technology can't match up in the thermos bottle time test.

It was good that I had brought some food because buying food was not easy for me. I was ignored in the dining car, which was incredibly filthy, and only finally got a bit of food through the kindly assistance of one of the very few English speaking Chinese on board. This young Chinese man had appointed himself guardian of Jean-Paul and me.

I had first met Jean-Paul in Canton at the CITS (Tourist Office) trying to buy a train ticket. He was on his way to Shanghai, and I to Hangzhou. We found one another on the train, and spent some happy hours talking, trading tourist information (much more helpful than the Tourist Office), and discussing the U.S., traveling, traveling alone, and traveling in China.

Jean-Paul had had the good fortune to receive a hard sleeper next to a young Chinese man who had just spent a year in England with his parents. His English was superb, and he spoke of how his parents had suffered in the Cultural Revolution, and how he was returning to finish college education in Shanghai. He was also helpful in getting me food, and in being sure I got off at the right stop.

At Hangzhou, Jean-Paul and our Chinese caretaker helped me to carry my bags off the train, and we wished one another well. I had said goodbye to my neighbors in the cubicle, and felt a certain pang of anxiety at saying goodbye to these two English-speaking traveling companions.

I shouldered my bags, took a deep breath, and went into the Foreigners' Waiting Room at the Hangzhou railway station. I had no place to stay. The CITS tourist representative stationed at the railway station looked more and more distressed as she tried in vain to find me a bed for the night. The places where foreigners were allowed to stay seemed to be full. Rightly suspecting I would sleep right there in the Foreigners' Waiting Room if she didn't find me a room or bed, she finally, and reluctantly, reserved me a place at a hotel meant only for Chinese. Another helpful lady negotiated a taxi for me after I was told that none were available, and I arrived at my hotel for the night.

A brief look around told me that I wasn't in the tourist, scenic area of Hangzhou. Unable to explain what she wanted to tell me, the clerk reluctantly picked up two of my bags and motioned me to follow her up and up and up and up and up five floors (there are very few elevators in China except in tourist hotels) to room 511. The building had a prison block look, and my room resembled a cell—complete with bars on the high windows that faced into the halls.

The price had not been high, although much higher than Chinese paid. The room had the barren look of a flophouse room. There were two beds, and I was not sure whether or not I had been charged for both beds, or would eventually get a roommate.

I had basically three needs at that time—food, showering off all the cigarette smoke from 30 hours in the train, and sleep. I found the ladies' toilet and showers. The shower only had one knob, which, as I expected, emitted only cold water. A Chinese lady motioned that I should bring one of the plastic washbasins. Being unclear just how to coordinate the water (there was a large, insulated boiled water kettle-type pot in a little room nearby), and not having the energy to figure it out, I decided to forgo the shower. I also ruled out food since I wasn't sure how to connect with food that would not turn on me, so I munched a little bread and decided I would last till morning.

The sheets could have been clean, or used. I couldn't tell. The pillow was quite dirty, but eventually the girl in charge of the 5th floor (occupants of the rooms do not receive keys and must request the room be opened by the floor attendant) brought in a clean pillowcase—with Mickey Mouse on each side riding a bicycle. There was something else American in the hotel besides me!

There was a practical-looking room with a row of spigots where people seemed to be washing both clothes and their teeth. I washed out my very dirty facecloth from the train ride.

In fastidious American style, I looked for the wastebasket. Finding only a spittoon-shaped thing outside the door, I dropped my carefully gathered trash into it, and discovered there was some water in it. It was indeed a spittoon! I had seen a sign in the hotel saying, "Please do not spit." However, it, and the spittoons were in vain. All around me, and all evening, I heard the unmistakable sounds of spit being gathered and emitted time after time.

My other need—sleep—also needed to wait a bit. The noise level was in the high decibel range with shouting, spitting, slamming doors, and televisions turned up for the hard-of-hearing. So, I turned on the tv and became engrossed in a Japanese picture dubbed in Chinese. It seemed strangely familiar. I couldn't quite place why until I remembered watching the Arab Friday night movie on tv in Israel with my roommate. As in this movie, the women were always pleading, crying, and in distress; the men were overbearing, nasty, and abusive to the women. With Mickey Mouse on my pillowcase, and an Arab-style movie on tv, I felt somehow at home.

Oct. 14, 1988

Pedicabs seem to be the best way to get around Hangzhou. The driver pedals a bike connected to a small carriage that can carry two Chinese-sized people. Negotiating a price before getting in is important, and always seems to be a reason for a crowd to gather around us. The pedicab drivers also seem to be the best source for changing dollars to *renminbi.* I'm sure they make more money as money-changers than pedicab drivers. At first I was worried because I outweigh these wiry men, but they hauled me around easily.

One pedicab ride was more like a roller coaster ride. We were on a hilly road with no cars. Sometimes I got out while the driver lugged the pedicab up the hill. Then, at the crest, he signaled me to get in and we whizzed down the hill. Of course, the little child in me just had to holler "wheeeeee" as we whooshed down. The driver looked back in surprise, and then he broke into a smile. We were like two children playing until a man dressed like a policeman stopped us. The driver looked suitably contrite and I knew our whizzing down the hills was over.

Oct. 15, 1988

Trying to plan ahead, I went to a government tourist office to see about booking a flight to Beijing. The following is the conversation I had with a clerk there.

Me: "I would like to buy a ticket to fly to Beijing."
She: "I can make a reservation, but I cannot promise you'll have a place on the plane."
Me: "When is it possible to get a ticket to be sure of a seat?"
She: "There are many people wanting to fly now. Some people must wait two or three days to get on."
Me: "In the meantime, I would like to have a tour of Hangzhou."
She: "They have been suspended. We have no cars or guides available.
Me: "Then, I would like to join a tour to Beijing or Xian."
She: "It is impossible to join a tour except from the country where you came from."
Me: "I don't intend to return back in order to join a tour."
She: "I understand, but it is impossible to join a tour once inside China."
Me: "So, I am indefinitely a prisoner in Hangzhou?"
She: "I can book a reservation on a plane or a train, but I don't know when you will be able to get on. Maybe you should go to our main office. But it won't help. They don't know either."

There don't seem to be any in between ways to visit China—either high first-class tourist, or the real, tough way.

I have learned my first Chinese word that sounds something like *meiyou*, which seems to mean, "There aren't any." "No more." "No way." "Go away." It is the standard answer to any question I ask.

Oct. 16, 1988

Ah, I have finally found some Chinese people whose interest in me and English extends far beyond, "Change money?" I went along the lake just to check out what Chinese people do on Sundays. I saw clusters of people. When I got closer to one group, I saw a rather embarrassed blonde tourist in the middle. Then, someone spied me and I was soon surrounded by excellent English-speaking Chinese students. What fun! I felt like I was back in my Shefaram English Clubs.

I had inadvertently walked into English Corner, apparently something informal that every city with a large number of university students has in a park on Sundays. They asked me many questions, and I pulled out of my pack a map I had of Israel. Few of them knew anything about Israel, but when I said Jewish, I once again heard the words, "clever" and "smart."

Since I wasn't having any luck finding an English-speaking guide to show me around Hangzhou, I took a chance and asked if any of these English speakers would be my guide. Three boys immediately agreed to accompany me. It was great being escorted and looked after by these three intelligent young men. While drifting in a boat around West Lake amid the islands, I asked them their names. To my surprise, they answered, Russell, Richard, and Bill, names given to them by their English teacher. One was a farmer's son, one a policeman's son, and one a construction worker's son.

They talked a lot and answered my questions readily. Their English was much better than I expected, but then, they were studying in a four-year university to be English teachers. They told me that students must work very hard to get into a good college, but did not study particularly hard once in college. They study only in the mornings and are quite free afternoons and evenings. When they complete their studies, they'll be assigned to schools back in their hometowns.

A big plus for me was that they didn't spit and didn't smoke, at least with me. As we visited some local sites, they were angered by everyone charging me sometimes as much as ten times more money than for Chinese people. They have invited me to visit with them at their school tomorrow.

Today made all the hardships of independent travel worthwhile. A tour tourist would not have the chance to see China this way.

Oct. 20, 1988

Today the boys borrowed a bicycle for me and we biked to some of the sights. They were a little surprised, but happy that I know how to ride a bike. They told me some Chinese girls don't learn how. But girls can gracefully ride "side-saddle" as a passenger on the backs of the bikes. I haven't ridden a bike for a long time, but there are wide areas separated alongside the road for bicycles only. It is a really useful mode of transportation here. Since privately-owned cars are rare, Hangzhou doesn't have heavy traffic. There are a lot of buses, but they all seem really overcrowded.

I am constantly surprised at the wide knowledge of these intelligent boys. Things American, such as Breakdance, have arrived, but much later than in Israel. I wonder how they can relate to American programs such as "Little House on the Prairie" that I've seen on television here. In a country which decides whether to fry or stew their dogs, it must be weird indeed to see a "typical" American lady on tv having her hair done in a beauty parlor while cuddling and hugging the dog sitting on her lap.

While talking to them and some of their roommates in their dormitory room, I have learned that their intelligence is not particularly valued and they are doomed to teach in small middle schools in their hometowns for poor pay. On the money and social status scale, they will be lower than bus drivers and waiters. How difficult it must be for these boys, particularly, who know English well enough to have acquired knowledge of the outside world, but no way to reach it. They admit they would like to get "out," but they don't see it as a realistic possibility, so they don't eat themselves up over it.

Does knowledge bring mostly contentment or discontent? Is it "good" or "bad" for a person, for a country? Certainly China has suffered for lack of knowledge, but how will it suffer with more knowledge? This makes me worry about my influence upon these boys and also whatever students I may have if I teach.

It bothers me that the guards at the gate of the hotel where I'm staying won't let Russell, Richard, and Bill in unless I'm with them. The treatment of foreigners is certainly schizophrenic, and makes me feel schizophrenic, sometimes feeling used and abused as simply a dollar sign, but other times I'm treated "special" because I'm allowed into places the Chinese boys can't go.

I invited the boys to see my room today. I was lovingly reminded of my Ethiopian boys when I went into the bathroom after they had used it and found pee all around the toilet. Why should they know how to use a western toilet? I only recently figured out which way to face and squat on their holes in the ground.

While in my room today, I turned my head at seeing movement and saw a mouse that stared back. I'm not sure which of us was more surprised and horrified! I told the manager that, either the mouse would have to pay for his share of the room, or he'd have to go.

Oct. 21, 1988

I invited Russell, Richard, and Bill to dinner at the restaurant in my hotel. We had a great time comparing different cultures, habits, gestures, and etiquette of eating. Sometimes they disagreed amongst themselves. Richard seems to be from a poorer, more rural village. However, they all have the chance to go to school together because education is free. Higher education is a matter of what one scores on a standardized test.

Logically, I knew that chickens had heads, but I had never seen chicken served with its head attached. They told me that chicken is more expensive than pork, which is the most common meat. And there's a lot of fish. Richard ate the eyes of the fish we ordered as well as all parts of the fish. He spit out the inedible pieces. That's just about impossible for me. First of all, I don't have the ability to roll the mouthful around so I can separate the bones and other inedibles. And westerners are taught that what goes into the mouth doesn't come out again. I suppose it looked silly to them when I cautiously de-boned each piece of fish before I ate it. The taste was great. Fortunately, my chopstick training in San Francisco's Chinatown restaurants came in handy.

Burping is apparently acceptable, as well as deeply slurping soup, which comes at the end of the meal. While I was blowing on food to cool it down before putting it in my mouth, they downed it without burning their mouths. And they ate an amazing amount of rice. Relishing each dish in turn, they finished every bit. They told me they had often been hungry in their childhood and never wasted an ounce of food. How spoiled we Americans are!

I told them Americans usually mix many dishes of food together when eating Chinese food. That horrified them. "How can you taste anything when you mix the dishes?" they asked. I suppose they'd hate American-style casseroles.

Watching the enjoyment with which they ate made me feel the $10 it cost me was spent wisely.

Oct. 22, 1988

"Hi, I'd like to teach English," was what I simply told some people at a place connected to tourism schools in Hangzhou. They scurried around to find someone who could speak English, contacted the principal of the Zhejiang Tourism

School in Hangzhou, and she said someone from the school would come out to meet me.

So, now it's all arranged. With help from Bill, I got a ticket to Beijing. It wasn't difficult for him to get me a soft sleeper bed. I'll return to Hangzhou in two weeks and begin my job as a teacher at the tourism school. Since I came into China on a tourist visa, I only got three months, so I'll have two months left to teach. Maybe the school can help me extend my visa a bit. I'll teach English conversation to a group of students training to be tour guides, and a group in hotel management. It's a two-year school following high school, so they're about 19 years old.

I met some of the students at the school today. They are an eager, interested, great group of kids with a decent start in English. I will have total freedom to do what I want as long as I improve their English and teach them about western culture. I'll have to develop my own curriculum because there are few materials here. The English books they use here are full of stilted, old-fashioned English like replying "It's my honor," when a hotel guest thanks you for something. My mind is already whirling with some ideas.

The school isn't offering a salary, but I'll get free room and board and they'll take me on weekend trips to tourist sites in Zhejiang, which is the name of this province. They've also offered to buy me a new bike.

Wow! I succeeded in getting a job as a teacher in China. Hope I'll be up to the challenge. How can I not love it when one of the students asked, "Can you tell me what apple strudel is?"

Oct. 23, 1988

"When the hotel said you had moved out, we felt a sense of loss," Russell said. He comes out with wonderful English phrases sometimes and has a store of unusual facts in his head. I had moved from my single room to a dormitory room to save money, but the hotel just told the boys I had left. Hotel staff can be quite inefficient too. Fortunately, they called back several times and eventually reached me. They're as delighted as I am that I'll be returning to teach in Hangzhou. Although their school is not really close to mine, we'll find opportunities to get together.

Oct. 27, 1988

Today I walked with Empress Dowager Ci Xi and the last Emperor, Pu Yi. I spent the day roaming the Forbidden City that I had read about in bed during cold evenings in Shefaram just about one year ago. I walked it, sat in it, and explored its nooks and crannies as best I could in one day. A little knowledge from Pearl Buck's book and the movie, "The Last Emperor," nudged my imagination and brought the cold walls and narrow alleyways to life. I thought what a shame it was that I should get here and that Russell, Richard, and Bill, who could probably appreciate its history even more than I, would probably never get here.

The scope of history in Beijing is overwhelming, as is the crush of people. I found an adequate hotel in a *hutong*, one of numerous narrow roads that lead to small neighborhoods and buildings built around courtyards.

Oct. 29, 1988

I must be wary of cheap tours because it can lead to mistakes, in this case a rather humorous one. I took a tour to the Ming Tombs and the Great Wall outside Beijing. There was no tour guide, only a bus driver who said what sounded like "One hour" when we got to the first stop. My usually trusty guidebook said that tours usually stopped at the Ming Tombs on the way back to Beijing. So, I prepared for the Great Wall in all its magnificence. There was, in fact, a wall and a great rush and crush of tourists and high-pressure souvenir sellers. It didn't look like the photos of the Great Wall I had seen, but I walked along the wall, waiting for the turn around the next corner to reveal that long wall snaking up and down over the high hills. It was pleasant, but not what I expected. I felt disappointed.

As we continued on by bus, we climbed into higher hills and the awareness began to grow in me that we were indeed still headed toward the Great Wall. Fantastic! The Great Wall of China, at least the little bit of it we were on, looked just like its photos. It was a thrill to climb the steep wall, and since it's so difficult to walk, my mind tried to grasp what torture it must have been for the workers who built it. Their blood, sweat, and tears were embedded in the stones.

The Chinese tourists were almost as much a spectacle as the Wall itself. I wondered how many people they lose over the side annually as they clamber in every crevice to be photographed. A horse and a couple of weary camels stood obligingly while people mounted and were photographed. The backdrop of the slinking wall, stark hills, and a fortuitously blue sky was truly spectacular. I bought some postcards of the Great Wall in the snow. That must be something gorgeous to see, but the Beijing cold of late afternoon and evening in October were cold enough for me.

Nov. 1, 1988

Today I made the contact I hoped to with someone connected to the famed Children's Palaces that I had heard about. Because of my membership in the same international organization that had given me a personal touch in Japan, I was assigned to a young apprentice named Miss Li to show me around play facilities for children.

Miss Li and her supervisor talked to me about two of the greatest problems in China. One is the "only child policy" implemented since 1979. An eventual nation of everyone having been raised as an only child has enormous ramifications, as yet unknown and unfelt. No one doubted the necessity of the "one child policy," but the reality of how it would change society was staggering to speculate about. The second problem looming was the huge generation gap because life has changed so quickly in China. The supervisor feels people are getting too selfish and money-hungry, but she also agrees that Chinese people have been too obedient and submissive.

The children's facility I saw had a strange assortment of children's entertainment. There was a physical sports center, a simulated airplane ride, a flag pole to learn flag raising and lowering, bumper cars, a roller skating area, a kind of pedal train on a raised track, a western birthday celebration with a birthday cake (but no candles), a cartoon center with Mickey Mouse and Donald Duck cartoons, a "playing" water fountain with lights and music, an art center with an impressive exhibition of children's art, and some simple, but cute playground equipment on concrete (ouch).

Miss Li told me that most Chinese people love China, but she also defended the younger generation's desire to better their lives. I thought how hard it probably was for intelligent and gentle people like Miss Li to survive China's more unappealing filth and roughness.

I gratefully accepted Miss Li's offer to take me on a bike ride through Beijing tomorrow. I bought some good Chinese classical literature books translated into English for a ridiculously cheap price. I also bought ridiculously expensive copies of two American magazines, Life and Reader's Digest, to use for teaching.

A short blurb about Israel on television reported a terrorist attack on eight Israelis near Jericho. Elections are today in Israel and it has been called a very dirty campaign. I immediately burst into tears. I can appreciate Israel more after seeing the extreme of China. I feel my attachment to Israel even here, and still hurt for her.

BICYCLING IN BEIJING

Bicycling is probably the most efficient way to get around Beijing, but one must first enter the "bicycle culture." If a visitor, and therefore not a bike owner, one must rent a bicycle. In my case, I entered a bike repair shop that also rented bikes.

The young girl clerk there didn't look up until addressed by my Chinese companion. She looked at me and snarled some Chinese, which my companion translated, "She wants to see your passport."

Being a tour book wise tourist, I knew she didn't want to just see my passport; she wanted to keep it until the safe return of the bike. Having read the tour book's advice, I offered her my expired U.S. driver's license. She looked at me in contempt, and demanded a deposit. I wanted to give her *renminbi*, the money Chinese people used. But she wanted only FEC, the special money for foreigners in China worth about double the *renminbi*. I produced all the FEC I had on me which was 150, and she reluctantly agreed to take 50 more in *renminbi*. She growled, "5:30," meaning to be back by then unless I wanted to take the bike for more than one day. The manner in which she gave me the bike was roughly akin to the way they throw food at you in restaurants in China.

I checked out the bike myself—tires, brakes, and seat. My companion told me that new bikes run about 300 *renminbi*, so having given the store the equivalent of 350 *reniminbi*, I doubted they cared whether they would see me again. As I left the bike shop, I hoped the bike would be friendlier than its caretakers.

Having little recent experience bike riding except for a few days in much calmer, quieter Hangzhou, I joined the streaming masses in Beijing. I did quite well actually except for nearly hitting one pedestrian as I mounted the bike awkwardly, and once causing my companion to collide with another cyclist because she had not told me to turn and then tried to avoid hitting me as she turned.

It's easy to learn the rules of the road—there are none. Learning how to deal with the chaos is another matter. I joined the other cyclists—those carrying incredible truck-sized loads on their bikes, mother and father with children perched on the bike or encased in an enclosed cubicle dragged behind the bike.

Cars and cyclists are theoretically separated, but this separation narrows with the streets. Intersections are another meeting (crashing) point. Since there are, in practice, no rules of the road, and no right of way for cars or bikes, they merge together. Cars and trucks don't necessarily slow down. These intersections separate the men from the boys, so to speak. It is not for the faint-hearted.

There are numerous dangers. One cannot daydream. It is not an outing, but a serious means of transportation. If the cars don't hit you, there is a steady cross-stream of traffic with other bicyclists in the intersection. This convergence reminded me of skating or dance routines in which one line of dancers crosses through and in between another line of dancers going in the opposite direction. But those routines are synchronized, choreographed, and carefully rehearsed. This was simply chaos. In addition, the test of a "real cyclist" seems to be whether or not s/he can negotiate all these maneuvers without having to set a foot on the ground and stop. They rarely do.

I felt a sense of confidence following my knowledgeable guide. But, then she said she hoped I could make it back on my own because she had to continue home in the opposite direction. I gulped and gamely replied, "I'll try."

And so, I set out on my own—more shakily than when I played duckling to the leader. Even though my path was simply to go straight, there was a considerable distance to cover. I began to doubt I could get back by that gruffly barked, "5:30." I pedaled furiously, weaving my way and clanging my bell, however still less incessantly than my fellow cyclists. I did, however, choose not to play "chicken" with trucks, buses, and trolleys.

It was now rush hour. Street peddlers joined business-dressed people with briefcases hanging over the handlebars. Most women wore various heights of high-heeled shoes. Some women's heads and babies' heads were enmeshed in a mesh scarf to afford some protection from unkind wind and swirling dust, both plentiful in Beijing.

As I pedaled faster and faster to arrive by 5:30, my mind began to develop a contingency plan. If I arrived after they closed, what would I do? I doubted I could convince a taxi to take the bike back to the hotel with me. How to get to the hotel by bike? I knew it was quite possible, but it was almost dark, and after the first turn, I had no idea how to go. I had taken several taxis along the same route over the past days, but the fare had ranged between 11 and 22 *renminbi*. Each driver had gone a different route, the higher fares doing a lot of unnecessary, but more costly backtracking. And then there would be the hassle of getting back to return the bike the next day.

At those thoughts, I pedaled harder, weaved in and out more erratically, and became more daring and careless. I'm sure I just seemed like everyone else.

I zoomed into the grimy bike shop at exactly 5:31. I was relieved to see even those scowling, unfriendly faces. I felt more rattled than the bike had. I felt I had survived a difficult experience. And I felt incredibly relieved that I did not have to travel like that to work every day.

BUS CULTURE

The "teeming masses" takes on new meaning at a bus stop in China. People stand impatiently squashed whether herded by rails or not. Most of the men chain-smoke. Children are hand carried which leaves no hands for maneuvering when the crowd surges and claws its way onto the bus. No consideration is given to women, children, or old people either getting on, off, or sitting.

In my American politeness, I tried to help one mother and her young child get on the bus. But the mother was scared, and rightly so. It is very dangerous. I don't know how she ever got to the bus stop, or how she ever left because there was always a crowd.

One young soldier literally leaped in front of me to get on. My sense of American justice riled, I pushed him hard with both hands. Even Chinese men are little, skinny people and I outweigh them all. It was like pushing a feather and he literally flew inside. I felt only moderately guilty.

Inside the bus is a crush. Sardines lie in luxury in comparison. It's a good thing Chinese men don't act like Italian men when they are pressed up against women. In this madness, a very determined lady shouts and expects you to buy a ticket. Somehow people manage to do so. The tickets are very cheap. Even so, there are checks during and at the end of the ride to make sure people have a ticket. There is no mercy from these ladies who will throw anyone off the bus if they have no money or no ticket. Sometimes, even outside the bus, someone demands to see your ticket when you get off. If you have somehow slipped through, they will demand a fine on the spot.

Perhaps the bus is where Chinese aggressiveness and rudeness comes through the most, although driving by bicycle or car is also rule-less and ruthless. Some bus personnel herding people outside the bus try to maintain a certain control and order, but the effect is generally unpleasant. Quarreling everywhere is common, but certainly obvious at bus stops.

Everyone agrees with the young student who told me, "too much people."

Nov. 2, 1988

Not only is this country contradictory, but I am also a schizophrenic tourist. Sometimes the grittiness and griminess of China gets to me, along with the rude, surly unhelpful response of most of the people. Then, I long to escape temporarily to a five star tourist hotel to once again be treated with a smile rather than a sneer, a polite "How may I help you?" instead of a brusque tirade in Chinese, or a turning away as if I had become invisible. Yes, if it were not for the fine people I've met, I would carry a very bad impression of Chinese who I mistakenly thought were culturally super-polite. They are a stark contrast to the Japanese Asian culture.

Nov. 5, 1988

This is my first visit to a Chinese family's home! I met a young student and his father who were traveling together in Beijing. They invited me to stop by and visit their home in Shanghai on my way back to my teaching job in Hangzhou. Their home is a welcome change from the unfriendliness of Beijing—and worlds cleaner too.

This is a hard-working family with above-average comforts and luxuries, such as a color television, but the apartment is still quite spartan. All hot water must be boiled. My hosts insisted on preparing a western-style bath for me with hot water. They boiled endless kettles of water, but it all took so long, my bath turned out quite tepid.

To accommodate me in their small apartment, the mother and father gave me their bed. They slept in their son's bed, and he was sent to a nearby Chinese dormitory hotel. Having guests is not easy in China.

When I took pictures of the family, the father wanted to pose in front of his turned-on color television. Another status symbol in their home was a large jar of Nescafe with a red ribbon tied around it. When I asked the son, Conrad, why, he said because Nescafe was western. He was shocked to learn that there are other kinds of coffee besides Nescafe. Of course, this jar would never be opened and used.

Conrad and I went to a western-style place for lunch and he used a knife and fork for the first time. He did a really decent job, but his awkwardness was apparent. The mother cooked dinner at home. When she finished eating, she said what Conrad translated as "Eat slowly." I thought I must have been eating too quickly, but this is the polite thing to say when anyone finishes and others are still eating. Instead of lingering at the table waiting for everyone to finish, each person gets up and leaves the table when finished.

Nov. 6, 1988

Today was filled with lots of impressions and tourist sights. Visiting Conrad's uncle gave me a perspective on recent Chinese history. Shanghai was once a very active, cosmopolitan, international city. He had learned English, but contact with anything foreign had been forbidden during the Cultural Revolution in the 1960's, and so his English had deteriorated.

Whereas people the age of my students had been very young during the Cultural Revolution, he had been middle-aged at that time. I tried to ask him some questions about the Cultural Revolution, but he didn't know how or if to respond. A curious thing happened when I asked. His leg suddenly developed a repetitive, nervous twitching motion.

He scared Conrad by telling him it was against the law for me to stay at a Chinese person's home. He suggested I go to a foreigners' hotel for the next two nights of my stay. When Conrad and I returned to his home, he told me to keep my head down and not to say anything as we passed the neighbors. When he told his father about the uncle's concern, the parents seemed unconcerned, caring more for hospitality than fear.

Of course, the neighbors have been asking about me. I'm not sure what he's told them. From what I've read, this isn't idle paranoia. Theirs is not a friendly government, even or especially toward its own people. Although more open now, the fear is there that it could revert to what happened before and somehow used against the family. Poor Conrad was scared because he is making plans to go to study in either Japan or Australia and doesn't want anything to jeopardize his chances.

In the evening, I took Conrad and his uncle to the Acrobatic Theatre. That was a rare treat for them. It's basically a tourist show, but well done and my FEC was able to get us excellent seats from scalpers that waited outside before the performance. Trying to get the tickets through the tourist agency earlier had been useless. It's just another way that independent travelers are punished for not coming with a group. There was that word *meiyou* again. The animal acts in the show gave me my usual repulsion and revulsion at seeing animals used that way, but in China, the cats, dogs, and monkeys in the show were probably better off than being eaten like their less talented comrades.

Nov. 8, 1988

During a boring 3½-hour boat ride down a very filthy, polluted Huangpu River, Conrad confided that he had had an unhappy childhood. He was raised by his grandmother from the age of two until she died when he was 17 because his parents had been sent away to a remote rural village during the Cultural Revolution. He said that was not unusual. The babies of the Cultural Revolution are now the young adults, and they spent most of their childhood far away from their parents.

I've been reading one of the Chinese classics I bought called Camel Xiangzi by Lao She. A young rickshaw runner tried to better his very miserable life, but failed. I kept waiting for a happy ending for all his hard work, but it was mostly depressing from beginning to end.

It was wonderful to be able to live with a family for a few days. And soon I'll be starting a new part of my adventure as a teacher in China.

4

TEACHING IN CHINA 1988

Nov. 9, 1988

Picture me, if you can, as the first model guest in the model hotel they are literally building around me on the small campus of the Zhejiang Tourism School. After putting up some knick-knacks and pictures I've bought along the way in China, it now has a cozy, homey feeling. It's only a little larger than my Kfar Saba room waiting for me in Israel. Like that room, this room has just one window that looks out onto fields of growing vegetables. The school is in the "suburbs," although picturing an American suburb can't conjure up what this looks like at all.

This room has a nice carpet, wallpaper and a color television that speaks only Chinese. The bathroom has a bathtub, but, alas, NO running hot water. My students have told me not to worry because they will bring me six large thermos bottles of hot water every night for bathing! The toilet is western style, but has already overflowed a few times. I suspect that western toilets have made it to China, but not toilet technology. I've never seen a plumber in the U.S. use a pink ribbon to fix a toilet like the plumber did this afternoon. Need I add that there's no heat in the room? So glad I packed my down booties. Apparently, I'm the ONLY resident living in the hotel now. It basically hasn't opened yet.

I'll be teaching 16 hours a week, although I'll also be invited to the English Corner evenings held by different classes. They wanted me to teach 40 hotel management students at one time, which is their normal situation. However, I pleaded the case for dividing the 40 into two groups of 20, which makes far more sense for teaching conversation. They agreed to do it. There are 25 in the tour guide class.

Nov. 10, 1988

Interesting, interesting, so very interesting. I went to the tour guide class today to introduce myself since the teacher had invited me. They actually applauded as I walked in. I felt my teaching "high" as soon as I began to teach. After I talked about myself, I asked each one to say something about him/herself. A few said they were lazy. One stressed that she liked reading, but hated class. One is a poet, and a few are writers. Many said they missed their parents and siblings because the distance is too great to get home often for visits. I wondered how many American 20-year-old students would say that. One boy said he liked catching dragonflies although he wasn't often successful at it.

Some are genuinely interested in becoming tour guides; some just accept their state-decreed professions. Most of their parents are traditional Chinese doctors, teachers, factory workers, or farmers. Actually, I use the word, "farmers," but they say "peasants." That isn't a derogatory word to them.

I spent some time after class chatting with their young teacher. His English is much better than some of the other English teachers whom I find very difficult to understand. That's because the older teachers have good English reading and writing ability, but had very limited exposure to hearing English pronunciation. The students today listen to short-wave radio programs through BBC from England and VOA from America, so their speaking is more fluent, with better pronunciation.

The young teacher, Mr. Chen, said the lack of freedom in China rankles him, but he seems to care about his students and how well they learn English. He told me that teachers must be careful what they say because everything gets reported. Hmmm! I told him of my dilemma whether or not to talk about travel because I don't want to frustrate them. He said that they realize they are different from me. And I know it's true that the seeds of knowledge are already a part of their personalities. I can only offer them my own world knowledge and opinions, and hope that expanding their world is not a disservice to them. But yet I worry that it may be wrong to fuel the dreams of these young students.

Nov. 11, 1988

Sleeping in isn't an option here. In the middle of the school grounds, directly under my window, the students gather at an absurdly early time in the morning and do exercises in unison to music blaring through the loudest speakers I've ever heard. I dragged myself over to the window and watched their exercise routine from above. And then I went back to bed. Exercise is good, but I won't be joining their morning routine.

I have had a nagging headache, which I suspect is from the heavy use of salt and MSG. Seems that Chinese believe food needs MSG in it to be tasty. The cook is trying hard to please me. They asked me what I liked to eat, and I mentioned cheese. That was not a good choice. Turns out they don't eat cheese or really any dairy foods. The cook went to a lot of trouble to get a piece of cheese for me that came from another part of China. It was truly terrible. I thanked the cook, but told him not to bother to get cheese anymore. In a small store near the school, I have discovered chocolate—which has the words "pit-filled chocolate" on the label. Like its name, it's really pretty awful chocolate, but the tastiest food I've eaten so far. I've lost my appetite—which isn't a totally bad thing if I lose weight. Thankfully, I brought a supply of vitamins.

I sometimes feel really cold indoors. In the classroom today, I noticed how red the kids' hands were. I wear my gloves in class, but they don't seem to wear gloves. Some of the students wear really beautifully hand-knitted sweaters made by their mothers. Their clothes are neat and clean. Instead of heavy jackets, they wear several layers of tops and pants over long underwear. But I'm glad I brought my down jacket.

I got my shiny new red bike today and went for a ride with Pearl, a bright, perky 2nd year tour guide student. Her spoken English is better than most of the English teachers at the school. The roads near our school are pretty bumpy. I have to pay careful attention.

I thought of my Ethiopian boys today when I saw news about Israel—strikes in the Arab sector, stoning, the razing of the Arab homes where militants live, destroying an Arab orchard, soldiers everywhere. Israel is like a sponge in my heart that keeps absorbing more and more pain.

Nov. 12, 1988

Russell, Richard, and Bill told me that, if they could, they would gladly give up their four years of education to become tour guides. The hotel management students envy the tour guide students. Even the teachers at the school would prefer to be tour guides because tour guides can go to new places and make more money from tips. Yet the tour guides lament that they will never be able to leave China. I try to give them hope because they are young and it is true that China is in flux and changing quickly.

I'm sure I'll come away from this experience with a greater depth of understanding that, while freedom does not always work well in society, the individual desire for it does not die. Freedom seems to be a basic need. There can be acceptance of circumstances, or resignation, but that doesn't quench the thirst. I never thought about freedom so much before coming to a country that has so little. However, to Communism's credit, it offers a very refreshing freedom from violent crime, theft, drugs, and pornography.

I found the first Chinese food here that I eagerly wolfed down. It's called *jaozi*, rather like a filled dumpling. Another of my tour guide students brought me on a long, hairy bike ride downtown. The restaurant, like most, was a government restaurant with unsmiling clerks who wear incredibly dirty aprons. There is often a shortage of chairs, so the patrons who are waiting stake out a chair and stand over you while you eat—quickly.

Nov. 16, 1988

"What kind of meat do you like?" I asked casually as I picked up my chopsticks.

"Dog," said a cute young student. With a sudden jolt, I remembered that I was in China where dog is a dish instead of a much-adored pet. I couldn't suppress a little shiver and suggested she not tell that to her future tour groups of westerners.

I have been their formal teacher for three days now and it has been great fun. The kids like me, and I like them. Some are quite knowledgeable, and yet others constantly remind me of how little they know of the world. It's also good to be working again.

Nov. 18, 1988

Today was precious. "Touch your forehead. Hold up your pinky. Stomp your feet. Shrug your shoulders. Wave to me. Wink at me." The kids adored it. They are not used to such active, participatory classes. But that's the difference that we foreign teachers can bring to them. Russell told me he was never so excited in class as when an American taught a few classes at his school.

From my short time in China, I've noticed that a sense of humor is sorely lacking. I want to put lots of humor in my class. So, we sat in a circle and I told them the story of Goldilocks. I'm so sorry I couldn't take pictures of their faces—good-looking 20-year-old faces enraptured with a simple children's story. I tried to burn into my memory the looks and excitement on their faces. For those minutes, we were all together in that time and place. I felt very happy to be there among them, and it made my decision to teach here even more right. We ended the class with my teaching them "Home, Home on the Range."

A teacher asked me to check over his English preface to a teaching booklet he has prepared. He had the peculiar statement in it that the book was immature and had many undesirable things about it. When I said that seemed strange to me, he said it was the Chinese custom of modesty. In the U.S., we would think he was fishing for compliments. I then spoke to some students about how different our culture is where we coddle everyone, and always try to build up self-confidence, not tear it down. We emphasize the positive and try to make the person feel good. And we are not very modest. It is hard for me to respond when they are always saying how bad their English is, how dirty the room is that they've just cleaned, etc. I think Chinese modesty will take some getting used to.

The school is taking me on a weekend trip to Thousand Islands Lake with one of the classes. Smith and his friend came to my room to talk to me. His English level is very low, but his determination to speak to me is high. He said where we were going was his hometown. I like when he points to his nose when he says "me" or "I." I've seen Richard do that too. Smith had actually written out a story for me about Thousand Islands Lake and its scenic spots. So thoughtful of him.

Nov. 21, 1988

These last three days have given me many highs and rushes of happiness. I was able to invite Richard, Russell, and Bill to come with us to Thousand Islands Lake. The school paid for me, but asked such a reasonable sum for the three of them to come along that I was thrilled to pay it.

Their individual personalities are becoming more distinct as I get to know them. Richard is the ebullient one who freely expresses his enthusiasm. On Friday, as we neared the power station, he became more and more excited. Russell is much more reserved, but his excitement began peeking through. He said to me a few times that this was a new world to him, and one he never thought he would see. His English vocabulary is quite extensive, and I could tell he kept trying out more difficult and sophisticated words. Bill is the most silent one, but his excitement was obvious many times. I had a couple of good conversations just with Bill. He thinks I'm very brave to travel around alone. He also told me he gets quite depressed about his future, and confided to me that he quarrels a lot with his parents although he can tell they're very proud of him for being the first college graduate in the family. When we were up on a mountain, his eyes glistened and gleamed as I tried to describe what camping was like in U.S. parks. Each one was very thoughtful toward me in his own way.

Each of them expressed sadness that the trip would end. I tried to emphasize that it was all locked into their minds to take with them forever. When we passed a secluded area with some farms, Richard said he loved scenery like that. I picked out a mountain and said that was "Richard's Mountain" for him to have a farm some day. I told him that nothing was impossible, although some things may be unlikely. We returned to the spot after dark, and he said excitedly, "That's Richard's Mountain. Do you remember it?" He had entered the dream.

Richard is actually the one out of the three boys with the biggest dream. He has hopes of going to France with the help of an overseas Chinese man who is living in Paris. Dreams, it seems, are universal. Without dreams and goals, one's spirit withers and dies. Their situation in life complicates having dreams. Being in China has helped me appreciate my options and freedom much more. But these boys really have so much going for them, I want them to realize it.

I had the honor of being allowed to sit on the deck of the little boat on the return trip. My caretaker, Elizabeth, made sure I was treated like an Empress. Everyone else had to sit in a stuffy, smoke-filled cabin that allowed little of the magnificent view to filter in. But, of course, I could not be outside without a companion, so they took turns being out there with me. When Russell was with me, he told me something about his family. He really disagreed with his parents on many things, but because he didn't want to hurt them, he pretended to agree with them. What a tremendous generation gap there must be between illiterate peasants, and a college educated, knowledgeable, bright son.

Each of these boys has the typical young 20's zest for life and desire to imagine all sorts of wonderful things that will happen in their lives. The gloominess and lack of choices in the reality of Chinese life weighs heavily on them.

I can only adjust so much to another culture. At other times, I'm just me. While returning on the boat to the hotel, there was a great stir of excitement when a swimming wild pig was caught and killed. Everyone on the boat was so excited. Only I felt sorry for the pig. It was hard for the others to understand my feelings about the pig. When they dragged the pig into the cabin, I went outside. Russell knew I was upset and followed me. He must have told the others because soon Richard, Bill, and Elizabeth came to join me. They were all freezing, not having the benefit I did of a down jacket, but they all sat with me to comfort me. I felt bad they were enduring the cold for my sake, but I did not want to be in there with the poor dead wild pig that had been so free and alive only minutes earlier.

I got to see an example of "losing face" later that evening. "Face"—losing it, gaining it, giving it—is a very complicated part of Chinese culture that I doubt westerners ever clearly grasp. That evening we all went to a local disco in the small town we were visiting. I was surprised that the music and dances were mostly ones I remembered from when I was in my 20's. The boys danced very well. I'm not a good dancer, but I surprised myself by keeping up with them and had fun. After awhile, the boys understood something that I didn't. They didn't want to tell me either. Apparently, the locals in the disco wanted to fight because they had lost face. How? Our group had better dancers! It did not end violently, but as the boys quickly ushered me out, I got beer thrown on my head. That led to a discussion with the boys in which I stressed that I prefer directness and openness and that they shouldn't try to protect me by not telling me things.

I must mention the beautiful places we saw. There was Monkey Island, Snake Island where I at long last had the chance to hold a boa constrictor, a temple built as a memorial to Hari who had been a benevolent ruler of the people and had even dared to criticize the Emperor. Then there were the fall-decorated mountains where I taught the boys the term "hairpin turns" and a newly opened Stone Forest that is probably similar to one in Kunming, minus the crowds of people. The lake and islands were like Puget Sound in Washington, Norway, Switzerland, but I've never seen such a clean, clear lake outside the brooks and streams of the Sierra Mountains or the Cascades. The lake is totally man-made—"all Chinese made" Russell proudly told me, in 1964. The islands are actually mountaintops. The depth and dimension of rows and rows of mountains reminded me of the Sinai area in Egypt I had hiked in. The water looked so wonderful, I would have gone for a swim if it hadn't been November.

The clear water also yielded an amazing array of fish. We had fantastic fish feasts. All different kinds of fish were cooked in various ways. I tried my best to dance around the fish bones. Every fish was yummy. But the best part was watching the Chinese enjoying their food with much shoveling and slurping and concentration and intensity. And how Richard can crunch those fish heads and spit out the bones on the table or floor. As the guest of honor, each dish was presented to me first as it was put on the table. Russell told me I was supposed to take the first piece before the others could eat it. It was hard for me to keep up. There are also parts of the fish that are thought to be more of a delicacy, and people kept putting these "best pieces" directly on my plate.

The bus rides were also Chinese adventures. It is amazing how those old wrecks of buses keep going. And it was much like Mr. Toad's rides with great speed and constant honking and beeping, and, of course, continually passing whatever appears in front of it. Actually, it's not too unlike Israel, only worse roads and more reckless.

Nov. 23, 1988

Teaching is hard work, but it's also fun. Sometimes I think I'll run out of ideas, but things seem to spring up. My students pay a lot of attention to me, giving me small gifts, coming to my room to talk, or taking me on bike rides. One girl, Diana, has invited me to visit her family in Hangzhou soon. We rode our bikes today to wonderful West Lake in time for sunset. On the way back, she wanted to talk about love. Even in their late teens, they don't date yet. They can't marry young because, by law, each must be at least 20 and their combined ages must equal 50 or more. And they are only allowed to live where their identity card is from, making it very hard for a couple to marry if they are not from the same area. So, getting married isn't easy in China. There I was pedaling home in the full moonlight talking to Diana about romance and the hardships of love in China and America. It all seemed so right.

When I got back, there was a message from Elizabeth that she would be taking me to Suzhou and Wuxi next.

Nov. 24, 1988

I got into a deep conversation over dinner today with Thomas. We talked about the differences between American and Chinese students and teachers. He told me that it is best to keep silent in China. He said, "Learning from Chinese teachers is like eating fish." He couldn't quite explain what that meant, but he and the other students at the table described a rather dry, dull, rote learning and regurgitation. And, it is not a good idea to disagree with the teacher. I told them that American students were encouraged to ask many questions and think for themselves.

I could see a certain excitement in him when I suggested he write out his thoughts and I would be glad to read it. He was surprised at my offer to read it. I think he'll do it. He seems to want to talk to me more.

Letters have begun arriving from the U.S. and Israel, so it's been good to catch up with my two homes. However, by the postmark I can see it takes at least one month to reach me! Mailing letters is different in China too. Most assumptions based on past experience of how things work can't be taken for granted. When they put an address on an envelope in China, the arrangement is completely opposite what I'm used to. In other words, the country comes first and then works down to the person the letter is going to at the end. The return address of the sender is under that address. There is no sticky part of the envelope to lick. Instead, a paste must be applied to close the envelope as well as put on the stamp. And the stamp can be placed anywhere on the envelope—including the back.

Nov. 25, 1988

Silvia, the bubbly Mistress of Ceremonies, announced, "We are glad to welcome Ms. Zima. She's an American from Israel." That's true enough, but we all cracked up laughing. It was an English party at the school. They hammed it up, sang those tired songs of the 50's that I think they think are the latest hits in America now. My contribution was doing the Hokey Pokey, which made them gape in amazement. Some joined in. They'll think all Americans are quite crazy after me.

These students are constantly surprising me. Yesterday, Thomas initiated a conversation about classical music and Picasso. The writing my tour guide students pass in is beautifully poetic. Letters turn into "birds that fly from one person to another." Sadness becomes a "shadow in my heart." And, I was touched by "I had to pretend all day. It's so tired." Even their mistakes in English can make poetry.

Nov. 26, 1988

Today, the three boys plus Conrad who came to visit us, wanted to talk about love and marriage. They said they don't intend to marry for at least five years so they can be ready financially. They had seen the movie, "Kramer vs. Kramer," and brought up divorce. I shocked them by saying that divorced couples in the U.S. sometimes remain friends and even continue to see each other. Russell called that "incredible." Apparently, there are no friendly divorces in China. Although divorces are far from common in China, they do occur.

Seeing Conrad together with the three boys made me think about the differences between them. He is much less shy, more open, spontaneous, and fun loving. I don't know anyone else from Shanghai, but I think being from a big city accounts for a lot of the differences. He has had more varied influences and has a broader outlook.

While in China, I am gaining an appreciation for Israel as well as for the U.S. I like certain American characteristics such as enthusiasm, directness, and lack of modesty. Although we have messed up the family system somewhat terribly, it is quite something to compensate by keeping a closeness after divorce, especially if there are children.

And yet, the shyness and innocence of these Chinese young people is very refreshing. In spite of being naïve, they are not shallow. In fact, I see them as deep, disciplined, and resilient.

Nov. 30, 1988

Russell had heard that there would be a black American breakdance troupe performing in Hangzhou. With the help of the boys, I got five tickets (Conrad's still here), from scalpers for about $10. How I loved hearing that black dialect ringing out in the gymnasium in Hangzhou. They moved like fluid. There was also a decent laser show. After the performance, Russell exclaimed with restrained excitement, "I've never seen anything like that before!"

Watching the performance reminded me of one of my tourism students asking me, "What is broken dancing?"

Dec. 5, 1988

Our happy group of the three boys plus Elizabeth and me set off for Suzhou. I was worried the school would not allow me to invite the boys, but they did. And the expense was, once again, fairly minimal. That tells me that tourist prices are far higher than the true cost. But, of course, we didn't go first class either. Actually, we took the all-night boat from Hangzhou to Suzhou. In our crowded cabin, we devoured chicken, laughed, played games I taught them like Hangman and Tic Tac Toe, and got into a philosophical discussion about the meaning of life after Russell shared an art book of famous western art pieces. When they finished a bottle of Chinese champagne, Richard said he was going to throw the bottle into the Grand Canal. I enthusiastically wrote a message to put into the bottle. And, since Russell said we would be passing close to his hometown, I added a note to his mom and dad telling them how much I enjoyed their son. Russell read it and then wrote a note to his parents saying that he had many stories to tell them about me. Richard wrote a wonderful note that expressed his happiness at being together on this trip. Bill just wrote his name. Then, we went to "launch" the bottle. The night was cold, but strangely beautiful, and we all felt close at that moment.

We remained a happy and playful group throughout the trip. We ended up staying in a very fancy hotel. It was the first time the three had running hot water, and they bathed <u>and</u> showered after asking me how to work everything. I taught them to lift the toilet seat on the western toilet. However, I neglected to tell them to lie between the sheets on the bed. The next morning, we all had a good laugh because each of them had slept on the top of the sheets <u>and</u> blankets, only using the extra quilts for warmth. They couldn't get over the softness of the beds. Russell said he had awakened at 7 a.m. and just walked around the room for a while.

Another new experience for them was an amusement park. They had never been to one before. They ran like 12-year-old kids to the ferris wheel and roller coaster. They came off the roller coaster quite terrified. "That thing is dangerous," Bill panted as he rushed to get off after the ride.

At a particularly beautiful scene of sampans on the lake in Wuxi, Russell said, "It is like something I have only seen in paintings, and you have given me the chance to see it." It was an eloquent thank you.

Elizabeth is a wonderful traveling companion although it's difficult to get used to the way she holds my arm when we walk. I've noticed my female students also hold my arm like they're leading an old woman.

There were several unpleasantries about FEC, and my not being allowed to stay in some places, but I'm too happy to think about that now.

Dec. 8, 1988

I love the unpredictability of each day here. Debbie, from my hotel management class, came to see me about stories from Isaac Bashevis Singer. She asked me about *Shabbat, Chanukah, dreidl, kugel.* What a kick sitting here, talking about the Western Wall in Jerusalem's Old City and showing her postcards from Israel.

The principal arranged for Elizabeth to take the three boys and me to a nice local restaurant to taste the specialties of Hangzhou cuisine—at my expense, but very reasonable. We had Beggar's Chicken (fantastic), which was originally cooked underground, Dongpu pork (good, but too fatty for me), West Lake fish (there's that dance around the bones again), and a special soup (with a slimy vegetable I didn't like). Russell was sick, but Conrad came with us. He has been accepted to three schools in Australia. But he got a worried look on his face when he talked about how difficult it was to get a passport. Being a citizen of China in no way guarantees one can get a passport. Of course, he can't get an Australia visa if he doesn't have a passport. They look at my American passport as a magic piece of paper that can take me anywhere I want to go anytime I want. They're right.

We are planning a visit to Yaoling Caves next weekend.

Dec. 12, 1988

I love caves, and this was an impressive limestone cave. The weather was turning nasty before we left, but we were lucky during the trip. I missed Russell who is still sick and wasn't able to come with us. We were a jolly group as we strode the caves, and later plied the river to a very beautiful hilltop from which an ancient emperor had fished.

I met a foreign teacher from Hangzhou University who has been in China five years. She is a middle-aged woman from Lafayette, Louisiana, who has been living around the world for the last ten years. She had one or more PhD's, but said she had started out as a banker. She had had a lot of money, but wasn't happy. Now she's happy in China and is even studying how to do Chinese painting. I borrowed some Christmas paraphernalia to use in my classes. She also introduced me to some Australian students studying Chinese and I arranged for them to visit my classes.

I am trying even more to savor every day because I know I will have to make plane reservations to leave China soon. It's hard to think about leaving.

Dec. 13, 1988

Tonight's English Corner was precious. I brought some paper to make Christmas decorations. Once they got into it, they had great fun. The little children inside them came out. It was absolutely wonderful. Being here is wonderful. I love the wonder of opening up other people's wonder. In fact, in being a teacher here, I think I have been the best social worker I have ever been. I have connected with that human core that lies at the base of humankind. I am exhausted and exhilarated.

Dec. 15, 1988

I spent a delightful day in the energy, exuberance, and freedom of young children. At my request, Debbie arranged for me to visit a pre-school. True, the children were much better behaved and more controlled than western children, but they were happy, learning, and having fun. Their teachers were caring and kindly. I was quite amazed when I went to an art class. The teacher was teaching them to draw a cat. Each child, with surprising concentration for only three years old, drew the cat <u>exactly</u> as the teacher did it. No artistic freedom of expression here. Debbie was an able interpreter.

Thomas came to talk with me again. He is a thinker stuck in a society that values rote memorization. He told me his father was extremely strict with him, even beating him as a child, and that he didn't want to be a father like that. However, instead of feeling angry or sorry for himself, he added that he was grateful to his father for teaching him self-control and never to waste time, money, or knowledge. I see frustration in Thomas' future. He's now reading Freud.

I'm learning a lot from these informal conversations with my students. They say things when they're alone with me that I don't think they'd say to other Chinese. Taylor told me that he had never really had a childhood because his father always insisted that he study instead of play. "What was I?" he said, resigned to his fate, "A little face with big glasses." But eventually, he turned study into play through reading books and was grateful for all the experiences he could have through books. Books could take him traveling to other times and places and the characters kept him company. Quentin said that he and his sister had spent much of their young childhood tied to a bed, able only to see a patch of blue sky out the window. "But, what could my mother do? She had to work in the fields and had to leave us alone."

Floyd came to my room eager to chat. He is adorable, intelligent, perceptive, practical, and quite sensitive. He said that the Chinese customs of being silent, not risking, not making mistakes because of losing face were not helpful, and even counter-productive in being tour guides. He felt he had to develop what he called "a double life." He said he wanted to prepare more material for me to look at, but had worried extra work would burden me too much. He thanked me many times for our talk and said how much he had enjoyed it. I had enjoyed it as much as he.

Dec. 16, 1988

The three Australian students came to my classes today. All went very well. They are an interesting lot—one born in Zambia, one in New Zealand, and one in England, ages 19, 22, and 23. When I said that I admired their traveling and studying in China, one said that he admired my doing this at my age. I do wonder sometimes what my life would have been like had I traveled like this when I was young.

Thomas asked some incisive questions of the Australian boys such as how they solve problems in their lives. He made a nice connection to one of the boys and has been invited to their foreign student dorm to come and talk some more.

Dec. 17, 1988

It is colder now and I have asked for a small heater in my room. At night I sleep inside my sleeping bag under the quilt, with two sweatshirts, two pair of pants, my hood, plus three pair of sox, down booties, and gloves!! My kind students are still dutifully bringing up six large thermos bottles of hot water for my bath every night. Coordinating the hot and cold water isn't easy, and the bathroom is so very cold, I don't want to undress.

The classrooms are also like refrigerators. I wear my down jacket, hat, and gloves, and at least I get to move around. To keep my students' circulation going, we periodically do exercises. I have even seen chilblains on some of their hands! I thought this was an old-fashioned word for something no longer seen, but they're very much here in China today and look quite painful. On the chance it might help a bit, I gave some of the students some cream I brought along. Although they always dress neatly and cleanly, I have noticed that they wear the same clothes over and over.

Dec. 18, 1988

Cultural bridges are sometimes unstable and today I fell off and got hurt. I was proud of the connection I had made with Russell, Bill, Richard, and Conrad. They had become friends. But they were lying to me.

I found this out after Diana took me to her family's home in Hangzhou. Her younger sister, Juliet, was there too. I found it interesting that the job of both parents was to translate English from chemistry research papers into Chinese. However, they had no English speaking or listening abilities at all. The father cooked a really tasty meal. I felt I had thoroughly stuffed myself, but they felt I ate practically nothing. I've noticed that, in spite of my weighing far more, there isn't a skinny Chinese person who can't eat more than I can.

Diana's home is closer to the teacher's college where Russell, Bill, and Richard study. It's impossible to reach them by phone, so Diana and I pedaled over to see if they were there. Russell and Richard share a dormitory room with six others. When I entered, I asked another roommate where Russell and Richard were.

I was shocked when the roommate told me that he would find Richard for me, but that Russell was still in the school hospital. All this time, Richard, Bill, and even Conrad had been telling me that Russell was getting better from whatever mysterious illness he had. It turns out that the illness is quite serious. They didn't know the word in English, but I eventually was able to determine that he has hepatitis.

When Bill and Richard were found, I was very angry with them for lying to me about Russell's health. In turn, they were shocked by my anger. What we had was a cultural miscommunication. As I'm trying to understand it now, in Chinese culture, people, even friends, don't want to give bad news to someone. The rationale is that, if the person can't change the bad situation, there's no reason to cause them useless worry.

I still felt they had let me, and our friendship down, by lying to me so directly and for several weeks. When I said I'd like to see Russell, they brought me over to the infirmary. We walked into a crowded room with four beds and a sleeping Russell. He perked up quickly when he saw me. I was incredibly happy to see him. He didn't look too bad. By chance, I had bought him a history of art book in Chinese just that morning on my way to Diana's. I gave it to him just as a nurse came in, looked at all of us furiously, and threw us out.

I learned that this is quite a serious epidemic going through the colleges. They may even close the colleges earlier for vacation to stop the spread. Bed rest and better food than usual seems to be the treatment. I hadn't heard about this at our small school because we are so far out in the suburbs, so our students weren't sick.

Dec. 21, 1988

The reality of my leaving now has a date—Jan. 12th, Dragon Air to Hong Kong. Before, I mentally toyed with it, but the pain of leaving is now beginning to sink in. I keep trying to capture the joy I feel with the students, the beauty of their faces, and of their unspoiled and innocent personalities—"pure" one teacher called them.

I don't know if I'll be able to see Russell before I leave. He sent me a letter in which he said he had told Richard and Bill not to tell me about his hepatitis. He said he hadn't even told his family! How very odd this silence about bad news is to me. I can handle much better what I know instead of fretting and being frustrated when I suspect something is wrong, but can't find out what. I wrote Russell back that this would be the start of what I hoped would be a long correspondence between us.

I got letters from Israel today, but none from the lawyer about the insurance money for my car. I am going to be in serious financial trouble when I eventually wend my way homeward. Oh well, how can I have any regrets about taking this trip?

Dec. 23, 1988

I am sitting by my little heater. It's a joy! The air is filled with the excitement of the Christmas and New Year celebrations tomorrow. The big winter vacation for the students won't come until Chinese New Year's, which they also call Spring Festival even though it falls in the winter months of January or February.

I am very proud of the progress I've seen in my students. The Chinese teachers downgrade them to their faces, but the students beam so happily when I tell them they are doing well. Some worry their English level will drop during the long holidays at home without hearing any English. I tell them to go for walks and talk English out loud to the rivers or the trees. When they laugh, I tell them that I have often talked to myself in Hebrew while I'm traveling to keep up my speaking ability.

Dec. 24, 1988

I'm not used to celebrating Christmas, but this has been my best Christmas ever. How I love being here. I expected to sleep in this morning, but Elizabeth came over early with the principal. She gave me a calendar to hang on the wall with pictures of Hangzhou, and two silk, embroidered decorative pillowcases. Conrad and his father surprised me by showing up at my door. We walked around the carnival the students had set up. The young American teacher they have found to replace me showed up at dinner with another Californian, and they helped me polish up "T'was the Night Before Christmas" for my part in the Christmas show.

Everyone felt truly festive and had worked hard decorating the rooms and preparing their performances. I received many lovely cards from my students and even some of the other teachers. Thomas sent me a card with a letter addressed to "Lady Chocolate." It was filled with caring, touching words of respect and warm-heartedness. He expressed his gratitude at my opening up his English. And it is as though there had been a dam blocking it and I had somehow unblocked that dam and released his English. He wrote, "In fact, it is you who makes me progress well on how to study English and help me learn more about lives and society. I really don't know how to express my gratitude. I can do nothing but keep studying hard and use English freely to show you my progress. Please believe me. I can!"

Dec. 25, 1988

After the joy of last night, I lay in bed this morning just to soak in how happy I am so that I can recall it all when I'm far away. The only blot on my happiness is another sore throat and cough that I certainly hope is not a bad sign of things to come.

I met Richard and Bill to celebrate Christmas together. I think I finally got through to Richard and Bill that I expect the truth from them—about Russell and everything else too. I hope they will be truthful in their letters.

We went to the nicest hotel I've seen in Hangzhou, the Shangri-La, to see the decorations, but it was deadly quiet there with very few guests. We did wander around and enjoyed the modern abstract art and sculptures.

Next, we took in the Chinese Christmas dinner at a western-style restaurant. It was really terrible food, and a hodge podge of western and Chinese foods and ways of serving it. It was quite funny and terribly expensive, but the place was decorated nicely with a gay atmosphere. I've now taught the boys to eat slowly, chat, and linger after a meal. So, we lingered long. For them, the "western style" was a new experience. For me, it was the first time I saw waitresses in China really working—not particularly efficiently, but not sitting around and chatting while the customers waited. We laughed a lot, knowing that our time left together was running out.

Dec. 27, 1988

Every day I mourn a bit more about the impending separation. I have a semi-cold that has dampened me a bit, and the news reports from Israel are becoming ghastlier by the day. Tonight there was a broadcast that 4 million gas masks are now being issued to Israelis in preparation for chemical warfare.

I was told by one of my students of a problem in China now with peasants not wanting to be peasants, but wanting a better life by becoming private vendors. He is from a peasant family himself. The selfishness of China's youth today worries him, as well as the drop in the number of peasants doing farming. But, he admits he wants a better life too. He accepts that he will eventually support his parents.

Thomas continues to come frequently for chats. I enjoy his insights, his youth, his thinking, his serious and handsome face, his grin and his shyness. He says he can be very open with thinking, but not doing. He speaks of wanting to help China develop, and is discouraged with the selfishness of his generation. He spoke sadly of a young man in his hometown that committed suicide because his girlfriend had jilted him after stealing all his property. Thomas said he would have been angry and taken revenge on the girlfriend instead of ending his own life. But he still felt sympathy for the young man because he had been such a kind person. I hope Thomas will be one of the ones who'll keep in touch with me. I'm quite curious about the sequel to his youth.

It may snow soon. I feel like an Eskimo who never undresses for long, wearing my meager winter wardrobe constantly. I have to admit I am looking forward to warmth and showers and food I like.

Dec. 29, 1988

Would I be brave enough to be in a country at war? There is the growing possibility of war in Israel. War doesn't make sense, but we Jews have nowhere to run to. I wonder what will be. It looks very bad.

Jan. 2, 1989

I passed the New Year with my traveling companions, Elizabeth, Richard, and Bill in an unusual city called Shaoxing. Sadly, Russell was still too ill to come. The weather wasn't great, and Shaoxing seems to be famous for people trying to cheat you, but one of my favorite times ever was riding down the river in a little black covered boat with a boatman who rows the boat with his feet. Even the fact that the boatman suddenly announced halfway through our ride that we must pay more or he'd leave us off right there in the middle of nowhere did not stop me from the pleasure of floating on the river, watching the countryside villages roll by.

We were a compatible, laughing foursome who thoroughly enjoyed our hotel rooms, which had blessed heat (I saw my arms again) and running hot water. Our pleasure was marred by a last minute switch insisting I pay either FEC or double *renminbi* for my share of the hotel. China certainly has its very grubby side!

I had a few quiet moments with Richard and Bill. Bill said I was his first foreign friend ever. Richard said he hopes he will eventually go to France and that I'd be welcome to come to Paris to live with him if there was too much trouble in Israel.

When we returned to Hangzhou, the boys and I sat at night by West Lake. The sky was so pretty with the silhouettes of the branches of the weeping willow trees that line the lake. The weather was not too cold, and lights shimmered around the lake. It was sad to end our last trip together. Next Sunday, I will see them for the last time—maybe forever. I will miss them so. They have given me faith that I am a lovable person who can do things that others appreciate.

And so, in this faraway place, I passed into the New Year, 1989, feeling a sense of peace and contentment while my little Israel spilled a lot more blood.

Jan. 8, 1989

I said goodbye tonight to my three special boys. It was so good for the four of us to be together again. Russell was pale, but okay. They gave me very beautiful gifts—a silk wall hanging of Hangzhou from Bill with the inscription, "To my best friend, Suellen Zima," special metal chopsticks from Russell like the emperors used to use that turn color if the food is poisoned, and perfumed bookmarks with ten scenic spots of China. There was also a metal cup and a boat made of wood chips because they remembered how I love the smell of wood, and some small figures of a water buffalo, a Suzhou boat, pandas, and a cock from Richard.

They were so excited to see the photo albums I gave each of them. They turned over page after page, treasuring our pictures taken over the last months. I then gave them each a stamped envelope with my Hong Kong address, an envelope to open after they graduated in June, and a "red envelope" for Spring Festival. They were surprised I knew their custom of giving "red envelopes."

After lunch, I urged Russell to lie down on the bed and rest while I played a James Bond video. I loved watching their faces while they watched the film. We then reminisced and I read to them from you, my journal. They were impressed with how much I had documented and they encouraged me to one day print my stories about us.

And then they had to leave. No taxis were out in our suburb at night. It was raining, so I put my scarf, poncho, and gloves on the recovering Russell, took my umbrella and we waited together in the dark at the bus stop. It was hard to talk because of the lump in my throat. We felt so sad. The bus came and carried them away.

Jan. 9, 1989

I'm semi-packed, but still I'm learning new things about Chinese culture. I knew the tour guides had a big test in another class. When I asked some students how they did, they replied "so-so," so I thought they were disappointed. But so-so means anything from "okay" to "very good." Guess that's Chinese understatement again. And I also learned that Chinese people smile at home and not outside. That's the opposite of us. We smile at strangers more than friends and family.

Jan. 10, 1989

Today was a precious day of goodbyes in my classes. It ended well with my letters to them, theirs to me, a last story of Little Red Riding Hood, and a circle where we sang Auld Lang Syne. It was a good ending, as good as sad endings can be. When I said class was over, everyone just continued to sit there. We didn't want to part.

Jan 11, 1989

More goodbyes—to my last hotel management class, to the Dean, to the teachers at a goodbye party they arranged for me. A conversation with a new student brought me back to how the seed of my wanting to go to China started. He had just returned from a year working at the Chinese Pavilion in Epcot Center in Orlando, Florida. It was there, in the replica of the Temple of Heaven at Epcot Center, where I had turned slowly in a circle fascinated by the huge faces of the Chinese projected on the walls in slides and movies. At that time, I thought, "I'd like to get to know them better." And seven years later, I did.

Russell's poem, written on Jan. 8th after we parted, arrived.

CRYING GOODBYE

A drizzling winter Sunday
Without sunshine;
When getting dark
It seems going to die.
Four lingering friends
Wandering in a sad sigh;
When the bus comes,
They are going to say goodbye.
Well, why so gloomy is the sky
Without anything bright?
Well, why so silent are they
With hard tries in each one's mind?
Oh, it's not meant to make you tired.
The sun has gone to the other side.
How could the sky
Be all the time bright?
Oh, life is doomed to bid
So many a goodbye.
Now it comes to another time.
Don't cry!

And I began to cry.

Jan. 12, 1989

I may not be an athlete, but I know what it feels like to stand on the winner's platform at the Olympics. This was what my last day was like at the school.

I went to the tour guide class to write a farewell message and leave a picture of me with a big smile since people always commented on my smile. I took a brief last look at them as they sat at their desks, and left quickly because I felt I would cry. I wrote parting words on the blackboard to the whole school. "It has been an honor and a privilege to be the first foreign teacher at this school. Thank you for the happiest two months of my life."

I went to the office. When I came out, several of the students were clustered in a group. The girls were crying, and the boys looked sad. I hugged the girls, touched heads with Debbie, spoke with the boys. I gave my thanks to the hotel staff that had taken good care of me, and patted my bike farewell. Several students carried my bags from my room to the waiting van, and I said goodbye to my room—my first real home in China.

Before I got into the van, every student of mine and some of the teachers gathered to wish me well. I shook hands with each of them in turn and we said goodbye with words and eyes. I shook hands last with the principal. She was fluent in Russian, but had never studied English so we had spoken very little to one another. Yet, she and I could speak with our eyes and they spoke a sincere "thank you" to one another. I got in the van and we all continued to wave until out of sight.

Then came the ride through Hangzhou, past West Lake, and to pick up Russell. Elizabeth had arranged for him to come to the airport to bid me farewell. Richard and Bill had to be in class at that time. He gave me letters from the three of them, and some "pit-filled" chocolate. He was excited about going to the airport for the first time. It had turned terribly cold out, but the warmth of our friendship kept us warm.

We ate at the airport restaurant. It was a desolate, deserted airport, unlike any airport I had ever been to. They were re-doing the whole inside of the airport, so we were supposed to wait in the cold for the plane to come in, let off its arriving passengers, and then let the departing passengers on.

Russell told me not to be sad, but we were both sad. He told me I had been very important to him, having come into his life during a difficult time. He said his letter would explain more of the details.

I knew that the weather might be warmer in Hong Kong, but that I would never feel quite as warm there as I did with Elizabeth and Russell. Waving goodbye, I walked out to the plane—and started to cry.

5

HONG KONG BALI SINGAPORE THAILAND 1989

Jan. 14, 1989

Hong Kong certainly dazzles the eye after the drabness of China. All the neon, the fast paced television shows, the sophistication, the wealth, make China seem far more than only a two-hour plane ride away. I have enjoyed the plenitude of everything, the ease of finding what I need, the food, "real" chocolate, but I walk around like one in mourning. Keeping busy helps. A few letters were waiting for me at the American Express office. One was from one of the Arab Interns for Peace who had been so sympathetic after my car was bombed. I've been running around getting pictures developed, mailing packages, arranging my on-going plane reservations. I'll be leaving for Bali a bit earlier than I thought because of the availability of flights. There's really no sense in hanging around here in the bad weather. It's warmer than China, but still cold and gray.

I do so miss what I left. Will I ever feel so totally fulfilled again? At least the photos are turning out well and the quality of developing is more consistent than in China. And here they put the precious negatives in little protective plastic rather than just rolling them up which ends up scratching them.

Jan. 16, 1989

It was that book on a dusty back shelf in the Kfar Saba library that made me decide to see Bali. Books in English were rather hard to find in that small library, and many were old books that had been donated. A young East Indian woman wrote about her journey to Bali in the 1950's. The glowing description of the place and the people intrigued me. It sounded like Utopia. She talked about a resiliency of the culture to change, but I had to wonder if that will still be true upon my arrival in 1989. I doubt it, but more up-to-date guidebooks still describe it as warm, lush, beautiful, uncrowded, filled with art, and a fascinating fun-filled culture. I am ready to see for myself.

Jan. 19, 1989

I awoke at 6 a.m. by chance with some vague idea of running along the beautiful beach here, but I promptly fell asleep again. Later on, I did wander onto the beach and had a massage by one of the Balinese women who stroll along the beach with numbers painted on their blue bamboo hats. Perhaps it's controlled somehow so that tourists aren't completely overrun by them.

Kuta is the most touristy section of Bali. My hotel has an inner courtyard, which makes it quiet and secluded. Just outside, it's a bustle of shops and people asking, "transport?" Young Australians are easily the majority of tourists here. It's a cheap destination from western Australia.

The English level of the Balinese is quite low, but they're good-humored and always smiling. Such a contrast from China! Although Bali is a part of Indonesia now, it has its own language, culture, and religion. Balinese are as beautiful to look at as the lush vegetation.

Although worlds different from China, I think I've found another fascinating place. However, it's hotter than I expected. I sweat a lot.

Jan. 23, 1989

Statuesque Balinese women walked to the temple with their fruit, flowers, and other offerings held high on their heads. They walked in a tropical downpour to the mother temple called Besakih on a mountain backed by a volcano. Some of the offerings were encased in plastic against the rain, while other women simply held a wide leaf over it. Rain here is just another part of nature—as are the people. I took a tour bus out here. The scenery and the people are a feast for the eyes.

I found out about a tourism school in Bali in Nusa Dua, not too far from Kuta. I called and the Director of the school invited me out to visit. He said it's possible for me to teach there through a U.N. organization. I don't know if I'm ready to give up Israel yet, but the time may come. It really appeals to me to go from exotic country to exotic country teaching English. I can tell that teaching is more right for me than social work.

Jan. 24, 1989

The tourism school in Nusa Dua is as beautiful as my school in Hangzhou was ugly. The flowers, the surroundings—everything is so perfect. These students are also handsome and pretty, like my Hangzhou tourism students. Good looks must be one standard used in all countries to choose tour guides and hotel staff. The school has a "model restaurant" and the students served us a marvelous lunch.

I spoke to two of the students who had a higher English level. They were much less shy than my Chinese students and were anxious to ask many questions. So different from my Chinese students who restrained themselves from asking me questions.

Jan. 26, 1989

I spent two and a half hours trying to call my father and finally succeeded. He confirmed what I had hoped he would not—nothing has moved on the car insurance money yet. Staying in a very interesting village called Ubud softens the blow because the idea of coming back here to teach is quite appealing. I might really have to leave Israel because I can't exist there without any savings. That may make my decision to leave Israel for me.

As I listen to the music of the rain on my bungalow in Ubud, I wonder if this paradise called Bali could work out for me. I remember Diana's family asking me if I had found a perfect society in my travels. I said "no," but now I think I may have.

MAGIC THAT IS NO ILLUSION

I once had a porch overlooking terraced rice paddies, waving palm trees, thatched huts, and high sloping mountains in Ubud, Bali. This is a place where everything seems interconnected—nature, people, community spirit, and art, incredible art. The art here is everywhere, from nature to the beautiful Balinese, to the small trays of offerings to the gods three times a day that appear everywhere—on shrines, on sidewalks, on the bus, in a telephone booth, on the table on my porch.

Art is in the color. Art is in the movement of the swaying of the palm fronds, the easy grace of the people as they carry huge loads effortlessly on their heads. The sounds are all a part of this melody with birds always chirping, the breeze swishing the lush plants and making the flowers bob on the trees, the crowing cocks. The smells are of warmth, flowers, water, pure air, and delicate incense placed among the food and flower-bedecked trays of offerings.

In Bali, nature reigns. It is not beaten, subjugated, destroyed, and smothered into obscurity as it is in so many parts of the world. Color is everywhere. There are hundreds of shades of green in the plants and trees and terraced rice paddies. Flowers contribute happy bursts of color both on the trees and bushes, and, I think most handsomely behind the right ear of the young men. The traditional batik sarongs wrapped around both men and women transform the people themselves into exotic flowers. The sky is multi-colored too, with an infinite variety of gray and white clouds patterning the shades of blue sky. And around sunset, all is suffused with soft, yet vivid oranges and yellows.

The Balinese seem to have found what eludes most countries. They are truly happy people. They are relaxed, and speak oh so gently to one another. There is a twinkle in everyone's eye, a lightness in everyone's step, a ready smile, and an easy laughter. I'm sure there is the gamut of human emotions here too, but there is an unstressed, un-tense interaction among people. A sense of peace, a sense of calm pervades.

Unlike the western world, Balinese do not segment life into roles. They combine work, recreation, business, religion, home life, and community spirit. They are hard workers, but without the intensity and ulcers of the western world. To me, they are more totally integrated than any other people I have seen. Their beliefs are complex and yet simple—the world is composed of good and evil forces always in battle. Both the good and evil spirits must be respected and given attention. Their religion, basically Hindu, is a daily part of each person's life, but there is no emphasis on sin, repentance, and self-sacrifice.

The Balinese have tightly-knit communities in which they are taught and required to show social responsibility. Individualism is not high on the priority list here. Each receives help when needed, and is expected to give help when needed. There is a strong moral code of right and wrong. Those who break it are punished severely by the community s/he has offended. The only real "social problem" I have heard of so far is that offenders who are sent out of their villages are never really accepted elsewhere.

But, the Balinese are not rigid. They were ruled by the Dutch for many years, among other conquerors. They are now part of Indonesia, but retain roots and customs distinct from other Indonesians. They can adapt to new ideas, and yet they curiously interweave new ideas and concepts into their existing culture so that their culture bends and sways rather than breaks under the pressure.

They like money, and tourism has brought them prosperity. But they have not yet gone to great extremes in chasing after money. They come after the tourist dollar with enthusiasm, but it is a good-natured banter and barter. No hard feelings if the final answer is "no." It is the only developing country I have visited where most people do not crave traveling to the west.

I'm sure there are some disadvantages in Bali. I just haven't found them yet—except perhaps that it is a bit too hot, chocolate loses something of its good taste in this heat, and it can take a couple of hours to make a long-distance phone call. Prices are rising, but not ridiculously. My room and view cost about $5 a day, including a hearty breakfast which includes the sweetest and prettiest two-colored bananas I've ever eaten.

Jan. 28, 1989

I had almost the most perfect room I could imagine. But today the guests next door moved out and now I have the most perfect room I could imagine. It gives me even more privacy because I'm in the end room, so no one has to walk by my room. Each room has its own shower and toilet, but what I especially love about this shower is that there's no ceiling. I shower while looking out upon the rice paddies and mountains. Whether in the bathroom or on the front porch, I'll never have another view like this!

I've been doing some day touring with a Canadian couple. Both are doctors traveling the world for six months or so before they settle into their own practice. We found a good *bemo*, taxi, driver for hire. He's not too fast or reckless. We returned in time to see a festival. There was a music competition between groups on the famous Balinese *gamelan* instruments, and then a truly wonderful dance performance. This one was for the locals because I saw a certain enthusiasm that was lacking in the tourist shows. And I enjoyed the happy Balinese enjoying the comedians.

The temperature doesn't vary in Bali very much any time of the year. But they have a rainy season and a dry season. Guess which one this is? Rain is just part of the ambiance of this place. It couldn't be so lush without it.

Jan. 29, 1989

During this year of my wanderings, I have known I have a home base—my little room with the big view in Kfar Saba. That grounds me. Could I make the jump to wandering the world with no home base? No permanent address? No place to go home to—only a series of temporary homes? Can I be that much of the proverbial wandering Jew?

I don't know. I'll have to think on it as I ponder the rice paddies. Perhaps the answer lies there.

Jan. 31, 1989

The Canadian couple told me they had been in China at a Lucky Draw held by the tourism bureau, CITS. The winners were chosen for a two-week trip through

China. They said someone from Israel had won. Well, I'm from Israel and I know I was one of the names in that Lucky Draw.

It's unlikely that my name was really chosen, but I took off on a flight of fancy imagining I was back in China with Bill, Russell, Richard, Conrad, my students. The thought gave me a very joyous feeling.

Feb. 1, 1989

Tonight, in the Asian New Year, the spirits of the ancestors return to the family shrine. As I sit outside at midnight eating a croissant and drinking a superb banana *lassi*, yogurt, I idly wonder if my ancestors could ever find me. Would they think to look on the idyllic isle of Bali in a 2nd floor room overlooking rice paddies in Ubud? Would they find me sitting amongst the symphony of thousands of night sounds, with the flame of a candle nudged by the soft breeze throwing a halo around the face of a small statue blending a Buddhist and a Hindu god?

I am lonely tonight. I would like someone I love to share this place with me. And yet I feel so very, very fortunate that I have lived and experienced the high joy of my China life, and the absolutely exquisite existence of Bali—one experience following closely upon the other. It is a rare happiness in one lifetime.

So, ancestors mine, seek me out for I am in and of this world still.

Feb. 2, 1989

For the *Galuggan* festival yesterday, I was lucky to be invited to be with Nadi's ancestors and family. Nadi's home is probably a quite typical Balinese family compound. The small houses stood around a courtyard. The banana trees and palm trees showed the way to the washing stream. Generations of the family were contained within its walls. The grandmother walked around in the old-fashioned way of not covering her shrunken and sagging breasts. The young women no longer expose their breasts. The mother walked around with the daily offerings, placing them everywhere, sprinkling each with holy water and words and incense. The rooster followed after, pecking away the flower offering and eating the food.

The sisters all returned scrubbed from their baths in the stream. They proceeded to dress in their holiday finery—a beautiful sarong wound ingeniously around, a girdle-like waist cinch, and a gaily-colored print blouse and ceremonial sash. Their tiny waists reminded me of Scarlett O'Hara in Gone with the Wind. They each came up to me timidly and tried out a little English. At Nadi's suggestion, I had brought a piece of material I'd bought in town and they showed me how to wrap it around myself. The effect was not the same.

The family shrine had been well decorated with cloth skirts and magnificently-arranged offerings of food. The people can eat this food after the gods have eaten the essence. The girls prayed to their ancestors with hands above their heads holding yellow flowers and sprinkling themselves with holy water.

They led me to the almost totally open-air kitchen where they cooked with wood as fuel. They gave me the special celebration food—spicy like the Ethiopians like—eaten totally with hands only. There seemed to be no gathering together to eat at this point.

When the group of *Barong* (Balinese mythical character) passed by, the families all came out and paid 500 *rupiah* for the *Barong* to dance. With cigarettes dangling out of the mouths of some of them, they were obviously a happy lot—the heat and monotony of a long route through many village streets not deterring them. Water to quench their thirst awaited them at the homes they went by. Tourists were accepted, but incidental. This was, after all, their holiday.

Nadi, my hostess, never did arrive. It turns out she had to work, but she gave instructions to care for me well—which was surely done. I felt, as with the Arab families I knew in Israel, the warmth and easy closeness of family familiarity and routine. One of Nadi's sisters put it well, "I left Bali once to visit somewhere else, but I don't want to leave Bali again."

Feb. 3, 1989

My mind seems to be awake and seeking. This place, Bali, somehow awakens my senses. It is so rich in other than money. It is so full. It is a feast of color, light, movement, beauty, sensuality. Its restfulness and peacefulness make it as fertile for thinking as its earth is fertile for rice and all growing things. Perhaps I am just another growing thing.

Feb. 4, 1989

I have two sets of sounds in my ears. One is the wonderful melody of the crickets and other insects in the rice paddies. The other is the awful imitation rock of a group brought to Ubud from Jakarta. They are trying to act like Mick Jagger and the Rolling Stones era.

Why do third world countries copy the west's worst points? There are hundreds of people gathered from around Bali. There are many stalls and booths, many selling clothes that advertise places and products from western countries. There are food stalls and families with little kids. The worst part is that an Indonesian cigarette company is sponsoring this big event. They are giving away a free pack of cigarettes with every ticket. How utterly disgusting to see these young lungs that have the pure air of Bali inhaling the noxious smoke.

The audience is just staring and standing. They aren't applauding, probably because, judging from local dance performances, it isn't in their culture to applaud. I wonder whether they even like the music. They don't know how to respond with adoration and yelling.

It's so absurd. They have what the west could never have again. It makes me want to put up a very high fence all around Bali. Perhaps I should come back here soon before it becomes like everywhere else that I prefer to avoid.

Feb. 5, 1989

Tonight I leisurely watched the colors of the scene change as afternoon gave way to dusk. The breeze lulled me into a trance and then—it talked to me. I was thinking about China and my Chinese friends celebrating their Spring Festival New Year holidays. I imagined them being together with their families, all happy, smiling, eating good food. I felt a keen missing for China and my newly made friends there. I felt my time in China had been cut short prematurely, that it was left unfinished.

As the breeze caressed me gently, I heard it say very clearly, "You can go back." It was such a simple message and yet one I hadn't really even considered. When I thought about the details of going back, I knew it was not only possible, but also the right thing to do.

Thank you wise wind. I will take your advice.

Feb. 6, 1989

A small sign outside a home advertised, "Massage." When I inquired, the young boy inside said his grandfather was out in the fields now, but would be home soon. I went back later and was greeted by an old man of some indeterminate age. I soon found out there was a lot of life yet in those gnarled fingers.

First, he dressed me in a sarong, sat me on the bed cross-legged, and went behind me on the bed. He put some rather icky-smelling liquid over me, but it didn't seem to be a massage oil. I hope not, because at some point he told me to drink it.

He massaged my back and neck and then my back again. We changed positions often. Sometimes he was behind me, sometimes in front, sometimes he kneeled or stood on top of me, or braced me against his knees while I was crouching down.

This was no relaxing Esalen-style massage. We both worked very hard. My body responded with numerous cracking sounds, especially my neck. There were pinches and pressure points, and some things he did even hurt. He gave me some of whatever he had rubbed on me to drink, and had me put it up and through my nose, somehow explaining that it would help my cold.

How do I feel now? My nose does feel less congested. My body feels tired, and my right elbow feels strained.

Feb. 7, 1989

I think I've identified that stuff the man gave me to drink and rubbed all over me. I think it might be breadfruit. I have fallen in love with a fruit called mangosteen which I've never seen or eaten anywhere before. It's the most exquisite fruit I've ever eaten with a thick purple skin covering white segments that taste divine.

My nose feels remarkably clearer, and my elbow is hurting less. However, my stomach seems to be unhappy about something. It hasn't felt normal for a while. That's a pity because the food here is good, well prepared, unusual, and reasonably priced.

Feb.8, 1989

I watched a fantastic rainstorm and a remarkable sunset today. Tourists aren't the only ones to appreciate the art of doing nothing. Every evening, I notice some Balinese who climb the unfinished building next door from which to view the sunset. Perhaps that is another part of Bali's success—never to take nature for granted.

Now I understand what the son of a friend meant when his mother asked him what he did in Thailand and he replied, "I looked and I thought."

Feb. 9, 1989

What has impressed me again is how very gentle these Balinese are. Wayan, one of the workers in the place I'm staying, just came over this evening to chat. It's a nice part of their culture, like the Arabs and the Israelis, just to sit and chat. Keeping others company isn't a waste of time to them.

Wayan talked about the friendliness of the Balinese, which is not like the Javanese who come to Bali because there's not enough work in Java. They are accepted in a community if they are nice, but only if they are considered a nice person.

Wayan cannot quite understand why some guests took offense when he asked how much they paid to rent their car. After all, he considers it his job to look after all the needs of his guests. I suppose we tourists must balance between suspicion of those trying to rip us off and those genuinely trying to be helpful.

When I mentioned that many Balinese had the same names, he told me that the children are named in the order they're born—the equivalent of one (Wayan), two (Made-pronounced as two syllables) three (Nyoman), and four (Ketut). If there are more children born, they just start all over again.

I daydream a lot about returning to China. It seems the only thing that will get me to move from here is the thought of returning to China after brief visits to Singapore and Thailand.

Feb. 10, 1989

Dear Russell, Bill, and Richard,

I want to tell you about my day today. It rained all morning, but rain here is not gloomy; it is pure and refreshing. After many hours washing down everything, the rain stopped. I sat on my porch pondering the terraced rice paddies and clouds covering and uncovering the mountains. This has always given me great pleasure, but another level of magic enticed me this afternoon.

I began to be aware that all my senses were becoming keener. The colors took on tones of incredible richness and depth. The mountains had an even more awesome presence. The sounds of the wind swishing and the steady gurgling of the water irrigating the rice became like voices. The feel of the breeze caressing me was delightful.

The Balinese are animists. They believe that rocks, mountains, trees, all have spirits. I have always perceived nature as such. Inanimate objects to me have a certain life and can communicate. Maybe that's what "communing with nature" means. To me, it is one of the highest joys in the world, and I felt it today in an extremely intense way.

As I truly felt connected to the vitality and aliveness and beauty around me, I thought only one thing could make me even happier—to be with you. And so, through the power of my mind, I brought you to me.

I closed my eyes and went into a half-sleep. I saw your looks of surprise and disbelief as you walked into your dormitory room with your bowls filled for supper and saw me there. We were all at a loss for words. I re-created the wonderful feelings we have shared together—the warmth, the smiles and laughter, the joy.

We traveled around China together—to the Great Wall and The Forbidden City in Beijing, to the soldiers of Xian, to the enchantment of Guilin as we floated down the Lijiang River. I was with you and your families on Chinese New Year's Eve as you told your families of our adventures. At Richard's, I could even see a water buffalo peeking through the window. We went to eat *jaozi* together in Hangzhou and we sat in the parks on the grass in the springtime and talked and laughed, laughed and talked. I showed you my pictures from Bali and Singapore and Thailand and tried to explain how truly close to perfection I found Bali and the Balinese.

I thought I would feel so sad when I awoke and found myself alone, but I didn't feel sad. I felt joy that we had been together at least in my mind as we were once together in China.

Love, Suellen

Feb. 11, 1989

I sent out my letter to the boys in China today. Even though I'm thinking strongly of giving up Nepal and going back to China instead, I didn't mention my returning in the letter because there are many details I need to work out first. Of course, there's a high likelihood that my letter will never reach them since I've learned that postal workers in Indonesia often rip stamps off the letters to re-sell them and just throw the letters away. Packages are often looted.

Feb. 14, 1989

I spent Valentine's Day in the delightful company of an English couple and their adorable four-year-old daughter. Sometimes I think I am being saved for something special because I've survived the roads of Israel, Egypt, China, and now Bali. The only time these Balinese are not in a relaxed state is when they're driving.

We visited a truly wonderful little deserted temple high up in Pulisan where we walked up lots and lots of stairs and literally stood in the mist and clouds. I found it very peaceful, a special place that invited contemplation. In Sangsit, there were fascinating temples because of their carvings that are quite different from the temples in the south. The carvings had a sense of humor too, with a man riding a bicycle with flowers for wheels, planes in a dogfight, and other modern innovations. Another place we went by looked just like a Rousseau painting. I could almost see his animals watching us. Each area I've seen in Bali has a certain sameness, but also something that makes each distinctive.

I left the young English couple trying to resolve the quandary of what to do with the rest of their lives. He can make money in computers, but doesn't like the work. He's trying to mentally adjust to returning to England after their six months of traveling the world.

I, too, am slowly adjusting to the thought of leaving. As I wanted time to stop in China, so do I want it to stop here too.

Feb. 15, 1989

I went over to the high school in Ubud today to see if I could help out with an English class. It turns out that they would appreciate a native English speaker, but the English level is exceedingly low. The principal invited me to his home. He has a homestay like many people in Ubud. He introduced me to a Dutch woman in her 50's who had been a social worker in Holland, but left her husband five years ago and had been a cook on a cargo ship with 11 men sailing around Africa. Now she lives six months in Bali and six months in Holland. Soon she will open up a restaurant with the principal's wife. Except for the fact that she smoked constantly, she was fun to talk to. I like meeting people like her because it shows me that being a nomad is just another kind of lifestyle.

I finally found a friendly dog to pet at his home. I have avoided dogs in Bali because they are neither cute nor friendly. Perhaps the Dutch woman living there has tamed him to like foreigners.

The principal is Javanese, and Catholic. One of the social problems of Bali is mixed marriages and being non-Hindu. When just the two of us were speaking, he brought up another social problem I had heard mentioned. They are the "Bali boys." Although I thought it would be mainly middle-aged women seeking them out, it is western women about their same age who want them as companions. They perform as guides, interpreters, and sex partners. He tries to counsel these students. Out of 29 male students, 13 of them were experienced "Bali boys" because Ubud is a tourist center.

The boys do it for the money, which is well accepted by their families. Balinese society and the Indonesian government ignore the problem, neither condoning nor openly accepting it. For the boys themselves, he says it confuses them. They come from poor families and walk perhaps 8 kilometers a day to sit in overcrowded classrooms of 40 to 45 students. What sense does education make to them after being treated to the rich life as a paid escort to rich, young foreign women? They no longer concentrate on their studies. He did not see this problem extending into the female Balinese young girls. The female prostitutes were usually Javanese living in Bali rather than Balinese. The Australian male tourists in the Kuta area looked mostly for Australian women.

Feb. 17, 1989

There is nothing quite so marvelous as a tropical rainstorm that washes, drenches, and swooshes down. I was feeling down because I finally made arrangements to leave this idyllic island. I wandered through an art gallery in a magnificent setting. I decided it was time for a walk, and I found a delightful, quiet place right among the rice paddies to eat. It was clear weather then, but it began to pour. I leisurely waited.

When it started to abate, I continued walking. And then the deluge came. I could have found shelter, or taken an opportunity to ride. But what did I do? I just kept walking and sloshing in the puddles just like the little kid I am. A family watching on their covered porch laughed when they saw my childlike delight. I thought of the happiest Mother's Day of my life when my husband, son, and I had all donned ponchos and walked through the rain in the hills.

It seemed a perfect thing to do today. Oh, how I have loved this island! How I want to return, especially when I read of the devaluation and inflation and low morale in Israel—and me with so little money.

Rushing, gurgling, thunder and lightning—quite a show by Mother Nature.

Feb. 18,1989

Come walk with me down Monkey Forest Road. Smell the cleanliness of the air. Feel the peace. Get in contact with nature that surrounds and envelops us. See the ancient banyan tree that reaches both up to the sky and down to the earth with its tangle of roots flowing from its branches. They are unique trees—ageless and eternal.

Hear the flowing stream and follow its sound down, down, down among the moss and the decaying temple. Step in its refreshing, cool water. Feel the fresh water flow from the spouts along the jungle cliff. Cleanse off your tension, your cares—all the physical and emotional dirt that accumulates. Feel the stream swirl around you as it gurgles on down its path.

Walk the dirt road among the rice paddies. Feel a part of the rice as it drinks and grows before it can nourish us. See the chickens running around, the rooster pursuing the hen, the baby chicks scurrying after their mother. Some day, they too will be on their own.

Marvel at how the women balance rakes and other farm implements on their heads. Say hello to the children who come out of their yards to yell "hello"—the only English word they know. Wave to them. Play with them. Laugh with them.

Watch the palm fronds wave at us with their coconuts dangling. See the healthy rice grow. Try to count the wonderful shades of green everywhere. Say hi and smile to the people we pass, for they are friendly and curious about us.

Let's eat lunch in a little place in the rice paddies while we listen to the hand-carved bamboo wind chime. Watch the child dance to the tune on a kind of bamboo xylophone played by a handsome young man and a beautiful woman. Talk with the friendly young man who sits next to us to chat, even though his English is quite limited.

Look at the black clouds gathering, telling us to head for home. Sit on my porch, protected by a wide, thatched roof, and watch the rain turn into a tropical deluge. The mountains have disappeared. See the woman over there hurrying home through the rice paddies, carrying a huge green leaf over her head for an umbrella.

Listen to the storm. Feel its power. Be awed at its intensity. Listen, listen, listen to nature talking to us, showing us she is still in indisputable command. Hear the irrigation ditches in the rice paddies begin to flow like rivers. Put on earphones and listen to Vivaldi accompanying the storm.

As dusk comes, watch the trees become silhouettes and those magical mountains rise again to their full height before the darkness makes them disappear again. Sharpen your ears to the night creatures that begin their incessant nighttime conversations and songs. Delight as the little flashes of greenish white light show us where the fireflies fly.

My time in China was the happiest in my life. My time in Bali has been the most exquisite. How connected I feel to China, and how connected to nature.

Feb. 19, 1989

The owner of the restaurant sat down to chat with me as I ate my late evening snack. One conversation led to another. He spoke of the problems of Bali, particularly the need for making connections with officials and paying bribes to get government permission. He spoke of how he had lived a simple life looking after his fields, but now he was a businessman who had more money, but also more worries. He said he was an artist who liked art a lot more than being a businessman.

He talked about the many foreigners who live in Bali and said they are accepted and even helped by the community if they are "good people." A German man who has opened a business lives with him. Since only Balinese are allowed to own land, foreigners must form partnerships with Balinese if they want a home in Bali.

My sad tale unfolded about the tension of life in Israel in general, and my life in particular. Without hesitation, he said I should move to Bali where I could have a good life. Even with all the problems, he thought life in Bali was basically good. He certainly wouldn't want to live elsewhere.

Feb. 20, 1989

It was fitting to end my time in Bali in a chance conversation with a young Balinese man who had graduated from the tourism school in Nusa Dua and worked on a cruise ship traveling the world. He had enjoyed Israel and the U.S., among other countries, but he wouldn't want to stay anywhere but Bali. He saw that everywhere else you have to work hard for the things you can get in Bali so much more easily because the village organizations help you. If you belong to a village, they cooperatively build a home for you and provide for you in many ways. Balinese only need money for ceremonies for their children, and for cremations. He spoke of his village community so lovingly, but he's no village hick. How it works so well here, I'm not sure, but it certainly works to everyone's advantage.

Balinese are gentle in everything but their driving. Their deep roots in their culture seem to make the difference. They truly know who they are and where they belong. This man is not worried about how Bali will change with foreign influence. Bali will, of course, change, but only skin deep. He is sure the rootedness will remain.

So, I listen to my last night symphony in Ubud—for now at least. While my mouth and taste buds enjoyed the food, my stomach remained uncharacteristically complaining. It was not the usual stomach problem that I could take medicine for. But my stomach was the only part of me that was not ecstatic in Bali. No matter where I may roam, it's so very good to know that Bali exists in this world.

Feb. 22, 1989

I slept last night in a 2 x 4 cubicle with only a mattress on the floor surrounded by a good number of sleeping bodies in a crash pad in Singapore. Tonight I have a bedroom larger than my entire Kfar Saba apartment, a magnificent penthouse view of the Singapore skyline, and a luxurious bathroom that looks out over the city from the 22nd story.

I have gone from rags to riches because I called Mrs. N. whose name had been given to me by the director of the tourism school in Bali. She insisted I stay with her and her husband while in Singapore. She's as unusual as she is generous. She is the mixture of an Israeli-Jewish mother and a Lebanese Moslem father. For the first ten years of her life, she went back and forth between Lebanon and Israel and remembers her Russian Jewish grandmother very well. Both her parents were doctors who met in medical school. Even though her mother was far younger than her father when they married, her mother died when she was only ten years old. Her father, then about 64, started moving with her all over the world—to the U.S., Peru, Argentina, and many parts of Europe. She didn't live anywhere very long, but she has an American passport and an American husband and considers herself both Jewish and American. She never saw her grandmother again and both loved and hated her father for dragging her around the world for so many years. In total, her father married five times both before and after Mrs. N.'s mother, but she was the only child from all the marriages.

Mrs. N.'s husband was sent by his company to work in Singapore. They live "high" in every way. Their apartment is absolutely huge, with more luxury than anything I've seen, and certainly much more than anyplace I've ever stayed. It's a peek into another foreign place to me—the world of the wealthy.

SINGAPORE

Singapore is a mixture of China without the dirt, India of the high caste only, and American values, looks, and money. One must admire an entire country that is squeaky clean enough to eat off subway floors, prohibits smoking in almost all places, has virtually no crime or drugs, and although home to a mix of cultures, demands integrated neighborhoods and no racism.

Singaporeans are neither friendly nor unfriendly. Bus drivers can speak English, but don't offer much help in getting around because they seem to know only their own routes. It is steamy hot like Bali, but not as gentle as Bali.

One should not judge cities too quickly, for each city has its blemishes and its good sides. Singapore has an emphasis on materialism much like the U.S., but without the crime and craziness, or democracy. But the dictatorial ways of the government have also given Singaporeans a good life. The government has myriad rules and regulations, which not only keep out pornography and drugs, but which even prevent traffic jams in the city by only allowing certain-numbered license plates to drive certain places on particular days.

Singapore has made me think of how out of proportion the world is economically. I paid $3.00 for a musical greeting card to send to a friend in China where

$25 is a monthly wage. And an East Indian Singaporean woman told me that her mother had shopped every day of her adult life but ten—on each of those ten days she had had a baby. The *amahs*, live-in nannies, did everything else.

Singapore has lush vegetation, cleanliness, efficiency, and a certain upper middle-class boredom. To me, it lacks the charm of Hong Kong. While I've penned these musings about Singapore in a Burger King, the employees have continually mopped and wiped around me.

Feb. 25, 1989

I was taken to the airport in Mrs. N.'s elegant talking car to catch my flight to Bangkok. I happily reunited with most of my luggage, which had mistakenly gone on to Hong Kong when I got off in Singapore. Fortunately, since I'd planned only a short time in Singapore, I had decided to leave most of my luggage at the airport and had everything I needed in my carry on. So, the airline just held the wayward luggage after it arrived back from Hong Kong to await my departure to Thailand. Strange how burdened I feel lugging all my luggage around the world, but how relieved I was to see it all again!

I particularly missed Mrs. N. when I arrived at the Bangkok airport and had to haggle with a taxi driver for the fare into the city. He didn't really know where the Youth Hostel was located in this vast city, but with my guidebook and his map, we finally made it.

The Youth Hostel was much more basic than I had wanted, but they did have a dormitory bed available. It was there that I met what I assume will be one of the most independent world travelers I'll ever meet. Although she was much younger than I, it was hard to tell her age because she had so many teeth missing.

She was from Poland, and had learned English on her own. She spoke it quite well and explained that she had just come from Hanoi which had been hard because it was difficult to get permission to travel anywhere in Vietnam. Her total luggage consisted of a tiny backpack made of old canvas. She borrowed my scissors and proceeded to cut her own hair while she told me about herself. She has traveled extensively in the world, can speak Spanish, and read and write Chinese. As a matter of fact, she had been in China in 1987 and loved it. The special foreigner's currency hadn't been any problem to her because she had only slept in railroad waiting rooms and Chinese dormitories, and always bought railway tickets at Chinese prices. She now travels only by boat everywhere to save money, and sometimes signs on as an engineer to repair a ship's engine en route. She has undoubtedly spent only a small fraction of what I have.

She was surprised that I have no desire to go into Campuchea or some other places she named I didn't know anything about. What happened to her teeth? She explained that she had an inflammation that she refused to have taken care of because she's afraid of dentists! So, as she traveled, each tooth had fallen out in its time. She figured it was better and cheaper than having a dentist pull them.

I had gone to a Youth Hostel specifically to make some helpful human contact. But she was a bit much for me. And, in the middle of the night, I woke up face to face with a young man I'd never met. The beds are extremely close together and males and females are not separated as they are in many hostels.

This was more togetherness than I wanted, so I walked around the neighborhood to find another place. All were cheap, but oh so dingy, so filthy, so absolutely grungy. Several looked like the sheets hadn't been changed in a long time. By sheer luck, I wandered into a place called Truly Yours that was clean and friendly. The room is ascetic and cell-like, but very, very clean with a bed and a fan and my own walls. For $3.20 a night, it's a good find.

Feb. 26, 1989

Finding a clean room of my own has helped to improve Bangkok for me. It is a terribly polluted city whose pollution my body feels in ways it has never felt before. Riding in a *tuk-tuk*, which is like an open taxi, puts you right on the level of the bus and car fumes.

They have an incredible array of street food, all quite artistically displayed. Pineapples on a stick are cut in beautiful patterns. Street vendors selling non-food items carefully and continually featherdust their wares. But, with the pollution and heavy traffic, it's quite useless.

"Beware of friendly people in Thailand," I had been warned by several travelers before my arrival. One had even been drugged over a friendly cup of coffee. He awoke without his luggage, passport, or money. As I was sitting on a bench in a park filled with intricate and colorful kites for sale, a young man sat down and tried to make conversation in poor English. A woman came along and offered to orient me on my map as to where I was. She said she was Thai and was visiting Bangkok from the Chang Mai area with her husband. She asked me if I had ever seen Thai dancing, and she told me there was a special show she was going to that night. Did I want to come with her?

I wondered why a Thai person would want to go to a tourist show of Thai dancing, so I just said "maybe." She produced a brochure and wrote down the information. Then, she said that she was going to a nearby precious stone shop that only Thai people knew about because she wanted to buy some stones there to re-sell in Hong Kong. Well, everyone has a get rich quick scheme. She asked if I wanted to go along with her.

Now, I started to smell a rat. Her husband said he needed to go to the bathroom, but she said he was going to look at the kites. I noticed that they didn't make any arrangements to meet each other later.

She and I took a bus. She was quite short, and I didn't really fear bodily harm from her, but I wasn't sure where this would lead us. It was then about 5:30 p.m. on a Saturday which didn't seem prime business hours, but this is Thailand.

We arrived at a big unlocked door that said "No Admission." Inside were several young girls polishing diamonds. A man rushed over to greet me in English and began to speak to me about sapphires. My "friend" Juanita immediately disappeared upstairs and I idly wondered if I'd ever see her again. Eventually, he took me upstairs too. I was rather surprised to see Juanita there. Another girl was waiting behind a desk to talk to me.

She was just about the most beautiful Thai girl I've seen, had wonderful dimples, and spoke good English. She proceeded to tell me how to tell a fake sapphire from a real one. I couldn't think of anything less useful for me to know, but I listened politely. Juanita said she had to go downstairs to conclude her sale.

When they took me downstairs, a girl led me outside to call a taxi for me. Juanita had somehow vanished. The girl said something about Juanita having to go to a bank (at 6 p.m. on a Saturday?) and asked me a strange, but familiar question—"Have you ever seen Thai dancing?"

I tried to catch a bus, but, for some reason, none would stop. So, I took a taxi. I'm not at all sure that it's safe to be on the streets of Bangkok after dark, but taxis and *tuk tuks* abound.

In retrospect, what did I lose or gain from that little adventure? I half-expected a set-up, but I hadn't found any of the situation threatening. I did make the mistake of drinking a coke that could have been drugged. Well, this time all ended okay, but I'll have to be more cautious in this so-called "land of smiles."

Feb. 27, 1989

I am standing on Khaosan Road at 6:50 a.m. waiting for a tour bus to pick me up. There are some strange and unusual sights. The city awakens slowly. Orange-robed monks are walking everywhere barefoot with their arms around a big rounded, covered bowl they are carrying. I learned this was to collect donations of food. Every Buddhist male, even the King, must give three months, often at ten years old, to live in a monastery and learn from the monks. Thailand is 95% Buddhist, 3 % Moslem, and 2% Christian.

Khaosan Road is a prime location for cheap hotels for travelers. Backpackers are on the move early. Their gear is fairly standard. I wish mine were as compact. Women walk by with yellow flowers in their hands—an offering, I suppose.

The street market is preparing to open. How Thais love their street food! It is so beautifully arranged—true folk art.

The driver, Eddy, came and picked me up in a car rather than a bus. My other fellow travelers were two people from Japan, and a tall, blonde girl from Denmark. We went through the crush of Bangkok to the countryside. We saw salt farms, and the more lucrative shrimp farms that raise shrimp to sell to Japan. There were some nice, classical teak homes on stilts. Sometimes they were on stilts so that the livestock could live underneath, and sometimes because of frequent flooding. On the opposite side of the road, there was a heavy flow of laden trucks driving rather crazily. Eddy said they had been driving all night from Malaysia bringing goods to Bangkok.

Tourists from other buses and cars converged at tourist spots, such as the Snake Farm. Here, cobras and pythons were handled, mishandled, milked, fought, and prodded to fight unwilling mongooses. Snakes are very plentiful in Thailand and one can imagine that Thai teenage boys learn how to catch snakes instead of fixing up junk cars. For a small fee, I got to wrap a very large boa constrictor around me. It was heavy and I marveled at the power I felt surging through its body as it wrapped around my body and down my leg. I have always wanted to do this with such a large snake. I have no idea why I wasn't afraid. Sometimes I had seen people just walking around Bangkok with snakes wrapped around their waists or necks—my idea of elegant apparel.

The Floating Market seemed more tourist than native, but it was interesting to go down the canals and see the houses and local residents. The array of goods on the boats was varied and attractive. It could be quite picturesque except that the tourist boats had huge, ugly, polluting, and noisy engines. Lunch was at a Crocodile Farm where, fortunately, I didn't have to watch crocodile wrestling.

After lunch, the Danish girl and one Japanese man switched to a car to go back to Bangkok, and I was joined by a British Guyanan man from Canada and the U.S. who is presently operating a bubblegum factory in Jamaica. He was another one of the colorful characters that one can only meet traveling. He had found U.S. life too fast paced. He said people were always telling him to move aside so they could pass. So, he had decided to open a chewing gum factory in Jamaica because there wasn't one. He had lost money the first three years, but had been doing okay the last two years. His wife wasn't crazy about traveling around, so she stayed home with the four children, ages 6 to 17. His doctor had told him to go away for vacation to cure his headaches and dizziness. And, so far, it was successful. I liked him. He was interesting and friendly.

In the afternoon, there was 90 minutes of instant Thai culture at a show for tourists, but it was informative and well done. Not every culture, or perhaps no culture can be like Bali where the culture is a daily, living, viable, integral part of everyday life.

Classical Thai dancing has some similarities to Balinese dancing, but it is more graceful and less interesting. They do have some variations like mock fighting with one holding a pole and another holding two pieces of wood over the arms to block the blows, fighting with two swords each, and dancing in between moving bamboo poles. Then, there was Thai boxing which involves kicking, and cock-fighting which is similar to Bali, but without the slashing razors on their feet. There was a wedding ceremony and a chance to see working elephants, which supposedly have strong relationships with their handlers.

Later on, while we were at a wood-carving plant exhibiting exquisite work, I heard Hebrew and asked the not-too-friendly Israelis how much the recent currency devaluation had been in Israel. It was a whopping 15%! In spite of their brusque manner, I felt a certain kinship with them. But their information about the sagging economy of Israel depressed me.

Feb. 28, 1989

Today was a strange compote of activities. I picked up a letter from mom at the American Express office. Still no word from the car insurance. I then went to a movie called "Scrooged." It was quite silly and sentimental, but somehow fitting America's loss of values. I felt a thrill combining Thailand and America in one place. As in Israeli movie theatres, they show many advertisements, previews of very violent movies, and cut off the credits that I love to watch at the end of a movie. However, unlike anywhere I've been before, everyone bounded to his/her feet when a picture of the King of Thailand came on the screen, followed by slides of the Royal Family and their good deeds.

This may be called the "land of smiles," but Thai people seem a hassled, burdened lot to me, and the crush and pollution of this city disturbs me physically as no other city has. Khaosan Road also attracts a very scruffy selection of independent travelers. I've met or overheard a few Israelis speaking Hebrew, but none has reciprocated with any friendliness. To me, it's a novelty to find Israelis during my travels, but there are actually large numbers of young Israelis traveling in Thailand because it can be quite cheap. I dreamed of one of my Ethiopian boys last night. As I usually do when someone I recognize enters my dreams, I sat down and wrote him a letter.

Out of curiosity, I checked into teaching English in Bangkok. The pay is very low—about $3 an hour for private tutoring, and $4 an hour to teach a class. Plus, because of visa restrictions, there is the necessity of leaving every two months. I have no interest in lingering in Bangkok. Although I've enjoyed some of Bangkok's unusual sights, this is a thoroughly disagreeable city to me. I will start seeing other areas of Thailand tomorrow.

March 1, 1989

Today I paid tribute to the men who built the bridge over the River Kwai. Being in that exact spot was far more moving than I expected even though the original bridge has been replaced. In some strange way, I was paying tribute to my father who could have been sent there in World War II instead of the European front. The people of Thailand maintain a cemetery there for the foreign soldiers who died protecting them. I walked among the sea of gravestones, and found a Jewish star among the crosses.

It took a long time to get there, but I was glad to be out of ugly, congested Bangkok. It was hard to put together the prettiness of the River Kwai area and the sickness, disease, and sheer agony of the men once so cruelly imprisoned there.

Will it really happen that I return to China in about two weeks? After such a perfect first experience there, is it tempting fate to return?

March 2, 1989

I overheard an Israeli talking while I sipped my banana shake. He was a typical curly-headed *saber*, native-born Israeli, and I became surprisingly homesick for Israel watching and listening to him. I listened to the easy banter between him and some young girls. Eventually, I spoke to him. He said he had left Israel a month ago, after an army stint in Gaza. He said that things were pretty bad. He nodded his head knowingly when I said I didn't think I was strong enough to cope with life there, and that it was a sad country. I continued on about not knowing how to deal with my Ethiopian boys going into the army all too soon, and telling him how hard it was to teach Jewish Israeli kids.

He was so typical—a *kibbutz* kid, and so beautiful to me. I felt a Jew to Jew kinship with him. Then, I thought, "How could I leave Israel?" But, "How can I stay in Israel?" quickly replied. I felt both relieved and sad when he said even he would be willing to leave Israel if he found a better place to live. "Perhaps Thailand," he said, "but I'll probably go back."

March 3, 1989

I can't seem to warm up to Thailand. I'm now in Chang Mai well away from Bangkok. It isn't really as polluted here, but I find the air of Chang Mai also still and stifling.

The train ride was okay. I do like being rocked by the cradle motion of a train. Inside, the train was quite wonderfully clean—so unlike China. I even saw them wash the outside of the train. I had an upper berth, which wasn't too hard to get up to, but was real awkward getting down from.

Mostly all independent travelers in Thailand choose to go on a trek to the hill tribes for three to four days. Reading notes from participants thoughtfully left behind in journals at cheap hotels note the experience as well worth all the physical hardships, but I'm really not into physical hardship. I just want to get back to China in one piece. I will do one-day tours instead and get a "flavor" instead of the full impact.

March 6, 1989

It seems I can't feel well in Thailand. Although nothing is seriously wrong, every part of my body seems "off." I dragged myself to a tour yesterday and was glad I did. We went to Elephant Camp where the elephants ate tons of bananas with skins, whole coconuts, and sugar cane. Their logging work looks very hard. We then traveled to a quite delightful place by a river. There were very few people there, and it was oh, so peaceful. We rode in a sort of box contraption on the back of an elephant with one young boy on the head of our elephant. I was glad I'd chosen the lazy man's way because the treks require days on an elephant.

Our mother elephant was followed by two of her sons, aged one and four. The youngest one always wanted to suckle, and the two brothers "horsed around" a lot. They all stopped very often to munch whatever leaves were tasty. It was a slooooooow trip. I wondered how Hannibal ever made it over the Alps at that rate.

Our group was congenial—two elderly French travelers, a couple from Canada, and a very sweet, very young guide. The young elephant drivers were from one of the tribes and had quite beautiful faces. After experiencing the side-to-side motion of riding on the back of an elephant, we had a short ride in an ox cart. The wheels, as well as the seats, had no padding. I was glad that very, very hard, uncomfortable ride was just a small taste of ox cart transportation.

We then got the lazyman's bamboo raft trip. There was hardly any water, so it wasn't quite white water rafting, which made it more serene and leisurely. A white on off-white butterfly settled on my foot as we glided down the river. For some strange reason, I imagined I was going down the Amazon River.

We visited two hill tribes. Of course, these were not the isolated tribes of the long treks because we drove there. Both tribes, the Lisu and the Meo, supposedly came from Yunnan and Guangzhou provinces in China 50 or 60 years ago. Some looked Chinese, but the younger ones looked more Thai. In the Lisu village, the young girls immediately surrounded us with goods to buy. They were tough bargainers all right, but quite cute, warm and friendly kids. We wandered the village and it reminded me of a few of the Chinese rural villages I had wandered through. Two little boys were having a wonderful time, one rolling a tire, and one rolling a farm tool down the road. The shacks were dank and unattractive.

In the Meo village, no one came to sell us anything. It was a curious mixture of primitive cabins with no windows and a fire inside which made it stifling. There was a color tv in the small store, and Isuzu trucks containing Honda or Yamaha motorcycles. They are partly in several generations. I don't know whether that makes them more content or less content.

The driver drove like a maniac in eastern style driving. I was reminded of the incessant honking and careening Chinese trucks and buses. Will my luck hold out surviving such wild, dangerous driving?

I wonder why I can't seem to breathe here. And I'm continually burping.

March 7, 1989

My companions on the tour were an interesting, international group. Two were travel agents from Australia, one of which was a girl of probably Chinese extraction who had been studying Chinese at Nanjing University in China. We traded China stories much of the time. From her, I also got the suggestion of looking into teaching English in Taichung, Taiwan, since I don't think I'd like Taipei. There was a young British girl working as a mid-wife in refuge camps in Thailand for the Vietnamese and Cambodians.

A middle-aged Chinese Singaporean told me a lot about his country, mostly in terms of money. He is proud of his country's admirable achievements in their economy and chance of having a good life, but he resents and regrets not having more freedom of speech and expression in their tightly controlled lives. The guide was a good-looking young boy who had just completed one of those grueling four-day treks.

We visited the Agha and Yao tribes. The Agha are a colorful, money hungry, and very grubby group (the guide explained they don't like to wash much), but the Yao are clean, short, and the older women have particularly beautiful faces. I was really struck by their beauty. The Yao came from Tibet about 200 years ago.

At the border with Burma, I gave out my U.S. and Israel postcards to the children. Many of the children just grabbed them, but some took them gently, bowed with folded hands under their chin, and said "*Merci.*" They were pleased with the postcards and even the filthy, deformed, pitiful Burmese children carrying babies and needing food took the postcards enthusiastically. They are allowed to beg inside Thailand at the border. I was so glad to see that there is some child part left in them that can delight in play. It really was heartbreaking to see them. I doubt I could stand India or Pakistan. I especially remember two very young tribal entrepreneurs who were dressed in their elaborate, colorful costumes and posed prettily for cameras for money.

The Golden Triangle, consisting of Laos, Burma, and Thailand, was prettier than any other place I've seen in Thailand. Once, the poppies grew there gloriously and once, mankind learned to tap them dangerously. But now one finds poppies grown only in smaller pockets of the hill tribes where opium is smoked on a small scale. It is astounding how mankind finds so many ways to destroy itself.

Money, money, money—one becomes aware all over the world (except perhaps in Bali) of the impact of money. It is not only the U.S., but most of the world both rich and poor that is obsessed by money on many different levels.

I will be glad to leave Thailand, but I'm glad I came. It gives me a broader picture of Asia.

6

CHINA March–May 16, 1989

March 10, 1989

I can see why Hong Kong has earned the reputation of being one of the most dangerous airports in the world. But, it is spectacular to fly right by the towering apartment buildings and land just before coming to a high mountain. The very first time I came was at night when, out of hours and hours of blackness, a profusion of colorful lights suddenly grew bright and we landed among them. As a concession to airplane safety, the neon lights in Hong Kong are not allowed to move or twinkle.

The airport may be dangerous, but it's very convenient to be so close to my familiar YWCA in Kowloon. I went into high gear taking care of numerous errands. First of all, I picked up many letters that were awaiting me at American Express. It was wonderful to read letters from the U.S., Israel, and my new China friends. I got another gammaglobulin shot to hopefully stave off hepatitis A, applied for another three month visa to China, got my Bali, Singapore, and Thailand photos developed, and now I'm working on getting a DragonAir flight directly into Hangzhou. I also need to book my return from Hong Kong to Israel via Paris since my one year ticket expires on June 15th and I must be sure to be back in Israel by that date.

March 15, 1989

Thanks to a cancellation, I got back to Hangzhou! On the plane, I had some moments of anxiety that I was making a terrible mistake returning, but once I landed, I felt great. There was really no way to contact Bill, Russell, and Richard, so I just took a taxi to their school. I had tried many times to envision the looks on their faces when I showed up, but their faces were just blank with shock. I'm not sure they really believe yet that I'm not just a vision. Richard wasn't at school because he's returned to his village to help with the harvest.

I excitedly talked non-stop and dragged out all the goodies I had brought for them, plus looked over the pictures which we shared with their roommates. We tried calling the tourism school to announce I was coming, but Alexander Graham Bell would be disappointed at the inefficiency of phones in China. So, we just flagged down a stray taxi that took us to the school.

I ran up to the 3rd floor classroom where most of my tour guides were. Such shock, surprise, amazement, and absolute love was there as word went out that I'd come back. Their new foreign teacher, Harriet, whom I had met before I left Hangzhou, was also surprised, but took it calmly and said that I could sleep in her room tonight.

But tomorrow, the complications of my staying in China begin. I can't stay at the tourism school because the police complained to the school after I'd left that I had not been properly registered as a teacher there. A foreigner can't live just anywhere in China, and places for foreigners are terribly overpriced. Well, we'll see. At least I'm here, and I'm still solvent—barely.

March 20, 1989

They say that love transforms. A person who looks just so-so takes on a beauty bestowed by the one who loves him or her. It's the same way with places. A quite common place is transformed in the lover's eye to a wonderful place. So it is with me and China. I love being back. Since coming back I have found the average Chinese in the street friendlier than before, or perhaps I'm getting better at getting a smile this time around.

With Russell and Richard's help, I went into the Foreign Affairs office of the University of Hangzhou and offered to teach in return for room and board. The person there was rather surprised, but eventually he took me seriously. There are two hostels connected to the university and I was able to move into one of the rooms temporarily. But after a couple of nights, I was told I'd need to move out to make way for someone else. But luck (a student suddenly leaving) and persuasion got me a place at the other hostel even if I won't be able to teach at Hangzhou University. I'm paying more than the other students living there (they're learning Chinese), but it's still cheap by western standards. It's a really ugly room and right next to some noisy factory, but it is a very short bike ride from here to the three boys' school. Hooray! They'll be able to visit me easily after their student teaching hours this semester.

Getting work will take a bit longer. So far, I have a private tutoring student from Zhejiang University for a couple of hours a week. The going rate for tutoring (just a little over $1 an hour) is even lower than in Bangkok, but I didn't expect to really earn much these next few months.

Russell and I had time to go out to what I had dubbed "my bench" last time on the causeway near the Shangri-La Hotel. We sat on the bench, ate some mediocre fruit, and took pictures. I tried to teach Russell some things about my camera since he bought a Chinese camera with the graduation money I had given him when I left in January.

I'm back to dressing in layers. Seems like it's spring only according to the calendar, not the weather.

As a gesture of gratitude for his help in my getting my little room, the man in the Hangzhou University Foreign Affairs office has asked me to write down my reasons for choosing not to live in the U.S. I've never really thought about my reasons, so it might be interesting to put something down on paper.

THE OTHER SIDE OF THE COIN

As I have traveled the world, I have become very aware of the awe with which the world, and particularly Asia, views the U.S. I am an American, yet I prefer to live outside the U.S. There are some very real positive aspects to the U.S.—what it has accomplished is remarkable. It is easy to see its accomplishments. It is more difficult to see what I call the "other side of the coin"—the part of America that makes me choose to live outside the benefits and easy life it offers.

The desire in me to live in a country other than the U.S. grew slowly and subtly. I wasn't sure why, but I felt a certain boredom and shallowness in the U.S. even though I lived in the east, west, and deep south. I had a good life there, and an active life, but I felt superfluous. After more than five years of living outside the U.S., I have come to understand more fully what urged me to leave. Return visits back have clarified and reaffirmed why.

Basically, it's the lifestyle I reject. In all its richness and materialism and "good life," I find a vast wasteland and a vacuous value system. The leisure that a technologically advanced society has made possible seems to have developed into a frantic, frenzied search for meaning in life. There is a rootlessness in Americans that sends them to extremes to feel connected to something. Some search for this connectedness in advocating for social causes, or in "doing good" for society. One's job is important in America not only for a livelihood, but also for a feeling of identity and self-worth, of connection to something more solid than oneself.

The family system in the U.S. has broken down to the extent that it does not contribute to a sense of connection, or to a feeling of belonging. While the pursuit of, and tolerance of, individualism has many advantages, the individualism that parents nurture in their children and demand for themselves, has eroded the traditions of closeness and responsibility as a member of the family unit. American society has devised clever ways to compensate for divorce such as joint custody, no-fault divorce, step-parenting, "blended families" of "his", "her", and "our" children, and even friendly divorces in which the parents both maintain interest and contact and may even continue family vacations together. However, these compensations cannot compare to the closeness and feeling of belonging found in Eastern culture families.

In contrast to Eastern families, American children grow up believing their parents owe them everything. This self-centeredness expands into the belief that society "owes" them everything. Therefore, they feel little social obligation. Organizations and charitable societies have been set up to provide the help that a family or community unit provides in other parts of the world. So, while there are services for poor people, old people, retarded people, sick people, lonely people, these take on an impersonal aspect.

It is written in the Declaration of Independence that everyone is guaranteed "life, liberty, and the pursuit of happiness." This pursuit of happiness has become a bizarre quest. Some try to pursue happiness through materialism until the waste and over-plenty assume unbelievable proportions. There is no end, no satiation for materialism because there is always something bigger, newer, more advanced, a prettier color, softer, more durable, etc. While there is too much by some standards, there is never enough for the American buyer's mentality, with big business and advertising aiding, abetting, and encouraging the normal greed of human nature.

While daily survival takes up the time and energy of much of the Eastern world, the search for personal fulfillment occupies Americans. Americans have limited obligations and a huge amount of freedom. But freedom can also be a burden because one must choose how to use it wisely, and where to direct one's energy. Having few societal rules and expectations to guide their lives, they are much more the masters of their own fate. But finding personal fulfillment is often more elusive and frustrating, and requires more creativity than hard daily labor for subsistence survival.

There are many signs of a sickness of spirit, a growing malaise in America. The high levels of drug and alcohol addiction, promiscuity, violent and senseless crime, random and impersonal anti-social acts such as poisoning yogurt in a supermarket—these are not signs of a healthy culture.

While there have always been some "crazies" who are responsible for horrendous murders, the truly strange, pointless, and extremely cruel crimes in America seem to be rising. I live in a country, Israel, which is always in a state of preparedness for war, but I'm more afraid to be in a New York subway or New Orleans street than to be in Israel. Perhaps the risk is not much different, but there are reasons for violence in Israel compared to a randomness and senselessness to the crime in U.S. cities which makes it totally unpredictable, and, thus, more frightening to me.

As I have had the opportunity to teach Western culture to Chinese students, I became more aware of, and grateful for, some of the truly wonderful American characteristics. There is in Americans an openness, a self-confidence, an optimism, and a sense of humor and fun that is sadly lacking in many of the Asian cultures. So, it is good to acknowledge, appreciate, and even imitate admirable aspects of the United States—but to do so without a reverential awe that blinds one to the other side of the coin.

March 19, 1989

How is it that I've never felt happier than sitting in a grubby Chinese university dormitory room watching the excitement and enthusiasm of Bill and Russell and their roommates playing Monopoly for the first time. Their eyes lit up with so much "money" in their hands.

I saw the English books Russell has collected stacked all along his bed since they have no bookcases in the dorm room. Literature and sociology keep him intellectually warm these cold nights. There's very little furniture in the dorm rooms, so one's bed becomes the only private space available.

Richard had come back to school, but I had told Russell and Bill not to spoil the surprise that I was back, so he was out somewhere when I came. When he returned, we didn't see him come in because the electricity had gone out in the whole dormitory. He recognized my voice in the darkness and rushed over to check if it was truly me. He was so wonderfully happy to see me. Good feelings flowed all around.

When I got back to my room, a bit less ugly since Diana had come over from the tourism school and helped me do some "light" decorating, I thought about how I would have to leave China and my friends again. How much more deeply it will hurt after having a few more months for our closeness to grow.

March 26, 1989

Even though I can feel I'm getting a bad cold, I went on an outing today with the three boys, Diana, and Cindy, who is a young American girl studying Chinese and living in the first foreign student hostel where I stayed for a few days. We rode our bikes out to a park where Cindy and I dressed up as Chinese Song Dynasty ladies and had our pictures taken while the boys laughed and laughed to see us dressed so.

Later, when I was alone with the boys, I surprised them by asking if being with me sometimes embarrassed them. Being with Cindy had made me very aware of how differently Americans and Chinese behave. They were quite amazed at my question and answered easily that they had always felt very proud to be with me.

I then brought up my insecurity about possibly leaving Israel and becoming a total wanderer. I spoke of how I felt I lived everywhere and nowhere, that everyplace was my home and no place was, and that I never felt I wasn't a foreigner even and perhaps especially in the U.S. Russell and Richard said they would always feel rooted to their hometowns, no matter where they roamed. They would change, and be changed, I'm sure, but they probably would always know where they felt rooted.

I also commented on their habit of reading everything they see on anyone's desk. They said it is Chinese custom, and that anything anyone does not want read by others would never be left out on a desk. I had seen Russell read a postcard in Cindy's room, and Richard read a receipt on my desk. I also remembered that Bill had picked up a paper on a school official's desk when he was helping me find work. They said they hadn't realized that this was "bad" in the eyes of westerners.

My job search is looking up. I've applied to teach staff at the Yellow Dragon Hotel and the boys have approached their school's English Department about my teaching there. All would be part time, but that's okay. It gives me more time to see my former students, now my friends.

March 29, 1989

Ah, young love. Russell came to my room to chat today. Richard had called Russell an "inside person," which, I think is a good description. So, I was particularly glad he felt comfortable enough with me to talk about his pain at just ending his first love relationship. He explained his reasons and said he had taken courage from an article in the Reader's Digest I had given him. The article was called "Take Charge of Your Life." I've laughed at similar all-purpose, pop articles, but they can be helpful if read in the right time and place. I'll never forget that Anwar Sadat credited a Reader's Digest article for an abrupt change in his attitude toward life. I ended up giving Russell an Ashleigh Brilliant cartoon I have been carrying around for years. It reads, "Due to circumstances beyond my control, I am master of my fate and captain of my soul."

We spoke of coping skills for troubling times in our lives, and I gave him some hard-earned advice about connecting with nature, crying, finding a safe person or place to express one's feelings, and to write out pain and anguish. He said writing hadn't been something he had been able to do. I told him to keep it in mind if the time came that he felt overwhelmed by inner panic. Then, I gave him a small journal with a sheep on it. Both he and I were born in sheep years. I also advised him to learn to know himself very well and to be able to detect if he is dipping into depression because depression can pull you down like quicksand. He seemed to appreciate our deep conversation.

Looks like I've gotten both jobs—teaching Hangzhou Teacher's College 2nd year students, and the Yellow Dragon Hotel staff. I'm looking forward to starting.

March 31, 1989

Today was a truly beautiful spring day, and the tourists have begun to come out along with the buds. I fell asleep by my bench. I was tired all day and slept and slept. My cold seems to be going into that dreaded bronchitis!

The boys have tried to teach me the Chinese way of dressing for cold weather. We westerners always like to be comfortable, so we put on and take off clothes according to the weather. We might wear a heavy jacket one day and be in short sleeves the next day. As I understand their system so far, they slowly acclimate their bodies to what season is coming up by adding or stripping layers. In cold weather, you must put on more clothes to go out than what you had on inside. And, once outside, you must not remove clothes. Before bed, you must wash your face and feet in warm water. As I saw when I slept in the girls' dorm one night in the tourism school last week, the girls sleep in only a top and underpants and lay their other clothing over them on top of the quilt. Then, when they wake up, they put those clothes on before they get out of bed. Sounds complicated, but it's worth trying if I can prevent future colds.

April 1, 1989

I am sick, and no April Fool's about it. I spent most of last night coughing which left me very sleepy.

As I was settling back in bed, Diana and Juliet came over. We went to a nearby restaurant for lunch. We couldn't finish everything, and I said I'd like to take it back with me to eat later. That was a strange concept to them because, apparently, Chinese never take food out of a restaurant after a meal. Nevertheless, they helped me find a plastic bag to put it in as though they were doing something very mischievous.

Juliet told me that the staff people at the hostel had asked her about me because I have so many Chinese visitors. They, in fact, have to keep a record with the identity card number of everyone who visits me. I hadn't known that. I thought these older women were there to take care of us and the hostel, and did our laundry by hand for a small sum. But they are also there to watch us for the authorities.

April 4, 1989

I pulled myself together for my first teaching hours at the Hangzhou Teacher's College. The English level of the students was better than I expected. And the magic was there—the high took over as soon as I started to teach. Again I forgot where I was and with whom, lost in a teacher's high not unlike the swimmer's high I've sometimes felt.

Russell met me after class and took me down the street for *jiaoxi*. I was feeling very weak from all my coughing, so Russell told me to nap in his dorm bed while he was at class until I could get up enough strength to pedal home. As I fell asleep, his roommate, Jerry, came into the dorm, saw me there, and gently laid another quilt over me. I've noticed before how thoughtful and gentle Jerry is.

April 5, 1989

I had my Yellow Dragon Hotel class today. They are a good-looking, well-dressed group of managers. Their English levels vary, but they are basically better English speakers than I expected. It should be fun to teach them except that they keep getting beeped and having to run out for a while. Conditions are good in the room where I teach them. At the very least, it gives me 90 minutes in a room with heat!

In class, I talked about the problem of lower staff people not smiling when they are serving western guests. I explained that westerners expect it. One of the managers said with a sigh, "It's very difficult to teach them to smile at guests if they've never been smiled at when in a hotel or restaurant." Yes, cultural communication is a complicated issue.

April 6, 1989

Thomas, the deep thinker, came over today and we talked about life, and what type of person we each want to be. Then, he came with Russell and Bill and me to see Alfred Hitchcock's "North by Northwest". Of course, Cary Grant and all spoke perfect Chinese with no sub-titles, but I enjoyed re-seeing it after 25 years or so with my Chinese friends in Hangzhou. Again, I wondered how they could relate to such scenes of America. They certainly perked up at the mild, mellow, pleasant love scenes.

ACUPUNCTURE

I walked into what looked like an ancient torture chamber. A woman sat in a chair with her arms turned upward, needles sticking out of her hands. An elderly man sat quietly with his shoes off and needles coming out of his feet, ankles, and on the sides of his knees. A man in a white lab coat came over and twisted the needles while the elderly man winced. A woman lay with needles coming out of her neck, forehead, and arms. Another woman had a box on her back with smoke rising out of it.

A foreign student brought me to the acupuncture clinic because of my hacking, bronchial cough. The place was dingy and dirty, which is not unusual in China. But the smiles of the doctors and attendants there welcomed me. One doctor approached me and, in decent English asked me what the problem was. I then sat down on a tiny stool and he put needles into my neck. He explained that Chinese people have words to describe the sensations when the needles are in there, but westerners don't know how to describe these feelings. For example, what is a "bitter" feeling in the physical sense?

I didn't have a lot of hope that these needles would work. The treatment was uncomfortable, but I can't say the needles were painful. Was it only coincidence that I managed to sleep through that night without coughing fits?

I returned for another treatment and was treated by an elderly doctor who didn't speak much English, but had the kind of face that made you trust him. He took my pulse for a long time, and said he would "strengthen my constitution." He had me lie down and placed needles in different spots of my body. Again, the sensation was one of slight discomfort rather than pain.

My cough continued to recede, and I returned for five treatments in all. They charged me the equivalent of $25 in all.

April 9, 1989

The ladies at the front desk of the hostel are surprised that I have so many "relatives" in China, as they call the many visitors that come to see me. "Chinese people don't visit their relatives as much," Russell said with a smile. My days are happily filled with so many friendly visitors. I do have a large, wonderful family in China. I feel it and am deeply grateful.

The Dean at Russell's school had spoken to him about me last week. He had stressed to Russell that the school had done me a favor by hiring me part time. Restraining his anger, Russell had told him that I was teaching there because I wanted the contact with the students and that I already was tutoring students from Zhejiang University—a "key" university, as well as teaching managers at the Yellow Dragon Hotel which also rings of prestige. I think I understand the source of the Dean's feelings about me because he had pointed out quite clearly to me that I am receiving per hour pay far higher than regular Chinese teachers. Chinese teachers really do suffer here.

Diana and Juliet came over while Russell was still here. The three of us went out for *jiaoxi* and topped it off with the most unusual ice cream and pastry I've ever had at a new pastry shop. I wanted to go out on West Lake. So, with some difficulty, we hired a boat and paddled around. It wasn't sunny, but it was pleasant. So many of the trees are starting to blossom beautifully and colorfully. We were a happy, congenial group just drifting aimlessly around the lake. I gave Russell my camera and he started experimenting with it. I think he has some creative talent in photography. The sunset was lovely.

When accompanying me back home, I mentioned that Richard's dad was visiting and that he was going to bring him over to meet me. Russell said he had been thinking about inviting me to his parents' home. He worried about where I could sleep because technically a foreigner cannot sleep in a Chinese family's home. He was also concerned about the culture shock to his peasant parents. Lack of common language would be the biggest problem. He was sure his whole village, mostly relatives on his father's side, would be welcoming and he felt I was easy to get along with. As we talked, he got quite enthusiastic about the idea.

April 10, 1989

Richard's dad is a very short man just two years my senior. He has a quiet dignity. He and Richard took me out for dinner and then came back to my room. Penny and her boyfriend stopped over, and together we looked at my photos. I've been surprised at some people's reaction to my pictures of Bali. They look at the thatched-roof cottages and refer to them as "poorer than China." Richard had told me with some embarrassment that his family's home has a thatched roof. He couldn't believe it when I told him that a thatched roof in Europe or the U.S. was very expensive.

Penny's boyfriend is studying photography, and he brought some of his photos and poetry to share with me. I'm not sure how Abraham Lincoln came up in the conversation, but Richard was amazed that his uneducated father had heard of Lincoln.

Through Richard's translation, his father thanked me for the musical Chinese New Year's card I had sent from Hong Kong. They still play it with pride when the neighbors come over. How nice to be where such a little something can bring so much joy! I was touched that Richard had wanted to bring his father to meet me.

April 11, 1989

After going to bed, I couldn't sleep. I was both very happy and very sad at the same time. It was weird. I was very happy about being here, and about feeling that my relationships here were developing well. Then, I was sad about leaving Israel and being away from so many people I care about. It was such a contrast of feelings! Even the music I was listening to sounded sometimes powerful and sad, or powerful and happy.

I found out today why Russell, Richard, and Bill never take books out of their library at school. Russell had mentioned to me how much he wanted to read some Shakespeare. Since I'm a part time teacher at their school, I thought I'd take out some Shakespeare books for him. Getting books out of the library involved having a librarian take me into back rooms where hundreds of books sat imprisoned in cages rather than within the reach of eager students. I didn't get to see Russell's face when he came back to the dorm and found Shakespeare waiting on his bed.

April 12, 1989

I finally had a really great meal! My Yellow Dragon Hotel students noticed how I practically salivated talking about western food. They told me that William could take me to eat at the western restaurant there and just sign for it. And so, sweet William took me to the hotel's restaurant to eat. I couldn't believe the wonderful taste of real bread and butter again, an actual lettuce salad, and a steak that I could sink my teeth into because it wasn't cut up into little pieces. The boss had even called ahead and ordered extra rolls and butter for me to take home. Yes, I guess there are many foods I've been missing on a limited budget. Western food, Chinese style of course, is only available in expensive five star hotels like the Yellow Dragon.

April 13, 1989

I didn't much like Cindy's father who had come to visit her while she was studying in China, but he was kind enough to invite a group of us out to eat. Cindy had met Richard, Russell, Bill, Diana, and Juliet through me when I was at the first foreign student hostel. The professor accompanying Cindy's group of American students also came. Richard had been nervous about arranging the small banquet at a nice restaurant for all of us. That seemed out of character for his easy-going nature, but he said he was afraid to meet other foreigners because he feared offending them. He didn't feel that way about me because he considered me Chinese! I thought that was a lovely compliment.

Surprisingly, I also felt strange and unfamiliar being around Americans again after so many months. Not only the speed of my English, but also my personality was different in the company of Americans. Also, on the one hand, I was glad to have given my Chinese friends the experience of broadening their life through contact with Americans. On the other hand, I had to admit to myself that I didn't like sharing my special friends with Americans who have so little concept of China and Chinese people. I met again my ambivalence in wanting to expose my Chinese young friends to a bigger world, and not wanting to be responsible for opening their limited world.

What was clear to me was how comfortable they felt with me compared to how awkward and nervous they felt around Cindy's father and the American professor. When the boys accompanied me home, Russell quite accurately pegged Cindy's father as a "lady-killer" and a "cowboy type." Richard was totally drained from the whole experience.

April 16, 1989

Each time the boys had taken me to a park in Hangzhou, I had wondered why the people never sat on the grass. So, Richard and Russell decided to take me to a park where we could see people having picnics on the grass. Our picnic wasn't particularly appetizing because we just bought some canned food, but the spot was delicious. It was by a quieter part of West Lake surrounded by mountains. The scenery and the pleasant weather reminded me at times of Louisiana, at times of Maalot in Israel, at times of any wonderful lake surrounded by mountains. Yet, this had its own Chinese flavor.

I was surprised when the boys just dropped the remains of our picnic on the grass. They said some old ladies had the job of cleaning up after us and we shouldn't deprive them of their work. I had noticed they threw trash out the window of their dorm room for the same reason.

Russell was feeling freer and more relaxed than I'd seen him for a long time. We were able to rent a small motorboat and he and Richard piloted us around the area. Russell and I took a lot of pictures of this picture perfect day.

April 18, 1989

How dear my Hangzhou life is to me! After my classes at the teacher's college, I spent some time with Bill and Russell. When Bill went to class, Russell and I took a walk to their new track and walked around and around reading some poems I thought he'd like. Then, we sat in the sun on the soccer field and read from Shakespeare's Sonnets, and then from Alice in Wonderland. He particularly enjoyed the dramatic quality I put into reading Alice.

That evening, Richard stopped by and we went for a long, lingering dinner during which we spoke of many things, including his "girl trouble." Sometimes, I think I'm becoming Dear Abby. We also talked about my upcoming visit to the classes he's student teaching.

April 19, 1989

The English level of Richard's students was incredibly low, but I felt the warmth of their welcome when I visited his classes. The teaching conditions are poor, with over 50 students to a class and very loud building construction noises from next door. It wasn't my finest teaching hour, but it went okay and the students welcomed me with flute playing, a "chop" with my name in Chinese characters, and some drawings. He was the only one of the three boys to invite me to his classes.

April 20, 1989

Surely this turned out to be my best and most unusual Passover ever. It was a letter from one of my friends in Israel that reminded me of the date that Passover fell on this year. I sat as close as I could to "my bench" in the evening because sweethearts take them over since privacy is in short supply here. And I began to feel very homesick for Israel. I thought of many Passover dinners that I had had with friends and relatives over the years.

I couldn't feel sorry for myself for long. The night was beautiful, and the draping weeping willow tree danced in the lake. I wished Israel and each of my relatives by name a Happy Passover. Then, I thought of my Chinese family here in Hangzhou and decided to have a modified Passover *seder* with them.

Excitedly, I went to a westernized shop nearby and bought good bread and other delicacies. Of course, it was all too expensive, but I pedaled over to the boys' dormitory and spread out a small-scale western feast. Although the taste was strange to them, the boys and their roommates consumed the food with great relish. I told them all the story of the Jewish holiday of Passover and we ate and laughed heartily.

April 21, 1989

Russell told me about a demonstration of college students he had gone to last night after I'd left. Apparently, frustration has been growing rapidly among the college students. They want more freedom, more capitalism, and less bureaucracy. I've noticed a definite boredom among college students here, and the energy of youth looking for an outlet.

We spent some time practicing on a TOEFL test because I have offered to pay for him to take the test so that he might study in a graduate school in the U.S. I think he'll be able to pass the test with an okay score because he has a good English vocabulary.

Since he's expressed interest in studying abroad, I took him to the western restaurant of the Shangri-La Hotel to taste some western food. While eating his hamburger, he kept drinking lots of water because he found it so dry. It also obviously bothered him greatly to hold the hamburger in his hands, but he persevered and helped the hamburger to his mouth with the aid of his fork. Although it was messy to eat, he claimed to enjoy it. He ordered apple pie and ice cream for dessert and truly loved it. Although just so-so in taste to me, it was an incredibly expensive meal!

April 22, 1989

I've entered a premature mourning because I am soon to leave my China life. It is difficult to predict where one will find happiness. I had no idea I would find it in dreary, drab, sad, troubled China.

With my last remaining money, I will leave Hangzhou with my three special boys on May 17th. They don't have to be at school because that's their time to do their project papers, which they said they'd prepare earlier. We will travel to a famous place they have longed to see called Yellow Mountain, *Huang Shan* in Chinese. We will then go on to Nanjing where I'll finally meet the professor I established letter contact with after reading about him in the Jewish newspaper in

San Diego. I'll then have a chance to visit Russell's home, followed by Richard's home. Getting hard sleepers for all of us to Guangzhou may be quite troublesome, but hopefully they will be able to bid farewell to me from Guangzhou after some time there. I'll go on to Hong Kong and they'll return to Hangzhou on June 3rd. My flight from Hong Kong to Paris will be on June 6th, and after a few days there, I'll go back to Israel.

So, my year-long odyssey, which could be named "The Strange Saga of Suellen," is about to end. I've learned so much, but I don't know what comes next.

April 26, 1989

I actually petted a bamboo tree today. Russell and I walked into the bamboo grove of a park, and there I saw something I'd never seen before—baby bamboo trees with a soft furry covering. It was so beautiful, and felt just like the soft fur on a dog or cat. On some I could see how the furry leaves part and fall off, and a young green color emerges.

We rested on the leaves shaded by the larger whispering bamboo trees. The artistic reflection of the bamboo stand showed in his glasses. Our conversation flowed without a connecting thread until we spoke of reading fiction. For some reason, Nancy Drew came to my mind and I remembered how I had loved her curiosity, courage, and sense of adventure. Russell said he rarely reads fiction because it draws him in and then he just wants to keep reading and forget everything else.

We talked about the meaning of life. He said he gets confused because things keep changing and it's not easy for him to change. He had been taught communism and caring for each other. But now, he thinks Chinese people are friendly only for what they can get from the other, so he doesn't know whom he can truly trust. I have heard that from other students too who live in the reality of China where *guanxi,* being able to make personal connections, makes all the difference in their lives.

The student protests are heating up, especially in Beijing. China seems to be entering a new stage of protest and discontent.

April 28,1989

I felt the warmth of being surrounded by my tourism school students when I visited them today. All of them are feeling nervous about their upcoming work assignments. For the first time, they have also been told they must try to find their own jobs, which can be very frightening and fruitless without *guanxi.* It was good to see Elizabeth again. I haven't seen much of her because she's been busy preparing for her wedding.

I'm trying to use the *guanxi* of having students at the Yellow Dragon Hotel to get train tickets for the boys and me to get to Guangzhou. Apparently, it's quite complicated for foreigners and Chinese to travel together. For example, I can get a ticket for soft sleeper, but the boys may be turned away even if they have tickets! When I complained about the discrimination, my student told me that, without this discrimination, foreigners would never get seats because Chinese business travelers would take them.

April 29, 1989

I was really impressed today with how Russell, Richard, and Bill know their way around a kitchen. They, along with Richard's girlfriend, invited me to lunch at a friend's apartment. The friend was away, but loaned them the apartment. Richard was the main cook, and he prepared a gourmet menu of river snails in chili sauce, pork and green peas and bamboo shoots, egg and bamboo shoots with green onion and ginger, fish cooked with ginger, green vegetable and pork, fish-head soup, and, of course, rice. It was the first time I sucked snails out of their shells.

Well fed, I went out on the balcony that had a nice view and let the wind blow through my hair. I was standing, but almost dozed. When I opened my eyes, Russell said he would like to take a picture of me that way. Once again the camera became a fun toy. How much I have come to love picture taking! These pictures are the most valuable material possessions I will ever have.

I had what might be called a "traveler's high" during our time together today. I felt so at ease and comfortable, I was suddenly shocked to hear Chinese music. I had completely forgotten I was in China!

I wanted to explore an area I had seen from the porch. It led to the countryside of Hangzhou on one side, and the encroaching city on the other side. They were able to point out and name several plants. We walked back slowly and joked about an apartment complex being constructed that they thought looked very nice and I thought looked like an ugly prison. Really, all the buildings are so dreary in China!

BLACK HEADS BOBBING ON A SUNNY SPRING DAY

On May 4th, 1989, Youth Day in China, I saw a sea of black heads bobbing as they marched along in the warm spring sun. They walked about eight abreast in a jovial, but orderly fashion. On either side, they held hands to make a human rope.

Baggy-green-uniformed police nervously preceded the marchers, some with loud speakers to keep the onlookers back. The marchers filled about one lane of the road, while bystanders, supporters, and those just trying to go about their daily work jammed the sidewalks and the other lane of the road. The traffic jam was of people and bicycles since buses and cars were not able to move.

The marchers held aloft a few banners proclaiming their demands, and leader/response slogans were chanted without benefit of loud speakers. These were the students of Hangzhou, China, answering the country's students' call to rally to the cause of freedom.

The students, young and fresh looking, did not have angry, demanding faces. Instead, they were smiling and seemed to be genuinely enjoying themselves, for it was a welcome break from the usual pervasive sense of boredom and frustration that one picks up from China's college students. Unable to choose their own careers, and shackled by a well-entrenched system of personal connections as the only key to upward mobility, or even to a decent lifestyle, these students don't feel they have much to lose.

Education and intelligence are not highly valued in today's China. To the contrary, one's intelligence often seems to be a liability, leading only to a dead end. Children of the terror of the Cultural Revolution, these students were led to believe that the only path out of a poor and common life lay in passing exams that would lead to a university. Their parents had pleaded, pushed, and sometimes even beaten them into studying harder and harder, desperately wanting their children to achieve what they had not. The students of today's China, many of them children who had never had the chance to enjoy their childhood, feel a sense of betrayal and broken dreams and promises. Their hard work and suffering, and their parents' sacrifices on behalf of their education, seem a cruel joke played on them all.

And yet they are now young adults—intelligent, and knowledgeable of western ways. Those that dare to dream (and many do not) dream of a China that will value them, appreciate them, free them to make decisions about their own lives.

The bystanders lined the streets, climbed up to higher vantage points, stared out from office windows and apartment balconies. They took pictures, applauded the demonstrators, ignored them, or looked on with pride, or amusement, or a sense of wonder that Chinese were again daring to criticize their government.

Some people eyed me curiously. What was a middle-aged foreigner doing walking alongside the march? One student said, "Walk with us." But, a woman sputtered in Chinese to me in worried fashion, urging me to stay away from the demonstrators. Without understanding what she was saying, I understood clearly her concern that there might be trouble. With her bicycle, she determinedly pushed me more and more to the side, out of possible harm's way.

I did not march amongst the students, for China is not my country. I am a visitor, and although I sympathize greatly with the students, especially after coming to know them intimately in these past months as their friend and teacher, this must be their struggle. They must reform their own country.

As I walked, my memory went back to other students, to another main street thousands of miles away and over 20 years ago—to Berkeley, California. Anyone who lived through the anti-Vietnam War demonstrations cannot forget the beauty or the pain of the late 1960's. In the end, the students there won out. It was not without a price.

As I walked, I wondered what price these students will pay for what they might dare to do. But this day, there were no confrontations, no violence, no guns, no blood. It seemed more like a festival, a spring celebration in Hangzhou.

And thus thousands of students spent this May 4th, the anniversary of a student movement of the past. They spoke out against what is, and dared to dream what can be.

May 5, 1989

There were so many precious moments today as my time to leave Hangzhou comes closer. Russell and Richard came by at 6:00 p.m. Once again we listened to music on my tape recorder, which has given us all so many happy, musical hours. We had a decent meal at the restaurant Thomas and I had gone to before and then I suggested we go home to my place the long way. We walked through a section of Orioles in the Willows Park, which was especially beautiful as it grew dark. We composed on Ode to a Chicken—a partially submerged boat except for the chicken head rising proudly. Those chicken boats they rent to go out on the lake have always made me laugh.

We then got on our bikes. Sometimes I rushed ahead with a flurry of energy and happiness. I even raced another cyclist on the road, but lost. We got to my favorite Su Causeway, putting on steam to make it over the bridges and then whooping on the way down as I had first done with the pedicab driver. It was such a beautiful and free feeling. We stopped to look out at, and listen to the lake. Richard fell asleep, and Russell and I sat on a bench. I thought dreamily of all the lakes and oceans I have listened to.

There was a little toilet across from the bench, which I used. When I returned, I could hear Richard talking but I couldn't see Russell. After a while, I thought he might have fallen into the trench toilet in the dark. Eventually, Russell showed himself up in a tree where he had climbed to hide on me.

The tree was hollow and we decided to leave a note in the tree just like the note in the bottle we had put into the canal on our boat trip up to Suzhou. We drank a bottle of yogurt I had with me and then inserted a note to Russell's parents saying I would soon meet them. We then made wishes while we threw coins into the tree hollow and the lake.

I jumped on a rock nearby and claimed it as "my rock." Russell claimed the tree as "his tree." Richard suggested we come back in the daylight and take pictures of this place. We were all very animated, our spirits soaring. We continued pedaling our bikes with great gusto and paid respect to "my bench" as we went by. That side of the lake was so calm and quiet compared to the other side we had been on. Russell said he had never realized how beautiful Hangzhou was.

It was so late at night that there were no cars and people to get in our way when we got off the causeway. It was as though only the three of us existed. Russell quietly said it was so perfect that he wished the sun would never dawn.

May 7, 1989

Today I discovered and <u>felt</u> the Chinese countryside in a sensual, deep, very close way. I went off for the day with Pearl, Russell, Richard, and Bill. Elizabeth had planned to come, but had to take care of something else at the last minute. In the outdoors, the boys seemed to need to smoke a lot, so I went off by myself to get away from that terrible cigarette smoke I've been trying hard to avoid all my life. We were in Pearl's hometown of Fuyang.

I liked a little street very much. I know well that I'm in the "real China" all the time, but that street was somehow even "more real." That day, I enjoyed being stared at by the locals. At a restaurant where we stopped for lunch, I played with a puppy—the first time in a year. I have missed dogs in my life. This little one got me all muddy, and I loved it. Richard had promised me that it was a pet and would not be eaten. The family that owned the restaurant saw how happy I was playing with the puppy and even brought out a little stool so I could be more comfortable.

Finally, when I stood up, I also looked up and saw what Russell had hoped I wouldn't see. The puppy's brother was hanging skinned above the door. It sickened me to think of that fate for my little playmate. Yes, that was a "very real" street in China.

We took a boat to a countryside village island a short way from Fuyang. It was quite ordinary and boring to the four of them, but quite a marvelous experience for me. When they claimed they were tired and wanted to rest, I suggested that I go on by myself for a half hour or so.

I felt a keen joy and elation being on my own deep in the Chinese countryside. I felt the strength of all the peasants who kept vast China fed. I walked down a little path and stopped to watch a man weaving a basket. The simple farmhouse behind him, his single-focused concentration on weaving a strong basket, and the warm weather all blended into a perfect moment stopped in time and space. It made me think of another sunny day when Reuven had shown me how Ethiopians knew how to weave a basket even out of plastic bags.

I felt a peacefulness in that quiet place. In that moment, the hardships of the peasants' lives seemed a distant reality. I sat among some trees surrounded by the fields. I wasn't ready to be with people again.

May 16, 1989

As I listened so many times to Barbra Streisand singing it on that tape the boys loved, "And so the word is goodbye. It makes no difference how the tears are cried. It's over," the precious last moments of my time in Hangzhou have ticked by. From my porch in Bali, I wasn't sure what would happen if I came back. But now I know that the risk was worth it. My little cell of a room has been a place of warmth and fun and love and companionship. It was a very busy, active, and once again fulfilling time. I've re-confirmed that my true career niche is being a teacher. Now I leave with two more fine recommendation letters and good, sweet memories.

So, today was one of goodbyes—to my Hangzhou Teacher's College students, to the track, to the boys' dormitory room that became my second home, to my bicycle, and even to "my bench" by the lake. The kind little lady at the hostel wouldn't even accept any money for doing my laundry, and the staff has been treating me extra well. So, no more Russell suddenly appearing out my window or at my door. No more Richard with his loud shoes coming down the corridor to check in on me.

Robert from the tourism school stopped by to give me some freshly picked tea raised by his family. He then brought me to a demonstration. Some Hangzhou students are now on a hunger strike in sympathy with the Beijing students on a hunger strike while the Russian leader, Gorbachov, is visiting China. Over 100 students in Beijing have already fainted from hunger. These young people have no meat on their bones, so they suffer quickly from hunger.

The boys will come by at 5:00 a.m. tomorrow to begin our last two weeks together. Goodbye Hangzhou! But thankfully not goodbye quite yet to China.

7

CHINA HONG KONG ISRAEL U.S. 1989

May 17, 1989

Well, of course, it was an adventure to get to Yellow Mountain. The bus driver was a compulsive horn beeper, which drove us all quite crazy. He was also a dangerous driver since he used one hand for the horn, and one for his cigarette. But some of the ride was truly picturesque. Russell was particularly appreciative. I hadn't realized that he has been longing to see Yellow Mountain for at least five years.

When we finally pulled into the stop for Yellow Mountain, we tried to buy tickets on to Nanjing in a couple of days. Again we heard that well-used word in China, *meiyou*, no bus tickets available for several days. Quickly, we were approached by local people who produced bus tickets for Nanjing anytime we wanted—but we could only buy them if we would stay that night at a particular hotel. Yes, capitalism is alive in China!

We spent the rest of the day souvenir shopping and enjoying the remote area. The women washing and beating the laundry in the pretty river was bad for the environment, but made a picturesque sight. We ate well because food may be quite expensive up on the mountain. Drinking in the beauty of the scenery will sustain us.

I think of the mountainous beauty awaiting us while I try to sleep through workers breaking up rocks outside my window. No wonder we had no choice where to stay.

May 18, 1989

It took us three hours to wait our turn for an eight-minute ride in a cable car up the mountain. The ride started out quite spectacular, but as we climbed higher, we also climbed into the mist and clouds. The mist definitely lends a certain mood. Whether or not tomorrow will be clear is a matter of luck.

On the mountain, Russell kept warning me not to fall off when I perched on a rock overlooking a sea of mist. I enjoyed looking out at the views, watching them appear and disappear in the mist. Anywhere else but China, they would have railings to protect people from falling over the edge.

As I sat or lay there looking out, hearing the voices of the boys talking, wondering, marveling at the beauty of nature, I didn't want it to end. I didn't want to leave China. I didn't want to be far away from my China friends. Life, I pondered from my middle-aged vantage point, is a continuum of losses that must be endured if we are to have gains to lose.

Getting rooms was an incredible hassle. Some people rent heavy blankets and sleep out in a good location for viewing the sunrise. That appealed to the camper in me, but horrified the three boys. So, we finally got three rooms. One is a double for foreigners, so I'll probably get a roommate some time tonight. The boys are two in one room and one in another double, which may or may not get another person. We stayed in one room watching a James Bond movie on one channel, and the student demonstration negotiations in Beijing on another.

At about 10:30 p.m., I looked out by chance and saw the moon lighting up the sky. I went outside and saw that the mountains had cleared and the scene bathed in moonlight was both magical and magnificent. I got the boys out of bed to take in the sights and sounds of the night and the mountains. Since almost all Chinese are fast asleep at this time of night, we actually found ourselves quite alone in this crowded place. Bill thanked me for giving him what he called this once in a lifetime opportunity.

I appreciated his gratitude and realized I had done something special by bringing these boys traveling to places they had only heard about. I really have very little money, but it is enough in China to be generous.

The harmonious whole of nature was at its very best tonight. I asked Bill if he heard the moon talking to the mountains. He said they had different dialects, but I said only mankind was stupid enough to have dialects and make separations. Nature behaves as an integrated whole.

May 19, 1989

Our second day on Yellow Mountain started very early with the thrill of a crowd of people gathered to see the sunrise. Russell ran around happily taking lots of photos. The day was wonderfully clear and Yellow Mountain showed all her beauty. We hiked a lot. Even though we came most of the way by cable car, there was still more "up" to go. I told Richard to stop counting aloud as he reached 1000 stairs. It was good that there were three boys with me because I needed them to push and pull me up those stairs. Alongside one edge of a particular cliff, there was a chain with hundreds of locks on it. These were locks that lovers bought and locked to eternalize their connection. So like the romantic Chinese!

On the way down what must have been thousands of steps to the bottom of the mountain, each boy took turns holding my hand to protect me from falling off. I was glad for the "sensible" shoes I had on for hiking and could only be amazed at the variety of what I would call dangerous footwear that I saw on the women and girls.

May 20, 1989

After the usual harrowing, bumpy bus ride with continuous beeping, and passing other drivers, we made it to Nanjing. At last I've met the professor with whom I've been corresponding since reading of his visit to Israel. He's a very interesting man who fell in love with Jews and Israel as I have with China and Chinese. He's going to take us around Nanjing tomorrow although he wasn't sure what would be blockaded. He said that Nanjing University, like other universities in China, has had to stop all classes during this time of student unrest and there are frequent demonstrations all around the city. Even workers were now marching and demonstrating.

May 21, 1989

Today was a very full day indeed. Conrad came up from Shanghai to join us. He's having trouble getting the documents he needs for Australia, but he wanted to take the last chance to be with us. We rented bicycles, and with the professor as our guide, pedaled around the sights of Nanjing. We spent quite a lot of time at an exhibition of rocks—wonderful, poetic, colorful rocks on display in water. I was touched when Bill bought a small rock for me to take traveling the world.

We went to the Confucian Temple and walked across a bridge over the famous Yangzi River. Nanjing was more active than Hangzhou in the number of demonstrations. That may be because they're closer to Beijing than Hangzhou and also have a large number of students. We saw many marchers wearing armbands and holding banners. They looked much angrier than the demonstrators I had seen in Hangzhou. At Nanjing University itself, a lot of students gathered around a central area of outdoor poster boards. I suppose these boards usually held posters for university events, but were now filled with demonstration-related material. We heard BBC being broadcast over loudspeakers. This was because

China was blocking news of the Beijing demonstrations and the students were learning what was going on through BBC short-wave broadcasts.

I got into a confrontation with a petty official when I left my bike among other bikes that I didn't know were illegally parked. I went to where I could change money. When I came back, I saw Bill tightly holding onto the handlebars of my bike and speaking angrily to someone who was trying to take my bike away. Bill explained to me that the man wanted to confiscate my bike so that I'd have to pay a fine to get it back. I didn't think the fine would be too high, but I was more worried by the inconvenience of it all. So, I grabbed the handlebars, looked angrily down at the face of the rather short, old man whose job it was to take it away, and said, "Let go of my bike." Of course, a crowd gathered as they always do around foreigners, and the people were saying things to the official. Actually, the man looked quite terrified and he let go. I jumped on my bike and pedaled away before he could change his mind.

Afterward, I worried whether that man had "lost face" in the Chinese meaning. The boys explained that he hadn't lost face because the people in the crowd were telling him to give me my bike.

May 22, 1989

The professor invited us over to his apartment for dinner. It was really an ugly, depressing place that didn't have enough room for all his books. This 41-year-old man has traveled the world. He is an accepting, optimistic sort who was banished for two years into the countryside during the Cultural Revolution, as were many intellectuals. He says he understands China and can accept the life there. He had studied for a while in the United States and showed us albums of when he lived there. I couldn't believe he was the same person because he was quite chubby in the pictures, but not at all now. He said he gained weight in the U.S. because he loved pizza and cheese. He showed me an interesting course on intercultural communication, comparing eastern and western customs. I asked him to get a copy for me because I think it could be useful for my teaching in the future. Although he says he knows Americans who have helped Chinese study in America, he didn't have any comment on Russell's wanting to study for a master's degree in the U.S.

He did, however, clear up some things I wanted to know about Chinese culture. For example, Chinese do not show gratitude in obvious ways, or in ways that westerners are used to. I asked him to explain more about that tricky, complicated issue of "face." He said that, for example, if someone says your wife is pretty, you must say she's ugly. You speak of your children as lazy and worthless.

Nothing seems to be done in the direct way. Russell used a descriptive word for this—the zigzag way of getting what you want. A Chinese person may say "yes," but how s/he looks saying it could mean something else. How a Chinese person counts out money will say whether or not s/he is pleased with the price. Parents don't hug their children or tell them they love them. When you give a gift to someone, you say the gift isn't good. That explained why Diana had surprised me by saying, "This gift is ugly," when she gave me a parting gift. And, you don't say "I'm sorry" to someone close. Instead, you just treat them like you normally do and that tells them all is well again. Also, as I had seen while bike riding, Chinese will lose their temper and patience quickly with strangers, but less so with friends. And, they don't thank friends for helping. They may be grateful, but they also expect help from friends. As for money, the friend who happens to have money at the time pays for everyone. When another one has money, he's expected to be the one to pay.

So, reading what's going on in the mind of a Chinese person can be quite complicated for a westerner. That makes me wonder how often I've insulted the boys or misunderstood what's gone on between us during some uncomfortable interactions. I know my feelings have been hurt on this trip when they spoke Chinese with each other and didn't tell me what they were talking about. I must admit I sometimes felt I was "added on" to the group instead of feeling a part of it until the time came to pay.

May 23, 1989

The train ride to Jiaxin near Russell's home was typically long and uncomfortable, certainly with all that cigarette smoke. Conrad returned with us as far as Shanghai and we had long conversations. He was particularly interested in understanding some of the western ways of asking friends for help. He also wanted to know if there were any ways he had angered or bothered me. And he said he hoped I would be able to help Russell study in the U.S. I was sad to say goodbye to him.

When we got to Jiaxin, Russell perked up and got excited in his "home territory." He quickly adapted to being our host. In contrast to the ugliness of Jiaxin, the area near his village was beautiful. We walked a bit on a path through the rice paddies and then a small boat took us by a small canal to his little village. They all came out to greet me—the first foreigner who had ever visited their village. My first glimpse of his mother was a very excited lady literally running to greet me, holding boots for me to wear because the heavy rain had made quite a lot of mud. She assisted me as though I was a senile cripple, but her tight grip on my arm and hand was welcome in the slippery mud. Without a common language, we babbled and laughed joyously. There was an unexpected instant chemistry between us that we each felt.

Just about everything in countryside life was out of my realm of experience. I watched Russell's four-year-old niece do something very peculiar. She caught a fly in her hands, tore it apart, and licked the inside of it which, judging by the look on her face, was not as tasty as she expected. When I mentioned this strange behavior to Russell, he laughed and said that she was copying what she had seen them do. One of the fun activities of countryside children playing is to catch honey bees that are in the mud fences, pull them apart, and lick out the honey. Richard, who had also grown up in the countryside, had surprised me by catching a bee and holding it in just such a way that the bee's stinger could only ineffectively "sting" his impenetrable thumbnail.

ROOTS VS. ROT IN THE CHINESE COUNTRYSIDE

It was a rare privilege for me to visit two families deep in the Chinese countryside. I was the guest of two friends, college students I had met in the city where I taught. In both their small villages, I was the first foreigner the villagers had ever seen. I came to understand the sense of roots that some of my Chinese students had received from their upbringing in the countryside, but I also came to understand why they feel they will rot if they remain in the countryside.

As I sat in front of the thatched roof cottage, I looked out upon a wide view of rice paddies in the growing stage that makes them look like a vast, green lawn. The tiny haystacks in front of the cottage and dotting the landscape were of dried wheat used to fuel the stove. The birds twittered, and there was a gentle peacefulness. It was not a wild, natural beauty, but it was beautiful. To me, it was lovely, quiet, and quaint. It was like going back in time to life before toilets and other modern conveniences. It gave me the feeling I have when I'm camping—a good feeling of being close to nature.

However, the peasants don't romanticize it. The thatched roof cottage and barn are quite dirty and undecorated by modern standards. The "simple" life is not so simple for the people who must draw water from a well, boil all water before drinking, and gather the fuel that must be continually fed into the stove when cooking. There are the animals to care for, the rice to plant and harvest, the rape to gather and thresh, the mulberry leaves to be cut for the hungry silkworms, the garden of vegetables to be cared for, the washing, and the babies to be tended to.

Men and women share most of the chores—each one doing whatever needs to be done at that time. In the families I visited, the fathers and sons in the family cooked, while the mothers constantly fed fuel through holes in back of the stove under permanent woks (deep, rounded frying pans) set into the stove. One wok was for steaming rice, and the other was used to prepare each dish individually. Since the cooking temperature couldn't be regulated, and the pot can't be removed from the stove, the cook must be constantly alert. The stove is an important part of the peasants' home, and has interesting symbolic hand painted decorations on it. The peasants greatly respect the stove because food is precious in a country that does not have enough to adequately feed its population.

In one home, the 70-year-old grandmother looked at me with some curiosity as I sat eating at their table. She had arisen at dawn, and had worked in the home and in the fields all day as she had done all her life. Although her life is physically hard, she rises each morning with a sense of purpose and responsibility that many of her western counterparts might envy. She said something to me which my friend translated as "It's very backward here."

I heard this reference to being "backward" several times while I was in the countryside. While they have little education and no refrigeration, there is limited electricity that brings radio and television into their homes. Television has shown them that their life is not modern. They do backbreaking work for hours and days that machines could do better in minutes. They freeze in their unheated homes in winter, and sweat in summer. They have no phones, and transportation is very bad. Even when transportation is available in a three-wheeled tractor vehicle, one must travel over unbelievably bumpy, rutted roads that tax both machine and body.

Brothers, sisters, neighbors came to stare fixedly at me. They watched how I sat, how I ate, what I wore, how I spoke. They seemed amazed at my ability to use chopsticks. Sometimes I was requested to show my ability to successfully pick up a cooked peanut with my chopsticks. I often felt I was a Martian who had landed on earth. But, they stared in curiosity, not animosity. When I looked them straight in the eye and smiled at them, they replied by smiling broadly. They treated me as a fragile, honored guest and tried to anticipate my every need and possible want. They prepared feasts of food in my honor. One of the fathers proudly showed me the eel—the largest one he could find—to prepare for my enjoyment. I was sorry when his son told him that Americans don't like eating eels.

They brought me hot water to wash my hands and face when they finally gave up encouraging me to eat more. Being so large and heavy compared to Chinese, they were amazed at how little I ate. Coming from an overfed western culture in which we must worry about the dangers of overeating, I took pleasure in seeing their total appreciation of food, especially the fat on meat. They insisted I keep sitting down and even followed after me with a little stool, and were horrified if I tried to do anything for myself. Helping out was definitely not allowed.

My two friends had been rather nervous and embarrassed about exposing me to such a "primitive" life. One neighbor asked how I could possibly be comfortable on their hard beds. Although timid about asking me questions, one group of neighbors asked me to show them American dollars and my passport. In the dim electric light, they peered unbelievingly at these treasures—unthinkable possessions to a Chinese peasant.

One of the families I visited was a wealthier peasant family. The father, who also worked in construction, was building a two-story home which is considered a sign of prosperity. He proudly showed me the western style toilet, which his son had requested he finish installing quickly in time for my visit. The mother and I liked one another instantly. We intuitively knew that, although from such different lives, we could have talked endlessly if we had had a common language. However, lacking common words, we had to make do with laughing, hugging and eye communication. I have never felt so warmly welcomed anywhere, nor my presence so appreciated. We brought each other honor. I felt honored to be there; she felt honored to host the only foreigner who had ever come to their village.

Both families gratefully appreciated my interest in their sons. Sons are the most precious possession of a Chinese family—and these sons had accomplished what few if any others in their villages had done—they were about to become college graduates. Unlike western culture, there are no hugs and kisses and words of endearment exchanged between grown children and their parents. But the closeness and love within the family comes through clearly and is, to me, the true beauty of China. What I could appreciate perhaps more than they can is the warmth of extended family living that modern western living has largely erased.

I left not only with the gifts they gave me, but also a fuller understanding. I could see how deep the roots are in the soil and hardship of the Chinese countryside, and the security that comes with a strong sense of place. But the students who have come from the countryside also feel they will rot if they remain in the village. And, in many ways, that is true. The rewards of the Chinese peasant are few.

To me, it was a short-term adventure, a sharing of the home lives and families of two of the students I had come to know and love during my time in China. But, to them, home is the place they love, and also wish to leave so that they can realize the dreams that intelligent young people have in their early 20's about their future. And the parents, mainly isolated, illiterate, and having suffered through China's traumatic recent history, also dream for their children as best they can. They do not wish to lose their children, but neither do they want them to remain in the village.

I helped the boys to appreciate some of the beauty of their countryside through my eyes—the peace, the quiet, the serenity. One of the boys had never noticed in the thousands of times he had drawn water from the well what a beautiful abstract kinetic art piece existed in his well. The boys helped me to appreciate their environment, their roots, and their conflict in mentally knowing the modern world through their exposure to it in their college studies, while stuck in the "backward" world of the village. For in China, college students have little choice about their careers or job assignments, and must return to work in or near their hometowns. I saw why they love the countryside, and why they want and need to leave it.

May 31, 1989

Today was the day I left China and the boys. My stomach, the repository of emotion for me, feels it. I do ache, but it is not with the unfinished feeling I left with in January. Now I feel I know China to a deeper depth.

I have not been hearing the news reports, but apparently, the whole world is hearing about China. Many of the foreign students have left because worried parents asked them to return home. I wonder if my parents might also be worried, but it probably can't be any worse than Israel. Obviously, the situation is serious. All students in all colleges are striking.

There is a more remote feeling about the demonstrations in Guangzhou, which is at the southern tip of China. In contrast to Nanjing, we didn't see any demonstrations in Guangzhou. Now that I've returned to Guangzhou after being in other parts of China, I can see the differences between Guangzhou and the rest of China. It is much more westernized. Bill and Russell said Guangzhou appeals to them, but Richard felt too "different" and shy when the people didn't respond in ways that were familiar to him. Even the language is not the same. They speak another form of Chinese called Cantonese (Guangzhou used to be called Canton) that has quite a different sound from the Mandarin Chinese of most of China. Apparently, however, the written language is the same.

We visited many of the traditional sights in Guangzhou, which the boys had only been able to read about. So, they were thrilled to see them in person. They can appreciate the history of what we saw much better than I. We spent one very strange night in an all-night movie theatre that showed three films. The first film took place in long-ago China and had wonderful costumes and scenery. Of course I couldn't understand any of the dialogue, but I appreciated the beautiful woman detective who could fight any man. Although it was new to me, Russell said it was quite an ordinary, common Chinese story. I never understood the plot of the second film, but the nature photography in it was stunning. Just as Richard was falling asleep, a Hong Kong action movie came on. The constant excitement woke us all up. The boys told me that Hong Kong action movies were something special to see and I can say it definitely kept us awake.

My dear boys are once again far from me. It was feeling so natural to have them around all the time, talking together, wandering together, being tourists together, exploring together, and laughing together. Russell had gotten his photos from Yellow Mountain developed just before I left. They were wonderful, so artistically done. He even had gone back and taken one for me of the bench, tree, and rock on the Su Causeway where we had biked one of the last nights we'd been in Hangzhou.

They walked me as far as they could to the boat that would take me the short distance from Guangzhou to Hong Kong—a short ride for me, but an impossible one for them because mainland Chinese are not allowed to go to Hong Kong. When Customs became once again the boundary—the border reminding us I am a foreigner and they are Chinese—I looked intensely into each one's eyes in turn. Their eyes met my eyes straight and sincerely and deeply. I said goodbye weakly and turned to go, sagging for an instant against a wall as if I needed help to bear my sadness. I didn't look back because I wanted the way we had held each other's eyes to be how I remembered them.

The raindrops running down the hovercraft window mirrored the tears of my face and those in my heart. And yet, I have a more satisfied, complete feeling at this, our second goodbye. I left China barely solvent, but having added the most unusual and interesting chapter—to date—of my life.

June 2, 1989

Today I presume the boys are enjoying their last day in Guangzhou before returning to Hangzhou. How they stay in my mind. I had copies made of the latest pictures and put together albums to send to them as well as my other friends. I am pleased with most of the pictures. I may be poor in money, but I'm rich in the treasure of pictures.

I'm enjoying some aspects of civilization, but to my surprise I find I'm not only missing the boys, but I'm also missing China. Somehow I no longer seem suited for the modern world, which is mainly geared to buying and selling, and hustle and bustle.

Hong Kong seems quite ruffled by all that is going on in China now. I called the man in Hong Kong whom I'd met at the Yellow Dragon Hotel to discuss a possible job teaching in Beijing starting next fall. He had told me to check with him when I was back in Hong Kong. But, when I called him, he said that he had called Beijing just today and they told him it wasn't safe to send foreign teachers there. So, once again that leaves me up in the air about what to do after I get back to Israel.

ONE MONTH LATER

One month ago, I was walking alongside the May 4th Youth Day parade of college students of Hangzhou, China. On June 4th, I again walked in a demonstration with Chinese people. But these were Hong Kong Chinese, and we were all in mourning for the many students killed in the Beijing nighttime massacre the night before.

As I walked alongside, a marcher called to me, "Join us," and held out his hand. I immediately thought of that other young man in Hangzhou who had said those same words to me on May 4th.

I joined the black-clad Hong Kong mourners. Young and old, children and even babies were there. We sweated together in the heat of the June sun. We passed the thousands of shops and skyscrapers that line Hong Kong with armbands, headbands, holding banners, chanting, or simply walking. On the roads not closed to traffic, cars and taxis honked continually and flew black flags from their antennas. People on the sidelines clapped, or made "v" signs with their fingers, or joined the marchers. One tiny, wizened Chinese woman waved a black flag angrily with tears in her eyes.

Most everything was in Chinese, but then I heard the familiar song in English, "We Shall Overcome." That brought me back to the other demonstrations and movements I had witnessed—the Civil Rights movement, and the anti-Vietnam War demonstrations of the 1960's.

I had left China a few days earlier. I had been missing my China life, and my diligent, sincere students. They had been excited about the demonstrations, about some action at last in their rather monotonous and hopeless existence. There had been speculation that the movement for freedom and democracy was growing, dying, or going underground. Even the peasants in the remote countryside had heard about the hunger strikes and sit-ins in Beijing and other cities.

In Hangzhou, my Chinese friends had innocently assured me that the government would never dare to hurt the students if the students remained non-violent. They believed that the fear of public outcry would prevent it. And the students everywhere in China had done quite an admirable job of remaining orderly and non-violent. I had not wanted to intrude upon their trusting innocence at that time. The massacre horrified me, but did not really surprise me.

As I stood on a Hong Kong street watching the news on a small television set placed by a local vendor above his shop, I watched the faces around me register stunned disbelief as they saw film clips of the tanks rolling down Beijing streets. With horrified fascination and disgust, they listened to gunshots and saw wounded, dying, and dead people.

I have lived in Israel where burning buses, tanks in the streets, and people being shot are often daily news there. But Hong Kong Chinese have relegated such sights to exciting crime movies. As my Hong Kong friend said to me, "Even demonstrations and protests are new to Hong Kong."

These Hong Kong Chinese are indeed a strange counterpart to their mainland Chinese brothers and sisters. They will unite politically in 1997. In contrast to my students, these well-fed, very westernized Hong Kong Chinese marched in Reebok sneakers and designer jeans with Gucci belts. They munched McDonald's hamburgers, and many carried radio-tape recorders plugged into their ears. The Hong Kong police looked authoritative in snappy uniforms adorned with a gun, nightstick, and walkie-talkie. I thought of the contrast they made to the nervous, baggy-uniformed drab Chinese police who look like little boys dressed up in their father's clothes.

The Hong Kong Chinese care about the mainland Chinese, and genuinely want to help them, but the gap is so very wide from so many aspects. I thought how hard it would be for my students from the countryside—thin, poorly-fed and poorly-clothed—to imagine decorating a car with banners and driving down the street honking and waving as a show of solidarity with Chinese students in China in their struggle for freedom and democracy.

The Hong Kong Chinese, already worried about the unification in 1997, are now understandably terrified of what 1997 might mean to the freedom they now take for granted. I, myself, had come to value my American freedom and choice much more since my students had expressed their envy of it openly and longingly.

I doubted that my Chinese students themselves knew the magnitude of what had happened in Beijing, or that the world was in outrage and mourning. I wanted them to know, and yet I wanted to shelter them from the full impact of the cruelty. I bought some newspapers to send them, and then was afraid they might get in trouble for having them. I wished they were safely home instead of still in school.

I thought of my first visit to Tiananmen Square in October. I remembered the monstrous proportions of the square, and behind Mao's huge picture, the gate of the Forbidden City, the palace for the Emperors of China. I thought cynically that the Emperors would have approved the action of the Chinese government. I cried for the students I knew in Hangzhou, and for those I hadn't known in Beijing.

June 5, 1989

I wait with a very heavy heart for my flight to Paris. I don't really want to leave. But what can I do? Even if I could get another visa to go right back into China, it would be senseless to return now. I can do nothing to help, and would probably only be a liability to my Chinese friends. I just want to know they're all safe. Russell, Bill, and Richard had train tickets for June 3rd to return to Hangzhou, but I've heard that all trains stopped running. Where are they now? What is the Chinese government telling them? I've also heard the government has cut off news reports. I've saved the newspapers from Hong Kong, but I don't think it's wise to send them.

Ah, my plane is ready to board. I said goodbye to Hong Kong—a city of mixtures I still find amazing and charming. I can't imagine I'm really finished forever with Asia.

June 7, 1989

My heart really isn't here in Paris. It is still back in China wondering how all my students are managing. I read that Shanghai is in a state of confused anarchy with no one in control. I do hope the boys have gone to their homes. The rice paddies seem a much safer place now.

My mind fantasized that, if the massacre had happened while the four of us were in Guangzhou, I might have been able to get the boys into Hong Kong with the help of the American consulate. Oh dear, I now understand more about the survivor's guilt syndrome I've read about with Holocaust survivors. I feel so guilty I didn't get them out. Logic can't dispel that awful feeling in my stomach.

June 10, 1989

I can once again see my big view from the little window in Kfar Saba. It really is beautiful and the colors change as lovely as I remember them. I straightened up and moved back in.

It's hard to believe that only one week has passed since that dreadful massacre that killed an unknown, perhaps never known, number of people. One of the first calls I made was to one of the only Israelis I know who has been to China. She gave me a quote from a book by John Fraser that seems very meaningful. "China is an ache that won't go away." How I felt that as I sat crying on the floor surrounded by my China souvenirs.

June 14, 1989

My body is in Israel getting reacquainted with so many things I enjoyed, and still enjoy, but my thoughts are far away in China. The news we get from what's happening in China is worse and worse.

Israel is the same, and yet different. It is tenser. It is sadder. It is harder to see West Bank Arabs in Israel. Jamal has told he is frightened all the time of both radical Arabs and Jews.

June 15, 1989

The moon is just about full again. It was only one month ago that I woke the boys up and dragged them outside to see Yellow Mountain in the moonlight. Russell had told me that Chinese think of a "lady in the moon," while westerners think of a "man in the moon." I never noticed before how sad that face in the moon is. I sit in the moonlight wondering and worrying, and listening to the tapes the boys made for me before I left.

June 18, 1989

I feel suspended—neither here nor there. Israelis seem so fat and hairy and curly-haired after the skinny, hairless Chinese. I am enjoying some familiar things about being back here. I visited my Ethiopian families and my Shefaram friends, bringing along my photos of China and Bali and tales of my travel adventures. But my head is in so many places at once—and mostly in China. What is happening there? My friends are probably okay, but terrified, as most of China must be under these conditions.

I wanted to find some Chinese people, so I went to several Chinese restaurants that have recently sprung up in Israel. I discovered that the workers are all from

Thailand, not China. But the other day I saw a young Chinese girl walking with her friend. I ran up to her excitedly and spoke to her in English. She turned to her friend and asked in Hebrew, "What is she saying?" It turns out that her family was one of a few Chinese let into Israel by Menachem Begin years ago. One of her grandmothers had been Jewish. She was a native born Israeli!

June 27, 1989

I feel I have entered the Holocaust—only as a non-Jew. All around me there is craziness. People are being stabbed, hacked, shot. Politics rage and people rage. Not only is the fight now between Arab and Jew, it is between Jew and Jew.

Survivors from Hitler's Holocaust are all around me in Israel. When an arm goes up in a bus to hold on to the top railing, the numbers on his or her arm glare at me like neon lights. I have begun to read any book on the Holocaust that I can find. I want to learn what helped to hold people together during that unbelievable madness. While life was rendered meaningless by cruelty, hanging on to the love of one of those meaningless lives is what kept some people sane. When inhumanity reigned, remembered vignettes—just moments of individual slivers of human kindness like a drink of water, a morsel of food, a kind word—became of supreme importance.

June 28, 1989

I wrote a letter to someone I don't know. I read her poetry in the Jerusalem Post and I wanted to write to her about how I'm going crazy trying to remain sane. I told her about my talent for fitting into many different cultures comfortably. But this flexibility, this "gift" I have, also has another side. I am rootless. While discovering my joy in China, I could separate that happiness from the pain of knowing what was going on in Israel. I felt the pain keenly, but I was able to compartmentalize it so that it didn't contaminate the joy I was experiencing. Now, back in Israel, I feel I am drowning in a sea of sorrow—the sorrow of Israel and the sorrow of China.

As I try to think of ways to help my Chinese friends, I feel like walls and bars are being put up between me and them. I think of the Jews trying to get out of Poland, Germany, Austria, etc. in the late 1930's and early 40's. Somehow it seems worse that I could get out so easily on my American passport, and my friends are so terribly stuck.

I try to do what people tell me about just going on, taking care of myself, looking after my own needs, continuing "business as usual." But the sadness, the hopelessness keeps oozing in, spoiling the taste of the ice cream, making the food tasteless. And so, I feel like I'm living in some kind of limbo, floating somewhere in between worlds and people.

I feel free, and yet trapped by my freedom. I try to make sense of it all, but there is no sense in madness. And the world is mad—in particular Israel and China, my two worlds.

June 29, 1989

Part of the madness is trying to get my money from the insurance company. The lawyer has wasted over 16 months now trying to settle my case. At first he said he needed a police report from the Shefaram police. He said he was afraid to go into Shefaram, and so kept writing for the police report. Nearly one year later, he received a simple report stating only in Hebrew, "The car was burned." He had told me before that the insurance company wanted the state of Israel to take responsibility for paying me for the car as they are responsible for acts of terrorism, but Israel had turned down the insurance company's request. Against my express wishes before I left last summer, he had filed an appeal to get the state of Israel to take responsibility. He asked me to be more patient and had given me a $3,000 advance from the insurance company in response to a letter I wrote him from China saying that I was coming home soon, and I was coming home broke.

There was a time I might have given up "fighting City Hall" to get my money, but now I know I really need that money if I am ever to return to China and help my friends.

July 1, 1989

As I sat having a root canal on my tooth, I casually asked the dentist what he used to fill the root canal. "Plastic," he replied. I pondered the concept of plastic roots. The subject of roots—my roots, where they are, how deep they go, where they lead to—has followed me around the world. I feel I am mainly rootless, having gone from one country to another, and from loving one person to loving another.

"But the tooth is still alive in your mouth," he explained. "The nerve is dead, but the tooth is still alive." Yes, I'm still alive somewhere deep inside.

July 12, 1989

As I feel myself sinking in sorrow, part of me wants to give in and just drown apathetically and quietly. But there is that little bit of buoyant spirit left that tells me to get my head up and breathe life. I don't know if I take up my pen more from desperation or depression, but I have begun to write.

I am writing my very first piece of fiction. The idea came to me while I was jogging in a nearby field. And, each time I return to run, the story unfolds in remarkable detail. It is as if it is writing itself.

The story is about letters between an American friend and a Chinese friend. It is no secret that letters are read and censored in China, so the two people must be careful what they write. They are writing to each other, but always aware of that third set of eyes reading their words. The main character is the censor who reads their letters and becomes emotionally wrapped up in their relationship.

Perhaps it is the focus on writing itself that is helping me because letters are always on my mind. I have written several to people in China, but nothing has gotten out to me. It's hard to know what to write. Even though I don't think any of my students were actively involved in the demonstrations, I have heard that students who have had a lot of contact with foreigners are being questioned. And, I remember well how all my friends had to sign in when they visited me.

I want very much to write often to keep up their morale and spirit, but a truly terrible thought struck me during a nightmare last night. What if my well-intentioned letters are getting them into trouble because the government is now very actively investigating students who have contact with foreigners? That thought truly terrified me! I want so much to hear from them, but I certainly don't want them to endanger themselves. And we all know there are other eyes waiting to read our letters. And those eyes are most likely much less sympathetic than my fictional censor.

July 30, 1989

My buoyancy finally seems to be pushing me up from the slime of depression and despair and feeling the victim. Anger helps, and finding out that my lawyer has been lying to me was the last straw with the insurance mess. I had finally decided to stop listening to him and check out myself why everything was taking so long. So, I went to the court office that decides when hearings will be held, and I asked about my case.

The clerk remembered the name "Suellen" (because of the television series "Dallas," of course), and said Israel had denied responsibility for my car months ago. He actually looked up my file in a series of what looked like shoeboxes on a shelf with papers held together by rubber bands. It was hard not to laugh at their "filing system" even though I was very serious about getting my case settled.

I explained that that decision had been appealed, so he called to another office in the same building and asked if my name was on a pending hearing. When none was found, he asked me to call my lawyer and get the case number to check it more easily. So, I called the lawyer who replied he couldn't find it at that moment, but that the court clerk should keep looking.

Only about 15 minutes later, while I was still in the clerk's office, the other clerk called back and said it was quite strange that someone had just come in and filed the appeal under my name. I was more than furious at being lied to and flew to the lawyer's office where his poor assistant had to listen to my screaming.

After firing my lying lawyer, I called the insurance company and said they had to deal with me now and I was very tired of waiting for a settlement. For some reason, they said they'd have to assign another lawyer, again at their expense. I didn't object, but said my case needed to be settled as soon as possible because I was making plans to leave Israel.

August 1, 1989

Leaving Israel isn't going to be a simple thing. Whether here or away, Israel is like a sponge in my heart that absorbs more and more pain. I feel that both the Arabs and the Jews are right, and my lack of foresight to see any solution makes me feel pulled and stretched in every direction. Israel is trapped, but it will not help Israel for me to stay.

After my year in Asia, I saw that I was still capable of being a happy, fulfilled, optimistic person. Back in Israel, I was again nervous, impatient, even yelling at bank clerks. Less than a month ago, I had traveled on the very same bus from Tel Aviv to Jerusalem only a day before an Arab passenger had grabbed the wheel and aimed it over a cliff. Fourteen people had died. The day after the attack, when I was riding back from Jerusalem to Tel Aviv, I had seen the scarred remains of the deadly bus being pulled up the cliff. It was chilling.

The simple truth that I am struggling to accept is that I am not strong enough to live in Israel. I don't have what it takes financially and mentally to survive here.

August 13, 1989

On someone's birthday in Israel, they say "Until 120." Today I'm 46, but I feel like 120. It is a joyless birthday. I've tried to rouse myself to go out, see friends, have some birthday cake. But all I do is lay on the bed and wonder and worry about what's going on in China.

August 15, 1989

Today was a day for rejoicing. I finally got a letter from Russell. He has received my letters and had written me two other letters that I never received. He is okay in terms of the authorities, but life is not easy for students in China now. He said he definitely wants to continue the plan of doing a master's degree in the U.S. and will take the required TOEFL English test as we planned. I've also received letters from some of my other friends in China. But I wonder how many of their letters never reached me, or my letters never reached them. However, I'm so glad to be in contact again.

I also received my check from the insurance company! It was about $1500 less than I expected. They said they had paid that money to my former lawyer. Contrary to the agreement that the insurance company would pay his fee, he had skimmed off what he considered his fee before giving me the advance. I called him and said that was my money and he said only that he didn't agree. That he considered himself worthy of any fee for all the work he hadn't done on my behalf really surprised me. But the fact that he refused to give me what was owed me spurred my pen into action. I wrote letters to English newspapers and to an organization he was president of telling them of his deceit. I also sent one to the Israeli Bar Association and decided to continue the fight for the money he owed me from San Diego where I'll be staying with my parents for a while.

To the insurance company, I bought the largest screw I could find at the hardware store, tied a big red ribbon around it, carefully encased it in a plastic bag filled with cotton balls, and sent it to them saying it was a token of my appreciation for how they had handled my claim. I added that, since they may not know the meaning of such a symbol in American culture, they could consult my former lawyer.

August 17, 1989

Happy Birthday, Russell. Tonight was a moon befitting your birthday. It was so perfectly round and solidly orange. It hung exactly in the middle of my window. I winked at it and was glad it would follow me to the United States while I decide what to do next.

Sept. 2, 1989

I continue on my trail of goodbyes in Israel. Yaacov, one of my Ethiopian friends, who had been at a different boarding school than the one in Maalot, came to spend *Shabbat* with me. He had been a good friend, and I gave him some of the furniture and things I didn't plan to sell before leaving Israel.

He came in his soldier's uniform and, as required, with his rifle. A chill ran down my spine when he laid the gun under the chair in my room. We watched an Indiana Jones movie on television. But when the part with the tank attack came on screen, I could only see Yaacov being shot at. His blood would not be ketchup and his wounds would not heal with holy water.

Sept. 13, 1989

Sometimes I can hold back the missing, and sometimes it floods in, around and over me—and makes me sad. I gave a stray cat a feast today. That made me happy. I said goodbye to my television, refrigerator, washing machine, beautiful table, and a poster that I loved. That made me both sad and happy. Leaving Israel marks a turning point in my life that is sad, but I'm happy that Jamal and his wife will give all my things a good home in their home.

I hugged many friends who came to say goodbye. That made me sad. But it also made me happy that they had been in my life and many will remain in my heart.

Sept. 29, 1989

Happy Jewish New Year! I'm spending it with my parents in San Diego. I've been having a nice visit, finding out again what good friends and family I have. But I'm also deep in culture shock, wondering how I can handle living in my birth land. And, of course I'm missing China and my China life.

This was the most incredible year of my life, for sure. But I don't want to be like the woman in a movie I saw who went downhill the rest of her life, locked in nostalgia for the best year of her life. I want intensity. I want to know I'm alive. I want to feel alive. I want more of those natural highs I've felt so strongly this year. But, I must accept the lows that can follow those highs.

No New Year resolutions, but I am, as usual, curious about what will be.

Oct. 9, 1989

Today is the Jewish holiday of *Yom Kippur*. Last year at this time I was sitting in the cemetery of a beautiful Japanese shrine. Today is a day we think of death. And I feel losses heavily today. I said the prayer for the dead for those Beijing demonstrators who died last June. And I now feel the pain of living outside Israel rather than the pain of living inside Israel.

Nov. 1, 1989

I'm thinking more and more about going to Taiwan to get back into Chinese culture and to do the teaching that I love. China is still in too much turmoil for me to return, but at least it's close to Taiwan.

In the U.S., I become too aware of worrying about health, boredom, and waste. But I don't regret spending this time with my parents who are, after all, my roots. It's pretty where they live. The days are almost always sunny, the mountains surround us, the sky holds nicely strewn clouds, and, of course, the moon is here, too.

Dec. 5, 1989

It has been good for me to see so many friends again, to come back briefly into their lives to share accomplishments, thoughts, dreams, indecisions, reconsiderations, and regrets. Old friends are also a part of my roots. Their years of history with me make them irreplaceable. Nature has also been my companion, especially at my brother's one-room cabin in the redwoods. We walked the woods, watched the dancing branches, and got thoroughly soaked in the wind and rain maddening the ocean's waves.

Welcome letters from China have been able to catch up with me in San Diego. Russell was able to pass the TOEFL adequately and I was able to get him accepted for graduate school at my undergraduate school. I wasn't sure how we'd find a sponsor for him, but I had some ideas. However, China has made it all but impossible to get a passport now. Students must work for five years after graduation to "repay" China for their education.

Dec. 31, 1989

It is the end of a decade. I don't see how the variety in my life could be topped in the next decade, but how can I predict anything about my life after this last unimaginable decade?

I have discovered the importance in my life of intensity and change. I have developed a deep joy in my own company, and in that of nature. There is the possibility that my life in the next decade will be fulfilling in ways I do not yet comprehend. While I may not be deeply rooted to any one place, nature offers to the tumbleweed places to roam and flourish, and so perhaps for human tumbleweeds too.

So, into the 1990's I go, with lots of memories and loose ends reasonably organized and packaged. I enter the new decade with relative health and vigor, excitement and interest. I'm going east again, curious about the Taiwan variation on an Asian theme. And, thanks to the car I loved and my former lawyer's fast response to being investigated by the Israeli Bar Association, I'm even relatively solvent.

8

TAIWAN Feb.–July 1990

Feb. 21, 1990

It has been an inelegant beginning—waking up on a tatami mat on the floor among ten sleeping boys, all young enough to be my sons. But I awoke with excitement, enthusiasm, and only a trace of nausea and exhaustion from that long flight.

So, I'm here and my luggage is here. As I look out into the grayness of a cloudy Taipei morning through a filthy window and listen to a cat yowl, I remember a sensitive and gentle conversation I groggily overheard between young English teachers. Most of this hostel is not for tourists, but for English teachers. I respect and admire these young people very much, but I hope to have a room to myself tonight with no smokers.

Feb. 23, 1990

I'm recovering from jet lag in a very strange little room with a large platform bed, a small desk, a mirror, a fan, a small window looking out at the temple next door, a picture of an elderly ascetic-looking Chinese man looking down at me, a small postcard of a seductive nude, and a large poster of a dove of peace and love on a very thin wall that leaks the sounds of the couple next door making love. There is a strange charm to this place, but I wouldn't call it ambience.

I've contacted a woman from that wonderful traveler's organization, SERVAS, and will soon be a guest in her cozy home for a few nights.

Taiwan is, on fast observation, a mixture of Tokyo's shopping, modern Hong Kong but less intense, and old-world China. The people here are better dressed, better fed, and more relaxed than in mainland China. Foreigners are strangers here, but not oddities. American goods are everywhere mixed in with goods from the rest of the world. Well-frequented Buddhist temples are everywhere.

I miss my China even more acutely here. The geographical distance from China may be less than 100 miles, but mail takes three weeks to get from here to there because of the political complications between China and Taiwan. There are two political parties in Taiwan in hot disagreement that erupted in unusual violence and rioting just in time for my arrival.

It's hard to believe so much rain can be in the skies. It rained all night and shows no signs of wearying.

Feb. 27, 1990

My first impressions of Taichung are good. Virginia, the lady from SERVAS with whom I stayed a couple of days in Taipei, is from Taichung originally and she confirmed that it would be a good city to find work in. It's a bustling city that is both very Chinese and quite westernized. As in Israel, it's probably a veneer of western culture that doesn't go very deep. Prices are high, and the level of English is very low. They definitely do need English teachers in Taiwan. Even the students studying English are totally tongue-tied.

Virginia is herself an interesting mixture of Chinese and western styles and values. She was born in Taiwan, but to parents who had fled from mainland China. She said she had suffered from prejudice against mainland Chinese settlers. She and her husband believe strongly in helping family members, so they willingly help to support their parents and siblings. She promised to keep in touch with me to see how I'm doing in her hometown.

I haven't really seen the beauty of Taiwan yet. For one thing, I have yet to see it in the sun. From what I can tell, cities here seem to have a uniform drabness and dreariness and deterioration. On the other hand, the streets are very lively and interesting. I've been applying for teaching jobs at several *booshi bans,* which are private, illegal language schools that are here in profusion. I feel I have come alive again.

Feb. 28,1990

Long shots sometime pay off. I am temporarily settled in the home of the mother and sister of a couple I met while I was in San Diego. I had called a museum that specialized in Asian art in the hope of being put in touch with someone from Taiwan so I could ask some detailed questions before I decided to come to Taichung. They gave me the names of a couple living in San Diego who visited me and reassured me that Taichung was a good choice for teaching English. They had also said that his mother and sister had a big home in Taichung and would love to have me stay with them.

True to their word, his mother and sister came to pick me up from the bus stop. Mama Chen was dressed exquisitely. She asked me some fast paced questions about my age, marriage, children, took me into a restaurant, asked me what I liked, ordered five dishes, and left saying she had an appointment. Her daughter, Emily, explained that they had already eaten. Then Emily and her little six-year-old, Theresa, took me to their home with several plastic bags filled with the food. I eyed the soup sloshing around in its plastic bag worriedly as we rode home. Amazingly, it arrived without spilling a drop.

Their house is huge. Mama Chen lives on the bottom floor. Emily, Theresa, and I live on the second floor. A family and a student rent the third floor. Emily brought into my room a gadget that combines a radio, tape recorder, and small television. The room is quite large, even including an air conditioner.

March 1, 1990

Emily introduced me to a friend of hers named Nancy whose life story had some similarities to mine. She is a native of Taichung, daughter of escaped mainlanders, who married an Australian and has lived in Australia the past nine years. She said she has changed a lot and re-evaluated her value system since living in the westernized world. She has come to appreciate her Chinese parts even more since living "outside," but it has also made her fit into Taiwan less and less. She is divorced, mostly she believes because of her Chinese habit of hiding her feelings and not telling the truth. Now, she values the privacy she could never have within her Chinese culture, and the need for her to decide her own future.

She is worried about the very recent prosperity that has weakened the Taiwanese traditional family and has made them indiscriminate consumers and racers after big and easy money. She has been to Bali and agrees that Balinese have something very special. Being outside Taiwan has helped her to see its faults more glaringly because of her wider view.

Her English is excellent. I hope I'll get to see her again.

March 2, 1990

I wandered to get the lay of the neighborhood. I found some stores I'll need to use. And I noticed some cultural norms—like small stores with puppies and dogs who come to work with their owners, afternoon siesta in offices after lunch where workers sleep somehow comfortably with their heads on their desks, and prized BMV autos driven right into the store for safe keeping. They can do that because the whole storefront has bars that can be pulled down and locked at night like in Israel and China. Most of the stores, by size and lack of stock and activity, make you wonder how they survive. There is the similar grittiness and griminess of

China, but also gaudy decoration that reminds me more of the Arab sense of décor I saw in Shefaram.

I walked into a residential side street, which ended in a garbage-strewn field with some dirty, stagnant water. Many white butterflies seemed not to notice the pollution. And there I found a little neighborhood temple. It was wonderful! It had the love and care that the streets and field did not. Brother Buddhas were locked behind a shrine gate. A fantastic tree came right through the temple—crashing through the roof and continuing upward. The branches were distorted and twisted, but that tree was very alive. It seemed to actually hug the shrine with its branches growing right around the dragon decorations. There was a strong sense of religious harmony with nature in that little spot that smelled of incense.

March 3, 1990

I'm settling into sort of a routine, but there's always the unpredictable. I got lost on the bus yesterday because the same bus number didn't work in reverse. I've started to get firm job offers at decent pay. When I'm fairly sure I'll be staying in Taichung, I must offer some money to the family I'm living with if they allow me to stay. And, if I accept teaching jobs, I'll have to enroll to learn Chinese at the local school for foreigners. That's the only way I can keep my visa to stay in Taiwan. It doesn't make sense to have hundreds of illegal English language schools that must hire teachers who can't legally stay in Taiwan without enrolling for Chinese language courses. But, it might be fun to learn Chinese.

March 9, 1990

I've begun teaching and love it. These students have the same quiet, respectful behavior with teachers as I found in China. Some have given themselves English names. One in my class today named himself Handsome. Chinese like their names to have meaning!

I've started studying Chinese six hours a week. It's clear already that I won't be a star student, but I do have a Chinese name given me by my teacher. Chinese words are actually written as characters and each character can have four different tones. So, even saying my own name is somewhat tricky. My name is Su Hua Lan. Su is just a surname. Hua with a rising tone is in the Chinese word for "China" and also means "brilliant" or "splendid." Lan, also with a rising tone, means "orchid". So, now I too have a name with a meaning. Splendid China Orchid—that's me.

This place sometimes lulls me into thinking it's western, but then I am shocked to see and hear small trucks carrying large gongs and strangely dressed people. I was told it's a kind of funeral. And there are so many motor scooters on the roads carrying entire families—dad driving, mom on the back carrying a baby on her back, with perhaps two kids squashed in between them plus one standing in front of the dad. I still have no answer as to why many people on motor scooters and motorcycles wear their jackets backward. Is it some kind of unwritten dress code something like the boys in China who ride a bike with one hand in their pocket? In a small park I saw old men having an amateur singing contest complete with electric organ accompaniment and microphones. It wasn't very melodic, but seemed much healthier than American retirees discussing their ailments and money. When I see these things, I know I'm not in the west.

March 10, 1990

Walking to a park in Taiwan isn't easy. The roads are hazardous to all—with barrages of motor scooters and cars and exhaust fumes. Normally polite Chinese turn into something else altogether when a car or a scooter seat is under them. It wouldn't be so bad if scooters and pedestrians could use the side lanes for bike lanes. But cars are solidly blocking the side lanes.

That wouldn't be so bad if pedestrians could walk on the sidewalks. But motor scooters are not only parked there, they are also ridden in both directions on the sidewalks.

That wouldn't be so bad, but the little cubicles called stores that line the street have no back entrance. Thus, loading and unloading takes place on the sidewalks too. Often a distrusting expensive car owner parks his car right in the store while he's working. That, by itself, wouldn't be so bad except that each store must have a puppy or small dog to sniff and challenge every passerby.

Now, that might be manageable except for the street and sidewalk vendors who set up shop right in your path. Little rocking horses might line the sidewalk, followed by piles of shoes.

I passed a store selling flashy new cars that lined the side of the road and, of course, the sidewalk. Next to it was a car repair shop for the many cars that lose battles in the fight they wage daily with too many other cars and aggressive drivers. Of course, they do most of the repair work on the sidewalk or side of the road.

Taiwan is by no means a poor country. Its prices rival the U.S., and money is plentiful. However, it retains a gritty, grimy, over-crowded, jumbled appearance more like mainland China than Hong Kong. They must prefer it this way.

A city park is like an oasis in the desert. It brings peace, serenity, some quiet, trees, flowers, and nature—while high buildings soar above and around it. Among the growing things are brightly dressed, running, hopping, playful children. It almost could be anywhere. However, the arched bridges over the little lake, the pavilions, the Chinese characters on the buildings, the old people doing *tai chi*, and the young people gaily babbling in Chinese distinguish it as a park on the island of Taiwan.

Everyone plays. The mothers and fathers play with the children. A quite pregnant wife runs heavily to pick up a fallen kite her husband is trying to keep aloft. A crippled husband, supporting himself with two crutches, plays Frisbee (but with a hole in the middle of it) with his wife. A middle-aged mother sits with her son who has no hair and looks like he will not live to see another springtime.

A mother comes by with an unusual assortment of children. Two are beautiful Chinese girls. A boy is an obvious Caucasian-Oriental mix. Somehow the physical characteristics of each parent look uncomfortably combined—Caucasian eyes with Oriental eyelids. The youngest little girl is blond, not at all Chinese-looking, and obviously underdeveloped and sickly. All eat strawberry ice cream cones with enjoyment.

The little boy begins to speak with me in fluent English. Then, his mother begins to chat with me. The two Chinese girls are her sister's children. She herself is married to an American and they live in the U.S., presently Las Vegas. She asks what I'm doing in Taichung. She explained that the little girl was born quite premature and has already had corrective surgery for a variety of problems. She told me about two big, new, glamorous hotels opening up in Las Vegas. She likes the idea of being able to buy a nice house in Vegas for a fraction of the sum of a house in Taiwan. Plus, her American passport renders her unable to buy a home in Taiwan.

She said she hardly knows her hometown, Taichung, after ten years away. I think of myself and how alien I feel in the U.S. now, and I understand. She then recommends several American style restaurants she has found in the area. She seems more comfortable in the pseudo-American environment than in her own. She excuses herself to go off to McDonald's. Then, back to the glitziness and glamour of Las Vegas.

I pass an old man who squats timelessly and silently by his fishing pole in the lake. On the way back home, I stop at the Buddhist shrine in the corner with the too-loud Chinese music blaring from a semi-elaborate puppet stage. I stop and watch alongside the sole spectator—a Down syndrome child dressed brightly in yellow. He sometimes seems to respond to the action of the play, and sometimes converses with an invisible friend. The puppets are dressed and masked rather elegantly, as in Chinese opera. They do not sing as in Chinese opera, but there is a lot of monotonous, loud music. The boy in yellow does not move from the spot, while other children playing on the playground totally ignore the efforts of the puppeteer and his smoking assistant who activates and shuts off the very loud music.

An older lady comes by on her motor scooter with groceries arranged efficiently in, on, and around the motor scooter. Without a glance at the puppet show, she removes her anti-pollution facemask and burns paper money to the gods in the shrine. This done, she scooters off.

Among the many things I don't understand is why the puppet stage is angled in a corner with little room and no chairs for spectators. But then, there is only one spectator plus me after all. The father comes for the boy in yellow. The puppeteer continues as though he is playing to a full house. Or, perhaps he doesn't notice, or doesn't care. He seems to be a man who plays with his work.

March 13, 1990

I have never felt so wanted as a teacher. I've been turning down job offers, and now I think I'll be offered a job in a university that I didn't even try to apply for. The Taiwanese lady in San Diego had asked me to call one of the nuns at the university she graduated from in Taichung just to give her regards. When I called the school and gave the sister regards, she invited me to come out to see the university. The university is an all-girls school outside the busyness of Taichung city. It's situated on a hill surrounded by other hills with a pretty campus including a great indoor swimming pool and a big library. She was enthusiastic about my coming there to teach English in the fall. She thought they could work out details of a visa without my having to continue studying Chinese. And they even offer very low cost housing on campus to the teachers. What's a nice Jewish girl doing teaching English in a Catholic University in Taiwan? Well, it seems variety certainly spices up my life.

March 17, 1990

I sit in Taichung on this St. Patrick's Day listening to Irish music on the one English radio station. No mail has reached me yet from China. Have my letters reached China?

There are many things I do not understand about the lifestyle in this house. Mama Chen seems to like me although all she can say to me is, "Ah, yes," without understanding a word. However, when I told her I wanted to begin paying money for staying there, she emphatically said, "No, no, no money." So, I try to do little helpful things around the house. I'm giving little Theresa English lessons. She's an incredibly spoiled six-year-old child whose mother chases her around the house feeding her with chopsticks because she won't sit and eat. So I was quite surprised to find that she can sit and concentrate on English with me for an hour.

In trying to be helpful around the house, I sometimes wash the dishes in the sink. The other day I cleaned the *wok* used for most of the cooking and stir-frying. But, some fish had stuck to it and I cleaned it too well. These pans are seasoned through layers of oil and years of cooking. In the morning, I saw the *wok* lying on its side on the floor with rust from where I had overzealously scrubbed. I washed off the rust and rubbed oil on it. It looked okay to me, but the next day I noticed that the offending *wok* had been carried off and banished to I know not where. A smaller, newer *wok* has appeared on the stove. No word was ever mentioned. Perhaps Mama Chen has forgiven me as a stupid foreigner.

Cleaning house is erratic. One night, however, at 11:30 at night, Mama Chen stripped to her panties and bra and started a frenzy of cleaning which lasted until after 1 a.m. Some cleaning was maintenance, but she included re-arranging some furniture.

Another puzzling aspect to me is the special code of shoes on and off, where which slippers can be worn, especially different slippers for the kitchen and bathroom, and only bare feet on rugs. On a very rainy day, I wore my flip-flops out in the rain. When I later used the same dry flip-flops in the house, Mama Chen looked down at my feet and uttered "Dirty."

Emily's English is better than her mother's, but I think she often doesn't understand me. However, like most Chinese, she pretends she does. Usually, as soon as Emily and I begin to talk, her daughter starts yelling in one ear, and her mother starts yelling in her other ear. So, my words get lost in the middle. We managed one good conversation when she came to my room at midnight, and we talked until 2 a.m.

March 18, 1990

Emily has taken me to her church a few times. The church invited me to visit Sun Moon Lake with them. Since Emily couldn't go, another lady was "assigned" to watch over me during the boat ride. I never feel so well cared for as when I am watched over by Chinese people, with every wish or fleeting thought of a need instantly answered. And I received my third invitation of a house to live in if I needed to move.

There are so many details about the look and feel of Taiwan that remind me of China. Being on Sun Moon Lake was reminiscent of parks and lakes I had seen in China. That reminds me that I still haven't received mail from China. However, someone from the church will be going to Hangzhou the end of the month and I'll give her some letters to mail from inside China. I'm thinking of going back to China this summer and traveling with Russell and Richard who'll be on vacation from teaching. Bill has been able to get a better, non-teaching job, so he won't get a summer vacation. So, I need to make contact to plan my visit. Fortunately, I have been getting some letters from the Ethiopian boys in Israel.

I keep getting two comments in particular that surprise me. Many Taiwanese ask me, "Aren't you cold?" when I wear short sleeves. I think the Chinese must have a different temperature regulatory system. The other surprise is that everyone thinks I look younger than 46, yet I feel Chinese women look a lot younger than they are. To my 20-year-old students, 46 is a very old age.

March 27, 1990

I put a lot of energy into my teaching, but I do so enjoy it. Today one of my students was very talkative. Frank wanted to know why I am so interested in mainland China. He spoke to me about his anxiety over needing to decide whether to take the examination for further study, or to enter the compulsory two-year military service. He envies Americans because they have so much freedom.

Although happier than China, Taiwanese live under many clouds of uncertainty. It is a troubled country in transition. The Taiwanese are frightened of being invaded by mainland China, and they are frightened by the political turmoil inside their own political system. There is an atmosphere of readiness to flee. Taiwanese who are rich enough hold passports in other countries, and many have bought homes in other countries as well. One person told me that he wouldn't even have to take a toothbrush if he fled from an attack by China. "There is no country spirit," was the way one foreigner with three years of tenure in Taiwan put it.

To me, Taiwan's fear of mainland China is quite similar to the fear between Jews and Arabs in Israel. They are like tragic family feuds that go on and on with no resolution.

March 29, 1990

Although I did not get to see the youth celebrating this Youth Day, I went with "my" family here to visit the father's grave. It did not have the sad feeling of visiting a cemetery in the western world. Instead, the family brought food and flowers. They washed off the grave, burned paper money, and bowed holding joss sticks. The fact that they are Christian apparently does not conflict. These graves are not grassy. I paid my respects to this gentleman who died seven years ago at the relatively young age of 63.

Who will visit my grave? Who will mark it or even remember it?

April 8, 1990

I learned that "No, no, no" can mean "Yes, yes, yes." Mama Chen had clearly told me "No, no, no money" when I told her I'd like to pay for staying at her home. But today, Emily's friend Nancy spoke to me in private and told me that the family doesn't understand why I don't express my gratitude for living in their home. I told her that Mama Chen had emphatically said "no money," so I bought fruit (which is incredibly expensive here) for the family, gave Theresa English lessons, and did other little things that I thought would show my gratitude.

Nancy gave me a lesson in Chinese culture. She said I must offer money, but, of course, they will refuse to take it. That is my cue to insist they take the money. So, I tried what she told me. I gave Emily what I had heard from other foreigners they were paying for rent. She refused to take it. It felt strange to me, but I insisted as best I could. She eventually relented, saying that it would help to pay for the gas cylinder that they had to buy to give me hot water in my bathroom. Curiously, Emily had earlier offered to pay me for Theresa's English lessons at the going rate of $14 an hour. I had said "no," and it was never mentioned again.

April 15, 1990

One of my tutoring students and her husband took me out to dinner at the Taichung Hotel. They are very rich and told me they own three houses in Taipei and one in Taichung, Hualien, Los Angeles, and New Zealand. The husband will continue to run his business in Taiwan while his wife and three sons live in New Zealand. He will visit them every couple of months. He said he wanted his sons to be educated in the westernized system of New Zealand rather than the strictness of Chinese schools. Because of his wealth, New Zealand was willing to give them New Zealand passports, which made them feel more secure in case Taiwan is attacked by China. Being separated like that sounds awful to me, but many Chinese and Taiwanese are ready to do it. That reminded me of a Chinese woman I had met who had lived away from her husband and six-year-old son for five of the child's six years.

Too bad starving for mail does not make one thin. I would be down to a wisp! One letter from the U.S. took eight days to reach me, and another took 20 days!! A few letters from China have dribbled in. There is so much sadness in the letters from China.

April 22, 1990

As I lay on my bed in Taichung listening to both the rain and a cassette of Israeli folksongs given to me by a thoughtful Christian missionary, I realize how important a year this has been for me. As the tears stream down my face when I hear those Hebrew songs from Israel, I know well who I am, who and what I love in the world, and what I am solidly connected to. I know where the pieces of my heart lay, and it's okay.

My personality is solidly American and I'm very grateful for the freedom that my birth land has given me. My roots are in Israel even though I may not be strong enough to live in my homeland. A big piece of my heart is in China, and my spirit is in Bali. I belong anywhere in the world I want to be. My heart is big enough to be divided among Israelis, Ethiopians, Arabs, Chinese, Balinese, and wherever else I may choose to be. My heart is a complicated jigsaw puzzle that fits together nicely.

April 28, 1990

For my Passover observance, I took a beautiful book on Jerusalem out of the library here and went to my favorite neighborhood Buddhist shrine and thought about Israel and my many visits in Jerusalem. I wished all my Jewish friends in all parts of the world a happy Passover. I also told my students about Jerusalem, which I believe is the most beautiful and special city in the world. The nuns at Providence University where I'll be teaching next fall invited me to their Passover meal. I wasn't able to go, but it would have been an unusual experience eating *matzoh* with Chinese nuns in Taiwan to celebrate the last supper of Jesus.

I am fending off more jobs although it hurts to turn them down. I put my limit at 30 hours of teaching a week, which includes adult classes, children's classes, and tutoring. I'm finally bringing in decent money that I'll need in China this summer. I'm also still taking Chinese lessons and can now say in Chinese, "Mrs. Chen is not at home," when I answer the phone. I must say it well, because people on the other end then begin to ask me questions I can't reply to. Maybe next year I'll be able to reply.

I have even greater admiration for how Israel teaches Hebrew to its immigrants without using any language but Hebrew. In Taiwan, many students who have studied English for more than seven years can't understand or utter a word. Judging from the students' fear of native English speakers who can't speak Mandarin Chinese, I think Taiwan's mistake is having Taiwanese English teachers who speak mostly Chinese to "explain" English. I saw this when I was invited to a *booshi ban* English class by a woman who I knew could speak English very well. In the 30 minutes I sat in her class, I only understood four sentences. All the rest was in Chinese.

Last weekend, Mama Chen had a *mahjong* marathon at her home. She and her friends began playing on Friday morning, occasionally slept a little in shifts, and continued until Sunday evening with an occasional time-out to eat. I have heard that *mahjong* clubs can be big money in Taiwan. People even borrow thousands of dollars from these clubs rather than from banks. I'm not sure how it works, but it seems Taiwanese trust them more than the banks.

May 10, 1990

I can't sleep through the night anymore. My mind stays actively churning. I have discovered wonderful cold coffee drinks that must have huge amounts of caffeine that I drink before teaching. When the caffeine and my teaching high kick in, I am usually oblivious to fatigue as I see those eyes so concentratedly watching me. My students may not be great English speakers, but they are dedicated.

Last night I got confused with the time I was supposed to teach that class. I kept the students one hour overtime. During the entire 2 ½ hours, not one student squirmed, left, or told me the class had ended one hour earlier. Quite astounding! American kids would have been out the door long before. And most of these night students come to class after long days at work.

May 12, 1990

I learn something new every day. On Mother's Day, the child wears a red carnation if the mother is alive, and a white one if she is dead. White is the color of mourning in Chinese culture. Thankfully, I'm still able to wear a red carnation.

I have finally understood what my students mean by a "double eyelid." Some Chinese are born with a small crease in their eyelid. This is considered very beautiful and can even be done by cosmetic surgery. Japanese are not born with a double eyelid.

May 16, 1990

My heart is full. As I sat in the teahouse surrounded by the warmth and goodbye gifts of my students, I felt a great sense of accomplishment. I can reach these young Chinese people, and they respond to me. And it doesn't take so long. Two months of teaching and I find a bond has been established with many of them. I like them so very much, and they like me.

I finally received that long-awaited letter from Russell. He talked in his letter of other letters he sent that just never arrived. I'm sorry not to be able to read his other poetic letters. He knows when I'll arrive in Shanghai because the Hangzhou airport has closed temporarily. He hopes he'll be able to meet my plane. I feel more relaxed hearing from him after so long.

I was treated to a steak dinner by a couple of my students. We started talking about the mainland Chinese kids. They are as curious about them as my mainland kids are about the Taiwanese. So, I got the idea to bring letters from them to my mainland friends. The mainland students need to know that the Taiwanese haven't forgotten them. And my Taiwanese students need to be educated about their mainland brothers. The boys even wanted to send some presents with me for the mainland boys.

My body rhythms continue to be confused. I'm still not sleeping through the night. And it's been 57 days without a period. Menopause would be a welcome relief when I'm traveling in China where they only have uselessly thin and meager pads.

DRAGON BOAT FESTIVAL

My mind is still filled with the wonder of it all—me in the famous, ancient city of Lukang celebrating the Dragon Boat Festival at the invitation of my student, Frank. Everything was in synch—a sunny day with blue sky, a holiday atmosphere, markets, carnival games, plentiful food, concerts, a puppet show, and milling crowds. What made it different for me was that there were also dragon boat races, foods I had never eaten, traditional Chinese music concerts, a traditional Chinese wedding procession, the incense of Buddhist temples, and many crafts that can only be seen in Chinese culture. Here are the details.

My host is a 22-year-old former student whose parents live in the countryside of Lukang. He is third generation Taiwanese-born. The most noticeable part of their home is a huge altar that houses three Buddhist gods. A large, tall wooden table with a lower and less ornate table under it holds three cans that have the

English word, "mango" on it. There are always offerings on the table, along with a container in which to stick the incense.

There are no warm hugs and words of greeting between Chinese children and their parents. The love between them is communicated in other ways I do not understand. The mother lights three joss sticks and bows to the gods three times and sticks them in the bowl of sand. Her son does the same.

Flanking this huge altar are a modern stereo, a television, and some straight-backed chairs. The house has some very pretty and modern parts, including very nicely carved wood. The kitchen is less modern. Pots filled with soaking vegetables and a freshly killed duck (chicken?) sit on the floor. The beds are mattressless. They put down a quilt pad when it is time to sleep.

The air is fresher and cleaner than I have smelled in the months of being in Taichung. Outside, the rice is quietly growing. The geese are honking as they run around the yard outside a picturesque barn that even has an old wagon wheel and an old, now unused rice-harvesting machine by the old brick wall. This is a family compound—uncles, aunts, sons, daughters, cousins—all live in the surrounding homes. The grandparents live in a very sparse home near the larger home of the parents.

I agree to ride on the back of a motor scooter into the city of Lukang. While it is too dangerous on the streets of Taichung, I hope that small-town Lukang drivers will be more civilized. At least, the traffic is not as heavy. And so I fly through the rice paddies nervously perched on the back of a motor scooter while the freshness of the air and closeness to nature cleanses me. The next day, I feel the elation of riding a bike through the fields. It brings back happy memories of riding my bike in Hangzhou last year.

My student explains many things to me as we pack in many activities in one evening and one very full day. His English begins to flow more naturally. He explains the traditional foods we eat, and helps me bargain for the small trinkets I buy to bring to my friends in China. He explains the Buddhist stories and beliefs. Does he believe in ghosts that must be appeased? Well, yes and no, but mostly yes, he admits somewhat shyly.

He also admires the Chinese crafts with a longing that I have become aware of in Taiwan. The Taiwanese Chinese, even three generations later, keenly feel their alienation from the mainland and the traditional Chinese roots. They do feel they are one people. I watch examples of the Chinese patience as a man creates an intricate animal on a heated plate. Eventually, he scrapes it off gently and hands the delicate lollipop to a waiting child. I watched as wide-eyed as the small children.

There is western cotton candy, and impaled small squid barbecued on a grill. There are men heaving huge tops that they tried to make spin by running and unwinding a thick rope around it. There is a contest of amateur singers singing in Taiwanese (which is different from Mandarin Chinese and has seven tones instead of four). Frank explains to me that the contestants must be old—at least in their 40's because their voices must be mellowed with age. I can only chuckle, for I feel like a wide-eyed youngster.

The unusual events, plus the special architecture of Lukang keep my camera very busy. I try many shots that can best be called experimental. I look long in order to at least register the sights and sounds in my memory just in case my mediocre photography skill fails me. I think so many times of my friends in China who I wish could be seeing it all with me. The narrow alleyways and unusual houses remind me of the alleyways I've wandered through in the Old City of Jerusalem. I feel again a joy and happiness for what I have chosen to experience in life. It is the "high" that keeps me going through the rough spots.

We sit and eat in a relatively quiet restaurant except for a very loud television blaring. I wonder again why the Chinese seem to thrive on noise. We discuss the young man's impending graduation and separation from his close friends. He is ending one stage of his life and entering another stage. He is nervous, understandably so. I try to remember my own fears at that age. It seems so long ago. I feel my middle age heavily.

And then he points out the window and there is a traditional wedding procession. I grab my camera, rush out, click in quick succession, angry at the spectators whose heads appear in the picture frame. There is an old woman being borne in a carriage on the shoulders of the coolies. She has a very beautiful and regal face. I try to frame it in my camera, but I miss. I run after her. The whole parade stops for a brief while and the inexperienced coolies set her carriage down ingloriously. She almost falls out, but her face stays regal and important in spite of a slight look of shock. I try again to capture her on my film, but it is almost the end of the parade, and the cars and motor scooters press around me dangerously close. Only one lane of the narrow road has been closed to traffic, and yet traffic follows hotly on the end of the procession, endangering the little children dressed in blue who are carrying the bride's dowry.

It takes a while to find my host again. We then go to enjoy the beauty of an orchid growing contest. Taiwan has good weather for orchids, and there is more variety and beauty in these orchids than I have ever seen before. I once again challenge my meager photography skills to capture it.

The festivities go on. I go home to think on it all.

June 4, 1990

I began to understand suffering when I made the decision to divorce. I deepened my acquaintance with suffering in Israel. It moved deeper in China. We had a minute of silence today remembering June 4th, 1989.

June 22, 1990

I came to Taiwan only four months ago, not knowing anyone. Last weekend I rode to Tainan in a very fancy car and was treated like a visiting dignitary by the family I'm tutoring that's moving to New Zealand. They showed me around their hometown, particularly an elaborate Buddhist temple in the mountains. Next weekend I've been invited to a wedding in Taipei at a fancy hotel. Teachers are truly treated wonderfully here by their students.

In the middle of all this opulence, I wear my grungy wardrobe over and over and over. I'll have to upgrade a bit when I teach next year. I don't think they'll appreciate "I Love Hong Kong" t-shirts. Since no store in Asia carries my size, I'll have to have my clothes made by a tailor. I've heard that's not as expensive as it sounds in Taiwan and China. I've already found out tailor-made clothes in Hong Kong are too expensive for my budget.

Another experience has been added to my life. The *booshi ban* I teach in at night was raided by the police. Now I'm on file as an illegal worker. I don't know what the repercussions of that may be. Sorry it had to come now so close to when I leave for China, but better now than earlier. Somehow, I think we were set up tonight. Strangely, the boss and none of the regular staff were at the school—just two new inexperienced clerks and we unsuspecting foreign teachers. When I questioned the police as to why they didn't deal with the owners instead of the foreign teachers, he garbled something unintelligible about the Chinese way. I'm sure it is, too.

June 26, 1990

Sometimes the way that Asian countries copy the west is just hysterical. One of my classes took me out for a fantastic farewell dinner at the "Gothic Artistical Café." It was a fancy restaurant that mixed several styles and motifs—Gothic décor, hostesses in Gone with the Wind southern belle dresses, a viola and piano concert, western food, and Chinese toilets.

June 27, 1990

My last Chinese class, my last yoga class, goodbyes and thank you's—yes, there is a sad part to leaving because these past four months have surpassed any expectations I might have had. And, I have paved a little future. Providence University awaits my return to teach in the fall. It seems my being caught as an illegal worker won't cause any visa problems.

I'm packing seriously now. I wish I could carry more gifts for my Chinese friends and their families. I do so want to bring some joy and fun to them. But this time I go to China having made many dear Taiwanese friends. I have become quite fond of this place.

June 29, 1990

More warm goodbyes and delicious meals with my caring students. Some have given me small gifts, including a cowboy boot keyring filled with beautiful polished stones from Alexander. He and I developed a good friendship. Whether deserved or not, he credits me with giving him a new outlook on life which has enabled him to get the courage to go study in the U.S. these next two years. I think he's mature enough to make good use of his studies there. It's nice to know I had a positive influence upon him.

Then there was the good bye to the crippled young man who had a nice smile for me every time I went to work at the night *booshi ban*. There he sat in his wheelchair selling the gum that the Taiwan government gives to disabled people to help them make a living. It's hard to be disabled anywhere, but particularly in Asian countries, even wealthy ones. We couldn't talk, but there was an unspoken contact between us.

So, as my mind travels to China and my reunion with my friends there, I am constantly reminded of all the sincere caring and kindness I've received here. I know I'm living my life fast, but I am living it full and I intend to continue doing it as long as I can.

9

HONG KONG CHINA TAIWAN 1990

July 3, 1990

I'm in Hong Kong again and have applied for my visa to China. The irony hit me of trying so hard to get back into that country when so many are trying to leave it in every conceivable and inconceivable way.

Waiting for the visa to China made me nervous. I felt agitated as I went up to Victoria Peak to pick up some gifts I had seen there before. But the artist wasn't in his shop. Another shopkeeper told me the artist doesn't keep any real schedule. But while hanging around waiting for him, I discovered a delightful walk on Victoria Peak that soon took me into unpeopled nature, a place where bird songs predominate, and the smell is not pollution. I felt myself calming down as it all seeped into me, and I into it. I loved Taiwan, but I was suffering from nature deprivation there.

This is my fifth time in Hong Kong, but I realized how little I've seen of it as a tourist. It has been the efficient place to get things done in between trips in and out of China. Yet, I really like this place. It's more beautiful than Taiwan. I need to be more of a tourist here sometime. Since Hong Kong is well known as a good place to buy cameras, I finally bought an adjustable lens that can take wide angle and telephoto shots. So, this time in China I'm bringing a new toy to play with.

July 18, 1990

How wonderful it was to see the friendly faces of Richard, Russell, and Bill at the Shanghai Airport. I really appreciated their effort because getting to Shanghai by train took them about five hours and then they ended up walking a long way since they didn't catch the right bus.

When we got to Hangzhou, I connected with many of my Hangzhou students. There is a deep depression covering China. My students look thinner from worrying and seem older in a weary way. Almost all are disappointed in their work, and their futures. Yes, it is sad to see the state they're in. Several said they had written me, but their letters never reached me. No one really knows quite what to believe about June 4th of 1989. Some believe the west has exaggerated what happened, but they don't believe what their government says either.

It was so good to be back with Russell's family deep in the Chinese countryside. However, his family works too hard to host me in what they consider the proper manner. They work long hours, and then prepare feasts. Since there is no refrigeration or modern cooking methods, everything is laborious. It is like going back in time. And, because foreigners are bigger and fatter, they insist on believing I must eat huge quantities. I feel like a stuffed pig. I'm sure they'd never believe I'd prefer a bowl of yogurt and some cheese and bread that are impossible to get here.

Speaking of good meals, I have a funny picture in my mind of the night I arrived where Richard is living close to his school. We got there at 2 a.m. after a very long boat ride. Since he has no shower, I sponge bathed at a water tap in the schoolyard by moonlight. The mosquitoes loved it. They hadn't had anyone with so much meat come to visit before. I felt like I was camping again.

Tomorrow Richard and Russell and I will set out to travel around China. Of course, that's quite crazy in this terrible heat, but it's the only time they are available. Bill must work because he's not a teacher, but we're hoping to meet in Guilin at the end of our trip.

July 27, 1990

Both boys are overwhelmed at being in Beijing. Rather than running all around to glimpse everything they have ever read about and dreamed of seeing, they have slowed down to a crawl. Richard says he wants to savor everything. It may be like the way I was so saturated by the beauty of Norway, I couldn't absorb anymore and had to rest. In their case, it is not feeling saturated by beauty, but being places they never thought they would be.

We are staying at that terrible hostel I stayed in my first time in Beijing. I don't know whether I dislike more the Chinese clerks who literally scream at the foreigners like naughty children, or the drunken British boys who sing under my window all night.

Before I go on with Beijing, I want to back up to our time in Qingdao about ten days ago. The three of us felt an amazing atmosphere of relaxation and friendliness of the people. Unlike other parts of China, the people there were well dressed, pleasant, and didn't push and shove their way around. This city was quite clean for China, with care taken in trees, parks and decorations. I'm a newcomer to it all, but Russell and Richard kept commenting on it. Even a money-changer took us to his home for a pleasant exchange with tea.

One reason Russell and Richard were anxious to see Qingdao was the chance to swim in the sea. Their first encounter with sea swimming was a rough one indeed. I rented inner tubes for each of them and then swam back and forth between them trying to keep them from drowning. That experience whetted Richard's appetite for sea swimming, but surfeited Russell's. However, we all agreed that it was a wonderful time and a very special place.

Another pleasant encounter for me was on the train between Qingdao and Jinan. I sat across from a 13-year-old boy who was curious about me, but did not look upon me as a freak. We played the card game War and shared some food. When I put my head on the small table between us to rest, he very thoughtfully placed a clean newspaper for my head to rest on. I was touched by one so young showing such caring for a stranger. I didn't think that would happen with an American teenager.

I've been writing this while under the gaze of Mao's bigger than life portrait in Tiananmen Square. He must have seen the thief who just stole Russell's bag!! I was so engrossed in my writing, I didn't notice that someone must have just walked by me and taken it from among the bags I have around my feet. Why am I sitting on the ground with my back against the little bridge and our belongings all around me? I was so angry that a ticket to visit the gate behind me was so expensive for me as a foreigner compared to the cost to Chinese that I told the boys to go on ahead and I'd wait for them here. Fortunately, Russell took his camera with him, but I'm sure he had other things in his small bag that he'll miss. Gone are the days in China when people didn't steal. Mao would not approve.

July 29, 1990

I've felt really guilty about my carelessness that caused Russell to lose some little treasures that are hard to replace like his address book, and the tapes that my Taiwanese friend, Frank, had given me to give him. Of course we reported the theft to the police who listened politely, but could do nothing.

The boys, and the other Chinese who gaily fly kites in Tiananmen Square, seem to have an adoration for this place. On the other hand, what I see when I look around is a stream of blood that meanders through the hugeness of it all. There's also a heavy presence of soldiers that wasn't here in 1988.

We stood sweating in a long line to visit Mao in his mausoleum. What was remarkable to me is that this is the only place where I've seen Chinese line up in an absolutely straight line and stay completely silent.

We were almost cheated by a moneychanger near our hotel. He had a strange way of counting the money out, and Richard didn't trust him. I trusted Richard's intuition more than the moneychanger, so I found a more reliable "businessman."

August 5, 1990

The group dynamics of our threesome keeps changing. There are many ups and downs both between the two of them and the three of us. Sometimes I feel left out when they speak only to each other in Chinese. Sometimes they are as silent and closed up as sea anemones. At other times, there is closeness, good conversations and lots of laughter. Russell and I laughed about the difference between my easy laughter and the way Chinese girls giggle.

As we see the famous tourist sites, I do feel a sense of pleasure in their enjoyment. However, my righteous indignation is often riled by being charged absurd FEC prices as a foreigner. Since I'm also paying for the boys, I can readily tell what a Chinese is charged compared to a foreigner. This applies to parks, tourist sites, and especially beds in the same hotel where I've paid four times their price. I have taken to intentionally crumbling up the always clean and new FEC before paying for something. Eventually, Richard and Russell told me that they understand my feelings but get very embarrassed when I do that. I guess they "lose face" somehow when I show my temper.

Xian has been a very happy place for all of us. We hooked up with three boys from Hong Kong and a Japanese girl who was assigned as my roommate in the hotel. One joy of traveling is the serendipity of these instant, congenial, short-term relationships that form between tourists. We ate tons of delicious watermelon to cool ourselves in this horrendous heat. I also saw here something I haven't seen in other parts of China. Prostitutes surrounded the hotels. I probably wouldn't have noticed because they didn't look very different from any other Chinese girls, but the boys picked them out easily.

August 6, 1990

I suppose conditions for cows are worse, but they don't have the mentality to understand and resent the way they're treated like I do. In China, we are herded, corralled, squashed, discounted, abused and dehumanized, especially traveling hard seat in a train. This is the way most Chinese travel—if they travel at all. It is as uncomfortable as could be—particularly for those who don't even get the "luxury" of a hard seat.

The train is a microcosm of the problems of China. Poverty, overpopulation, overcrowding, lack of respect from petty railroad personnel who I even saw hit an old man who didn't have a ticket, government corruption and inefficiency—all with an overlay of dirt and grunge. As some compensation, a certain camaraderie does develop between fellow sufferers who attempt to maintain their dignity as best they can.

Russell tells me he simply empties his mind to deal with the boredom of long train travel. I, however, cannot seem to do this. Instead, I find it's a good time for peoplewatching. I had a lot of time to observe a group traveling together. They were only teenagers and a fairly scruffy looking lot. They had been able to get tickets for seats, and they felt proud of this power over those unfortunate unseated souls who tried occasionally to squeeze half their bottom on a mere corner of a seat. While I and others periodically gave up our seats or a portion thereof to accommodate the huge, unseated population of the train—some children and tired-looking old people among them—these six jealously guarded every inch of "their" seats.

The group reminded me immediately of the old "Our Gang" movies I used to watch as a child. The leader of this motley group was the shortest boy. His manner left his leadership in little doubt. He loved being the center of attention. Thus, all his actions were conspicuous and exaggerated. For example, he took wads of money out of his pockets and stuffed them into his t-shirt. Later, he took them out, arranged them, and slowly and repeatedly counted each bill. It may have been the group's money perhaps painstakingly saved to bring home because I noticed it was all in small denominations.

They passed the time chatting, smoking cigarettes, eating, and sleeping. One of the boys and one of the girls sat on the seat for two. The boy rarely spoke, often smoked, and gruffly kept pushing a tired lady who kept trying to sit on a small portion of this seat. His girlfriend wore a discolored bruise on her arm, which I had no doubt he had given her.

The other girl sat next to me in a coveted window seat. She was a chubby, plain-looking girl who was presumably the girlfriend of the leader, which she showed by being as disagreeable to him as she dared. When he tried to do something nice for her, such as buying grapes for her, she promptly rebuffed him. However, she only went so far in acting brazen and rude to him, and ultimately always relented.

Three boys sat across from me. Of course, the leader took the best seat near the window, which he never gave up to anyone, including his friends. The boy next to him had a very pale, sickly complexion. He exhibited what seemed to me like a genuine rather than self-serving deference to the leader. In turn, the leader treated him with good-natured contempt. The third boy was the healthiest and best looking of the group with a bland, congenial, undemanding personality.

Most of the endless hours were nighttime hours. They were the most interesting for observing. The girl next to me, and the leader opposite her, had an enviable ability to sleep through many hours of hard seat misery. She put her head on her bag placed on the small table between them, and scarcely moved. The leader kept changing position often, imposing his head and body on the lap of his kind companion who cradled him rather tenderly. Sometimes the leader rejected his touch rudely, but at other times demanded a soft spot on his neighbor's lap. In time, the third boy was crowded out altogether, but affectionately gave up his seat to the reclining sickly boy and leader who snored away. Since there was not even floor space because all space was occupied by the unseated, he resorted to draping himself over the narrow edge of the back of the bench.

The most active one during the night was the bruised girl. She often played with smoking cigarettes—a rather daring act for a Chinese girl. And she did it as grotesquely and as obviously as she could manage. She seemed to be a moody and sad girl whose unhappy future I mentally predicted.

I have often noticed that Chinese show little delicacy when waking someone up. She displayed this by extremely rudely pinching the sleeping girl next to me. She did this several times in the course of the night since she dared not wake up her grumpy boyfriend to get near the window. She first woke up the girl because she wanted to sit on her girlfriend's lap and stick her head out the window to chant a long, lamenting refrain over and over. She next woke her up when she wanted to brush her teeth and spit out the water into the middle of the night. And, exactly at 3:30 a.m., she again woke her to sit on her lap while she slowly applied her make-up for the day. The sleeping girl tolerated it well with the resignation of one quite unable to control her friend.

Trying to sleep in such hot, unbearably stuffy trains (for some inexplicable reason, the fans are never used on summer nights) must be experienced to be understood. It is anatomically and mentally anti-human. The contortions one tries approach the acrobatic. I had watched the undemanding third boy finally receive a piece of seat from his sickly friend. He gratefully sank immediately into a deep sleep, only to be painfully awakened by his friend pinching his eyelid! His friend then murmured a couple of words, and pushed him off the seat again.

By 7 a.m., I had lost all curiosity in the human interest aspects of Chinese hard seat train behavior. I laid out my plastic poncho over the trash and spit and cigarette butts and crawled under the seats. Sleeping amidst the rubbish seemed worthwhile in order to spread out my fatigued body. As I extended my leg, a hand grabbed my foot before it crashed into his face. Another under-the-seat squatter had set up his turf, complete with a mat, tea, and cigarettes. I carefully angled my leg away from his face, and we both settled in for a snooze.

To add yet another insult to my human dignity, I was stopped as I was leaving this train of horrors to pay an additional 50 FEC because I was a foreigner!

August 9, 1990

I have had the longest, hottest, dirtiest trip of my life getting to Lijiang in Yunnan Province. We took the train from Xian to Chengdu where we got off for a few hours and tried to eat. However, the food in this part of China is much too spicy for any of us to eat. As a matter of fact, the boys really haven't enjoyed any of the food since we left Hangzhou. It's too different from what they're used to. We boarded another train for Jinjiang. And, we arrived at Jinjiang just in time to catch the ten-hour bus trip to our destination, Lijiang in Yunnan Province.

Although we were thoroughly exhausted, the bus ride to Lijiang was spectacular, with gorgeous terraced rice fields and banana trees, interesting villages and minority folk along the way. Our bus driver must have been practicing for a race because he sped along wildly with me hanging out the window snapping pictures as we careened around curves. In a remote area, we had to rest because the driver had blown out two tires. Since he only had one spare, we had to wait until another bus came by and loaned us another one.

After days on trains, my main need was for a shower. We were able to get into a dormitory, but the group showers with hot water had been turned off for the night. Very early the next morning, I woke the boys up and we moved to another place where I got a double for them and a single room for me. It wasn't the right time for showers there either. Chinese believe that people should shower in the evening before bed. The western habit of showering in the morning, or perhaps twice a day, makes no sense to them. However, I took thermos bottles of hot water for drinking and washed my filthy hair. The basin turned positively black with dirt.

Once we all recovered from the rigors of getting to Lijiang and were once again clean, we looked around and saw what a nice city it was. Lijiang has a charming old city with a large population of a minority called Naxi. It's one of the few matriarchal societies. Thankfully, it was also cool in Lijiang, so cool in fact that I bought a sweater for Russell and a jacket for Richard.

Our spirits soared up into the deep blue sky and the marvelous mountains. We breathed the unpolluted air greedily. Some local girls, attracted to these Chinese young men from the richest part of coastal China, showed us some of the highlights of their very beautiful hometown. To my western eyes, the four of them acted more like teenagers than in their early 20's.

Both boys thought they must be in heaven. They said they wished it could go on forever and didn't know how they would be able to deal with their boring, confining, small hometown jobs.

August 10, 1990

I sit amidst some of China's mountain beauty and am closer to Tibet than I'll ever be. We even needed special tourist permits from the Chinese government to come here. The scenery could be many places—Switzerland, Austria, Washington state. This way—a snow-capped mountain. That way—a green-treed slope. Down there—a powerful gorge. In the gorge, the water runs, jumps, skips, flows, falls. It reminds me of life—racing to where, to what, why? It doesn't make much sense. Nature makes more sense. At least it's following gravity. What am I following? I don't know, but I, too, keep on going.

It's not silent in the mountains. It has voice and sound and timelessness. And most of all, it has the wonderful ability to release me from the burdens of emotions and relationships.

We are on a tourist trip, so the boys are enjoying our international companions. Russell particularly keeps looking at a pretty, long-legged blonde from Sweden. Later, he says to me with a little self-conscious laugh, "Maybe hairy legs aren't so ugly."

August 13, 1990

I've turned 47 in the very picturesque town of Dali in Yunnan Province. The boys gave me some cute little gifts. I bought myself a special Dali blue tie-dyed skirt and top that fits well, but turns my skin blue. My birthday dinner was Hungarian Goulash, the best I've had. Because Dali is small and gets a lot of foreign tourists, there are some good restaurants here that have learned and copied as best they can recipes from homesick foreigners craving familiar food.

This is a big minority area too, so we went out to the Sunday Shapin Market where the boys were a particular hit with the local Bai women. They bought tie-dyed vests and matching hats, necklaces and bracelets that make them look like tourists.

August 16, 1990

The bus ride from Dali to Kunming may not have been the longest I've taken in China, but it was definitely the bumpiest. Sometimes a work crew was only yards in front of us working on the road. There was no heavy equipment, only dozens of men breaking rocks with pickaxes like a chain gang.

Kunming is a beautiful city. I think the bright blue skies, cool air, and wide, uncrowded streets help to make it so. I'm trying to mentally prepare myself for our 33 hour train trip to Guilin.

August 18, 1990

I suppose that my memories of this long summer trip will be divided into small moments and poignant encounters. I can't get the beautiful face of a beggar boy out of my mind. He was lying on the sidewalk next to the railway station fast asleep. Maybe he was about 11 years old. Both he and his clothes were absolutely filthy. I assumed the bulge in his stomach was from malnutrition. The boys and I had just come from eating dinner where I had complained about my chicken, cut inedibly into what another tourist had called "chainsaw chicken" due to the way Chinese cut up whole chickens. How that little boy would have loved what I had left behind! I felt ashamed.

Later, when the train made a stop at a small station, an old man with one leg and one arm approached my window on one crutch. I'd been repeatedly warned by my friends not to give anything to beggars who are, they assured me, mostly just pretending. I handed him a banana. He sent me a grateful thank you with his eyes and hungrily proceeded to tear off the banana skin with his teeth.

Later on, something was announced on the loudspeakers in the train, which the boys translated as "Watch out for your things on the small tables by the windows." At the precise moment they finished the translation, some food zipped off several tables. The boys said street urchins did it, but I was sure they must have been magicians.

For some of the ride, the train was thankfully not overly crowded. I went out for a change of space to the area between the cars of the train. One other weary traveler was there, sitting on a piece of newspaper on the floor. I had noticed before that Chinese don't like to sit directly on floors or even grass. I was wearing jeans and just sat down on the floor. The man kindly reached for his newspaper seat, took off another page, and silently offered it to me. We sat together in that small space with our own thoughts for quite a long time. Too bad we couldn't talk.

There was another problem to overcome on this train trip. We were able to buy hard sleeper tickets for the boys, but I could only get a hard seat ticket. The boys were willing to sleep together in one bed and give me the other bed, but the railway clerks were known for coming around at night to check the number of "feet" sticking out of each sleeper. This required some intrigue as we carefully planned our timing so that they wouldn't be caught sleeping in the same bed. Pure luck was with us.

August 22, 1990

We spent only a little time in Guilin and then went to Yangshuo where the boys were interested in doing some amateur spelunking in one of the many caves there. I was glad to send them off with a guide and a young English girl whom I'd met because the hotel put us together in one room. Alison was pretty, bold, and always in third gear. She went from spelunking to a long swim down the Li River with nary a breath in between. The boys enjoyed her thoroughly and told me they had never met such an active girl.

Most foreign tourist boats go down the Li River from Guilin down to Yangshuo with fresh fish caught, cooked, and served while on board. We took a less-used tourist boat ride from Yangshuo up to Guilin without the fish feast. The scenery, however, was just as magnificent as the looming karst formations reached out of the river. During this ride, certainly one of the most picturesque and unique boat rides anywhere in the world, Richard read a book and Russell fell into an exhausted heap. I was sorry that Bill had not been able to join us in Guilin.

August 24, 1990

I can't remember what my very first plane flight felt like. So, I vicariously felt what a first flight is like. Neither Russell nor Richard had ever flown, and I couldn't imagine another endless train ride back to Hangzhou, so I bought us plane tickets from Guilin to Shanghai. Most everyone else on the plane was a first-time flyer. Excitement literally crackled in the air when the plane took off. There was a communal "Ooooooh" when the plane took off. When the plane leveled off, people started taking pictures of each other on the plane. Next, they opened up the little gifts the pretty flight attendants handed out with a snack. When the time came to land, there was an air of nervousness on the part of the first-timers. Richard gripped my hand. Safely down, everyone applauded loudly and immediately stood up to get their luggage from the overhead bins before the plane could stop. Of all the flights I've taken, this will definitely be one of the ones I'll remember.

August 25, 1990

No matter how many difficult times we had had together on our trip, I still became sloppily sentimental when it came time for us to part. They were going back to the little towns where they worked, and I was going on to Hangzhou. I gave them each an envelope with money in it. In the Chinese way, they didn't open their gifts in front of me. So, I missed seeing their reaction to my goodbye letters and counting the money. And, in the Chinese way, they never really did say "thank you."

Sept. 1, 1990

We all sang Happy Birthday to Thomas's father on his 50th birthday, which would be considered his 49th birthday in the U.S. The discrepancy of one year is yet another confusion between east and west cultures because Chinese start life as one year old instead of zero.

I've once again been able to come to lovely Thousand Islands Lake because that's where Thomas's parents live. Of course, I wanted to swim in that pure water, but again the weather did not cooperate. It was cool and rainy.

Thomas is easy to be with. His careful thinking and analytical mind has helped me understand more about Chinese behavior, which has helped me to at least intellectually understand some of the miscommunication between Russell, Richard, and me on our trip. According to Thomas, Chinese read a lot of cues about what another person is feeling or thinking. They rarely, if ever, actually check out with the other person what they think the person is thinking. And, they rarely express their own feelings, especially anger, directly. He could not find a way to explain how gratitude is expressed, if at all.

Another piece of useful information from Thomas was about the countryside boy who comes to college in the big city. The countryside boy has already developed a different thought process based on his isolated village culture. Eventually, the countryside person begins to act more citylike, but is copying or mimicking what he sees. It is not truly an internalized part of him. Thomas understands this process in reverse because he spent his earliest years in a big city, and then moved to a small place.

I suppose my behavior is as much a puzzle to them as theirs is to me. I think of one of the couples, an American woman and a Chinese man, that I met in

Lijiang. I remember her face as she told me how hard it has been for them to stay together. Their love holds them together as their cultural differences try to pull them apart.

Sept. 3, 1990

I got to see some of my other friends again before leaving to go back to Taiwan. Debbie took me to the place in Hangzhou where they grow and dry the famous Dragon Well tea that I've come to enjoy so much. She shared with me her frustration and sorrow with her low-paying job. Her misery seems to be the common Chinese young person's lament. Another former student told me his story that is like a record stuck in the same place—his sadness and loneliness and lack of hope for the future.

It would be so much easier to leave China if I knew I was leaving my friends to happy, challenging, successful lives. Instead, I feel like I'm abandoning them while I go back to my comfy-cozy life.

Sept. 5, 1990

I went to a feast last night with Pearl's family and their ancestral ghosts. We biked a long 45 minutes out to her family's home. When they burned the paper money, the ashes rose quickly and floated down like ash snow covering the room and food. Then, the mother waved a hat, and all the ashes floated away from the food. I like the way Chinese culture continues to incorporate the dead family members into their lives.

Sept. 8, 1990

The air is heavy with expected rain. I feel leaden with the necessity for me to leave China once again. How did I become so involved with these young people and this depressed country? I have enjoyed being Santa Claus, handing out helpful gifts that can encourage one's art talent, buy new glasses for another, pay for something special one had never hoped he could afford. At least I know I'm going back to a good job in Taiwan where Chinese people are happier, live more comfortably, and don't have to suffer so much for being Chinese.

I got to say goodbye once again to Bill, Richard, and Russell. Richard, Russell, and I unquestionably went through some hard times together on our long trip. In spite of that, we parted with a deeper closeness and caring smiles. I don't feel this is a permanent parting from China. When will I be back? Maybe in four more months to welcome in the Year of the Sheep—Russell, Richard's, and my year according to our birth years in the Chinese zodiac.

Sept. 20, 1990

Tonight is the Jewish New Year. I'm sure it is one of great trepidation for tiny, beleaguered Israel. Israel is getting very close to the brink of war. Iraq is close enough to send missiles directly into Israel.

What will next year bring? I assume I'll spend it here in Taiwan, happy at times and crying inside for China and Israel.

Oct. 2, 1990

"What is that terrible smell?" was the first question I asked the other teachers the first night I was settling into my new home at the teacher's dormitory in Providence University. I was told that there was a big dump behind the school that couldn't be seen, but could often be smelled. Ugh! This may be a big problem for me.

Otherwise, my accommodations are fine. My one room has a little balcony and its own western toilet and shower. We all share a kitchen. It's convenient and cheap, only costing me about $44 a month, including all utilities. That's good, because prices in Taiwan for other things are very high.

Other benefits are that I can easily walk to work, and I have a big indoor swimming pool and library in my "backyard." A disadvantage is that my room has no view on my side of the building, but if I go to a common sitting room on the other side of the building I can watch the huge ball of a fiery sun setting over the ocean. I don't think I've ever felt so close to the sun anyplace else. Another disadvantage is that the mountains obstruct radio reception. Therefore, I can't listen to my short-wave radio, which is my English lifeline to the news of the world. The dump is the major disadvantage because they burn the garbage several times a week, sending a smell and smog over the campus that gets so bad some teachers even cancel classes.

I like my classes and the students except that my conversation classes have about 55 students per class. It's like teaching a mob after my 20 students of last year in the *booshi bans*. New challenges for me are teaching an oral presentation course and a composition class. The composition class takes a lot of time because of correcting their writing, but I'm also using the assignments to help me understand more about the Chinese culture in Taiwan. The students in that class are English majors who can write English much better than they can speak it.

Girl students in Taiwan are different from the girls I taught in China. Taiwanese girls giggle a lot, act and speak softly. Their dainty mannerisms remind me more of Japanese girls. That makes sense because Taiwan was under the domination of Japan for 50 years between 1895 and 1945. Many of the older Taiwanese can speak Japanese because they were required to learn it.

Oct. 21, 1990

The air pollution at the school is awful! My body doesn't like it at all. My nose fills with an allergic reaction. I sometimes go into sneezing fits, and my eyes feel terrible. Often I even find black ashes covering my balcony. People here don't like the soot and smoke, but either their bodies don't react or their minds can block it out. Taichung city had bad air, but this is worse even though it's on the outskirts of the city because of the dump right behind us.

If there is war in Israel, I will go back. Even if I don't need to march to war, I don't see how I can continue to teach here next semester. I wrote an impassioned letter to the mayor of the city about the air pollution problem. He responded politely. Basically, it is not only the dump that is the problem. People come out to the mountain area around us to illegally burn their own trash. This apparently is not just residents, but also businesses that come here to burn chemicals as well as trash and garbage. Even though it's against the law for them to do it, the authorities don't have people patrolling to enforce the law.

Garbage is a big problem for this island. I have seen myself that a lot of the problem is the excessive packaging of just about everything you buy in the stores. In our school alone, thousands of lunch and dinner boxes made of styrofoam are discarded in numerous plastic trash bags every day. I suggested that students could bring their own bowls and utensils and be responsible for cleaning them. That is what the students in China do.

My classes at the university take a lot of preparation time, but I've also started some private tutoring. It's so easy to find work here in Taiwan. One "student" is an adorable four-year-old girl who spent a little time in kindergarten in the U.S. She uses only four English words—"mine," " no," and "go away." I've nicknamed her "One Tough Cookie."

Nov. 7, 1990

There were two astounding pieces of news today. One was a tiny little clipping in the International Herald Tribune that said Ethiopia would now let all its Jews go! Hooray! All those years of trying, hoping, pleading, bribing—my kids will all have their families with them again.

The other news was that Meir Kahane was shot dead in New York. I can feel no sympathy for him.

Nov. 11, 1990

I realized once again how much I am a product of those idealistic, non-realistic days of the 1960's in America. Rose, one of the Taiwanese English teachers, and I are becoming good friends. She spent some time studying in the U.S. when she was in her early 20's. She especially liked being in America where each person is independent and can do what he or she wants without group censorship. In Taiwan, she feels her behavior is always being watched and judged. That's a major difference between "groupy" Asian cultures and the American emphasis on individualism. So, she likes to talk to me because we can chat about all sorts of things she wouldn't talk about with her Taiwanese friends.

She introduced me to the audio-visual department of our university where we can watch movie videos on small screens and listen with earphones. We just saw the movie, "The Dead Poets' Society", which I thought of as a movie memorial to the "Seize the day" spirit of the 1960's. How much of the 1960's is left in the U.S. now, I don't know. But it is left inside of me. Perhaps that is why I'm here watching this movie with Chinese subtitles.

Dec. 2, 1990

I have moved into the home of a kind American musical missionary only a 15-minute bus ride away from Providence University. So, now I'll be able to come back to teach here next semester after my visit to China during the long holidays in January for Chinese New Year. The air here is definitely not great, but it is farther away from the burning dump.

I knew I had to make a drastic decision to either quit or move out when I began to have nightmares of not being able to breathe. Visions of my mother and my dear friend, Carolyn, gasping for breath, made it crystal clear to me that breathing is my priority no matter how good a job I have.

I came to Miranda because she knows a lot of families at Tung Hai University, where she heads the music department. I thought she might know of a family who would be interested in having me live with them. She offered to take me in herself at no charge. This dynamo of energy is from Texas, but has been in Taiwan for 25 years and speaks, reads, and writes Chinese fluently. She has a charming old-style Chinese wooden house in a park-like area for faculty housing. Her faithful companion is her small dog, Viola, who is ugly enough to be cute. Viola has the habit of going out for a walk with Miranda, and then simply lying down on the sidewalk until she's carried home. The biggest and most loved object in the house is a grand piano that Miranda plays and on which she teaches some very talented private students. Many of the friends she invites over are also musicians or opera singers, so a casual evening together always ends up in making music. Thus, either "live" or on tape, the house is always awash with magnificent melodies.

I have not had good impressions of missionaries in general, and especially in China where they infiltrate China in every way they can, including masquerading as English teachers so they can proselytize and convert. While staying at hostels in Hong Kong, I have seen young groups of missionaries preparing to go into China by hiding Bible tracts in among personal items they didn't think would be checked by officials.

Miranda's group of missionaries does not proselytize. They believe that they can influence people through their behavior, friendliness, and ability to communicate directly in Chinese which all of them are required to learn very well. So, even though I sleep under a quote about Jesus from the Bible, it is in Chinese and Miranda never mentions religion to me.

MEANDERING WITH THE WANDERING JEW

I'm sure I am quite crazy—dancing with a dog and singing Christmas carols to harp music in a missionary's home in Taiwan. A thrill ran through me yesterday when I looked around my class of friendly Taiwanese girls while singing an off-key "Rudolph the Red-Nosed Reindeer" to them.

It's Christmas, a new year, an upcoming trip to China and my kids, a chance to act like Santa Claus, a nice university job to return to, and a lovely room made of wood instead of concrete to live in away from the burning dump.

My Christmas Eve was wonderful, with variety—my spice of life—predominating. Rose joined me for a Christmas Eve celebration at the church Emily had taken me to when I lived in her house. It was fun to see some of the people who had been so kind to me my first four months in Taichung.

Then, I returned to Providence University. Standing all the way on the bus, my mind wandered over other roads I have taken around the world. At the convent at Providence University, I had a leisurely chat with two of the American nuns. They said that the Catholic Church was becoming less rigid. I told them about the night I woke up in the mountains of the Sinai and saw more stars overhead than I could have ever imagined.

At midnight, I attended a touching Mass with the nuns. They wish everyone *pin an*, the Chinese word for peace. It seems a futile wish now as Iraq prepares more and more for war. The Mass was all in Chinese with a very capable Chinese-speaking American priest. I wished him *shalom*, the Hebrew word for peace. Besides hearing Chinese, I could tell I was in the Chinese culture because they brought incense as a gift to Jesus, and had a Chinese gong.

When I got locked out of the building where I was staying that night, I was led by the hand of a Chinese angel named Angela to an open door.

Jan. 16, 1991

Is there war in Israel yet? I wonder as I sit here listening to a student concert at Tung Hai University. I ponder the paradox of humans who can produce both music and war. One can make one forget the other, but only temporarily. I see the snapshot in my mind once again of an ugly Uzi rifle placed next to a delicate violin on which the soldier-musician had just played a very beautiful concert. It was during my first time in Israel in 1982 when I was a volunteer on a *kibbutz* and the Lebanon War broke out. I may be far away in distance, but the pathos of Israel is always with me.

10

CHINA TAIWAN 1991

Feb. 8, 1991

Once again I am a fairy godmother, Santa Claus, confidante, companion, and a precious treasure that is passed along lovingly from one to another. I've made a varied schedule to make use of my vacation time, seeing as many of my friends as possible. So far, I've walked with friends around wonderful West Lake and sat on "my bench" on the Su Causeway, eaten the Hangzhou specialty of Beggar's Chicken that I like so well, chatted with Thomas, Jerry, Smith, Pearl, Diana, and Debbie. I was truly pleased to learn that Russell and Frank have been keeping up a frequent correspondence in spite of the complications of Frank writing Chinese in the traditional style of Taiwan and Russell in the simplified style of mainland China.

At such moments, it doesn't seem to matter that I caught cold again, or that I couldn't take a bath or shower because the water temperature kept changing radically. Then, I couldn't turn off the bathtub faucets at all, so an attendant had to come and bang the faucets closed. The cold and the discomfort somehow blend into a general feeling of happiness, of never having enjoyed spending my money so much.

Feb. 11, 1991

The New Year of the Sheep is fast approaching. Russell, Bill, and Richard accompanied me to Xiquo to meet some of my tourism school students who are working here now. Last night we went to a "dancing party." Richard has been practicing and is a very fluid dancer. He and my tourism student made wonderful dancing partners. The steps are the same ballroom dancing I tried to learn long ago as a teenager. I surprised myself at still having stamina for fast dancing. I particularly enjoyed when special lighting turned us all into slow motion dancing figures like in old-time movies.

I discovered that Bill sings very well. It was the first time I saw Karaoke, but I've heard it's very popular in Asia. I'm not sure if it has caught on in the U.S. There is a screen with pictures and the words of a song accompanied by music. The singing is provided by whomever holds the microphone. I liked listening to people with good voices like Bill's, but I didn't enjoy those with bad voices. Since my singing voice is not good, I can't imagine wanting it to be amplified. However, the boys explained that there is a good reason why even people with bad voices like to sing Karaoke at dancing parties. That's because Chinese culture makes it difficult to talk about their emotions. But there are no inhibitions on singing one's emotions to others, and no criticism of bad voices.

Feb. 12, 1991

The day dawned at the same time as the attendant entered my room, threw open the curtains, and left a thermos bottle of hot water on the table. Chinese have no concept of locks on hotel doors or sleeping in. Involuntarily awake, I felt playful. The bed was rather high off the ground, and the floor was fairly clean, so I decided to play a joke on the boys.

When they entered the room, I was nowhere to be seen. They called around for me and discussed possibilities of where I might be. But they saw that the waist belt holding my money and passport was still there, so they didn't think I'd gone far. When they went to check out the lobby and yard, I scooted back under the puffy quilts. When they returned, I was lying in bed "asleep." They peered over the quilts in disbelief. They claimed I had not been in the room when they looked before. I assured them I hadn't moved from under the quilts.

I don't think I'll ever tell them the truth. It was too perfect.

The day was equally perfect with blue skies and warmish weather. Colorful quilts decorated the railings of the bridge next to the hotel. People love airing everything on warm, sunny, winter days.

Feb. 16, 1991

The New Year of the Sheep—my, Russell and Richard's year—is here for its once every 12 year cycle. I'm writing in front of Richard's home. The sun is setting. The air is nippy, but fresh and clean and light, not heavy like in Taiwan. The view is far and green, and the feelings are warm and friendly.

I judge my happiness by whether or not I want to be anywhere else or with anyone else at this time. And I don't. The whole cold, uncomfortable time has been exactly where I've wanted to be and with whom. It is an accomplishment to be here that took planning, persistence, guts, and money. Few Americans have ever heard old Chinese instruments bringing new-year luck to a poor peasant family in rural China. I'm a beloved guest as I go from one family to another. My gifts—both large and ridiculously small—have been received with great pleasure. I feel like the Pied Piper. On a walk through the village rice paddies with Richard, we looked back and saw that people had come out of every home we had passed to get a better look at "the foreigner." The many children in the neighborhood gather around me to play with the various simple toys and games I brought. They don't get to see many toys in their childhood, especially western children's toys. One of Richard's little nephews thinks my name is "Hello" because that's what people tell him to say when he sees me. The plumpest lady in the village came by to check whether she or I was fatter. I'd say it was a draw.

One of Richard's sisters sews pants in a factory. She made a pair to give to me. Alas, she proportioned them for a Chinese girl's figure. She kept stitching in more and more material to make them fit me. It was embarrassing for both of us. They were more successful in hand-stitching a pair of shoes for me. I've never had hand-stitched shoes before.

A PEASANT MATRIARCH

She is short. She is strong.
She has false teeth and clear eyes.
She stoops over agilely to pick up the leavings from her sweeping.
She enjoys the sun while her nimble fingers stitch a homemade shoe.
She speaks little.
She goes to bed early and rises with the sun.
She knows where she is rooted, to whom, and why.
What goes on in her mind, I do not know.
She is the matriarch of a family—a dynasty of her own.
She is a peasant grandmother in rural China.
She and I are friends of a sort.
We cannot talk, but we share mutual respect.

PEASANT AND PARADOX

A simple life. A pure life. Not without its pain, but also not without its joys. It is a closely-knit family system in which the main goal is a full rice bowl and to propagate itself. It is physically a hard life. It is spiritually almost one-dimensional. It offers everything to the parents, but much less to their few college-educated offspring. Sometimes the generation gap becomes a generation gulf. Life, meaning, love, purpose, stimulation. Can an educated mind be filled by a peasant's life? But, the intellectual son is often a much less fulfilled person than his peasant father. Is there any resolution, or just the bumbling along of living a paradox?

Feb. 19, 1991

On that day in Taiwan when I heard the missiles exploding in Tel Aviv, I was quite sure I would return to Israel after China in time of war with Iraq. Thanks to the technology of instant news around the world, BBC on my short-wave radio recorded the explosions precisely as they fell. I screamed as I heard each one hit. They were not screams of fear. They were the primal screams of grief as I mourned for those who might have died with each loud boom.

In Hong Kong, I called the Israeli Embassy to discuss returning to help in the war. A kind lady said I certainly could return if I wanted to, but realistically what use would I be without medical training? Fortunately, I don't have to make the decision because war with Iraq seems to have been averted, at least for now. So, I will return to Taiwan to finish out my teaching year. However, I know the bad air will drive me out of Taiwan after the school year finishes. Where after that? I don't know. It was so hard to leave Hangzhou and know I'll once again be too far to chat with my friends, too far to laugh together, too far to walk around West Lake together.

A SUBJECTIVE PERSPECTIVE ON TAIWAN

Taiwan was once a beautiful island peopled by aborigines who lived a close-to-nature lifestyle much like the American Indians did. The Chinese from Fujian Province in China came over long ago and pushed the aborigines into the mountains. Basically untouched by white men, except for a brief time by the Dutch, the Hakka people developed into Taiwanese. Japan occupied Taiwan for 50 years from 1895 to 1945 when the Taiwanese threw them out. In the present generation, there appears to be little anger left about this occupation, perhaps because the Japanese instilled a certain orderliness and modern technology that made it easier for Taiwan to become a "developed" country.

In 1949, Chiang Kai Shek escaped from mainland China with innumerable followers to set up the Kuomintang government on Taiwan in defiance of the Communists. In the process, the occupiers murdered thousands of the Taiwanese.

And there it rests today. The aborigines have become a focal point for Christian missionaries, as well as a tourist curiosity. The present day Taiwanese-born whose parents came from mainland China feel they are in exile from their motherland. Even Taiwanese from Fujian extraction feel they are connected to China by being Chinese.

Though physically indistinguishable to me, there is tension between the Taiwanese and the Chinese who arrived after 1949. The older generation of Taiwanese hate the mainland Chinese for their cruelty to the Taiwanese and the systematic degradation of the Taiwanese culture, especially the Taiwanese language which is different from the mainland Chinese language and is not allowed to be spoken in school or government.

The Kuomintang government remains in power, although it has been losing power to the DPP Party, which calls for Taiwan's independence. That means that Taiwan will no longer be a province of mainland China, which the Kuomintang and Communist China claim it to be. Like David and Goliath, tiny Taiwan lives in dread of being attacked by the gargantuan mainland if Taiwan declares itself a separate country. China constantly renews its threat of invasion. Taiwan, like Israel, lives in constant fear and preparedness for war.

What are the people of Taiwan like? Like most of the world, they are in awe of the U.S. and its lifestyle. However, having become newly rich in the last ten years or so, they can teach even Americans something about materialism. They flaunt it every way they can, in as obvious and gaudy a way as possible. Everything is overdone. If budgets allow, they are willing to pay any price and have little regard for quality. They pay out money as freely as they make it. They are generous in ways and to a degree that Americans aren't. A lot of the generosity is kind and sincere, while some is for gaining "face."

While Americans stress self-respect, Chinese want the respect of others. This emphasis on acceptable codes of behavior reminds me of both the Arab and Ethiopian cultures, which rely heavily on a group mentality. And, like Ethiopians and Arabs, they also have a very strong, durable, devoted family system. The father rules, and girls are of less interest and value. There is a responsibility to each other, and respect for the old. Arabs, Ethiopians, and Chinese make the best students because of a solid respect for teachers ingrained in them.

In bureaucracy and politics, Israel and Taiwan seem similar. Both say what they feel they have to, but do what is expedient. What Americans call "lying," Taiwanese and Israelis might call "survival." And, if a law is not liked for whatever reason, it will be ignored if possible, or circumvented if necessary. Rarely would it be openly challenged as in America because that's inefficient, a waste of time, impolite, and unnecessary.

As in all cultures, there are the paradoxes. The polite, gentle, kind Taiwanese become something else when behind the wheel of a car or motorscooter. Even Israelis would find it a challenge to cross a street in Taiwan, or drive down one. The only other place I have seen such aggression is in competition. They are bred for competition from an early age since their educational system is limited and geared for the best. This unfortunate fact has put too much pressure on little ones who need play as much as study. Some teenagers dump responsibilities and join the pleasure circuit, which has led to a higher juvenile delinquency rate, as well as a climbing crime rate which includes arson, kidnapping, and extortion as ways to get rich.

Another paradox is that this Chinese culture, which is able to paint, draw, and compose delicate verses to the beauty of nature, defiles and violates nature flagrantly and unabashedly. This does not only apply to garbage being strewn carelessly, but the worse pollution in every category. The wonderfully sensitive and aesthetic Chinese have turned their water and air into an abomination, and they have constructed the ugliest cities of any I've seen in the world. Only the wild, uncooperative mountains defy destruction. In conjunction with a mentality that lags behind its technological capabilities, safety standards of all kinds are far behind western standards.

How do they differ from their mainland Chinese brothers? Basically, the Taiwanese have kept traditions that communism has destroyed in China. Buddhist temples here are very alive with children, parents, and grandparents in contrast to the temples in China filled mostly with curious foreign tourists. Religion is part of their daily lives, filled with superstitions and ancestor worship. I find their caring for dead ancestors a very effective way to feel rooted to something, to feel a part of something bigger than oneself.

Taiwanese girls differ from their Chinese mainland sisters in giggling more and being more delicate and traditional in spite of the fact that their ideas are more westernized.

Of course, the biggest difference between Taiwanese and mainlanders is that the Taiwanese are free—free to think, free to choose, free to leave, free to do. However, the hardships of the mainland young people have forged a deeper character, yet purer and more innocent.

Taiwan is in many stages of transition. I am grateful to Taiwan, my Taiwanese friends, and my Taiwanese students for warmly accepting me into their homes and hearts. I value them, and I value what Taiwan is—and is becoming. It's an exciting place to be. If only I could breathe here, I'd linger longer. I'm sure I will never find a place that will offer me as many jobs or make me feel more wanted.

March 3, 1991

In the dark of night, it is gaily colorful to see the young people and children wandering around carrying lanterns for the happy and beautiful Lantern Festival. I'm here in Taipei with Rose to celebrate. The delicate Chinese traditional art contrasts with the abstract sheep under laser lights.

This morning, surrounded by paper flowers and artfully composed bouquets with a reminder of Matisse on the wall, I sat in a Taipei street. Taipei, Taiwan, is a mixture of both life and simulation of life, boxed-in-store next to boxed-in-temple, each adored by the same people. Bald, nude, wig-coifed western mannequins lined the streets and boxy shops. Those that were clothed were dressed gaudily, exotically, girlishly, ugily. The air was deadly, but the streets were alive on this Sunday morning during Lantern Festival that traditionally ends the welcoming of this new year—my year, the Year of the Sheep.

March 4, 1991

I finally got to meet another member of the SERVAS group, Fiona, who graciously took me out to eat. After the meal, she deftly picked her nose with the long fingernail of her pinky finger, and then delicately inserted her findings into the empty clamshell on her plate. She then took a toothpick and politely put one hand over her mouth while she picked her teeth clean. All meals I've had in China and Taiwan end with a busy toothpick in one hand while the other hand shields the mouth. It is impolite not to do so.

I most likely won't get to see Fiona again because a fortuneteller had told her she must leave Taiwan soon and she has already quit her job and bought a ticket to the U.S. Such is the power of the words of a fortuneteller to many in China and Taiwan.

March 17, 1991

Happy St. Patrick's Day! It doesn't create much of a stir in Taiwan. I'll always remember the deep green of St. Patrick's Day in New Orleans.

I am fortunate to have my own apartment now around the corner from Miranda's home. She knew an opera professor who had gone on sabbatical and asked her if I could stay in her apartment for the rest of the semester. The air is still deadly, but the view is more open. I'll enjoy it for the next few months, but

I've already given Providence University notice that I will not return to teach next fall. The Chairwoman of the Department really wants me to stay and has made me an attractive offer, including a rare work visa. She can't quite believe my decision to leave is final. Rose and the other teachers also find it difficult to understand how I can give up such a good job. They agree that the air is bad, but to give up a good job because of air pollution? But I made a promise to my body that I would get us out of this deadly air if I could keep my health until it was time to go.

March 19, 1991

I finally got the answer to a question that has been puzzling me since I first started teaching in Taiwan.

"If both you and my mainland Chinese students speak the same native language, why is their English so much better than yours?" I bluntly asked my Taiwanese students.

"Mainland students are more desperate," was the reply that made the most sense. Taiwanese have money, options, and opportunities that my mainland students don't have. Every one of my former students in China is desperately unhappy with his or her job and future prospects. It is not that they are overworked. On the contrary, the boredom at work is part of what depresses them. They must come and put in their time, but they say they can do all their work in perhaps 30 minutes and then spend the rest of the day drinking endless cups of tea, chatting, and reading newspapers. China has too many people who need to work, so the government hires and supports most of them with housing, medical care, and a small salary. Predictability, security, and a guarantee of three bowls of rice a day sounded good to those who had suffered so terribly during the cruelty, insecurity, and famines of the Cultural Revolution. But my students were only babies in the late 1960's.

Now in their energetic 20's, they complain bitterly of being "stuck" for life unless they give up their secure, dead-end government jobs and risk going into a joint venture company. Most of the joint venture companies with other countries deal with import and export and they need people who are fluent in Chinese and English, the international language of today. So, lacking money and options, English has become their key to a better life.

March 21, 1991

The air here doesn't allow me to even think of jogging around the track or doing strenuous exercise. But, the swimming pool is indoors and I love to swim. So,

Rose comes by after my last class on Tuesday afternoons and we go to the pool together. Afterward, we go to a steakhouse on campus. The steaks come out sizzling on hot platters, and I love the ritual Taiwanese have of holding a big napkin in front of their chests when, with a flourish, the waitress takes the top off the sizzling platter.

March 29, 1991

Today was a school holiday, so I went to an American movie with Miranda and Rose and had the chance to compare movie cultures. In Taiwan, movie theatres are often located on upper floors reached by narrow, long, winding staircases with no exits. People smoke anywhere they want to. Unlike Israel, there are no previews of coming attractions or advertisements, and they flash phone messages on the screen to people in the audience. Although no country I've been in loves to munch through movies as much as Americans, Israel absolutely forbids eating inside the theatres. In Taiwan, like Israel, they cut off the ending before the credits. Then, everyone exits crowded together on the narrow, long, winding staircases. I began to have the same sense of panic rising as I did back in New Orleans when I was caught once in a surging crowd on Bourbon Street during Mardi Gras.

April 3, 1991

The Buddha stands; I sit. Perhaps we are both listening. Listening to what? To the clean air as the wind rushes past us.

Wind, where are you rushing to? River, where are you running to? You rush; I rest. Your rushing helps me relax.

I have been too long out of nature. I have been too long out of air. I need nature. I need fresh air—the kind that you can't smell, the kind that is light and colorless and kind.

Why is mankind so unkind to the air? But air will have its revenge on us.

I am spending some much needed time with Smokey the Bear's Taiwanese cousin, Smo Wang Lee. He lives in Taroko Gorge on the eastern side of the island of Taiwan. I have discovered Santa Barbara's twin sister, Hualien, a small city neatly tucked away between the ocean and the mountains. I have also found California Route 1's twin brother. The two sides of the Pacific are identical, no matter how many thousands of miles divide them.

For three days now I have actually been breathing. It's a wonderful feeling. I have discovered that good air is the absence of what you can see and smell and taste. And oh, it is so light! It floats around you and in you in a way I can appreciate much more since I have a deeper acquaintance with heavy, smelly, thick air that corrodes my innards.

Coming here was an adventure on a rather frightening road that can barely be called a road at all. Nature and this eight-hour wonder of a path crossing the mountains are in constant conflict with portions of the road regularly dropping into the abyss or being covered by mudslides. It was spectacular, to be sure, made more exciting by coming in above the clouds and looking down only on fog. We were driven by your typical impatient, betel-nut chewing and spewing bus driver who hates being behind schedule no matter what the road conditions. The corkscrew road added nausea and people throwing up all around me to this mixture.

I came here because I thought I would go absolutely crazy if I couldn't breathe some air that didn't feel like lead in my lungs. Rose told me to go to Hualien during our few days of vacation because that side of the island isn't heavily populated or polluted.

Once I saw, and felt in my lungs, how wonderful Hualien is, I wondered about finding a teaching job here for next year. However, less population also means fewer schools. I've applied to a Buddhist nursing school, and I met an aborigine girl who suggested I apply to teach aborigines at the Bible College. I tried, but was told that all their teachers must be Christian. I was a bit upset about that, but then realized I am the citizen of a whole country that requires its immigrants to be Jewish.

Not much hope for work in Hualien, but I got to breathe good air for a few days and have seen, literally and figuratively, another side of Taiwan.

April 16, 1991

I have already experienced many things in life I never expected. And, it's happened again. I'm a grandmother! Elizabeth, my companion at the tourism school, wrote that she has had a baby girl and formally asked me to be her foreign grandmother. I feel so honored. She has asked me to give her an English name. I want to follow the Chinese tradition of naming a child something with a meaning, so I'm thinking carefully about it.

May 3, 1991

"I'm not sure whether I'm alive or dead," was the way Russell's letter began. Getting mail from China has been additionally unreliable because Providence University has never quite figured out who and where I am. So, it was really just chance that a student of mine eventually saw it somewhere and brought it to me.

I was distressed enough to make the impulsive decision to go to China for a week or so because there's no way to reach Russell by phone. I've found substitutes for my classes, bought my ticket, and now sit surrounded by my rushed packing for China. It will still take me a few days to get there because the political divide between China and Taiwan won't allow direct flights. I have to go through Hong Kong and apply for a visa into China.

Russell's skin disease has plagued his body and burdened his mind since high school when he first got it. Although I've heard of no cure for this skin disease, Russell still desperately wants to find a cure. He has been to a Chinese witch doctor who chanted for his health, axed a certain tree to make a paste of its sap to rub on his body, and has taken several smelly Chinese herbal remedies that seem to weaken his body and his liver more than help the disease. He wrote that this outbreak has been so bad, that he is now trying a treatment that requires him to be caked in mud for most of the day. Not only is the disease torture, but so are the ineffective treatments.

I'm not sure what use I can be, but I feel I want to be there to offer whatever comfort I can. The other teachers were really sweet about substituting in my classes.

May 17, 1991

Through no fault of my own, I'm having the rare treat of sitting in business class with classical music, a super wide seat, and a seat upstairs in the bubble of the plane I've always wondered about on a 747. Definitely "a new taste" as Richard would say. Except that the smokers are not too far behind me since there isn't really any separation of smokers from non-smokers in business class. They upgraded me because of a lack of economy seats. The flights between Hong Kong and Taipei always seem full. In this comfort, I can mull over the whirlwind trip I've just had to China.

In spite of the emergency nature of it, I enjoyed being there very much. For whatever reasons, I am never happier and never feel better than when I'm in dirty, inconvenient China. I was able to breathe cleaner air and felt the comfort and serenity of nature in the countryside. I was even able to sleep better in China. I grow more at home in China and think more often of coming back to live and teach in Hangzhou.

I was able to contact Bill by his work phone and he met me in Hangzhou and then accompanied me to Russell's countryside village. At the bus station in the small town from where we had to walk to Russell's village, an actual circle of curious Chinese formed around me. I knew it was curiosity, but I thought they would simply look at me and then go on about their business. However, they just kept staring at me. So, even without being able to sing or dance, I was a "hit" with the local people.

Bill and I wound our way on the narrow paths through the rice paddies and eventually came to Russell's home. Needless to say, the family was quite shocked to see me but immediately welcomed me warmly. Russell's deep depression lifted a bit while I was there. I felt the relationship with his parents deepening, non-verbal as it must be.

Russell was not the only one who is depressed. The depression was very obvious in all of them—Jerry, Richard, Thomas, Diana, Debbie. They can't see any future for themselves. We did have some time for fun and laughter. I think bringing them joy is my joy. Russell said he is mobilized now to mentally endure six more weeks of that terrible treatment. China, China, "the ache that won't go away."

I made plans with them for my return to China after I finish the semester in Taiwan. These days were perfect weather in Hangzhou, but when I come back, it will be very hot, especially for traveling around China together. Even so, I will be so glad to be on the arrival side of the airport rather than the departure side.

June 9, 1991

There was a different air around the campus yesterday in addition to the pollution. It was graduation day, and since this may be my only year as a university professor, I wanted very much to go.

The campus had flags flying and was filled with happy parents, grandparents, and siblings all busily taking pictures of their daughters, granddaughters, and sisters in their black caps and gowns. It is a Taiwanese tradition for the girls to carry a bouquet of beautiful flowers. And so the girls made a wonderful garden together.

I went into the auditorium, which had been transformed into a garden too. The front of the stage had several large pots of flowers with ribbons and Chinese writing. As a professor, I got to sit in the front row. Soon after I walked in, the ceremony began. All the officials of Providence University marched in, plus what looked like an important man because of several security guards. The guards were not dressed in uniforms, but they looked all alike in navy blue silk suits, intense watchful eyes, and one earphone.

I wondered at all the security, but I had never been to a big event here, so I thought it might just be normal. Two people sitting next to me were asked to move and were replaced by two silk-suited men.

Not understanding the speech, I entertained myself by watching the security guards. The ones next to me never took their eyes off the speaker. There were three men on each side of the stage, but not on the stage, whose eyes continuously swept over a very defined area of each part of the audience. When some people from the audience crowded forward to take pictures, the security men next to me got nervous.

I looked at the cameras. It was better than a camera exhibition, and represented enough money to build a small university. After the crush of photographers left, a young man came up with two magnificent Nikon cameras with different lenses. He very carefully arranged each photo before taking it. The slow, deliberate way he framed each picture reminded me of the way Russell takes pictures.

When the important man finished his speech, all the security men rushed forward to flank him as he walked out of the auditorium followed by the enthusiastic camera-clicking group. I asked the man next to me who the speaker was. "The President," he said. "The President of what?" I innocently and ignorantly asked. His reply, however, was drowned out. Later, I learned that it was indeed the President of Taiwan.

I loved watching the students receive their degrees and have their tassels placed on the opposite side of their mortarboards to signify "graduate." There was an orchestra playing traditional Chinese music as the graduates marched. How nice to be at a Chinese graduation! However, I felt sad that my mainland students graduated without any ceremony, caps and gowns, pictures and bouquets.

While watching the ceremony, I had a little chat with a very huge picture on stage. In the Chinese way of idolizing leaders, the huge picture was placed on the even huger flag of Taiwan, which I've been told is also the Kuomintang flag. I thought the good-looking face up there belonged to Chiang Kai Shek, the Kuomintang leader, and I thanked him for my good 18 months in Taiwan. I was later told that this beloved man was Sun Yat Sen. But, perhaps he would forgive me, a dumb foreigner, for such a mistake.

I doubt I could have been happier had it been my own graduation. I thought back to how I had cried in 1983 on the day I received my Master's of Social Work and knew I was soon to leave the U.S. to emigrate to Israel. It's only a ritual, to be sure. But I have come to appreciate such rituals.

June 22, 1991

It is once again a sleepless night. I have had so many of them in my 1 ½ years in Taiwan. I so hope I will leave this insomnia behind when I leave Taiwan. My body tires, but my mind doesn't. Instead, it flits from here to there, thought to thought, solving problems and mentally writing "to do" lists.

Flit, flit—Taiwan has not been at all good for my body, but strangely my face looks younger. Perhaps it is only an optical illusion, but it seems true that my face looks better, but is stuck on a fat lady's body.

Flit, flit—It's so hard to break engrained belief patterns, even in the face of reality. To Chinese, Americans have blue eyes and blonde hair. So, in answer to a final oral exam question to describe me, several of my students turned my brown eyes to blue, and my very brown hair to blonde.

Flit, flit—I'm not at all sure what this summer in China will hold, but I'm anxious to go back.

Flit, flit—to Les, my former husband, who is turning 50 when I knew him at 16. The years have not exactly flown by, but a lot of years have passed.

Flit, flit—I remember the atmosphere of Bali as I listen to the music of Bali on the tape. The music does not help me sleep, but makes me long to return. Bali was not a dream. My knowing it truly does exist helps me to accept this world.

Flit, flit—I must find some time to write my friends in Israel before I go back into China. Israel is never very far from my thoughts. Israel and China seem to crowd my mind at times.

Flit, flit—I will have to leave the good parts of Taiwan along with the bad air. Except for the gruesome air, Taiwan is a sweet memory. I hope at least Rose and Virginia will keep in touch.

Flit, flit—I will never really get used to goodbyes even though my life lends itself to many and continuous goodbyes. It is as true today as the night I rather hysterically composed it years ago—

Piece by piece,
Goodbye by goodbye,
I die.

11

CHINA MACAU Summer, 1991

July 17, 1991

I sit on the highest floor of the highest building in Ningbo watching the sunset over the river. It is a wonderful room arranged by one of my former students. They do take good care of me and their job connections in tourism sometimes make that easier.

Before Ningbo, Richard, Russell, Bill and I took the boat out to Putho Island. We swam in the ocean and Bill thought I was a wonderful swimmer. We walked along 1,000-Step Beach (Chinese seem to love hiking up and down steps), and wandered through the medieval city, which looked even more dramatic by candlelight because the underwater cable bringing electricity to the island broke. It had a bit of the Old City in Jerusalem feel except for everyone being Chinese.

The three of them are finding it harder and harder to communicate in English since they aren't exposed to English as they were when they were students. They are taking the vitamins I brought them, but also smoking (although away from me). Bill has tried to explain to me that smoking is culturally mandatory for Chinese men. Offering cigarettes to other men and chatting while smoking is an expected cultural ritual that makes business and socializing friendlier. Although I have seen a few Chinese men who don't smoke, I have to admit that most of them do seem to enjoy these social cigarette exchanges. Fortunately for me, it is rare to see females smoking. Apparently they have other ways to "bond" socially.

Next, it's back to Hangzhou where we'll re-group, pick up Jerry and go off to Wenzhou, which they've told me is an up and coming city of businessmen.

July 24, 1991

We sometimes resemble a comedy team, which makes it easier for me to keep my sense of humor when the group dynamics get rocky. Indeed, our trip to Wenzhou started out rocky when we took a crowded all-night bus ride from Hangzhou. Besides exhaustion, there was extreme discomfort all the bumpy way in the very back of the bus with only one brief pit stop at a toilet that was too disgusting to use.

I guess I could call this time together a fiasco with fun sprinkled here and there. Jerry, more serious and sophisticated than the others, was in shock at all the dirt, travel difficulties, weird interpersonal relationships, and being slapped by some hooligans at the bus station which equals a large loss of face to a Chinese person. He also left his camera behind at one of the hotels we stayed in. Fortunately, the staff people saved it for him. Richard doesn't feel well and he confided to me privately that he had gotten into big trouble on his job and didn't know yet how he would be punished. Russell is physically quite weak and is a picky eater who can't eat many foods that interact badly with the Chinese medicine he's taking. Bill hasn't been too communicative with anyone. Unlike my tourism students, none of them is very good at negotiating details like transportation, finding our way, getting accommodations—things I depend upon them to do.

I think I've enjoyed the trip more than any of them. Wenzhou is a bustling city on the move. We went out to some mountains outside Wenzhou that are known for having beautiful waterfalls. But, like people, nature also has its "moods," so the spectacular waterfalls had dried up for lack of rain this season. Still, it was pretty in the mountains. I swam in a natural pond with water that felt so clean and good. The air was fresh and my insomnia only crept in occasionally. I loved the walk we took in the mountains with a wizened old guide who could explain about the temple we visited high in the rocks. During the trip, there was sometimes laughter among us, and some good chats with each boy. We may not have gotten along so well together, but in some strange way, I feel we are closer and more familiar with each other.

August 2, 1991

I am out at sea (hopefully not lost at sea) on my way to Dalian with only Russell. At this moment I am one of the very few awake as bodies lay strewn about. Although the boat is filthy, I feel quite clean and cool. I went out into the open air to sleep. There I was on my trusty purple plastic poncho, new blow-up pillow (how did I ever survive China without one?), and quite comfy remembering last year out on the deck of another boat with Richard while he told me stories about the constellations. Then came a strong bolt of lightning and I imagined myself electrocuted on the steel deck. "Strange foreigner fried on deck of boat somewhere between Shanghai and Dalian," a newspaper headline might read.

I then put the poncho on and enjoyed the bigger and bigger drops of rain. It gave me the cleanest feeling I'd had all day. And, of course, I breathed the air deeply. I was thankful for the air and the rivers of rain dripping down my body that were not the rivers of sweat that I'd felt earlier in the hot day. I stripped and washed in the ladies' room while a couple of Chinese girls tried not to notice my flab.

At the last minute, Richard backed out of coming with Russell and me for our long summer excursion. He was too worried about the ramifications of his punishment at the school where he works. Since he has a government job, they can't fire him, but they can demote him from a teacher to a worker in a factory. He felt he must give up the trip to stay there and learn his fate.

August 3, 1991

And so today we are still on the sea on our way to Dalian. We should arrive tomorrow morning. Out at sea, I didn't sweat all day! It was a pleasant enough day. The group in our cabin didn't smoke inside the cabin and I engaged them in playing Old Maid. I have sponge-bathed both nights at midnight and feel relatively clean.

I spent a lot of time on the bow of the boat, especially at night alone. Probably only the captain of the boat and I were awake. It is often quite easy to find privacy in crowded places in China because they are so group-oriented. You can rarely found one alone anywhere. I breathed the air and felt and watched the sea. My mind wandered many places it had not gone in a long time—no spectacular revelations, but with a certain nostalgia and peace.

August 8, 1991

Dalian has offered some good, some bad, and some ugly. I endured the humiliation of being charged as a foreigner four times the price of Russell's bed. In this hotel, as in many, a Chinese person pays for one bed in a double room and is given a roommate. However, a single foreigner is charged double the price for each bed in a double room and must pay in the inflated FEC money.

Being by the ocean, I expected Dalian to be beautiful, but we found out that its beauty is only selectively true. We were so disappointed when we went to one beach and found it garbage and trash-strewn. However, on the "other side" of Tiger Beach, we found a beautiful California look-alike beach that was picture perfect among some large boulders. I let the sounds of the waves clean out my mind.

We took a tour out to what is advertised as The Colorful City. And, indeed, it was a very pleasant departure from the usual drab Chinese buildings. Every building was new and clean. The palette of colors reminded me somewhat of residential streets in San Francisco. We walked around a lot, soaking up this unique décor.

August 11, 1991

The "best" time to see the northern city of Harbin is in the dead of winter when the city comes alive with massive ice sculptures. I can't imagine myself ever being here in such cold weather, so I had to settle for seeing it in the summer. Unfortunately, some of its prettiest parks are closed off because the Song Hua River has risen too high and may flood.

The northern Chinese are much taller and fuller than their southern counterparts. They eat much more meat and wheat. In some places, I can even find tasty hard bread from Russia because we're so close to Russia up here. We usually ordered way too much because the portions were so huge compared to southern China. In one restaurant, one of the local young men was so excited at seeing a foreigner up close, he asked me several questions through Russell. Then, he ran out of the restaurant and returned quickly with a gift of a fan with the city of Harbin on it. I felt like a movie star.

On the other hand, people notice my shabby clothes, especially my well-worn sandals. Because I'm always traveling in dust and dirt, I dress accordingly. Not so the Chinese. They may not own many clothes, but they do not dress shabbily. Russell overheard some Harbin residents muttering that I must be Russian because Americans are rich and dress well, complete with gold jewelry.

Harbin's residents love to socialize. In the wintertime, there are many large areas set aside for ice skating, complete with music. In the summertime, people gather at these same locations to dance with each other until late in the night. A man from North Korea asked me to dance. Unfortunately, with our language barrier, we didn't get past "One, two, three."

August 12, 1991

We arrived in the cool, neat, small city of Qiqihar with the goal of seeing the Zhalong Crane Reserve. At the train station, we were "adopted" by a father-daughter team who drove a taxi. Apparently, they expect to be our transportation all the time we're in their city. Even though the ticket agent said there were no sleeper tickets for the train to our next destination, Hohhot, the daughter promised to get us sleeper tickets. Can we trust her? Generally, the people here are a mixture of minorities, quite friendly with lots of smiles.

We took the long ride out to see the cranes. It was such a pretty marsh, I spent some time lying on the ground by myself and talking to the spirit of the marsh.

Marsh: "Hello. Welcome to our spot. Nice to have a new visitor."

Me: "Yes, I'd like to rest a while and join you and your friends. It seems like a truly wonderful spot."

Marsh: "Yes, it's nice to live here. The air is fresh, the breeze is sweet, and the cranes and other birds liven up the place every year during their migration."

Me: "Looking up I can see the waving reeds and the wide, blue sky with puffy clouds stretching across it."

Marsh: "It's a good place to rest. I can tell your eyes are ready to close. I'll wait with you while you rest."

Me: "I feel like I'm sinking into the ground and joining the marsh. It feels like a friendly, nice place. And the sun feels good on my body."

Marsh: "Yes, it's quite a nice spot to drift into sleep."

Me: "You know, tomorrow's my birthday. I'll be 48 years old. That's not particularly momentous, but I wonder if I should think momentous thoughts now about my life up to now."

Marsh: "Oh, that's not necessary. Just join us in our serenity. I get the feeling you want to come closer to nature."

Me: "Relationships with people can be quite confusing and troublesome. I want a deeper relationship with nature, but maybe it's also hard to be close to nature."

Marsh: "Don't worry about that now. Perhaps it will get clearer as you get closer."

Me: "Actually, except for some sagging parts of my body, I feel very, very healthy and well. I am quite lucky really."

Marsh: "Yes, you look strong and healthy compared to a lot of Chinese people. But their lives are hard."

Me: "That's true. I've had a physically easy life and good nutrition. If my health lasts, I can do everything. If it doesn't, I'm not sure I'll mentally be able to cope with that. But, for now, I can enjoy my feeling of health."

Marsh: "It's true that nothing stays the same. Our marsh is in a good mood now, but sometimes it's in a terrible mood and then I'm not sure you'd like it."

Me: "That sounds like the young friend I'm traveling with. He is often in a silent mood, and sometimes a dark mood. It puzzles me why I am sometimes miserable with him, but miss him when he's not around."

Marsh: "Sorry, I can't help you figure out loving and caring for others. I've never figured it out either."

Me: "I have a peach and a banana here. Would you like to share them? I'd like to eat here with you. I feel so relaxed now. The sounds here are really wonderful.

There is silence, and then the voice of the reeds as the wind comes through. This place has something to touch every sense. I travel the world and I seem to need change. Does it ever bother you to stay in one place all your life as you do?"

Marsh: "I never thought about it. We who come from nature do not think like you who are human. I feel content here most of the time. In the bad times, I do my best. I don't have a long life, after all."

Me: "Well, I probably should rejoin my friend now. He didn't want to come out here, but I'm glad he didn't because I wouldn't have had this chance to talk with you. And I wouldn't have been able to join the marsh like I have. I do want to thank you for your kindness in helping me to enjoy this place so much. You didn't treat me like a weird object like many Chinese treat foreigners."

Marsh: "To us in nature, there are no foreigners."

Me: "Oh, my! That crane just flew so close. It is so very beautiful to watch him fly by. It is a special treat as I'm ready to leave."

Marsh: "Remember that the Orientals consider the crane to be the symbol of longevity. Happy Birthday!!"

August 15, 1991

They did it! The father-daughter taxi team asked me to buy a carton of cigarettes as a "thank you" to their source of tickets for sleepers to Hohhot. They took us to pick up the tickets. Who was their source? The man who <u>prints</u> the tickets! Thankfully we were able to get some sleep on the long trip to Hohhot.

Scott, one of Russell's classmates whom I'd met at school in Hangzhou, welcomed us to his family's home. This city is very big. Scott and his sister have led us on some long bike rides to introduce their hometown to us. Scott has been an avid stamp collector for many years, and showed us his impressive collection. Although he has stamps from all over the world, I like the ones from Asian countries best. They are like little elegant art pieces. He'd particularly love more stamps from Taiwan.

Tomorrow we are going out to see the Nadamu Festival. It is a massive event, bringing in thousands of Mongolians from the outlying areas to compete in horseback riding and camel racing.

August 16, 1991

We saw Mongolians racing bareback on their sturdy, small Mongolian horses, and others sped on the backs of camels. I'm so glad our visit coincided with this incredible festival. The Mongolians had set up *yurts* that we were invited to visit. Mongolians are nomadic. This is the rounded home that Mongolians set up wherever they live. Inside, it was spacious. And now I have the indelible memory of being welcomed by a Mongolian official inside a large *yurt* at the festival. As a foreigner, he honored me by asking a woman with him to sing a Mongolian song in greeting.

After the melodious greeting, he asked me to sing something. Actually, I have quite a terrible voice, but how could I say "no" to this VIP without offending him? So, I sang a rousing "Jingle Bells" to honor the occasion. At least it was peppy and not too out of tune.

August 17, 1991

Who knows why something pops into a traveler's head and must be obeyed? Although I'm not much of a horseback rider, riding a horse across the grasslands sounded like something I had to do in Mongolia. And Russell had told me that he always wanted to ride a horse. So, at my request, the family arranged a day's outing to the grasslands. They couldn't see much point in it themselves because the landscape gets quite boring after a while.

However, there was something special about being on a horse in the grasslands. I wish I could say I galloped across the grasslands, but I wasn't capable of that. Russell got to go a little faster for a short time. I just let my imagination fly over the grasslands on horseback and felt very satisfied—and safe.

August 17, 1991

I was rudely routed out of my bed at midnight by the police! They took me from Scott's home where I felt warm and wanted and put me into a Chinese hotel since all the hotels were full of tourists for the Nadamu Festival. My blood boiled. My fist hit the wall in fury at this segregation and humiliation over and over again in China.

Russell explained that the north of China was stricter about the government policy of not allowing foreigners to sleep in the homes of Chinese people. Scott was angry and his family looked miserable. They had tried to convince the police that it was not comfortable for me to be in a Chinese hotel where no one spoke English, and all the hotels for foreigners were full. But, they were fined anyway. They wouldn't tell me how much they had to pay.

How can they understand how I feel? They have never known respect and freedom in their country. Maybe what they felt was losing face in front of an honored guest. I do not have Chinese patience and obedience, and I never will.

August 18, 1991

We tried rowing on a very beautiful, large lake today, but there was a plant taking over the water that made it quite impossible to row through it. The effect was more like bumper cars with the other boats that were attempting to plow through the water too. We didn't get too far out into the lake, but the day was warm and lovely. The colors of the water, surrounding mountains, and sky enhanced the backdrop for taking pictures. There is an arid feel to this area that reminds me of Israel.

Scott is making plans to join a joint venture company and start building a better future than he can have in teaching. He has a girlfriend he wants to marry, but she comes from another province. He isn't ready to give up yet, but it's very hard for two people from different provinces to get permission to marry.

Russell's unwillingness to translate much of what is going on has worn on me. I feel like an inanimate curio that is always being talked about. I'm looking forward more and more to being back in my own culture where I can understand what's being said.

August 23, 1991

Hohhot was an endless train ride from Hangzhou. We stopped in Beijing for some Peking Duck, a hot shower, and some sleep. As we were nearing the stop closest to Russell's village, his eyes and face lit up with excitement. He said excitedly, "I am of this land. The land will not perish. I will not perish either." I was glad to see his exuberance. Sometimes it takes going far away to appreciate coming home.

August 27, 1991

Today I bathed in a river and went to the "toilet" in a clean pigsty complete with two pigs looking at me. After a truly horrendous eight hours eating dust on a bus from Hangzhou, Robert and I have arrived at his home in the countryside. It is absolutely the most beautiful countryside I have seen so far. His village is nestled in the mountains like a Swiss hamlet look-alike. The air and water are pure—a rarity in this world. Life and work are hard here and people age quickly, but the peace and serenity make it unlike China.

The corn grows high next to the chili peppers and around the rice paddies. Can these people care if Russia has now killed Communism and the Baltic States claim independence? Time here is as it was almost centuries ago. The tea grows and the nut trees decorate the mountains. The river flows amazingly clean through the village from the mountain springs.

The durability of the Chinese family is like the durability of these mountains. Their lifestyle remains undisturbed, as does the air that is polluted only by the smoking men. No technology but broken-down buses reaches here. Only one foreigner—me—has reached here.

The villagers are kind and curious. While visiting one of Robert's neighbors, an old lady sat close to me. I felt a brief poke in my breast. Of course, she had never seen anyone with such big breasts before. She must have wondered if they were real.

I could visit perhaps in another hundred years and not find it very changed. Will the children like Robert who learn of the world and yearn for it make it change? The long arm of the government reaches here, so perhaps knowledge of the rest of the world will reach here too. For better or worse?

Settled tonight in Robert's old attic room with real wood walls in the cool mountain air makes the discomfort and inconvenience of the third world more bearable.

Sept. 2, 1991

Richard and Diana took me to the airport to catch my plane to "the other world," as Richard calls it. Richard's punishment is to be demoted from a teacher to a worker in a factory connected to the school. I encouraged him to think about trying his luck in private jobs, maybe in a place like The Colorful City. He really has nothing to lose now. He listened carefully, and then eagerly.

I have said my goodbyes with a sigh of wistfulness. My plan now is to check out Macau as a possible place of employment, and then return for a few months to visit my parents and friends in the U.S. I look forward to getting back to life with no salt, no oil, no smoke, and no rice. I feel rather certain that I'll return to China, but there's always that little pang of "What if I don't?"

Sept. 3, 1991

I was entertained the entire two-hour flight from Hangzhou to Hong Kong by the abstract city in the sky formed by the clouds. Huge vertical clouds made fanciful skyscrapers. I imagined seeing the complete city of Oz as Dorothy might have viewed it. I have now flown this path from Hong Kong to Hangzhou and back several times and have been impressed by the complexity of the cloud formations more than once. It's the only route where I've been treated regularly to such an artistic extravaganza in the sky.

Sept. 7, 1991

Here I sit atop a hill in Taipa Village on the first island next to Macau. Macau is actually located at the tip of the mainland peninsula, plus two islands that are connected by roads. Taipa used to be an old Portuguese fishing village and still retains circuitous alleyways, and pastel-washed homes with small family businesses on the street floor. Peculiarly, there are people-sized statues of bottles of Coca-Cola, Fanta, and other drinks all around the island. That's a first for me. There are Chinese shantytowns of tin boards as well as manicured gardens. There's Chinese food and wonderful Portuguese food served delicately and relatively cheaply. There is order, grace, and lots of police. It seems to be several places in one.

I think Macau may be a well-kept secret. In Hong Kong, only an hour away by jetfoil, people are hurriedly walking around in silk suits, holding mobile phones and worrying about making more money and escaping Hong Kong before it returns back to China in 1997. The part of Macau connected to China has the densest population in the world. But, here on this island only a short bus ride away over a bridge, the pace is easy, restful, very laid back, unhurried and unworried. Macau will return to China's rule in 1999, but Macau doesn't seem as worried about it as Hong Kong. I'm not sure why.

The University of Macau is on Taipa island. It may be possible to teach English there. Just across the bridge back in the city, there is the Canadian College of Macau that also has English-speaking high school teachers. I'm checking out the possibilities here for the future. The pay is good. It's a highly livable place that quite enchants me. I know that one of its charms for me is that it is close to China for frequent visits.

Sept. 8, 1991

I'm still tired from all my recent travels, but I'm in a wonderful place to feel tired. I am sitting on a beach in a cove on the island of Coloane, Macau's second island also connected by a short bus ride. I purposely chose a Sunday to come here so I could see just how noisy and crowded the beach would be. But it is neither noisy nor crowded. That is a delightful surprise in a place that has continued to pleasantly surprise me.

The beach is quite lovely and easy to get to. I got to see a baptism in the sea, so there must be Christians here. The people on the beach seem well behaved and thankfully don't carry big boom boxes to the beach with them. The water looks inviting, and there are areas to sit in shade.

The whole island seems worth exploring with its own little village, including, surprisingly, an English bakery, an aviary, a park, and two beaches. The air is free and clear. Remembering my misery in Taiwan's air, I asked about their dumps. Apparently, they don't burn their garbage and trash. Instead, it goes into landfill.

It has taken me several trips to Hong Kong before I made the short journey into Macau. The combination of good pay, good conditions, pleasant lifestyle, clean air, and being in the Far East close to China are quite irresistible. I'm definitely going to keep it in mind for future employment.

Sept. 13, 1991

This is probably the only time in my life I'll get to celebrate two Friday the 13^{ths} consecutively. Friday the 13th is "my" special lucky day because I was born on Friday the 13th. Because of the time change, I left Hong Kong in the morning of Friday the 13th, and arrived in the U.S. on the morning of Friday the 13th!

Soon I'll be back in San Diego visiting mom and dad, and a simple phone call away from my American friends. It's back to letters only with my Chinese friends—for a few months at least.

12

CHINA 1992

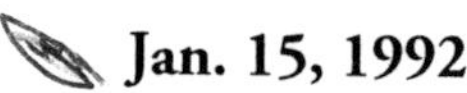

Jan. 15, 1992

As soon as the plane started circling Hangzhou for a landing, I looked down excitedly and truly felt my heart leap up from the ground and reunite with my body. The purity of the emotion made me gasp in surprise. It was extraordinary to feel so aware that I had left my heart in China and it was drawing me back.

While I was contemplating the joy of arriving in China, the people on the plane started drawing out of their bags extra pants, sweaters, and jackets to prepare for the cold of the Chinese winter after the temperate climate of Hong Kong where we had boarded. We all hurriedly added layers before the plane landed. So, without having any idea of my future plans, and wearing three pairs of pants, three sweaters, three pairs of socks, two pairs of gloves, I exited the plane to greet the three boys waiting for me.

I arrived in time to be an important guest at Richard's sister's wedding.

THE MATCHMAKER BRINGS THE CHAMBER POT

The night before a rural Chinese wedding, it is a good sign that all will go as planned when the groom's matchmaker brings the chamber pot to the bride's home. As with other parts of the peasants' life in China, there are changes taking place. But the changes in the countryside are far behind those of the city dwellers who are adopting more western culture.

A peasant wedding has a great deal of ritual that is still practiced and is very important. And there are many differences from one village to the next. In this wedding, the bride and groom each came from tiny villages a thirty-minute boat ride apart. When the groom's matchmaker brought the chamber pot, the bride's family sent their matchmaker to collect the money for the bride's family. A poor family may pay the equivalent of $200 to $300 for the bride. And each member of the immediate bride's family receives some of this money. The night before the wedding, the bride's matchmaker sleeps in the groom's bed. He sleeps elsewhere.

The bride's family put into the chamber pot, which is a very practical gift in a place with no toilets, two red eggs for fertility, waste grain which is a play on words (in Chinese it means "stable," a good wish for a marriage, and the same word in their local dialect means "waste"), salt to urge them to have a baby early (Chinese couples often have their one allotted baby under the one child policy during the first year), and candies for a sweet life. That night, the bride's family carefully rolled many colorful quilts they were presenting to the new couple, slipping candies inside. They also tied red yarn to the hope chests and furniture that the bride would bring to the marriage.

Very early on the wedding day, the bride went off to have her hair styled and her face made up. They prefer a whitish face with prominent rouge. Still very early in the morning, I was awakened by musicians clanging and drumming their way to the bride's home. Except for the bride and groom, the musicians and guests don't wear special clothing. As a matter of fact, in response to the question, "What does one wear to a Chinese countryside wedding in January?" (a popular time for weddings because of the upcoming Chinese New Year usually in February), I have to respond, "Everything one can put on." Since heat is used sparingly only in the north of China, it is considered unnecessary in the south of China which is cold enough to get snow.

Dressed in four pairs of pants, three sweaters, a down jacket, scarf, and gloves, I greeted the musicians whose faces registered shock when I appeared. The group, including the groom and his close male relatives and the two matchmakers were invited in for tea and the perennial weed in China—cigarettes. They had also brought with them two large baskets of food for the bride's family.

Eventually, male members of the bride's family carried the dowry outside the home, receiving a small amount of money from the groom. Time was given for all to properly appreciate the pieces of furniture, hope chests, and large tape recorder that represented what the bride had been able to buy from her savings as a worker in a sock factory. The bride's family then gave permission to take it away, and the groom's relatives took the dowry to the waiting boat. While the musicians clanged and drummed to urge the couple to hurry to their new room at the groom's family's home, the groom asked the bride, "Can we go now?"

The musicians played and the firecrackers popped as we all walked to the waiting boat. The bride, dressed attractively in a red silk padded jacket, looked very serious. As a special guest, I was allowed to ride to the groom's home along with the musicians, bride and groom, matchmakers, and four girls the bride had chosen to accompany her. The parents of the bride stayed at home to prepare to meet their relatives who would be coming to their home in the afternoon.

The villagers stood on the bank to wish them well as the bride changed into new red shoes before stepping onto the small boat. I carefully balanced on a small plank and made my way under the crowded canopy. The youngest sister took a bucket of water from the river, which somehow insured a safe trip. Then, the pole had to be maneuvered properly to quickly and easily propel the boat on its way while keeping the tip of the pole under the water. Otherwise, it would be rude and bad luck. The chamber pot accompanied us in our cramped quarters in the boat.

Waiting excitedly were the relatives and villagers of the groom's family. The new mother-in-law invited the bride to come into the house. The mother-in-law is indeed an important person since the bride becomes a member of the groom's family and will hereafter visit her parents' home only as a guest. In fact, she usually severs relationships with her own aunts, uncles, and cousins.

Inside the groom's home, the bride and groom stood before a long table that held vases of paper flowers and two large red candles. With one of the musicians officiating, the ceremony was brief as the marriage certificate issued by the government (physicals and blood tests and permission having been taken care of earlier) was read and the new couple bowed to the groom's parents and to each other. Someone preceded them with the two lit candles into their new bedroom in which the four bridesmaids and all the bride's dowry were waiting.

The bride, still looking serious, was introduced formally by her mother-in-law to each new relative. She called them by their new titles—aunt, uncle, etc.—and they each gave her a red envelope containing a gift of money. To the younger nieces and nephews, the bride had to give a small amount of money also wrapped in red. The distribution of small bags of candies by the bride to relatives and friends seemed to be an important component of being honored. The bride bestowed several upon me.

Before all could eat, the bride's brothers had to come into the home and be seated. They were served sweets, nuts, sugared water, and yes, of course, cigarettes. Then, they were given regular tea with tea leaves after which a brother placed a red envelope on the table and only the brothers got up and went outside. They returned immediately, and then the eating began in earnest.

The small red envelope left by the brothers was for the person who dutifully fed the fire from behind the stove. Surrounded by baskets holding mounds of cut up meat and vegetables, a hired cook stood in front of the two woks permanently set into the stove and, with a cigarette constantly dangling from his lips, produced perhaps 30 freshly prepared dishes for each table of guests. The groom's family served the tables graciously and kept each guest well supplied with wine or a soft drink. I, who well outweigh mostly all Chinese people who can eat much more than I, disappointed them by my meager appetite. However, they were impressed with my skill in using chopsticks.

They were all naturally very curious about me and often wandered over my way to stare at me. We couldn't speak, but we smiled a lot and they got the impression, according to Richard, that I was friendly. Since I had brought my camera along, they happily requested family pictures. A camera is an expensive rarity in the countryside, so most adults tended to look very serious when they posed, while some children even broke into tears at both the foreigner and a strange object looking at them.

Eventually, the bride and groom changed clothes, and the groom successfully put out both candles at once with the swish of a straw hat, and we made the return visit to the bride's home where the bride's relatives eagerly awaited us. The feasting began again with another cook, cigarette dangling, preparing a similar number of freshly cooked dishes.

Toward evening, the four male relatives who accompanied the groom began to clash cymbals to urge the new couple to return to their new room. The bride lingered, as is customary, but at last they set out again to greet the groom's relatives waiting for them in their new room where they played intentionally embarrassing games such as making the bride and groom bite the same candy on a string.

On the morning of the third day, the new couple returned to lead the immediate female and male relatives, including the bride's parents, to the groom's family for another feast where they were the guests of honor. There is a great deal of required visiting (no honeymoon off by themselves) during the coming days and the days of Spring Festival, which is the Chinese New Year. A nice meal is always served, often including a side of pork, which is an expensive sign of respect and honor for the new couple. They also receive a rice cake with a cooked red bean inside, symbolizing a baby. These cakes can sometimes be distributed to all the villagers of the groom's family.

As is generally true in Chinese culture, there is a great deal of protocol that must be followed to insure good relations in the years to come. There were almost no similarities to western weddings, except for the high spirits of the relatives and friends who gathered to give the new couple a good beginning.

Jan. 23, 1992

Unfortunately and predictably, I caught a bad cold right after the wedding festivities. A cold is a big nuisance anywhere, but in the Chinese countryside in the winter, it is more than uncomfortable. Richard's mother checked every day to make sure I was wearing several layers, and his sisters graciously washed out the rags I used to blow my nose. Richard explained that they didn't understand why I preferred to blow my nose into rags that had to be painstakingly hand washed rather than blowing my nose between my fingers and flinging the snot to the ground. I had to admit that the Chinese way made sense, but I just couldn't do that.

They all seemed to bear the cold inside the home better than I in spite of my layers plus down jacket and down booties at night. I even slept in a ski mask and was very glad I had brought it because my nose would have succumbed to frostbite, I'm sure. The children managed to get through the cold with various layers topped by a beautiful hand knit sweater made by someone in the family. However, their little cheeks were red and sore—the cheeks on their faces as well as the cheeks on their behinds in their split pants which facilitates toilet training in a country without diapers.

When only the tail end of my cold remained, I felt an extreme urge to have a shower. Richard explained that many of the older people, including his parents, never fully bathed or showered during the winter. They did not consider it healthy. In warmer weather, there was the river to swim in and get cleansed. However, nearby in a small town, there was a public bath that offered hot showers. I went eagerly. The inside was steamy and foggy, but I could quickly see that the big pool was not only filled with children and their mothers, but also a lot of soap scum as they rubbed in the pool. I thought rather longingly of those wonderful, super-clean public baths in Japan that don't allow you to go into a pool until you have thoroughly soaped and scrubbed off at least one layer of skin. One cannot say that all Asian cultures are alike.

I stripped off my layers of clothes and found a shower in the steam. As I was enjoying the streams of water washing away the dirt of all those days, I felt the eyes of a short little old lady peering up at me rather like I imagine Jack must have viewed the giant at the top of the beanstalk. She then went to the other side of me and peered up from that angle. She was not unfriendly, just curious. What kind of a monster I must seem to these short, skinny people!

Feb. 8, 1992

I greeted the Year of the Monkey with Russell's family. Spring Festival is not a good time to be a visitor in Asia unless one is with a family. People gravitate to their hometowns for family celebrations, clogging the trains unmercifully trying to get home in time. There are many traditions associated with this time of year.

Along with the children, I got a red envelope with a little bit of money from Russell's father. His father still observes some of the Buddhist ritual of remembering their ancestors at this time. I wonder if Russell's generation will carry on that tradition.

There is a flurry of cleaning just before the new year, but no housecleaning is allowed on the day of the new year. The year should start harmoniously, so there is not supposed to be any yelling, arguments, or criticism between people. Dressed in all new clothes and on good behavior, the year begins peacefully after the noise of the small fireworks that each countryside family lights as the old year leaves and the new year begins. Since Spring Festival is such a long holiday in China, visiting other relatives begins in earnest after the first couple of days. All China seems to be on the move, from family to family.

Bill came to pick me up and took me over to stay with his family for a couple of days. I love these circuits of going from home to home.

Feb. 11, 1992

I am back in Hangzhou as happy as a clam in my room at the Xi Hu Hotel. This time I was very lucky and got room 2329, which overlooks West Lake. I've been told this hotel will eventually be torn down to make way for a modern, expensive hotel, but for now, it's my home. The room is dirty, grungy, and ugly, to be sure, but the view is wonderful and I have everything I need. There are communal hot showers available most of the day in the next building. I think they're actually for the staff, but they let me come in too.

The room has no toilet, and the walls are crumbling around the cobwebs, but it has the look of a once elegant lady now dilapidated from lack of care. Instead of wallpaper, a flower design is painted up and down the walls. The room is an odd, nondescript shape and was perhaps once the bridal suite because it has a double bed and the double happiness symbol of marriage decaying on the wall.

At night, the unmelodious attempts at karaoke intrude rudely and loudly into my room that sits above the speaker that is outside to attract customers. But somehow that seems to fit the overall atmosphere, and it's bearable if I plug my radio into my ears. Plus, I have toasty warm hands and feet with a small electric blanket and non-leaking water bottle. And all this I can have for the affordable price equivalent of $5 a night.

Anywhere else, I might consider living like this slum living, but I love it. I take walks along West Lake just across the street. Occasionally I get up early enough to watch the old people doing *tai chi* exercises at sunrise. I enjoy just looking out my window, which sits near the treetops. Strangely, I have sometimes imagined having a room like this in Montmartre in Paris where I could write and be creative. If I don't find work, I can imagine staying here and writing my book while watching spring turn the tree branches outside my window to green.

Feb. 13, 1992

"I'm going to have an abortion tomorrow," Ginger said over the waist-high partition as we stood up face to face after squatting over the Chinese toilet trough. I was the only one she was willing to tell. I didn't want her to go through that experience alone, so I told her I would come with her. I wasn't at all sure what to expect.

The father of the baby was a 32-year-old African student. There was an agricultural school in Hangzhou that had many African students. Their countries sent them to study in China for five years. All were young males. Without any African girls in China, they found girlfriends among the Chinese girls. This caused many problems with the Chinese males of Hangzhou and many fights broke out between the groups. One can hardly imagine two cultures that differ more in just about every way. Marriage was hardly an option for the mixed couples, but the relationships could go on in secret from the girl's family for several years. I had already met the African boyfriend of another of my students. Their relationship was gentle and sweet, but destined to end.

Unlike the U.S. where I had passionately fought for the woman's right to abortion, it is not difficult to get abortions in China. In fact, it is mandatory for unmarried pregnant women, and those who already have one child. Villages and neighborhoods actually have their own local spies who report the pregnancies of their neighbors to the government. Abortions are also quite cheap.

Ginger, however, had chosen to go to a special clinic where abortions were done by inserting a pill in the uterus to cause contractions. By Chinese standards, this cost quite a lot, but women chose it because it was considered to be less painful. I had never heard of early term abortions being physically painful or dangerous if done by a doctor in a medical facility. I found out the difference in China was because there was no anesthesia given to dull the pain, as is also true in childbirth here. Her boyfriend gave her the money that was necessary for the "easier" abortion.

Well, I've been to many places I never believed I'd actually get to, but here I am sitting in a place I had certainly never thought of being. I'm sitting next to Ginger's bed while several women are on other beds chatting in between episodes of violent throwing up. They constantly eat bowls of soup with noodles, believing it is better to throw up with something in your stomach. Many of the women have their husbands with them. It's a sad time for them because most would dearly love to have a second or third child. However, I've never met a Chinese person who does not agree that the one child policy is necessary. We get to know each other a bit. Some of the young women have already had as many as five abortions!! Why? The preferred method of birth control in China is the IUD, but the technology of the ones being used is quite old and unreliable.

From time to time, a woman gets off the bed to squat over a chamber pot. Unlike westerners unaccustomed to squatting, she does not teeter over the pot. She is rock solid on her feet. After she passes blood, she looks through it thoroughly to find the tiny fetus. A doctor or nurse confirms that the baby has indeed been aborted, and we all congratulate her and feel happy her ordeal is over—at least this time. The beds begin to empty. Ginger remains. She has a second pill inserted. The doctor will not insert more than three in one day. She is in pain, but manages to keep up her end of our chatting to ease the waiting. We go for a short walk. When we return from walking, the baby gives up and ends its brief, unwanted life.

As we leave, the doctor comes over to me and says, "Come again." I look at him incredulously. Ginger is elated that it's over. I feel totally drained.

Feb. 20, 1992

My short-term future has been decided. My book will have to wait because the professor I know in Nanjing University has been able to get me a job teaching this semester. Nanjing University is probably rated in the top three universities in all of China. My students are quite literally the cream of the crop, skimmed from every province throughout China based on high test scores.

As a full-time teacher, I teach conversational English 12 hours a week. In return for my teaching, I receive a luxurious (by Chinese standards) room all to myself. It has a private bathroom with running hot water, but the water constantly changes from warm to scalding. Nanjing is nine hours north from Hangzhou by train, so I was extremely glad to learn that the room has heat. Alas, I found out they only turn the heat on 30 minutes every evening. I also receive two to three times more salary than the Chinese teachers, but it still only adds up to the dollar equivalent of about $135 a month. At least it's income rather than all outgo.

Like the other Chinese students, Nanjing students have the same dexterous ability to twirl their pens around one hand in a swift motion. And, they trace the letters of new words with a finger on the palm of their hand. But these students are obviously much brighter than any I've ever taught, or known. I couldn't teach them anything except English. Many seem to come from educated families and have higher hopes and aspirations for their futures than my Hangzhou students. Probably, their families have more *guanxi,* connections, to help them along. Like other university students in China, they are not particularly studious because they have already achieved getting into an excellent university.

Feb. 26, 1992

I sit in the welcome midday sun on my little concrete balcony and look out upon three tiled roofs that have that Oriental tilt upward at the corners. The buildings look old, but that doesn't always mean much in China. The newer highrise buildings of Nanjing loom beyond them, giving an anachronistic confusion of time and age.

The sounds around me emphasize the time warp because the construction workers re-constructing the insides of two of the buildings pound, clang, and hammer in the way I imagine construction technology was in the Middle Ages. But, probably modern construction workers who maneuver large cranes and sophisticated building equipment do not sing and chant as they work.

It will take far too long—much longer than my four months here to finish their tiresome work. It will take great energy, and long days and nights to do what machines can do better and more easily. But China is a third world country, and China is overpopulated. So, these men need jobs more than they need machines.

And so the wheels of the present grind slowly and cacophonously as China builds, tears down, and re-builds.

March 4, 1992

It is early in the morning—much too early for me—and I have once again been rudely awakened by hammering. So, I have come out to see why.

A young man is the direct cause. He holds a hammer perhaps 1 ½ inches wide and a small chisel. It is a ridiculous way to make a building, but this is China. In whatever wisdom, they have decided to make kitchens for the teachers in the Foreign Experts Building—kitchens that could be made during the summer vacation when it wouldn't disturb anyone.

On Sunday morning, they began the destruction of the wall that was once the end of the building. Now, it is harder to know what they are doing—perhaps evening it off—but no, he is going farther than the space they need for the door. Chips are falling around me. It seems childishly easy to destroy a wall, although agonizingly slowly with a tiny hammer and chisel.

The cold air blows through the big hole. What it will be, I do not know. Perhaps they also do not know. There is access to the outside through a slide. The leftover bricks and long pipes lay all over the proposed "kitchen."

The ladder is a strange looking, inefficient and uncomfortable affair. The ceiling is concrete. It is hard to imagine what it will look like. Nor will I most likely get to see it completed. Now some metal pipes are going out the hole in the wall. To where?

It taxes my patience and makes me angry—angry that the young workers aren't wearing any protective clothing, or anything to keep their lungs from inhaling the copious dust. I'm angry that they are waking me up for nothing!

March 15, 1992

I had to do something about sleeping or give up a job I really enjoy. The administration knows the noise situation is bad, but is unable (unwilling?) to change it because the university is preparing for a big 90th anniversary celebration of its founding. The noise is now going on 24 hours a day. When I was consistently being jolted awake by hammering, my stomach always feeling awful, and I was even starting to mix up words when I spoke, I realized I was showing the effects of noise stress. Some of the foreign teachers have taken to pills or even drinking to put them to sleep. I took a more practical approach. I moved out.

I independently went to the Foreign Students' Dorm and rented a room. I've had to give up a phone and a toilet and bathroom in my room. It can't really be called "quiet" either since only the Chinese countryside is quiet. Otherwise, Chinese only feel secure in lots of noise all the time. No matter how low level the technology is here, the loudspeakers boom out from everywhere—terrible quality, but very loud. At least the noise is now somewhat further away from my ears.

So, I am now in the absurd situation of having two rooms and four beds in Nanjing. Even though the price for this room is cheaper than what the Foreign Affairs Office pays to the Foreign Teachers' Building, they insist they must continue to keep the other room for me since I'm a teacher, not a student. That means I will have to pay for the second room myself, which costs more than my entire monthly salary! Oh well, by Chinese standards I'm a rich American, so a good night's sleep and some quiet time to think is worth the expense to me. I'm still not sure whether I'm renting the entire room, or only one half the room. I do go back to my first room daily to check for mail and use the refrigerator in my room.

The package of letters sent by my parents finally arrived, and I hungrily devoured them. I miss mail. That is a big disadvantage to me of leading a wandering life. The authorities had opened the package, but not the individual letters.

My classes are going very well. I also gave my first lecture in the big auditorium for anyone in the university who wants to come. There must have been over 200 students there, making it my largest audience ever. I spoke about Israel, and especially the similarities I've observed between Israel and China. It was well received by the students. They don't know very much about Israel. There certainly haven't been a lot of Israelis for them to meet in China. However, the professor here who helped me get this job is creating a center for Jewish studies at this university. He has already translated the English versions of some books written by Israelis into Chinese. He is a Chinese who loves Israel; I am a Jew who loves China.

March 25, 1992

The weather here is cold, rainy, and awful. However, it snowed on March 17th (Happy St. Patrick's Day!) and was quite pretty. My little room seems a tad warmer than the big one in the Foreign Experts' Building. It turns out that both the Foreign Affairs Office as well as the other foreign teachers are miffed at me for taking matters into my own hands and moving out of the noise and dust. They feel somehow it wasn't right to take unilateral action. That's my American sense of independence, I guess.

Although I think it's ridiculous to have to pay the tourist price for this room that exceeds my monthly salary, I'm enjoying my little room. One reason is that I love curling up under the quilts on cold weekends and reading through a whole Pearl Buck novel. I knew that she was actually a teacher at this same university in the late 1930's, so I asked in the school library if they had her books. I rather doubted it because she and the Communist government hadn't gotten along well. Holding their grudge against her, the Communist government had even canceled a centennial celebration in her honor.

To my surprise, they had a wealth of her books hidden behind the stacks. I loved reading her when I was back in the U.S., but it was something very special to read her books right there at the same university where she had taught. Now that I was experiencing China personally, much of what she wrote held even more meaning for me. She was like my teacher in Chinese culture.

My students did not know about her. When one asked me to recommend a good book in English, I suggested Pearl Buck's The Good Earth. "Why would anyone write about something so common?" was the student's response when I asked her if she had liked it.

March 28, 1992

My housing problem has been solved, but now I must take drastic action on another major problem—eating, or more correctly, not eating. My alternatives for meals are not appealing. The school cafeteria is like eating at a salt lick. All I can taste among the oil is salt. It's difficult to eat at a Chinese restaurant by oneself because meals are geared for two or more who can share a few dishes. One dish of something is too monotonous. Plus, several teachers have come down with food poisoning from the only Chinese restaurant near here that has an English menu. There is another restaurant serving pseudo-western food with an English menu I can read, but the food's truly terrible.

I have been surviving on hot powdered milk, bottle after bottle of cold sour milk that tastes like yogurt (I wish they had that in Hangzhou), canned peaches, crackers, lousy chocolate, and those tasty sweet potatoes that vendors cook in big barrels along the street. Although I've often doubted my body's need for any food, I have been getting occasional dizzy spells that I believe are directly caused by not eating enough.

Out of the blue, an interesting solution struck me. Each of my students must eat one meal with me. Since I have 70 students, that means I'll have to eat at least 70 times. Since they don't have enough money to go to restaurants, we'll buy food from the cafeteria and take it up to my big room to eat. We'll eat Chinese style, but chat western style while we're eating. That will be their mid-term exam. It won't improve the taste of the food, but will force me to eat more often and make for an unusual test in a one-on-one situation. I'm curious to see how it works.

April 5, 1992

As she walked down the street pushing a younger child in a homemade baby stroller, she playfully let it go a few feet down the slope of the street. I thought of Reuven's faraway brothers and sisters in Israel and yearned to be with them again.

When the girl noticed me, she drew to my side as though magnetized. She did not abandon me even after her attempt to speak Chinese to me clearly indicated I could speak no Chinese. She walked alongside me, and I gaily chatted with the toddler in the carriage, telling her I had a Chinese granddaughter about her age. The older girl and I smiled widely when we looked at each other. It was clear to each of us that we liked one another.

When I said goodbye as I turned the corner, she happily turned to go down that street also. We walked like a pair, and several Chinese eyes took in the scene. When she turned into an alley that was home, we said goodbye to each other reluctantly. When I walked on and looked back, she was standing there still waving goodbye.

The serendipity of these unexpected moments of connection is a joy of travel.

April 7, 1992

Today was one of those days I came to China to have. My mid-term exam luncheons and dinners with the students are working out remarkably well. The students feel free to tell me many personal things they would not say in a group. One girl told me she had seen a soldier's body burning under a bridge in Beijing on June 4th of 1989. She had never told anyone about that horrific scene which she said had changed her forever. Another one wanted to talk about the things her boyfriend was doing when they were alone that he claimed couldn't get her pregnant. I know Chinese smile when giving bad or sad news to soften the blow, but I wasn't prepared for the sweet smiling girl who started our lunch conversation with, "My mother hates me." I never expected such openness and personal disclosures from them.

Tonight I had dinner with James, a very intelligent 19-year-old sophomore. He dressed for the occasion and took me out to the Pizza Place I hadn't found yet. There we ate pizza, spaghetti, garlic bread, French fries, and cucumber and tomato salad with a very decent oil and vinegar dressing. We munched and talked for three hours about many things.

This boy is bright, deep, speaks English wonderfully, and has a sense of humor. He is a very traditional Chinese, a modern young man, and a young adult trying to decide on his value system—that touching and somewhat tragic combination one can find in the Chinese students of today.

April 8, 1992

Ah, I loved it. At least 200 beautiful Chinese students' faces were turned upward hanging on every word of Snow White and the Seven Dwarfs. There were many faces in the auditorium I didn't know, but there were also the faces of my devoted students beaming up at me. Part of the reason I'm so fat must be because so much of me is pure ham.

My topic was "Tall Tales from America." They sat spellbound even through my faulty black southern accent telling "The Tar Baby" from Uncle Remus. The most successful was the children's fairy tale I slightly feared might be beneath them—"Snow White." I played it to the hilt. I was rewarded with smiles and applause. The teacher designated to take care of me while I'm teaching here ran down to the stage afterward, his eyes shining as he said, "That was the best lecture I ever heard."

I couldn't have had more fun than I did tonight doing anything else, anywhere else.

April 17, 1992

Dear Mom and Dad,

You have asked what keeps drawing me back to China so many times. At last you are coming to see for yourself what keeps bringing me back. And, you will get to meet my friends whom you have only "met" through my descriptions and the many things I've asked you to send to me for them. Here's the way the plans for your visit are shaping up.

I'll be able to get a week off from my teaching at Nanjing University and will meet you at the Shanghai Airport, hopefully with a couple of my friends. The next day, we'll go by train to Hangzhou where you will be enthusiastically greeted by many of my other friends. We will stay in Hangzhou from May 3rd to May 6th. On the evening of May 6th, you will host a scrumptious 50th Anniversary banquet arranged by the same tourism student who did the calligraphy piece hanging on your den wall at home. I'm inviting about 36 people, most of whom I believe will come. We should be able to feed them a reasonable banquet for about $200. This banquet will give you great face, and hopefully a lot of fun. I'll bet you never thought you'd be celebrating your 50th anniversary in China!

On May 7th, we'll go out to stay with Russell's family in the countryside. Be prepared to walk a bit since there are no roads directly to his home. We'll spend May 8th with Richard's family and stay at a small hotel not too far from there.

From then on, you'll be on the independent tour I've been able to arrange through a travel agency in Nanjing where the wife of one of the professors works. The rest of your time in China will be pre-paid, with a guide meeting you at each airport to accompany you on whatever you wish to do and see in those cities. I'll have to return back to Nanjing to teach. Since it's an independent tour, you'll be able to do what you want at your own pace with no group to keep up with.

The professional, very expensive pre-paid portion will probably go much more smoothly than the Hangzhou portion, but keep in mind that the professional portion will show you the tourist sites and scenes, while the Hanghzou portion will help you experience the "real" China, warts and all. Reality is often different than Tourism Bureaus would like.

Please be open to new adventures when you come. You will be very honored guests, which means you must try to eat as much as possible. I'm sure you will disappoint them in this way as I always have. Although the food (which I will request be made without salt or MSG) will probably not be too delicious to you, please keep in mind that the families will spend more money than they can afford to provide it for you. Of course, the perennial problem I've never solved, especially at the banquet, is that none of the others will like the food without generous amounts of oil, salt, and MSG.

Mom, at Richard's home, you can compare your $8000 false teeth with his father's new $20 false teeth. Dad, I think your idea of bringing some silver dollars to Richard's and Russell's fathers is good. Also bring some small books and postcards of California to show people where you live. I'm sure a couple of those small pocket radios you like to listen to would be appreciated. Include some small toys for the little children. And, of course, taking pictures with your Polaroid and watching the pictures develop will be a treat for all. If you wrap gifts, don't be surprised if they don't open the gifts in front of you. That's not considered polite. I'm sure they will also increase your luggage with small gifts.

On the subject of luggage, be prepared that your bags will be an incredible drag. Dealing with it, especially on the train, will be rough. Do you think you could carry backpacks? Just kidding. Don't panic, but your bags will surely outweigh the people carrying them. And, if I could wear the same clothes for three months on end, it should be a piece of cake for you to pack for just 18 days of good spring weather. If you have a spare corner in a suitcase, please throw a Hershey bar into a Ziploc bag (neither is available in China) and hope it doesn't melt before I devour it.

Dad, I know you're a good driver, so I feel the need to prepare you for the drivers in China. Drivers always only use their bright lights at night. They honk continuously day and night. In the rain, for some strange reason I can't fathom, they continually turn the windshield wipers off and on rather than leaving them on. There are seat belts in the front seats only, but I have blackened many a blouse trying to put on a seat belt that has only been used as a dirt collector that came with the car. Most of the time, the belts don't even buckle. Seat belts are considered an unnecessary nuisance that insult the skill of the driver. The behavior of drivers resembles a perpetual game of "chicken."

Be sure to bring all your medications. And it would be a good idea to get a gammaglobulin shot as some protection against hepatitis A.

I'm looking forward to sharing my world with you. I'm sure the trip will not be an easy one, but it will be the most unusual trip of your lives and provide a very memorable 50th anniversary celebration! Start practicing your chopstick skills.

April 18, 1992

The classrooms are bare and cold. By the time my classes meet in the evening, the smell from the toilet troughs down the hallway sometimes make me gag. But, our classroom is filled with laughter and the whir of busy brains churning English around the room. In response to a homework assignment on describing someone, one of my students wrote the following piece.

"Firstly, I must tell you that this person is not of my nationality. Secondly, I must use 'she' to refer to this person. Thirdly, she is middle-aged. Let's come to some specific ones. I dare say she is not very slender. If you think she is strong, I can't very well say no. Her height is average. But there are some more wonderful details. The short and puffy and wild hair, the lively and various facial expressions and the habit of wearing red all show us that the person is not quiet. During her teaching, she moves wildly all things on her body which can be moved to make us understand better and participate more easily. I really regard her as a very good teacher. But, who is she?"

April 19, 1992

It was just another day in China. When they had assigned me to 301 Foreign Experts Building, I noticed there were some unnecessary doors to my room. "Why is the peephole on an inside door rather than an outside door where it would be possible to see someone knocking?" I also wondered at the peculiar position of the peephole. It was off to one side and quite low. I could guess it was low because the Chinese man who put it in was probably short, but why off center? I speculated that the previous teacher had arrived in pre-peephole days and had put up her name card in the center of the door. The man installing the peephole hadn't dared move it.

This morning, at 7:30, there was a knock on the outermost of my several doors. Not having a peephole in that door, I sleepily opened all the doors to the hallway. Three Chinese men stood there. One held a can of red paint. Another held a small paintbrush. The third one held nothing. They eyed me suspiciously, wondering what possible reason I could have for not arising at a suitable hour. The spokesman of the group spoke to me in Chinese. When I indicated I couldn't understand Chinese, he yelled louder.

Bewildered, I asked the help of another teacher passing by. "Oh," the other more talented Chinese-speaking English teacher replied after the spokesman repeated himself, "they're here to paint identification numbers on your bed, desk, and chairs so you won't be able to take them with you when you return to America." Why hadn't I thought of that? The three men marched in officiously and performed their duty.

As I was settling back to sleep, I heard a loud chanting outside. I looked out curiously from my narrow balcony. A column of yellow-hatted little men were marching by, each with a hammer in one hand and a chisel in the other. They stopped at the building next to mine, and began their attack. Later, someone explained that the building under attack had been especially renovated to be a guesthouse for the important 90th anniversary celebration. Now that the celebration was over, it was to be gutted and rebuilt as a sports arena. "They change buildings like shirts," I thought sleepily.

Soon I heard the metallic clink of the hammers outside my several doors. The kitchen construction that had chased me away to the Foreign Student Dorm a couple of months earlier was being dismantled!

Just another logic-defying day in China.

May 10, 1992

Wow, what a week it was! My parents entered my world and found it both profound and enjoyable. Mom didn't complain about any of the many inconveniences and discomforts. Can you imagine four hours in the doorway of a hard seat train sitting on her suitcase chattering gaily with people sitting on the floor all around us and the smell of the toilet wafting through?

Mom's rapport with all my friends was mutual and instantaneous. Richard said excitedly, "she's even better than you." Juliet and Diana's parents welcomed my parents to their home and presented them with a large gift indeed—a ceremonial sword. Mom hugged Juliet's mom enthusiastically, at which the poor woman froze. I had forgotten to tell Mom that Chinese are not used to friendly hugging like westerners.

We made a hit wherever we went, even causing a fist fight between two boatmen who vied for the chance to take us across West Lake. Riding and rocking in the back of a tractor, the only vehicle that could handle the narrow paths to Richard's home, didn't faze Mom a bit. I got a precious picture of her daintily washing up at the well in front of Richard's cottage. And one of her draping her shawl around her and Richard's grandmother together. They are actually the same age. At Russell's home, his mother, unable to verbally express her exuberance at having my parents at their home, took Mom's hands and danced her around the large earthen floor.

As an added bonus, we were also able to visit Debbie and her newborn daughter, my second Chinese grandchild. Debbie and the baby were staying with her in-laws for a month after delivery. Chinese believe women who give birth must do nothing but rest and eat healthful foods for a full month after delivering a baby. Others take care of her and the new baby. How different from American women who get very short maternity leaves from work and don't have help in the home. I've heard that Taiwanese have set up centers in the U.S. for rich Taiwanese women to be taken care of after birth. They go to the U.S. late in their pregnancies in order to give birth to babies who instantly become U.S. citizens by being born there. Taiwanese are ever mindful of their political insecurity next to the giant China.

Mom and Dad were good sports throughout discomforts. They got through a sleepless night on a roped bed rather than a mattress. They endured eating more than they wanted to and did a decent job of using chopsticks. Dad's sensitive stomach longed for familiar foods. And his tongue swelled uncomfortably once after drinking bottled mineral water. But, all in all, it was their self-proclaimed "best trip of our lives."

The 50th anniversary banquet, starring Mom and Dad, was absolutely magnificent! The good food and drink, my friends, the warm feelings—all flowed along joyfully. Mom and Dad have often worried about my leading an untraditional life that they could never have imagined for their only daughter. But now they've entered my world and understand me better. Mom was enchanted by China and my Chinese friends. Dad was awed to see Mom as she'd never been before. Come to think of it, we three impressed each other.

May 16, 1992

"I hope you can be my mother, another mother," Benjamin wrote me before he asked me face to face. Benjamin was one of my youngest students, starting Nanjing University at the tender age of 14. At 17, he was a fascinating mixture of brains, maturity beyond his tender years, plus normal teenage emotions—certainly a complex boy. He had already read every Agatha Christie mystery, and gobbled up (and guessed every killer halfway through) the Sue Grafton mystery books I had requested my parents send for him. He was impatiently waiting for some Perry Mason mysteries and books on playing bridge that my parents had sent for him. When he said he wanted to go to Harvard to study computer science, I knew he was capable of doing just that.

When I asked him how his mother would feel about him having "another mother," he explained that parents could select "another mother or father" for their children, but that children themselves could also ask someone to take that special role in their lives without their parents' permission. He said that my becoming his "other mother" would mean that he would take responsibility for me as he would for his parents. Why he would want to take on an added burden was strange to me, but I was more concerned about how his mother would feel about it.

At my request, he wrote to his mother and she replied (through his translation) with a very touching letter.

"My honorable teacher,

First, I'd like to thank you for your good care to my son. You came to China as a representative of an excellent nation. You've tried your best in order to develop the friendship between our two countries. Each Chinese people will be grateful to you. It's obvious that you have given your love to your students since you can win the trust of your students. We can see how precious the friendship between two countries is from you.

We welcome you to visit our family very much. You stimulated Benjamin's interest in English. How lucky he is! If he can be successful in the future, your work is very important. We'll be grateful to you forever!

About your willingness to give Benjamin your love as a mother, I can understand you with the heart of a mother. We can see your love is from your heart. It's his good luck that he can own two mothers. I'm in no way hurt to hear Benjamin say that. You'll be helpful to his growth. I'll only be glad for him for that.

It's our honor if you can visit us. We are always ready to welcome you and hope you will like the visit to our family."

June 14, 1992

I'm beginning to get that sinking feeling in my stomach when I can see the end of my time in China approaching. I've just given a paper at a Foreign Teachers' Conference in Suzhou. We foreign teachers in China are a strange conglomeration. Some are masquerading missionaries. Many are misfits in their own countries. Some have a long history of teaching and are being financed handsomely by their governments or organizations, complete with paid transportation to and from China. Others, like me, took the opportunity to teach as a tool for getting to know the Chinese culture without learning the Chinese language. And, quite a few men and women are finding Chinese marriage partners among their students.

One of the Americans in our group from Nanjing University seemed to hate China. I had personally seen her banging her fists on the chest of a man leading the pack of people crowding onto a train as we were struggling to exit. "Why do you people act like this?" she cried out in her frenzy. I had heard her loudly yell other complaints about China more like a two-year-old having a tantrum than the Rhodes scholar she also was. Catching her at one of her calm times, I asked her why she had come to China when so many things about it bothered her. "I love the students," she replied simply. That part of her I could understand well.

At the end of the term, I'll return "home" to Hangzhou for several days. Benjamin and another one of my students, Peter, will come to Hangzhou together a few days later to meet my Hangzhou friends. Then, we'll go on to Benjamin's home, an arduous 26 hours from Hangzhou by train. Peter's home is along the way. After spending some time with Benjamin and then Peter's family, we'll go together to Shenzhen and Zhuhai. I'm interested in seeing these places because they are special economic zones near Hong Kong and Macau. Like Hong Kong, only mainland Chinese with special permission are allowed to live there. But, unlike Hong Kong, Chinese mainlanders are allowed to make brief visits.

After that, my finances are telling me I'll definitely need to do some serious job hunting. My chances in Macau are dim, but I'll give it a try since I can't return to the air of Taiwan and, for a while at least, I need to make more money than I can in China.

June 20, 1992

In spite of having sometimes slept in my bathroom as the quietest place in my room at the Foreign Expert's Building, and walking around with a hot water bottle between my freezing hands in the winter, I'll be leaving Nanjing with the realization that I have taught some of the brightest young minds of China's future. I asked my students to evaluate our time together and received this extraordinary reply, which I intend to include as a job recommendation letter.

"Dear Zima,

The end of the term came much too soon. Now we have to say farewell to you, but I still remember vividly the first class you taught us at the beginning of this semester. We students were waiting expectantly for the new teacher to appear. Before long, you came in. You are an impressive-looking teacher. Your eyes were lucid and bright, and your smile made students feel warm and trustworthy. You spoke without condescension, voicing a welcome message of friendliness and understanding. You had a way of dangling before us part of a story. You let us move around in the classroom and do some interesting exercises—your teaching methods are very fresh to us, and your lessons are really attractive. An unexpected feeling of happy stirred in me. From that moment, I thought I was very lucky to be your student. And at the end of the lesson, I felt as if I had known you for several years.

I think you gave us the greatest gift a teacher can bestow—an awakening of a passion for learning. You have traveled around the world; you have interesting and abundant experience, and you acknowledge the differences among all kinds of cultures, and you do want to part your knowledge on to us. So the contents of your classes are colorful and helpful. Besides, you are able to hold the attention and interest of your audience. You are a clear speaker, with a good, strong, pleasing voice that is fully under your control. And you can act what you are teaching, so that makes its meaning clear. And by some devices you led us to an appreciation of the beauty and perfection of English. I think you are one of the best teachers I've ever known because you are always patient and fair. I admire you and respect you very much.

This term I made a lot of progress in English, especially in speaking and writing. But in the latter part of the semester, the load of our courses is heavier, and sometimes I am very lazy. So my assignments are sparse. And I seldom review or prepare for my English classes, so I have some kind of retrogress. I want to apologize to you for this.

Though I like writing in Chinese, and also like reading English novels, I never thought writing English compositions was joyful before. I thought it was a painful task, because with limited vocabulary, I could only write what I could write, but not what I wanted to write and what I was thinking. I couldn't express myself freely and thoroughly. But you always gave me encouragement. Warmed by such confidence, I felt I had to justify it by giving more than my best. And I tried. I want to thank you for your help and encouragement. I don't know whether I can improve my writing ability in English steadily or whether I will take a career related to writing in the future, but now I am sure writing English compositions has become one of my hobbies. If I can write a paper worth to read, I will mail it to you.

You are the most unforgettable teacher I've met. I really appreciate your teaching ability and your personality. And I think your writing is quite moving. When you finish your book about your memories and experiences, please let me know. I think it will be beautifully written and I will be able to understand its meaning and your feeling that you express in that book.

I hope I can see you again soon. If one day you want to come to Beijing, please write to me or send a telegram. I'll meet you at the airport or train station. You'll be assured of a hearty welcome from all my family.

If you go to a new place, would you like to tell me some of your impressions and experiences? I will look forward to hearing from you."

July 10, 1992

I am having one of those, "If I could leave China in a minute, I would" days. Communication is a true nightmare here. I'm in Hangzhou, but I can't seem to reach Richard, Bill, or Russell. Jerry has gone off to Shanghai. There is no trace of a telegram that Benjamin is supposed to have sent telling me what train he and Peter are taking to Hangzhou. I've already gone to the train station to meet a couple of trains they haven't been on.

I have had enough noise to last me forever. It kept me up all night. Yet it's too warm to close the windows. The fan above the bed has only one speed—hurricane speed, and it is precariously "secured" into the ceiling. I can imagine it falling down, chopping away as it goes.

All I can think of are the difficulties of the long train ride to Benjamin's home, and then the discomfort of going to Shenzhen and Zhuhai with so much luggage. Of course, I don't need my down jacket in the heat of the summer, but I must carry everything with me for the four seasons. I am an overloaded turtle carrying my home with me on my back.

I wonder where I'll find work for September. In many ways, I've had enough of China for now. But I'll probably begin missing it as soon as I leave.

July 12, 1992

The weather's no cooler, but I've cooled down now that the boys have made contact with me and Benjamin and Peter have arrived. Richard met me with a funny story. He had received my April Fool's letter back in April when he was with some of the other people in the factory where he's working. Of course, none of them could read English. They crowded around him and asked him to tell them what was in the letter.

At first, he felt happy to be the center of attention, but "I started to sweat," he told me. I had written the letter with every word backward as an April Fool's Day joke and he couldn't make head nor tails out of it!

Both Richard and Russell talked a lot about the effect meeting my parents had on them. Richard said he actually stopped smoking after my mother's health lecture, made stronger by how her smoking had given her chronic asthmatic bronchitis. He said he can already feel a difference in his nose and throat. There have been several letters back and forth between them and Mom. I feel an undercurrent from both boys that they resent the fact I'm not my mother. They miss her.

July 15, 1992

Benjamin suspected there was a problem when only his 80-year-old grandmother met us at the train station. His father had been in the hospital for several days with fluid in a joint. His mother was just hospitalized for a high fever, and his brother is now in the hospital with a high fever. His granny is the strong one holding it all together.

July 22, 1992

I can see a corner of blue sky with two thick lines of dirty white clouds. There is part of a balcony and an old shingled roof in my view. Some scraggly red flowers make a nice contrast with the open blue door. A small mirror with a crane wrapped around it stands on the desk across from the cranes on the curtains. The squares of tile add color to the floor. The artificial wind of the fan stirs the curtains, calendar, and embroidered blue and white tablecloth. It helps a bit in bearing the heat.

The fan also adds a whirring sound to the plethora of human sounds that surround us constantly, except in the deep of night when I, alone, like to be awake (unless, of course, there's a "hot" mahjong game that goes throughout the night.) The little children of the kindergarten downstairs make a constant and confusing din. The apartment is located somehow inside a square of apartments, which magnifies sounds as though we are inside a tin can.

Surprisingly, I hear no shuffling feet in the apartment. That is rare, since everyone in the house shuffles rather continuously from place to place, each with his or her own gait and rhythm.

Benjamin is calmer now and more at rest than I ever saw him at the university. He obviously loves being in the warmth of his family, especially his granny who dotes on him. His granny had been a teacher and had taken him to school with her when he was little more than a toddler. At one part of his life, he had lived with his grandmother while his mother and brother had lived elsewhere. Then, because of his high intelligence, he had been sent off to the university at the tender age of 14. Benjamin's future is the focus of the family. The pressure on him is intense, but at least he has a brother with whom to share the burden of high expectations. The "only children" of China's future will feel the full weight upon them with no siblings to dilute the pressure.

I can see many ways in which this family is different from the others I have visited. They are educated, and I have even read a few of the books in English in their home, which belonged to Benjamin's grandfather. They also seem to have more money than the other families I know. They even have a refrigerator—the first I've seen in a family's home.

However, the family doesn't eat much. They all wolf down bowls of rice with liberal servings of chili peppers. Since I can't eat such spicy food, the grandmother buys and prepares different food for me. Benjamin explained that she doesn't like to spend money on food. When Benjamin's uncle came to visit from Shenzhen, he hosted a large banquet for us and many other relatives. Granny couldn't get over how much money he spent.

His uncle is an interesting man. Although we are unable to communicate verbally, we took an instant liking to each other. He calls me the Chinese for "elder sister," and urged me to call him the Chinese for "younger brother" that indicates a warm relationship. He has a factory in Shenzhen that produces women's handbags. He gave me a couple to see if I could find U.S. companies that would buy his bags from China. Foreign trade, import and export, seems to be what China is hoping will bring it into the rest of the world. The uncle is already rich by Chinese standards. Benjamin's future is heading toward foreign trade.

I've met some of Benjamin's friends who all seem fascinated with video games, bridge, soccer, and computers. I went with a group of his high school classmates to visit one of their former teachers at his home. Once again, I really appreciated the interest and warm feelings that bond teachers and their Chinese students permanently.

July 27, 1992

The earlier plan had been for Peter to come all the way to Benjamin's home and then we'd all go to Peter's home together. However, as the train had come closer to Peter's home, he said he was missing his parents too much after all those months at school and couldn't wait any longer to see them. Benjamin and I reunited with him at his home before going on to Shenzhen.

Peter's home was also incredibly hot in the Chinese summer, but his family's apartment had a view of a nice, cool river. I couldn't blame the children from the area who played and swam in the river to cool off. But the place where I saw polluted water from factories gushing into the river definitely kept me out of the water.

Peter's mother worked for a factory that made ramie cloth. The homes of the workers were right around the factory. At one time in California, I had organized a teenage girls' group and we had gone to a pickle factory. After that, I was hooked on seeing any factory I could get into. So, I appreciated a very complete tour of this cloth factory.

Since I was a foreigner staying in their home, Peter's family applied for permission for me to stay there. I had to go with him to the government office to get the chop of approval for a few days' stay.

August 4, 1992

Imagine a city that is being built before your very eyes. Roads are being constructed in front of you. The dust never settles. Somewhat whimsical skyscrapers are growing like weeds. It's hard to find an old person. The children that you see are mostly beggars who follow you tenaciously around the railway station. It is a society of young adults, scurrying around with dollar signs in their eyes. I've been told that the young girls here use their looks and sex to get what they want. With some exceptions, most Chinese who have permission to live here are not allowed to go into Hong Kong, a tantalizingly short subway ride away, but still a world forbidden to them. Although Shenzhen isn't Hong Kong, you can immediately tell it's not like any other place in mainland China.

Shenzhen also has something most of mainland China doesn't have—McDonald's! The fame of McDonald's had spread in China long before McDonald's arrived. My parents told me they had visited one of the first McDonald's in Beijing. It had rows and rows of shiny cash registers and animated young clerks taking orders.

We got the traditional cheeseburgers, fries, and sodas. The boys were uncomfortable with picking up the cheeseburger in their hands, so they wrapped napkins around it. As they lifted the cheeseburgers up, their noses crinkled in distaste, asking what that awful smell was. They struggled through the evil-smelling stuff. Compared to the multiple dishes of a Chinese meal, one boy asked me how such a little thing to eat could be so filling.

The next day at dinnertime, I headed toward a Chinese restaurant, but the boys lagged behind. "What's wrong?" I asked. They all agreed, "We want to go to McDonald's again!" No, they hadn't liked the food. Yes, it had smelled nasty. But the lure of the western way of eating overcame everything else.

13

HONG KONG MACAU 1992

August 13, 1992

I'm 49 now in Hong Kong, although in the U.S. it wouldn't be my birthday quite yet. My day is going well. Sentimentalist that I am, I decided to try something new and something old.

I began at Stanley Bay. Since it's not a weekend, it was relatively uncrowded and very pleasant. It's a new side of Hong Kong for me. I liked it. I like being by the ocean. Perhaps because of being raised by the water, I feel good when I'm near the sea. There was an occasional breeze, which helped on this blistering summer day. The worry of finding a job only quietly nagged at the back of my mind.

I thanked whomever, whatever for my continuing good health. And, although poor, I'm still solvent. I have a lot to look forward to now that I'm approaching my 6th decade and half a century mark. I watched some kids at the beach learning, mostly unsuccessfully, how to windsurf. I wished that they were my mainland friends I'd left behind.

I even found a temple where I lit incense to many of the people and places I love. The smell of incense and the temples brought fond remembrances of Taiwan.

I'm now ending the day with the inspiring magnificence of Victoria Peak and a quiet night stroll in the park—just the crickets and me, a few runners and lovers, and a dog I shared my birthday strudel with. There is a bright and beautiful full moon to start my 49th year. I'm already looking forward to returning to the Kowloon side on the way back to my hostel and admiring the mouth-dropping view of Hong Kong's skyline across the harbor. I never tire of seeing that, whether by day or by night.

August 22, 1992

I've settled into the hostel to await word from the Polytechnic in Macau as to whether or not they are going to hire me to teach there in the fall. I'm in a room of ten women, squeezed into bunk beds. Nothing's very spacious in Hong Kong. Even the schools put their playgrounds on their roofs. Fortunately, I have a lower bunk. Much like the Chinese kids in their dorms, my bed has become my own little world with books and daily items I use arranged around the bed. I've even utilized the bars of the bunk bed to drape towels and laundry like curtains for a bit of privacy.

Some people are actually living at the hostel because they've found jobs locally. There are both long-term and short-term tourists who come through. Most are younger than I, but not all. One old woman asks me over and over who I am, where I've come from, where I'm going. Some of us worry about her when she goes out and feel relieved when she finds her way back to the hostel. One girl had a high fever for over a week and we brought her food. I remember one woman who never could manage to get to the airport in time to catch her scheduled flight. She finally had to sleep at the airport in order not to miss her flight. Most try to be considerate when others are sleeping, but there are always those who have no concept of how noisy the crinkling of plastic bags can be when someone's sleeping. Life in hostels became much more bearable to me after I discovered ear plugs.

There are often romances that form quickly, and usually end quickly. There are also fledgling friendships that begin in hostels. I've been fortunate to have some continuing relationships that began in hostels. Here I'm becoming friendly with a middle-aged New Yorker who regularly comes to visit Hong Kong for about a month every year. She's a psychologist. It's interesting how people at the hostel seek her out for some free counseling. She helped me solve a mystery.

A young Chinese American girl was staying in an upper bunk that looked down on my bed. She was going through some kind of emotional turmoil because she would sometimes get up on her bunk and just cry and sob. One day, she greeted me with "I don't want to ruin your life, but I can't be your friend." After that surprise announcement, she ran out of the room sobbing. I hadn't a clue as to what that was all about. We had hardly exchanged anything more than mere pleasantries.

Very late that night when the psychologist returned, I heard the girl climb down and ask her if they could talk. The next day, Vivian, the psychologist, told me that the young girl was convinced I was a lesbian who wanted her desperately. Vivian didn't know me very well, but she felt the poor girl was going through some identity crisis. Shortly after that, the girl just disappeared, leaving her belongings. The people at the hostel said it happens occasionally that people just suddenly disappear and leave behind everything. In her luggage, they found a book written by a famous Chinese American woman.

This incident brought to mind again the complications people face who are torn between different parts of themselves. I'm glad I'm not biologically mixed racial. I am 100% Jewish, but, through living in other countries, have happily and voluntarily become a multicultural mixture.

August 26, 1992

Hanging around waiting to hear from the school in Macau has given me the chance to read Myself A Mandarin by Austin Coates. Although the book was written about Hong Kong in 1968, his perplexity at dealing with Chinese people often matches my own. "To anyone trying to understand other races in the world, the Chinese surely pose the greatest challenge…In everything to do with my Chinese friends, I was invariably either a bar late, or else playing in the wrong key…Beneath the surface of every day lies a continual struggle to understand the deceptively different realities underlying the visible nature of things."

He and I might have had quite a conversation sharing our China experiences.

August 29, 1992

Much of life in Hong Kong requires traveling like a mole beneath the earth, burrowing from place to place through the subway tunnels. It is, however, Britishly clean, efficient, and convenient. Vivian and I left the comfort and convenience of Hong Kong temporarily to visit Macau. She was interested in seeing it, and I had to go there for a job interview.

Although our Hong Kong hostel wasn't particularly special, we missed it when we were in Macau. We ended up staying in an old, decaying, cheap hotel with a very bizarre configuration of rooms. It all made sense when someone told us it had formerly been an opium den. There was, however, nothing historically significant about the piles of dirt and trash among the decay. A couple of rather large rats as roommates pushed us out of that place.

Sept. 2, 1992

I was getting nowhere waiting for the Polytechnic to notify me as to whether or not I could work there this fall. They just kept putting me off with "next week we'll let you know" as I was running out of money. I decided to take the leap over to Macau and find other job possibilities.

And so I have arrived at a different hotel, which well may have been a defunct opium den too, but cleaner than the other one. In contrast to the hugeness of the rooms in the first hotel, this one is divided into cells in which an oversized bed, sink, table and chair, and overhead fan just fit. It also has a very frail balcony, which I don't trust to hold my weight. There is no room to move, but then I suppose that people inhaling opium weren't too active. A lattice high up on the walls up to the ceiling offers more circulation of air. Several peepholes in the walls are covered over with "pasties."

Mostly workers live here, and I'm sure pay only a fraction of what I'm paying. The iron Jewish star in the railing around this strangely pie-shaped building makes me feel just a bit more at home. However, the smallness of my cell is closing in on me. It is even too dingy and depressing for my standards. There simply aren't the variety of cheap and somewhat decent hostels in Macau like there are in Hong Kong. Much as I enjoy Hong Kong, I don't want to live in its busyness and congestion. And work permits for Americans aren't so easy to get. Therefore, I must make my stand in Macau to find work.

So, armed only with the hubris of overconfidence that I'll find some gainful employment in Macau, I have decided to go apartment hunting.

Sept. 6, 1992

As yet I have no job, and no work permit to remain in Macau past 20 days, but I've signed a two-year lease for probably the most unusual apartment I'll ever have. I'll try to describe it.

I had quickly decided that I didn't want to live in a highrise in the very congested main part of Macau, so I headed for Taipa Village on the first island connected by bridge. Without much of a clue as to how to proceed, I stopped to buy a bottle of water in a small shop on the first floor of a row of homes. The teenage girl who took my money started a halting conversation in English. I explained that I was looking for a small apartment. She said to wait a minute, and left. Some minutes later, she came back with a woman who had a connection with an apartment for rent very close by. We went into a building just a few houses down.

What has become my room in Taipa Village is a medium-sized light and airy room with a high ceiling. Two large doors open up into a long balcony with a bamboo rod high up for hanging clothes to dry. There is also a large window, and a hallway that includes another large balcony, a slab sticking out from the wall that I finally understood was my "kitchen," and a small room with a squat toilet. There is a cold-water spigot low on the wall near the squat toilet and one at foot level from the balcony off the hallway. When I asked about a shower, the landlady said they could put one in for me next to the squat toilet.

There is another apartment off the hallway, and a stairway leading to a third apartment upstairs. Underneath is the unused first floor of the building, which once was an office but is now only used for storage. All space is shared with an infinite number of cockroaches and geckoes.

Ah, the view! The view is best. I see green everywhere. From my second floor balcony, I look out upon a small, decoratively tiled public water area combined with a tiny Buddhist shrine across the narrow street. Behind these are some magnificent trees and luxuriant foliage climbing up the hill as only the tropics can grow them. Next to the shrine is a wonderful old, abandoned building that has been well reclaimed by nature with vines and flowers crawling everywhere.

When my new teenage neighbor, Bobbie, explained to the landlady that I had no furniture, I returned to find a table, chair, and what must be the very first version of a sofa bed in the room.

I only pay $100 a month, which is probably double the going rate for a Chinese person. As a foreigner, I never would have found this place without Bobbie's help. I think I'll be happy in this total Chinese environment. Actually, it's much more like mainland China than Hong Kong or Macau city.

I'm ready for a modified "nest," not unlike the several birds nesting in the eaves of my front balcony—not too permanent, but "home" nonetheless. But can I find a job with a work permit that will let me stay?

Sept. 10, 1992

My persistence and obstinacy have paid off! I have a part time job teaching English to hotel staff at a new, big, fancy hotel called The New Century Hotel. That won't get me a work permit, but some good luck did. A job at the Canadian College of Macau (which is actually a high school) opened up unexpectedly when a new teacher backed out at the last minute. Fortunately, I had left Bobbie's grandmother's phone number with the principal even though he had told me all the jobs were filled. Without a way to speak to me, Bobbie's grandmother had stood under my balcony one afternoon yelling and clapping her hands until I came out. She then gestured there was a phone call.

"Can you teach math?" the principal asked me hopefully.

"Not even to kindergarten," I replied with a sigh.

Desperate as he was at the last minute, he decided he would teach the math classes and I could teach social studies, geography, and literature to the high school students. Most of the students are Chinese, but as an international high school, all subjects are taught in English.

Hooray! Let my Macau adventure begin!

Sept. 13, 1992

"Very lucky. I can see that next month you'll be very lucky," he said as he came into my vision. I had been walking deep in thought and wasn't prepared for this turbaned good-looking young man with a magnificent curled moustache. After all, I was in Macau where Chinese make up 95% of the population. This member of the 5% "others" category kept muttering about my good luck and pointing to a piece of red showing out from his turban. If this was supposed to have any significance to me, I disappointed him.

Slowly, I grasped the thought that he wanted to tell my fortune. Perhaps that's what he wanted, but he was already walking on. I called after him, "Oh no, I don't want to know my future." And so I don't, and haven't ever really wanted any fortuneteller—no matter in which country—to tell me my future. After all, curiosity is a major force that drives me and keeps me interested in living.

My curiosity has led me to my room and hallway in Taipa Village in a country where I celebrate Moon Festival, but not Thanksgiving. It has led me to places where I am always a part of that small "other" category of residents, where an Indian man can appear before me as well as an international mixture of kids at the Canadian College of Macau.

Here I share my room with one tiny mouse who comes back to his hole every night about 10 p.m., and lots of geckoes who (thankfully) like the supply of mosquitoes that invade my room. I light my camping stove with joss sticks and live near several Buddhist, rather than Jewish, temples. The mob scene of Macau is a sharp contrast to little Taipa Village and even more of a contrast to wonderful Coloane, which offers rolling hills to climb as well as ocean swimming in a picturesque cove, or in a delightful public pool I recently discovered across from the cove.

Of course I still miss China, but it is not so very far away. I'll be able to go back often while I live in Macau.

October 15, 1992

I am living amid many contradictions—the old and the modern, quiet and noise, good air and bad, the poor and the rich, the east with a touch of Europe. There is more variety than I ever imagined in the 6.5 square miles that comprise Macau.

I have added a clever European hot water heater to my shower that heats the water as I use it. My little "kitchen" has expanded to a cabinet for pots and pans and a miniature refrigerator. I usually take the handy camping stove out to the railing of my hallway balcony to cook the little that I bother cooking. I call it my "kitchen extension." A large plastic bowl on the slab is my sink. No wonder Chinese don't lose mobility as fast as old Americans. Nothing, including the water spigots, is at a convenient height. Squatting to reach the water spigot, and squatting at the toilet, are daily challenges.

In my "main" room, I have added a plastic closet, some lamps, a very comfortable chair for reading, and a mosquito net above my bed that somehow ends up strangling me by morning. It's really quite a cozy home, although the bars on all the windows seem somewhat prison-like.

I can tell the time of day or night by the noises that surround me. Very, very early in the morning, I am awakened by the chairs and tables being set out in the alley next to my home. Workers stream in for breakfast noodles or rice, noisily greeting each other and chatting loudly as though they aren't sitting next to each other. I wake up long enough to put in my earplugs to soften the din. The scraping of the chairs and tables and dismantling of the makeshift restaurant a couple of hours later wakes me again in time to get up to go teach.

The evenings are lively because of all the restaurants hiding in the alleyways around my home. Outside the restaurants are many cages holding animals I can't identify. They come and go and are advertising the menu of the day. I always feel sad for these victims awaiting execution.

The narrow street in front of my home is filled with frequent noisy, smelly buses and cars. Since tiny Macau has so few places to drive, rich teenagers are fond of riding by over and over with their customized cars and blaring radios for all to admire. After the buses have stopped running, and the joy-riding teenagers have gone elsewhere, my home becomes deliciously quiet. Soon, the clink clink of the mahjong tiles becomes audible as the mahjong parlor just in back of my home begins in earnest for the night. These games, with excited yells when a game gets hot, often go through the night.

I have no interest in getting a television, but I'm kept well informed and entertained by BBC on my small short-wave radio. Now that I'm so close to Hong Kong, BBC reception is clear and easy. I don't have to hold my radio and keep moving it around to pick up the signal as I do in China. There is much more on BBC than the news. I'm surprised at the breadth and depth of their programs compared to Voice of America, which offers some entertainment and a lot of American propaganda.

I have many choices for food here. I can eat bagels, lox, and cream cheese, pizza from Pizza Hut, European espresso coffee, great chocolate, or any kind of Chinese or Portuguese food. I know I'm in Macau when someone orders a lemon tea or lemon Coke, takes a spoon and thoroughly and methodically mashes the many lemon slices to a pulp before drinking. There's wonderful imported juice in the supermarkets. I miss juice so much when I'm in China! Even some of the five-star hotels in China pass off Tang as orange juice. When I told someone in China I missed juice very much, he asked what juice was. When I explained that the juice was squeezed from the fruit, "What a waste of precious fruit," was his reply. As I thought about it, he was right. I remember ordering a glass of juice at juice stands in Israel and noticing how much fruit it took to make a glass to drink. Still, I'm so glad to have juice back in my life.

For a bit more than I pay for my room monthly, I have joined the Hyatt Hotel's fitness center. Here I work out as many times as I wish each week in the exercise classes run by gorgeous, muscular Australian young men. Afterward, I pamper myself with the sauna, steam room, and jacuzzi. And as often as I feel I can afford the $25, I have a massage by a masterful Filipina masseuse.

Standing alongside the human-sized statues of Coke and Hi C, the trees in Taipa are quite magnificent. Some are two trunks intertwined. Massive banyan trees wrap themselves into creative designs. An old temple down the street is slowly falling apart. It has lost its ceiling, but a tree and its roots actually form the roof. I don't understand how it is even possible, but I can look up and see its root structure with my own eyes.

My home was most likely built by a Portuguese merchant who needed to be near the sea where the ships loaded with tea and silk anchored a hundred years ago. The sea has been banished from those shores in a land reclamation effort, but a quiet, lovely park remains, along with a couple of old, restored homes and a museum to remember the glory of Taipa's past. I walk there often.

If Macau is most like a modern city, and Taipa is a quaint suburb, then Coloane is the picturesque countryside that offers trails along the hilltops overlooking the Pearl River and the South China Sea beyond. From here it is hard to tell that Macau is booming and pounding. Here the birds sound louder than the explosions, grinding of steel, and violent sounds of rearranging the earth. The trail I like the most goes from the sea on one side, through some hilltops, and down to another beach enclosed by hills.

The sand on this beach is scratchy and feels like a foot massage on my feet. How many voices the water has! Little brooks babble, streams gurgle, rivers rush, and the ocean speaks many sounds. The water can be serene and restful in its monotony, or it can be full of swishes and swirls as it curls noisily around the big rocks. It can leap playfully upon rocks as well as the unwary people walking on the rocks. And, it makes an audible swoosh and shoosh as it crawls over the sand.

In Macau, I can find pieces of Hong Kong, China, Portugal, Britain, the United States, Santa Barbara by the sea, and a unique blend of all of them. I can live in an old Chinese village, work for a Canadian school, get a massage at a five-star hotel, and see an American doctor connected to a Baptist Clinic at $10 an office visit. I am living in a time warp, and a place warp.

Oct. 31, 1992

The fall season is the best season in Macau. Not only has the terrible heat of the summer cooled off, but there is an annual Music Festival and an international fireworks competition. Once a week, for several weeks, one country sets off a 20 minute extravaganza of its newest, most creative and artistic fireworks. These are easily the best fireworks I've ever seen. A winner is eventually chosen. The Music Festival provides a series of delights, sometimes performed in halls and sometimes in gardens. The culmination of the festival is an elaborately staged complete opera that is attended and lauded or criticized by just about every Portuguese person living here.

I spent this Halloween at a concert I found out about by chance from reading a poster advertising it. I was hungry to hear some live music, but had no idea what to expect. In came 50 or so mostly Chinese men and women dressed in traditional ancient Chinese robes. In sharp contrast, the conductor was dressed in a formal tuxedo. Most of the instruments were ancient Chinese ones, which came in a very wide variety of shapes and sizes, and especially sounds.

I can't appreciate the nasal, high-pitched singing of Chinese opera, but the sounds of the classical Chinese instruments totally delighted me. These marvelous instruments can bring alive sounds I never even suspected exist. Their music evokes in me a state of conscious suspension in which I relive the warmth of some of my indescribably high and happy times in China.

I am always envious of the way musicians themselves become totally engrossed in the music they are producing. At the end of a piece, a brief expression of surprise flit across their faces at finding themselves on a stage in front of an audience. At the conclusion, the conductor and soloists bowed and awkwardly accepted huge bouquets of flowers that seem to accompany every performance, be it professional or amateur, in Hong Kong, Taiwan, and Macau.

Sometimes the beep of beepers, the ring of mobile phones, the rustling of programs, and the general chatting of the audience broke the spell momentarily. The contrast between the often crude behavior of Chinese and the delicacy of their art and music regularly confounds me.

Nov. 10, 1992

"As anyone who has lived among Chinese people will testify, Chinese friendship, once established, is of the truest." This quote from Austin Coates in his book, Myself a Mandarin, has been on my mind lately. I have received some letters from a few of my Taiwanese students who have been studying in the U.S. on an exchange program. Independently of each other, each girl has written me of her confusion and disappointment in friendships in America. Those American girls they thought of as friends turned out not to be their friends at all. One girl had even felt so friendless, she had decided to quit the program and return to Taiwan.

I, too, have come to see that the concept of friendship is different in the Chinese culture. I am only beginning to understand the complications. Chinese, whether poor or not, rely heavily on relatives and friends. Independence is not valued in the same way as westerners value it. You feel free to ask of a good friend whatever you need. This is considered helping out, not "using" in the bad sense. When the helper needs help, the help is owed and repaid. That is why *guanxi*, connections, are even better than money. In Israel, I also noticed the importance of connections built up from school years and army years together, which new immigrants had never been able to develop as a support network.

In China, help is expected from friends if it is within their power to help. And, the closer you are, the less gratitude is expressed directly. To us, it may even seem like ingratitude, "using," and keeping a scorecard of favors. To Chinese, western friendships seem polite, superficial, and shallow.

I was surprised once when Richard said that he didn't want more friends because friends required care, nurturing, and obligation. I have come to understand that attitude better now.

Nov. 16, 1992

The impossible may now be possible! My part time job at The New Century Hotel has brought me into contact with the woman who regularly goes into mainland China to recruit staff for the hotel. They recruit kids from Shanghai and Guangzhou basically because it's cheaper for the hotel. The recruits are put into crowded, but clean dormitories. Their salary is low for Macau, but higher than what most can earn in China. They don't get Chinese passports and can't get Macau passports (which are actually Portuguese passports because it's still a Portuguese colony), but they get special work permits that allow them to travel only between Macau and China. After working at the hotel for two years, they can return to China if they haven't worked out any other options. Many do find ways to stay in Macau. Of course, the hotel is exploiting them, but it's also a chance for exposure to a richer, more westernized lifestyle and better working conditions.

There are several pitfalls along the way, however. Among these good-looking, ambitious, young mainland recruits I am teaching at the hotel, I have heard that many of them succumb to temptations that would not be found so easily back home. The boys often gamble away their hard-earned money in Macau's casinos. Since the bank that pays them their salaries is located in one of the biggest casinos, some don't even get out of the casino before losing their entire month's wages. If they should happen to win, they get hooked even faster.

Pretty girls in my classes show up wearing expensive jewelry that advertises the benefits of extracurricular activities easily found in an entertainment city that Asians from other countries flock to. Limousines even come to the dorms to pick them up for a night out. It's predictable, but sad.

So, there really is a chance for me to be the *guanxi* that some of my mainland friends need. And, it wouldn't cost me any money. I could set up meetings between them and the recruiter when she goes to Shanghai next. But would it be a good thing? I'm both excited at the prospect, and worried about the huge responsibility of changing anyone's life so drastically.

Nov. 19, 1992

Good news! Thanksgiving is alive and well in Macau. The American expats here manage to get some turkeys from Hong Kong, and the rest of us bring potluck dishes. The principal of our school says that he waits eagerly every year for his chance to enjoy Thanksgiving turkey. I'm rather excited too about tasting a freshly roasted turkey with all the trimmings. The diversity of the spices of life in tiny Macau never ceases to amaze me.

Dec. 1, 1992

I've been meeting a new friend weekly at a very special library in Macau that is a replica of an ornate library in Toledo, Spain. Her name is Mary Gaunt. It doesn't matter that she died before I was born. Lest I think my adventures as a lone woman traveler in China were extraordinary, she has left behind a book called A Woman in China with a copyright date of 1914 that shows me we would have a lot to talk about together. This old book is too precious to take out, but I'm welcome to visit Mary in the quiet and dignity of these unusual surroundings that neither of us would expect to find in Macau.

I worry what will become of Mary's old book along with the other dated treasures of this library when Macau reverts to Chinese rule in 1999. The librarian has told me that these books will not be allowed to return to Portugal after the handover. With such an uncertain fate, the library is attempting to put them onto microfilm for posterity.

CONVERSATIONS WITH MARY

Mary: "I had reached China, the land of blue skies and of sunshine; the land of desperate poverty and of wonderful wealth; the land of triumph, and of martyrdom, and of mystery."

Me: "Even in 1988 when I first came to China, it was an unusual destination for an American woman alone. China's past of deep poverty and extravagant wealth still seep through the sights one visits even though communism has leveled the excesses in the present. As a third-world country, it all seems poor to the eyes of a westerner. You would be disappointed in how polluted those blue skies have become as coal and smokestacks obliterate the blue. The mystery you felt remains."

Mary: "…in all the towns I passed through I was a show, and the people stared, and chattered, and crowded round the carts, and evidently closely questioned the carters…What romance they wove about me, I don't know."

Me: "Yes, I know what you mean. It was a new phenomenon for me to be looked at so continuously and so carefully everywhere I went in China. In the U.S., I blend in anonymously and attract no attention at all. I know that it bothers some foreigners to be scrutinized so constantly, but I accept it as the curiosity of a country that has basically been closed to the outside world for such a long time. I particularly remember a man walking along a railroad track who was obviously shocked to see me looking out the train window. He studied me with an intense stare as though I surely was from another planet. I broke into a smile. Then it struck him that I was just another human being. Whereupon, he broke into a big, wide smile and we made contact."

Mary: "When first I heard of the wolves, I laughed. I was so sure no beast of prey could live alongside a Chinaman for the Chinaman would want to eat him."

Me: "It was in the markets of Canton, now called Guangzhou, where I first watched snakes being stripped of their skins, saw eels swimming around, and cage upon cage of miserable animals that I couldn't even identify. Dogs lay bleeding and half dead, waiting only for some gourmet to put them out of their misery. I never saw cats wandering the streets.

But food is food. And Chinese have suffered from starvation. You were in China long before Mao and the terrible famines, but the Chinese have had to endure starvation often. In truth, is a squid, octopus, sea cucumber or jellyfish any less edible than a lobster or shrimp? When I ate eel, I liked it—until someone said that it was eel. So my friends knew never to announce we were eating eel. Although possibly delicious, I never intentionally ate dog or monkey brains, but I did actually enjoy eating a pig's ear once."

Mary: "A man with a birdcage in his hand, taking birdie for a walk, is a common sight in China...but I have never seen a man followed by a dog."

Me: "It seems to be the delight of older men in cities to take their birds for a daily walk. They hang the cages in the trees and listen to their lovely songs while they gather for a smoke and a chat with their human friends. I have heard that swinging the cage gives the bird the illusion of being free. I wonder if that's true.

My countryside friends have told me that they sometimes have pet dogs. I met one of these dogs, but it was not used to being touched or played with. My friends expect their pet dogs to be short-lived. It is no surprise when, one night, the dog doesn't return home. One friend even told me his mother went out looking for their dog and caught a neighbor in the act of skinning it.

The close relationship that we westerners might have with a pet dog is reserved for the peasant and his water buffalo."

Mary: "The average Chinese mind is essentially orderly, and never dreams of questioning rules...their faces are impassive, smiling with a surface smile that gives no indication of the feelings behind."

Me: "Events in China between your visit and mine have held much sadness and repression of both thinking and action, but these observations are as true today as they appeared to you in 1914. The inscrutability of the Chinese must be attributable to their culture more than their politics."

Mary: "Squeeze seems to be the accepted fact in China."

Me: "Bribery and corruption certainly remain in China. Proper "connections" can make or break one's life. My friends have told me that *guanxi* is interwoven into the very fabric of life in China, much like a sweater that would unravel without it. They may not like the system, but they can imagine no other."

Mary: "The foreigner in China is divided into two camps. He is either missionary or he is anti-missionary. Both sides are keen on the matter...I began to think and to say that missionary enterprise, which I had always thought should turn its attention to its own people, was at least justified in this land of China where no provision was made for the sick and afflicted, and where charity was unknown."

Me: "You would be surprised to know that all the missionaries were kicked out of China by the communist government. This did not mean, however, that the sick and disabled have been cared for by anyone else. Train stations are filled with unfortunates who stick the stump of their arm into your face to beg for money. Painfully thin children stick out bowls to you as a way to tell you they are hungry. My friends assure me that begging is organized and big business, but my western eyes see mostly desperation on these faces. Are children really intentionally maimed by their parents to evoke more sympathy for begging? Perhaps so.

Missionaries are sneaking back into China in any guise they can. Their goal is more conversion to Christianity than helping the poor. Deprived by the government of their traditional Buddhist rituals, the Chinese of today seem starved for some sense of spirituality. Some of my students have asked me about god. As China opens its doors more and more, many religious groups are poised to jump in and fill the spiritual void. In Macau, there is a large group of the Baha'i faith biding their time as an international school and preparing their strategy for encouraging converts. I even met a couple of Messianic Jews assigned to infiltrate China and quietly introduce their religion.

I'm sorry to say that missionaries will once again have their day in modern China."

Mary: "...and when I inspected the room offered for my accommodation, I only wished drearily that there had been no room in this particular inn, and that I might have slept out in the open...When I smelled the smell of the rooms, rank and abominable, and reeking of human occupancy, I envied my mules sleeping outside. The Chinese, as a rule, have not much use of fresh air. They all bear a strong resemblance to one another, the rooms of these Chinese inns."

Me: "Although probably not as bad as where you stayed, the sameness and dreariness of the cheap hotels I stay in can get rather depressing. The carpets are always stained. Nothing seems truly clean. Rarely do things like toilets, showers, lights work properly. And the room, sheets, pillows—absolutely everything reeks of cigarette smoke from many former occupants. They are places to be endured rather than enjoyed."

Mary: "It marked a wonderful stride in Chinese feeling that a Chinese should come to the assistance of a foreigner in distress."

Me: "The first time I knew I was being cheated by a street vendor was the look of triumph on his face and the laughter of the crowd that had gathered to watch our transaction. And Richard, Russell, and Bill explained to me once that a watermelon vendor had chastised them for not helping him to cheat me. He told them he expected their help as Chinese to be on his side. But then I remember a woman who stopped by while I was negotiating for some fruit. Even though I couldn't understand her words to the vendor, it was clear that she told the vendor not to charge me more than a Chinese person. Other pedicab drivers in Jiaxin also told one of their own that he had overcharged me and pressured him to give me back some money."

Mary: "But since the interpreter knew even less English than Tuan, whom I had left outside, there was really little else to do but smile and look pleasant."

Me: "Smiling and looking pleasant is often the only option in a country where you are reduced to an illiterate deaf mute. Being speechless in a different country is a humbling experience indeed."

Mary: "In truth, the civilization of China is still so much like that of Babylon and Ninevah, that it is best for the poor man, if he can, to efface himself. He does not pray for rights as yet. He only prays that he may slip through life unnoticed, that he may not come in contact with the powers that rule him, for no matter who is right or who is wrong, bitter experience has taught him that he will suffer."

Me: "My friends have told me of a Chinese saying that the nail that stands above the others is the first to get hit by the hammer. So, it is still true today that they don't want to be noticed too much. Yet, there is something else stirring in the minds of the Chinese of today. The educated have been awakened by what they've learned of the world. For peasants even in the remotest villages, the television has brought knowledge of other worlds to them."

Mary: "Today, the spirit of the West is breathing over her and she responds a little, ever so little, and murmurs of change, yet she remains the same at heart as she has been through the ages."

Me: "China is a vast country of over a billion people whose history spans thousands of years. I cannot comprehend these numbers in any meaningful way. How fast can a behemoth change? What parts of its culture should be kept and which parts thrown away? Are the western ways better?

I cannot guess China's immediate or distant future. Part of the fascination for me is being here watching what happens and somehow being a part of it all."

Mary: "One thing seems certain, between us Westerners and the Chinese, is a great gulf fixed. We look across and sometimes we wonder, and sometimes we pity, and sometimes we admire, but we cannot understand."

Me: "I do not understand the bond that has grown between me and China, between me and my Chinese friends. Yet I know it is there because I feel it strongly."

Mary: "...and again I questioned the curious fate that sent me wandering uncomfortably around the world, and sometimes actually—yes actually getting enjoyment out of it."

Me: "I just think of it as a very special magic that has captured us under its spell."

Dec. 20, 1992

In the cool winter night snuggled under my quilt on my vintage sofa bed in my cozy room in a Chinese village in Macau, I think about the coming year—1993. I'll miss my afternoons with Mary in the library while I use my winter vacation break for a jaunt to China and then time in the U.S. to catch up with mom and dad and my friends. It feels good to have my job and home here to return to. And I must think about my summer plans because this is the momentous summer I'll turn (gasp) half a century old!

14

CHINA MACAU ISRAEL 1993

Jan. 2, 1993

"The fact remains that Nanjing is seldom agreeable in terms of weather and the consequent atmosphere. It's so old a city with so many pieces of broken things, or persons thousands of years ago wandering in the air. Even the dusts smell heavily." This graphic description, written by one of my Nanjing students, came to mind when I took Richard, Russell, and Thomas with me to visit Benjamin, Peter, and my other students who were still studying there.

There were the usual problems with finding accommodations. This time I had to pay for an entire dormitory room of six beds because this place wouldn't rent to foreigners and Chinese together and there were no other foreigners there that night. The night was so cold in that unheated room that I used all six quilts from the six beds.

Besides the fun of reconnecting to my Nanjing students, I was able to introduce the boys to some historic scenic sights and first time experiences in Nanjing. I took them to their first buffet in one of the nice hotels in Nanjing. Thomas looked wide-eyed at the lavish, aesthetically arranged food. In one of the old museums in Nanjing, I was trying to read all about the history of China on display while Thomas was practically running through the museum. When I asked him why he was going so fast, he said, "I'm not interested in old things. I'm interested in what's new." I could see his point. He is part of the educated modern generation that is looking forward rather than backward. I know he's been changing jobs trying hard to find a way to enter the world of business. Because of Nanjing University's reputation, companies are already courting Foreign Trade students such as Benjamin and Peter to come work for them immediately after graduation.

Richard was quite depressed about his dead-end job, but the traveling changed him back, at least temporarily, to the joking, laughing boy I knew. Russell's restlessness about getting out of teaching is now overcoming his depression. Bill may be getting married next year. The boys told me that there are certain basic requirements to get a "yes" answer to a marriage proposal. In addition to furniture, they must be able to buy a color television set, preferably foreign made, a refrigerator, and some gold jewelry for the bride. Housing is usually provided at low cost through their work unit.

I talked with many of my Hangzhou friends, both male and female, about the possibility of coming to work at the hotel in Macau if they could meet with the recruiter when she came to Shanghai. The thought of going to live as far away as Macau in such a different lifestyle was both attractive and somewhat frightening to them. Several said they'd like to meet the recruiter. Richard was the most enthusiastic about making such a drastic change.

My grandchildren are doing well. I'll need to keep visiting regularly so they can get to know me. I love bringing gifts to them and watching the smiles on their faces.

Feb. 7, 1993

My visit back to the U.S. was short, but sweet. I flew as a courier for Jupiter Airlines and it went off without a hitch. Not only is the ticket price low in exchange for giving them the opportunity to use my luggage allowance, but they put couriers in Business Class if a seat is available. Wow! That's the way to travel. I'd better not get too used to such luxury.

Mom has quite an active correspondence going with several of my friends she met during her visit to China. I know where I got my love of writing letters. Richard, Juliet, Russell and his sister are frequent correspondents with mom. Although I grew up with the heads of a Chinese man and a Chinese woman hanging as household decorations in all the homes my parents had lived in, I learned for the first time when I was back that these two Chinese people were the very first home decorations my parents had bought after they were married. In the 1970's, my parents had chosen Hong Kong as one of their first foreign countries to visit. Now they've been to China, and my life is mostly centered in Asia. Interesting coincidence?

Getting into gear for teaching was tough. I'm not sure how I'll do with my 7th and 10th grade courses. They are not the highly motivated Chinese mainland kids I prefer to teach. The difference is money. These wealthy kids know that their parents' money, rather than brains, will make their opportunities for them. At least I'll learn a lot about history and geography.

My colleagues are definitely enjoying the upgraded wardrobe I brought back from the U.S. Each day I wear something new and colorful. I like looking less monotonous. But I'll always have a special feeling for the unusual blouse and pants that were so skillfully made for me by a cross-eyed tailor when I was teaching in Nanjing.

I'm excited about my Taiwanese friend, Virginia, coming to visit me in Macau next week. Rose from Taiwan will be coming later in the year. I've also been getting some new SERVAS visitors since I'm the only SERVAS hostess listed in Macau. I enjoy my guests, but I have the restriction that they must be thin to sleep at my home. That's because I only have an old folding cot that I found to accommodate them. I can't give up my bed because I'm too fat to fit the folding cot.

Feb. 14, 1993

Change is all around me on this Valentine's Day. The sea is changing into land through land reclamation technology. My sleepy Taipa village set in the past is changing into a mini-Hong Kong. Parts of my aging body are rounding out, while other parts are sagging down. The winter weather in Macau changes daily.

When I asked my students what comes to mind when I say "Chinese," one American boy in the class said "a beeper and a mobile phone." And so the rings and beeps of the omnipresent beepers and mobile phones disturb me everywhere—on the street, on the bus, at concerts, in the movie theaters, on the beach, and, alas, even in the classroom. In mainland China these are still too expensive for most people, but the appeal of the status symbol is strong. Unable to afford the real thing, I've even seen mainland children carrying toy mobile phones.

Age changes, time changes, places change, and I change too.

INEXORABLY ONWARD TOWARD WHAT?

It is painful and sometimes humorous to watch a country struggling to come out of the Third World. Sitting in a hotel restaurant in Macau, I watch the mainland Chinese businessmen who easily stand out among the diners as they chainsmoke through their meals and busily talk on their mobile phones. Chinese are generally fond of status symbols, and it seems that these trappings of the "developed" countries seduce them easily.

Macau is a greedy place today. Having spent years as a fairly sleepy Portuguese enclave in Asia, and eventually as an escape haven for refugees from China, it leaped into materialism when it caught sight of the economic possibilities as the 1999 reunification with China neared. Looked down upon by the neighboring Hong Kong residents as a city cousin might look down upon a country cousin, Macau nevertheless became the place many Hong Kong people are making investments just in case their troublesome 1997 reunification between Hong Kong and China goes badly. Macau, with its Portuguese government, has had a much more harmonious relationship with China than has England and China over Hong Kong. Life and trade may change much more drastically for Hong Kong than for Macau after reunification although you can still find many Macau residents planning to make use of their Portuguese passports to get out.

Why the difference? I have been told that corruption lies at the root of Portuguese and Chinese compatibility. Both are cultures based on favoritism and personal connections. Furthermore, Portugal has never been able to resist what China has commanded in over 400 years of being a colony, mainly because Macau is geographically connected to the tip of the Chinese mainland, which provided food and water to Macau. Historically, the Portuguese were given permission to remain in Macau because the Portuguese sailors were effective in keeping the waters free of marauding pirates. In contrast, Hong Kong was taken forcibly in a humiliating treaty between England and China.

Most of the Portuguese in Macau will return to Portugal in or before 1999. They have had a good life in Macau with higher pay, better conditions, and a more impressive job status because most of them have government jobs. They have been tolerated rather than liked by the 95% Chinese majority in Macau. In earlier years, there was integration and intermarriage that resulted in the mixed Chinese-Portuguese Macanese. In the present 600,000 population, there are three distinct societies—Portuguese, Chinese, and the Macanese. The distinctions are not by law and all carry Portuguese passports, but, as just one simple example, one public swimming pool seems to attract mainly Chinese, while another mainly Portuguese. Even the streets show this duality in having both a Portuguese name and a Chinese name.

The people in the middle—part Chinese and part Portuguese—fit in both cultures, and in neither. They will have the hardest time after 1999. They will not be very welcome in Portugal. And, even though most speak fluent Portuguese and Cantonese Chinese, as well as a local patois, they won't quite fit their native land either after 1999.

Macau's main attraction is not business and trade, but gambling. Compared to Hong Kong's illegal gambling, Macau showily flaunts its many casinos. Starting on the hovercraft from Hong Kong to Macau, you can begin gambling. There are other attractions including temples, historical sites, museums, and nature trails in the hills of Coloane, which is the second island connected to Macau. But, without gambling, what would Macau be? Some say assuredly "nothing."

It is because of the large revenues from the controlled gambling that the income tax in Macau is so low and some public facilities are so well funded. The crime is growing, but is still relatively confined to the triads—the Chinese mafia—with ties to Hong Kong and China. There are periodic grisly discoveries of body parts in dumpsters, but almost all the violence on the streets is somehow linked to the triads. Otherwise, the ability for most people to walk around day or night without fear is what makes the major difference between Asia in general and the west in today's world.

Given the rapid and unsightly building boom in Macau (Hong Kong has already run out of room), Macau and Hong Kong are getting to look more and more alike. Macau, the little sister nobody much noticed, is coming into her own. But, in many ways, she is becoming a Hong Kong look-alike, both in the look of her buildings and the look of her people. For example, take hairstyles. Both Macau and Hong Kong residents prefer hairstyles intentionally cut to fall over one's eyes and into one's face. While teaching at a high school in Macau, I regularly see a variety of hair curtains falling in front of my students' faces when they bend down to write. Some girls use their ears to temporarily pin their hair back, while other students develop a certain repetitive cock of the head to clear the hair from their eyes. Those who try to dye their black hair invariably come out with a most peculiar and similar off-red color.

Although richer than mainland China, Macau is still unsophisticated in some ways. The fine arts are limited in Macau, but are an occasional treat. Western classical concerts are very well attended, but accompanied by active milling around, chatting, and even talking on mobile phones during a performance. They also love to gleefully clap to the music whether it is classical or popular music.

Since Macau, plus its two islands, totals only about 7 square miles, a car becomes more of a toy. They are often customized by distinctive two-tone paint jobs, and many display a row of stuffed animals lining the back window. Macau hosts the annual Formula 3 Grand Prix, during which a large portion of the city is turned into a racetrack.

I was fortunate to come to Macau in time to live in an anachronism—an old Chinese fishing village on Taipa, the first island connected to Macau. There is one much-overused bridge linking Taipa and Macau, as well as a super new bridge shunned by local residents because a cemetery was disturbed to build the on-ramp.

The homes in the main Taipa village have the appearance of large dollhouses, many with the front room open to the street also serving as a store with an unpredictable variety of food and odds and ends. Small Buddhist altars with the smell of incense hug the corners of the narrow alleyways between the houses. The houses are washed with pastel yellows and greens. These color washes are much faster and cheaper to apply than paint, but don't last long in the humid climate. Very soon, mold begins to add its decorative touch.

High, ugly, and mostly uninhabited highrises loom all around the village, and the character of the village itself is beginning to be destroyed by re-building some of the old buildings into higher, charmless, unimaginative expanses of concrete. Both Macau and Hong Kong have perfected the art of making outdoors as claustrophobic as indoors. There are many small, but well-known restaurants tucked into the alleyways of the village. Perhaps it is these restaurants that will save my village for preservation as a tourist attraction.

Hong Kong and Macau are more alike than either of them and China. The Cantonese language, spoken only in Hong Kong, Macau, and the most southern province of China, is, to my ears, a whining, discordant tune that seems to always be shrieked instead of spoken gently. Because of the way the mouth forms around the Cantonese words, Cantonese speakers have a much more difficult time with English pronunciation than Mandarin Chinese speakers. Cantonese speakers of English clip the sounds mercilessly. The more melodic tune of the Mandarin speakers lends itself more smoothly to English pronunciation. Cantonese and Mandarin are written in similar characters, but are not identical because China developed simplified characters used only in China.

The different history of China, Hong Kong, and Macau has influenced the culture of each place. Certainly, Hong Kong and Macau are not third world economies. But, in spite of enormous complications and challenges to be faced, many mainland Chinese are now dedicating themselves to closing the gap by consuming as conspicuously as they can.

Feb. 18, 1993

My decision to pass my 50th birthday this summer in Israel was made easily. It was there in the Japanese garden next to the wild mountain above the valley that I faced my 40 to 50 decade with optimism and excitement. It gave me renewed energy and helped me find my balance. Now, I face my 50 to 60 decade. There are many birds singing today in Taipa. My heart sings with them because I'm quite certain that I will draw closer to nature in my next decade. What else will fill my next decade? I'm happy and feel I can enter my next decade with perhaps less energy, but still excitement and awe.

April 5, 1993

I paid my respects to Bobbie's deceased grandfather today during the *Ching Ming* Festival. Once again, I was impressed by the light, holiday atmosphere of the Chinese memorial day. I love being with Bobbie's huge family. Although our age difference is vast, she's become a good friend from the first time I bought water in her family's little store. So, I joined them as they carried a small, whole roasted pig along with other food. They burned paper money, and "useful" items like cars and houses made of paper that the deceased might want. They cleaned up around the tomb and respectfully washed his picture on the tomb.

Other families also gathered in jovial fashion to honor their dead. Some graves and coffins lay open since it's Chinese custom to exhume bones after a certain number of years. I don't know what they do with them. No matter how long one lives in another culture, there always seems to be so much more to learn.

Having taken care of the deceased, we ended the afternoon with another succulent meal cooked by her father at his restaurant.

April 6, 1993

My same old bags are packed once again for a rather short trip to China. Living so close to China makes these short visits possible. I'll go over to Hong Kong where I'll run around like crazy as usual doing last minute gift buying and getting the immunizations I'm due for. I already got my visa to visit China in Macau.

Russell will meet me at the Hangzhou airport, but he may not be able to accompany us to the mountains because he has finally succeeded in getting a promising job as an English interpreter for an import-export company. He had to pay bribes and figuratively kowtow which he truly hated doing, but it seems to be a Chinese ritual of manhood. Now that he has passed it, he wrote me a letter of exhilaration. Even if the job is lousy, he has at least extricated himself from the quicksand of doom and gloom he was sinking in.

Since Bill is preparing to get married, at his request I've bought gold rings for him in Macau, which is known as a center for buying gold. Buying the gold was an interesting procedure that even included getting official certificates documenting the weight and worth of each item I bought.

So, off to Hangzhou I go to see those wonderful faces I love waiting for me at the airport!

April 20, 1993

Even though I've been to China so many times, there are always unexpected adventures. This time, a group of us went together to some beautiful mountains. All Chinese seem to love standing in front of a stone marked often in red Chinese characters with the name of the scenic spot we are standing on. I have zillions of pictures of people taking pictures of other people. No one can understand why I like to take pictures of the scenic spot itself, without anyone in it.

As we were walking down a particularly steep trail, I began to wonder if I'd be able to climb back up. Curiously, a young man carrying a rope started to accompany us. I didn't know why he kept following us, but his mission soon became clear. These are young mountain dwellers who sell their services to carry people back up the mountain. Other helpers and sedan chairs await down below while he tries to "rope in" riders. The rope becomes useful when you agree to hire his muscles.

I was somewhat dubious that they could carry me up the mountain since I easily outweighed two of them together. However, I also knew I'd have quite a time walking back up. So, I hired sedan chairs and carriers for each of us. We must have made quite a sight indeed snaking back up the path. To my relief, their wiry legs were capable of carrying even my weight, and they slid into an easy swaying rhythm that felt like I was softly flying slightly above the mountain trail. I gasped a bit when I saw we were about to cross a stream, but they didn't even break their stride. I was both relieved and sad when my first, and perhaps only, ride in a sedan chair over the mountain paths came to an end.

Russell was able to come with us to the mountains, so we had some time for him to explain more about the complications of being a worker in China. Apparently, you must reach a delicate balance of relationships with bosses and co-workers. Excelling in your job is dangerous because the other workers get jealous and will make your life intolerable. Russell said they will even try to destroy you. Keeping on the good side of everyone requires talent and finesse. If you don't have the necessary skills to maintain the relationships, you will be miserable and never progress. I can only partially understand the tension Chinese must feel every workday. It seems much more cutthroat than merely competitive.

The zigzag way Chinese approach social relationships still befuddles me. The following conversation is self-explanatory.

Russell: "Richard is hungry."
Me: "Are you hungry too?"
Russell: "Of course. If I didn't want to eat, I wouldn't have told you."

Richard told me he's excited at the prospect of coming to Macau to work. He's even started learning Cantonese in preparation. The recruiter is coming to Shanghai sometime next month. Russell said he might also meet her just in case his new job doesn't work out well. And Thomas and Jerry want to meet with her as well. Maybe I really will be their *guanxi* to leave China and find other careers.

The evening before I left, several of us celebrated a pre-50th birthday party for me. I've seen some unusual cakes in Asia with real fruit on top. But I had never seen a cake like we had for my party. It was topped with chocolate and two white pigs!

May 8, 1993

How I do love my crazy life! No two days are the same. I went to Hong Kong Friday night so I could dash over to my travel agent's office on Saturday a.m. and sit there until we had worked out my summer trip.

I stayed at the same hostel as before where I am known as "Zima." Since the staff seems to stay fairly constant there, and since I lived there for a month last summer, it is a kind of home. I even had my old bed again, one of five bunk beds squeezed into a room. I can never return without acknowledging the ghosts of those hearty travelers I have met there on previous stays.

This time I met a young Israeli girl who is about to go into China. We spoke in Hebrew and I did better than I thought I could. When I begin to talk about my experiences to these young travelers, I feel old indeed because so much has been packed into the last ten years.

Then, there are the resident "crazies." Still there is a young Chinese girl from New Zealand who has been working there many months. She speaks English, and it seems to be fluent until one tries to make sense out of what she says. She is an "inside bag lady." Surrounding, under, and on her bed are infinite numbers of plastic bags with who knows what in them. She still has the habit of returning at about 11:30 at night and transferring things in and out of the myriad plastic bags for at least an hour and a half. That rustling sound is somehow worse than a clanging bell when one is sleeping.

Hong Kong is such a wild place. People look so serious and are so dressed up as they hurry along looking anxiously at their beepers and clutching mobile phones in be-ringed hands. As many times as I've been there, I never can keep all those mammoth buildings straight with their pompous British names.

When I finished at the travel agency, I called about having a mammogram done since there's no adequate place available to me in Macau. The girl on the phone was rather mystified how I could be so sure I wasn't pregnant when I hadn't had a period for almost three months. They stayed open in the afternoon, so I went to have a very expensive mammogram plus ultrasound exam. During the ultrasound exam, the doctor bad-mouthed the Japanese, whom he hates, while I spoke of my love of China. He is Chinese, educated in England, and commutes from Australia.

Martyr-like, I successfully avoided all the foods I so love to eat in Hong Kong. The western food in Hong Kong is more varied than in Macau, but since my weight is inexorably rising, I want to at least stem the tide even if I can't reverse it. Living in a society of thin, little people makes me feel like Gulliver.

As usual, I was overwhelmed by the gaudiness and persistence of the "consumer society" which exists in Hong Kong and Macau. I returned to Macau and stopped at a famous Japanese shopping center that has just opened up. In the middle of the shopping center were three fancy cars plus pretty girls to promote them. I outwardly laughed at the absurdity of being so attracted to cars in a place that can be driven end to end, including two adjoining islands, in no more than 20 minutes. Besides, the bus system is the most convenient and frequent I could imagine.

As I laughed at their wastefulness and materialism, I realized that I had just that day spent $2200 for plane tickets—and considered it a bargain! I'm sure they would consider me equally foolish with the extravagance in my close-to-impoverished state.

Chicken in western styles has been entering Asia. Even Kentucky Fried Chicken is opening in Hangzhou in China. The top floor of the new Japanese shopping center in Macau has a Food Plaza with a variety of relatively inexpensive food. As for what sounds familiar to westerners, it must be kept in mind that it is easternized western food. I left one place because no one would wait on me because I could only speak English. At the chicken take-out, I ordered. The girl, who had studied English I'm sure for at least six years as a required subject in Macau, looked at me as though I'd spoken Greek or Hebrew. We then resorted to pictures.

The people in Macau are somewhat behind Hong Kong and Taiwanese in western eating. My grilled chicken was served without a knife and fork. Instead, since Chinese do not like to eat with their hands, there were thin plastic gloves included. When I sat down to eat, I laughingly packed the gloves away and picked up the chicken with my hands. The woman at the next table looked at me in curious disgust as I ate the chicken and licked my fingers. No doubt the Chinese word for "barbarian" came to her mind.

When I got home, I greeted my room and found a note from Bobbie inviting me to her mother's birthday dinner. I love being with her big family anyway, but an added bonus is how good a cook her father is. I also found a telegram from Richard telling me he's going to stay in Shanghai waiting for the lady recruiter from The New Century Hotel. He had missed her during her last trip because of the time it took for my telegram to reach China, and then for him to get to Shanghai. He's really hoping he can be chosen to come to Macau in the near future. Russell and Jerry had managed to see her last time, and she did offer them the chance to come, but they turned down the opportunity because each has already just started a new job and they want to see how it goes. I sent telegrams to many of my Chinese friends—both male and female—and feel good that I at least gave them all equal opportunity. They must take it from there.

I took the plastic gloves that I didn't use for the chicken, and wore them to open up some de-humidifying and anti-mold packets to put in my cabinets and plastic closet. I remember a foreigner wrinkling up his nose when he said, "There's even mold in the glasses." Now I know what he means. It is so humid that the mold thrives—even on my jacket.

I know that I must seem comical in my version of "home" as I de-mold and keep a watchful eye on the cockroaches ever since one dive-bombed me while I was in the shower. I laugh at myself sometimes when I get tangled up in the mosquito net I sleep under, or even find to my horror that a sneaky mosquito is inside the net with me—a huge slab of meat to him/her.

Such is my present life as a wandering Jew.

May 24, 1993

Wonderful news! Richard has been accepted by the hotel and will arrive in Macau while I'm still on my summer travels. A new part of his life is opening up.

That long lost package I've been waiting for finally turned up in Macau. It looked as though it had come over with Thor Heyerdahl on the Contiki raft. I barely got it home from the post office before it literally disintegrated. But all's well, thanks to Ziploc bags mom used to pack things.

Hooray! Another piece of good news is that I won't be teaching the high school kids next year. Even though discipline is not a big problem at our school, I'm really not an effective teacher with unmotivated students. So, I'll be teaching in the night school program. Those students are in their 20's and 30's, both Chinese and Portuguese, and are working during the day. So, studying is their voluntary decision, which they, not their parents, pay for.

I've finally solved the mystery of so many parked cars with one windshield wiper beckoning upward. Apparently, it's a sign for people who ride around on bikes with buckets on their handlebars to wash the car. How they get paid remains a mystery to me.

June 14, 1993

Ah, quiet at last. The little village is now what a little village should be like. The one road through the village and under my balcony is almost silent. The fancy cars advertising blaring sound systems have gone elsewhere. The noisy buses have ceased for the night. Two people pedal their bicycles, and a car hiccups as it is programmed to do when its master arrives. The six swallows are crowded into their nest near the roof of my porch, and the two extra swallows have found my bamboo pole for hanging laundry an adequate "annex" to the nest. Amazing they don't tip over in the night and fall down. Birds seem to be heavy sleepers.

During the day, there's a new addition to the general cacophony—the thwump, thwump of the pile drivers as the little village becomes squeezed on all sides by "progress." Pooh to progress—but it will come anyway. Perhaps the village will be saved as a tourist oddity because tourists flock here much like the swallows who nest in the village in large numbers.

I should be sleeping. Why aren't I? My memories are vivid—everything and nothing makes them spring to the surface. I play a beautiful Chopin tape and remember Taiwan and living with the musical missionary, Miranda. The Bali tape makes Bali come back to me and I am homesick to be there. My mind flits, much like the swallows, although perhaps the swallow has a purpose, and I don't. I'm excited about my summer vacation to friends and relatives in the U.S., and to Israel for my 50th birthday. Then, when I return to Macau, Richard will already be here.

I loved the letter I just received from Bill. He wrote, "I admire you very much. You are a good traveler, deep thinker, fantastic photographer, and a very kind and warm-hearted woman. I hope you'll have a good time every time, everywhere."

June 29, 1993

This is my summer of going home, and home, and home. The word "home" can be a confusing word. For me, it is divided into three parts, but each one is sufficient within itself.

First, there is home—where my parents live in the U.S. It is not the city where I grew up, yet the massive U.S.A. is all quite similar after all. From my parents, I have received my genetic code, and my upbringing. My face shows my mother's side of the family, and my body shows my father's side. From the U.S., I have developed the personality I have—independent, a deep sense of fairness and justice, an "I can do it" attitude, and a 1960's idealistic social conscience. And I am unendingly grateful for the freedom my citizenship allows me, especially after time spent in China.

So, I will go home to the land of cotton candy, the land of overplenty and oversimplification, of sleepwalking, rootlessness, and random violence, which is nonetheless pretty and nice and non-smoking (ah, sweet air!). I will visit old friends in this homeland. They are pieces of my unchangeable personal history. And, I'll visit an additional new friend who was a former student from China now living in Chicago.

And then I will go home again to Israel—the little country where those who aren't writers are poets. Home to the land with a long history that gives me a sense of roots and connectedness. Israel is the mixed miracle by the sea. It is first of all a miracle that it exists at all. And yet it remains troubled, both a young and old country—a country of Arab cousins and neighbors, aggressive recent Russian immigrants, and beautiful and gentle brown Jews from Ethiopia. How will it appear to me now? Will the Wailing Wall remember me now that I live closer to the Great Wall of China? Will the fruit and vegetables still taste splendid to me? Will I feel the tension that drove me out? Will my wonderful Japanese garden next to the wild mountain give me as much peace and excitement facing my 50 to 60 decade as it did my 40 to 50 decade?

And then I will return to my newest home—China. Back to where I feel comfortable, where I love and feel loved, where I can speak no common language yet communicate eloquently, where I feel a sense of purpose and fulfillment, where I feel both anticipation and fear for the accelerated pace of change and movement happening there, and where I want to be.

And, now it's time to board the plane.

August 13, 1993

I am sitting in my special garden again. And I am 50. The garden looks somewhat the worse for wear, as do I, I suppose. Sadly, the weeping willow tree near the pond is in the process of being taken down because it caught some dreadful disease. But I can easily tell it is the same Japanese garden whose serenity helped me realize back in 1982 that I was ready to move on from mourning over my divorce to looking forward to my future. It was most likely right there that I also reached the decision to come to Israel as an immigrant in 1983 when I finished my Master's in Social Work degree.

In the summer of 1982, I was often alone there after my day's work as a volunteer at the sister *kibbutz* next door. But, on my 50th birthday, there were some Japanese gardeners there who wished me a happy birthday and told me that today was the Japanese holiday of the stars. In the magic of Israel, Japanese gardeners and an American/Israeli Jew speak immigrant Hebrew to each other.

The view from the garden still fascinates me. I find some philosophical meaning about life in having a meticulously manicured Japanese garden end abruptly up against a totally wild, un-manmade mountaintop. The view sweeping down to the long valley is still alluring.

My former *kibbutz* looked remarkably unchanged since 1982. I still enjoyed greeting the cows on my way to the communal dining room in hopes of being able to get permission to sleep in an empty bed in the volunteer's quarters. Unfortunately, my story of coming from China just to be here for my 50th birthday because being a volunteer in 1982 had changed my life was just too far out for the people in charge. They softened the rejection by saying there was no room. But I already had found out that there were two empty beds.

So, now I'm 50 years old, hot, tired still from jetlag, but I made it back to my garden and what was once my friendly *kibbutz*. Of course I'm disappointed at not being allowed to sleep overnight, yet I wanted to make it here on this day and I did! I have called Druse friends in Shefaram and I will go there to finish my birthday. We share a celebration on August 13th. It's my birthday and the couple's wedding anniversary.

August 14, 1993

We shared our celebrations last evening and feasted on the Arab food I remember enjoying so much. My friend made the special dish she knows I love—*tabouli*, which is mostly chopped up parsley and bulgar wheat with spices. Fortunately, I could recall enough Hebrew words to have good conversations. Their family has grown from one child to five. It was a happy reunion filled with laughter and the ease of good friendship. At night, I taught my friend and her oldest daughter how to wish on a star.

Have I found some direction for my 50 to 60 decade? I'm not sure at this point, but I am glad to be back. So many parts of life are "for better and for worse." Israel is still a country in deep pain. And it definitely still shows the effects of ubiquitous nervous tension. I have reconnected to many friends and discovered I am still loved. I still find joy and beauty in the places I'm re-visiting. It is not bad to enter my next decade so.

August 29, 1993

I am back in the hodge-podge that is Jerusalem—and Israel. I sit once again at the Panorama Café with high prices to match the view from on high. I have overlooked this view several times over the years. In some ways, it has changed, as have I. In other ways, it is the same, as am I.

From my bird's eye view, I can watch the *hassidim* in their heavy black coats in the sweaty summer sun. I can see the tourists from everywhere in shorts with necklaces of cameras around their necks. And I can hear the half-pathetic, half-intimidating old beggar woman. She, perhaps Russian herself, doesn't even try to extort sympathy from passing Russians.

It is the time of day when the golden city turns even more golden. A bright green crane stands loftily over it all, contrasting with the golden white stones of Jerusalem's buildings and the trees. It is still a city of magic, of the past and the present, of high and low, of good and bad, of beauty and ugliness.

Except for the workers at the restaurant, I seem to be alone here. I feel a sense of peace and quiet in this otherwise noisy, crowded place. I was also sometimes alone in parts of *Yad Vashem*, that saddest of all places dedicated to remembering the Holocaust. I visited some of the additions that weren't there before. The candle light that fractures into a million pieces to represent the Jewish children who died, and the huge stones representing all the Jewish communities that were wiped out by the Nazis were poignant reminders of who I am and why there must be this happy/sad, old/young place called Israel.

As the rock turns more golden, the almost full moon waits for the sky to darken. In the distance is the ugly color of smog. The smell is not of smog, nor is the wind. The smog is undoubtedly a change for the worse.

Yes, Israel goes on without me here although I still feel the guilt of leaving it. My legacy remains because my Ethiopian kids and families remember me and respect me as a permanent memory. My Arab and Israeli friends also treat me as a welcome guest. I did invest a lot of myself in my six years here.

The golden dome of the Dome of the Rock is not sparkling in the sunset. It is being reconstructed. Its green crane rises above it, but with no flags of Israel waving in the breeze such as adorns the crane on this side. And so, the separation of Arab and Jew remains.

Sept. 2, 1993

Almost a decade ago, in 1984, I was one of very few non-Ethiopians who attended a group wedding for new immigrant Ethiopian couples in Israel. They were caught in a sad conflict between Jew and Jew because laws for marriage in Israel were set by the Orthodox Jews, who didn't accept Ethiopians as Jews without a ritual conversion. The Ethiopian Jews, who had guarded and preserved their Jewishness through much oppression in Ethiopia, were humiliated by such a demand and refused to go through even a symbolic conversion. So, several couples were married in this ceremony in the Ethiopian tradition by their religious leaders with the grooms wearing red headbands.

The wedding I attended in 1993 was quite a different affair, which affirmed the Ethiopian Jew in Israel. It was quite an incredible mixture of American, Jewish, Ethiopian, and Israeli cultures and customs.

The wedding was held in a typical Israeli wedding hall. The Israeli man in charge of the hall had the looks, demeanor, and personality better suited to an undertaker, but the wedding guests looked more like movie stars because Ethiopians are generally truly beautiful. They have bright, white, strong teeth, regal profiles, and large eyes with long, curly eyelashes. There was an old woman dressed in the colorful traditional Ethiopian dress wearing sneakers, and a traditionally dressed Ethiopian man wearing a snappy Stetson hat. Some guests were dressed casually like a day around the house, while others had on elegant attire. Some flashy suits reminded me of the zoot suit era of blacks in the U.S. in the 1970's.

The invitations said 7 p.m., but meant 8. It had correctly added that the party would continue until the light of day. Pink envelopes were handed out at the door in which guests were expected to put money and drop it in a convenient box for that purpose.

The officiating rabbi was Israeli, and the wedding ceremony was a rather bizarre collection of rituals—Israeli handclapping, the western song, "Lady, Don't Hurt Me," eastern ululating followed by the Jewish custom of the groom breaking glass under his foot.

The food was bland Israeli instead of spicy Ethiopian food, and the dancing alternated among Israeli, black American, and the competitive Ethiopian upper chest movements. A few photographers went around taking pictures of guests, developing them, and then offering them to the guests for a price.

It was hard to place them as the patient, starving Ethiopians plucked from refugee camps in the Sudan, or more recently brought from Ethiopia in planes that literally catapulted them out of the third world into the modern world. They have an air of self-confidence now, of belonging to Israel, but they have not yet acquired the abrasiveness of native Israelis. Their smile is still too quick, too warm, and too shy. But Israeli ways such as heavy smoking are appearing more and more. Integration of cultures is always a mixed blessing.

Sept. 14, 1993

I had a perfectly wonderful summer in all respects. And, fear and hesitation aside, how nice for the peace agreement between the PLO and Israel to happen when I was back in Israel. My 50th year is off to a great start!

Being back in Asia and Israel has reminded me how nice it is to walk so much and enjoy street life. The U.S. caters to cars instead. It's a difference that strikes me every time I'm back with my parents. In most places, sidewalks, if there are any, are deserted. I am reminded of an exchange student from Europe that I met in the U.S. who lamented that he walks and walks, but never gets anywhere.

I'm on my way for a short visit to China after a brief stop in Macau to see how Richard is adjusting to his new life. With daily showers and the use of the sauna after work, I've never seen him cleaner or more relaxed. He's even gaining weight with the substantial food provided for the workers at the hotel. He describes himself as "90% happy." The only cloud over him seems to be that his roommates speak the Shanghai dialect amongst themselves and they look down on him because he's from the countryside. I've heard my Hangzhou friends complain before how snobbish Chinese from Shanghai are toward everyone else.

Sept. 20, 1993

And so today Russell is 26 and I am here in Jiaxin with him. He is not the optimistic, excited, and energized boy of last April. The euphoria has been overwhelmed by the reality of life as a businessman in Jiaxin.

His life has a series of complications, including a badgering boss and unfriendly, envious colleagues. Yet, he wants to stick it out because he wants to get a house that is promised to him at very, very low cost from his work unit. But he doesn't like the dirty side of business, and that's what seems to be growing.

Corruption is rampant as the old order is breaking down and chaos is getting the upper hand.

Unlike many of my former students who tell me they are given very little to do on their jobs, Russell is kept endlessly busy rather like a rat on a treadmill. Can his sensitive, artistic nature sustain the abuse? He has just called to wish me good-night before going off to the first night of a computer course he's taking. It was good to hear some enthusiasm in his voice because he will learn something new that might help his future.

Oct. 10, 1993

Jerry has been sent to work in Hong Kong by his company in mainland China. With special permission, he might be able to come over to visit me in Macau. I'm so happy to have both Jerry and Richard close by. Their worlds are expanding.

And so, apparently, is Peter's life in the new development city of Shenzhen from which he wrote the following:

"I am working well here. But I am not a real businessman yet for I dare not cheat others. I am still a pure and honest boy. I do not know if there are gentle-men in the business circle. If there are, I would be one.

Shenzhen is a corrupted city. I am at the edge of corruption. People here think pureness is unnormal. They try to tempt me to be corrupt. I should resist it, for I still have dreams.

Today is my weekend. I will go dancing with a previous classmate. Now I find I enjoy dancing because there are pretty girls at the ball. Disco is also a sport for me since I sit in an office all day. I am lucky that I have eight University class-mates in this city, so I can chat with them and play together and not feel lonely.

Some classmates will go back to Nanjing for a party. I feel sorry that I cannot join them. I often recall my University days, especially in the fall when there are golden leaves on the trees. There are pretty and pure girls walking along the ave-nue and there are lively boys playing soccer on the playground. How I love the old days!

Please drop a line to me. My postbox is a hungry fish."

Oct. 31, 1993

Yesterday I stood in the front row to see the President of Portugal. This wasn't too difficult because he was right on the street under my balcony in Taipa village. He was a kindly, grandfatherly-looking man who seemed tired and too old for all the activity. The primary school children waved their flags enthusiastically as they were told to do. But colonies generally lack the adoration of its citizens, and so it was a subdued affair except for the police motorcycles and plainclothes guards with earphones protruding from one ear.

The night before, after working all day, Richard also worked all evening as an extra waiter at a Presidential Banquet. He said a huge amount of food went to waste, but the hotel only paid the extra waiters about $2 an hour. Disgusting how Chinese exploit Chinese.

Nov. 5, 1993

It's great fun to introduce Richard to the "outside world" and see and hear his reactions and observations. We are getting to know each other even better, and I'm learning new things about the Chinese culture from him. For example, he has explained why Chinese hairdressers always want to make me look like Princess Diana. Chinese don't like curly hair. They think it looks dirty and messy, so they make it behave in rounded waves. He also told me that he, Russell, and Bill always cringe when I buy something like a chocolate bar and divide it up into little pieces for all of us to share. And, he regretfully told me that Chinese find the smell of westerners quite offensive. It might have something to do with the cheese and dairy products we consume. That most likely explains why a lady on the bus put her hand over her nose when I sat next to her.

Max, Richard, and I have been spending a lot of time together. I first met Max when I started working at The New Century Hotel. He's from Shanghai, but working at The New Century Hotel in Personnel on a two-year work permit. He has paid special attention to Richard because of our friendship. They often come over to my place at night where we drink juice, chat, and often study English. Now that I'm happily teaching adults during the evening, I have a lot of good advanced material to use with them.

Sometimes we go to concerts together. I particularly love Chinese music on traditional instruments, but recently we went to a rousing western music concert. Richard seemed to be enjoying it. When I asked him if he liked the music, he said he wasn't sure because this kind of music was "outside," rather than "inside" him. I thought that was a good way to describe what I've felt watching Chinese opera, or Japanese Kabuki.

Nov. 7, 1993

I have come to my favorite place in Coloane to listen to the quiet, and enjoy the blue sky, the brown South China Sea, the green of nature around me. While I was eating a chicken leg on the beach, a dog that looked just like the dog I had for 12 years bounded by dragging its owner. The dog's eyes were lighter than my dog's were, but quite uncannily this dog stared into my eyes for a couple of seconds. I telepathed, "Hello, Taffy" to it. The Chinese belief in mediums and ghosts helped me believe that this dog was inhabited by Taffy's spirit at that time. For one magical, meaningful moment, I felt Taffy with me again.

The Year of the Dog, 1994, will be here soon.

15

CHINA MACAU MALAYSIA 1994

HAPPY NEW YEAR OF THE DOG

It is Chinese New Year's Eve day in the countryside. Bill and his wife are playing mahjong in the winter sun along with relatives they see only once a year at this time. Little four-year-old Chi-Chi watches me intently as I write English words. I can hear the rather continual frustrated and bored "baa" of the sheep as it tires of its small 2 x 4 enclosed life. The 85-year-old grandfather energetically cooks for the New Year's Eve feast while the 81-year-old grandmother chainsmokes as she feeds fuel into the back of the quaintly beautiful and always hungry countryside stove.

This morning I watched a duck bathe in the fishpond just beside the house. It enjoyed itself as much as I do when I'm in the water. It stood on a slab of rock slanting into the water and dipped its head, throwing the water over its back as it came up. It pecked and picked and rubbed its wings over its back very much like hands. When it got out of the water, it raised its wings like arms and fanned itself dry.

Next to the bathing duck, a woman patiently washed her clothes. She pulled them across the scrubbing-board rock and kneaded them like dough. A woman squatted near her, cleaning a freshly killed chicken. She dipped its insides into the muddy water and cut open the intestines with an efficient Chinese scissors. Not very far away, another woman squatted while cleaning out a large wooden chamber pot. When the chicken cleaner left, the mother of the family I was visiting came out with a basket of glasses and washed each one thoroughly in the pond. I looked upon the peaceful countryside scene and couldn't help wondering if my hepatitis A gammaglobulin protection would be strong enough to balance the mixture in the water. I was slightly reassured when I found out that our food and dishes were rinsed in well water.

Last night I slept like Empress Dowager CiXi in a bed beautifully crafted by the grandfather, whose hands are still slender and agile enough to do carpentry. Nights in the countryside are as cold in the winter as they are hot in the summer. In summer, I like the multitude of frogs and crickets serenading. In winter, I like the warmth under the quilts that provides an environment so totally different from just a nose-poke outside the quilts.

Bill spoke to me with such animation and love about how glad he was to share his new wife's family with me. He was raised as a city child in a small family, and even looked down upon the countryside people. But last year he had come to be inspected by his intended's family and found a lifestyle and family-style he had never imagined. The warmth of the large family and the peace of the countryside combined to enchant him.

I felt him relax as this usually tense boy allowed the same sense of serenity and well-being he had experienced at their home last year to calm him once again. I felt the love with which he had brought me into it. He said, with an unaccustomed gleam in his eyes, that he had nothing else to put his mind and attention to over the holidays except enjoying and relaxing, talking and eating. And so we have talked and eaten and relaxed and walked the village, feeling the pleasure of togetherness and acceptance.

It is good to see him at ease because he has also felt the heavy burden of responsibility as an already married, yet still about-to-be-married man. It is a particularly People's Republic of China predicament—they are considered married by law as soon as they receive the unceremoniously handed-over government certificate. But the actual wedding party, which sometimes includes some kind of ritual ceremony, can be many months apart depending on several factors. This husband will only feel like a husband when he has decorated and furnished their partially-government-subsidized apartment (a recent change in China from being totally given by the work unit). They will have a countryside wedding for relatives eventually, and a city wedding dinner for friends. We of the west have only one ceremony that changes us from unmarried to married. And so, he and his bride sleep together in the city, but here in her home this year, they are not considered married and must sleep separately.

I find myself taking pictures of things that might be considered either worthy of the trashcan or a museum. It is like having traveled backward in a time machine to an era of long ago and unknown to the modern age. But yet it is only part of the time warp and confusion that China finds itself in. The educated children want a modern, wealthy life. Some of the houses in this village are of relatively rich peasants and bear a definite architectural resemblance to open, spacious Arab homes in Israeli-Arab villages where I've been. And yet, next to the newer home is the hand-built home of earthen floor with the warmth of wood walls.

A cousin in the family talks about negotiating for a more highly paid job in southern China which would probably sink if all the Chinese people who want to move there were allowed to. My friend, Bill, has been to Indonesia for a month through his job and has had four university years that filled him with a broader worldview. The father asks his daughter to dye his white hair black because he wants to look younger. Why? I can't imagine because he rarely goes far from the confines of his many-walled house. And I have yet to find a mirror on any of the walls that would make him notice his "youth."

They wash clothes and dishes in a muddy pond, use a chamber pot for a toilet, and recommend to an uncle deteriorating from a liver disease to eat several apples a day to cure it. The push and pull of China today, the race toward money, the pain of its recent past, the weight of such severe overpopulation, the dedication of its highly-motivated students, the pervasive corruption in contrast to the purity and depth of children raised by parents who were once under the spell of Mao, the delicacy of its ancient artistic culture and the crudeness and rudeness of some of its social behavior—all this is China as it enters the Dog year. I am no fortune-teller, but I predict another chaotic year for China—one of progress and regression, hope and despair, dreams and nightmares.

Today is New Year's Day beginning the Spring Festival, but the hail came down and now it is raining with an unSpring-like cold. For this Spring Festival, I am dressed in four pairs of pants, two sweatshirts, a down jacket with hood, a scarf, and two pairs of gloves. My feet are my main problem. Three pairs of socks, including one woolen pair, seem like nothing through my padded shoes on the earthen floor of the old house, and the even-colder cement floors of the adjoining new house. Because I've been to China during Spring Festival several times before, it does not surprise me to feel like a block of ice.

Visiting and eating are the main occupations of the day. Over my years in China, I have observed many customs and I now understand more. During the New Year feast, I am indistinguishable from the Chinese guests except that I wear gloves, cannot spit out fish bones very well, and my arms seem shorter than Chinese because I often must stand up to reach some food across the table.

Two apprentices and their brides have been invited for the New Year lunch. The host is the husband of Bill's bride's eldest sister. While Bill's bride and the mother freshly cook each dish, the husband sits at the table and urges his special guests and some family members, including children, to eat. More and more food comes, requiring a second story of delicacies to be balanced precariously on top of the existing plates of food. The host often puts choice morsels directly into his guests' bowls. Proper manners usually require a refusal to accept more food at first, but the guest inevitably backs down and eats it. When a guest goes to the kitchen and takes a bowl of rice, he signals he is nearing the end. It is, after all, not polite to take too much food because the rest of the family promptly eat the leftovers. Like cooks everywhere, they get to eat the colder remains. As each person finishes, he or she leaves the table saying the Chinese equivalent of "Eat slowly" to the others. Lingering over coffee and dessert until everyone is finished is a western tradition I miss in China.

With my stomach full and my pockets filled with wrapped candies, I wander over to the house extension where the old grandparents usually cook. Bill acts as my interpreter as the grandfather and I chat. He remembers that he was born during the dying years of the Qing dynasty. He had a primary school education, but says he did not learn the range of subjects children learn today. When I ask him what he wishes for the new year, he says to stay strong and happy. I ask him what was the best time in China, and he replies without any hesitation, "now because the economic situation is getting better all the time." He appreciates the leadership of Deng Xiaoping.

He speaks with a clear memory of the past. The worst time he remembers was the Japanese invasion of China when the Japanese took everything and left the Chinese to starve. After the Japanese left, his carpenter's hands made him rich enough to build a villa and be the richest one in his village. But, in the 1960's, he was declared to be a "landlord," and his house was taken away. During the Cultural Revolution, both he and his wife were arrested and tortured by the infamous teenage Red Guards who hung them by ropes from the ceiling. He spent eight months in prison and was a poor man again because he had had to divulge where all his gold and valuables were hidden.

"Does he hate the Communists?" I wanted to ask. But Bill said this would not be a proper question to ask because it was still against government policy to speak against the government. China is changing very quickly, but some old fears are still necessary.

The grandfather asked a few questions about America. "Does it have pigs and sheep? Do you have fish like we ate for lunch?" Food is a basic concern everywhere. He asked my salary in Macau (a typical Chinese question) and said the interest would be enough to live on. But I had Bill explain that prices are also very high so that I am rather poor after all.

Since my parents are aging, I asked his advice on living well in old age. His advice was relatively simple and wholesome.

Don't eat cold food. (This one puzzles me because I've never understood the Chinese concept of foods being hot or cold. It is not based on the temperature of the food. Chinese people just seem to know which foods are hot or cold without being able to explain why to me.)

Don't drink cold drinks.

Don't sleep too much, or in the middle of the day.

Be happy in spirit.

Keep active and busy.

He seems to live his philosophy successfully and still earns money for the extended family by his carpentry skill.

While China hurtles into the modern age at dizzying speed, the daily life of the countryside seems to stay the same. These wealthier peasant families in Zhejiang Province near Hangzhou have become wealthy quickly. With their money, they have built taller homes—a form of status. These homes may be more decorative, but don't have the conveniences that could make life more comfortable. The cement locks in the bitter cold of winter more than the old style farmhouse. There is still no hot water except what must be heated rather laboriously in an old countryside-style stove. Keeping one's body clean is a challenge. Keeping a hygienic kitchen is hard to imagine. The Chinese custom of putting chopsticks into the food in the communal serving dishes and then directly to the mouth and back again easily passes along illnesses.

Bodily functions and needs become a major concern. Consumption of food and elimination are not the simple matters they are in modern society. As a westerner, I dread both in the countryside. Food is heavily salted, which helps in preservation without refrigeration. All meals seem large to me, and as a guest, I am forcefed much like a pig being readied for market. It is uncomfortable both to say no and to say yes to such exaggerated hospitality. During Spring Festival, one munches constantly between large meals—seeds, nuts, fruit, candies. Even at my size, I cannot begin to consume what the smallest Chinese person eats. I would die without a supermarket, so it amazes me how self-reliant they are about the food they eat. There is a room full of grains and roots and "stuff" which somehow turns into edible food. To a city westerner, it is magic.

The members of the family who are not cooking are happily unmindful of the cold as they laugh and shout over endless games of mahjong. The small children play and cry like any other cousins. Their unmittened hands seem warm, but their unnaturally rough-red cheeks and rotund layered bodies are signs of the cold. Accustomed to living with the cold, they laugh at my now five pair of socks that I remove when I practice the wonderful Chinese custom of soaking my feet in a basin of warm water before going to bed. I'm sure they have no concept of how much my feet feel more like icicles than a warm-blooded human.

This is a big family and they all share in the many chores. The men readily join in all the washing of dishes and clothes, cooking, and child-watching. One night the grandfather prepares the meal for 14 people. It would not seem like a paradise to anyone else I know, but I believe this grandfather will not be as happy in heaven as he is these days.

And now I have left the family and am sitting in a bus to Hangzhou on a tiny, nursery school-sized stool squashed in between men polluting my air with their constant cigarettes. I had a ticket for a seat, but that meant nothing in this bus that swelled with those who pushed their way on or had *guanxi*, connections with the driver.

It was to be a two-hour ride, so I put my gloves on to grasp the cold bars between which I could balance myself as the bus swayed. I put on a facemask to help me endure the smoke. I felt my nose and throat and lungs filled with the mucous of a heavy cold and wondered anew why I put myself into such discomfort. How can China keep drawing me back for more physical abuse? Why do I still feel its pull after almost six years?

My Chinese friends tell me they can close their minds on long, uncomfortable bus and train rides. But my mind becomes activated and busily wanders fruitlessly from thought to thought. Chinese vacillate between courtesy and discourtesy toward strangers. I have sometimes observed a loyal sense of actual camaraderie on long trips. On this bus, they take a little pity on young children and allow them to sit on the engine (which is inside the bus) cover between the driver and his scowling girlfriend who sits in the other front seat. She takes a young baby from its mother's arms to sit with three other children all squashed in together.

Since it is Spring Festival, this little baby is dressed in a newly hand-knitted sweater and pant set that is basically blue with many other bright colors. The effect of a clown is accentuated by the clown hat and colorful pom-poms. As the Chinese get richer, the only child allowed to each couple becomes dressed more and more like a precious gift box. This baby registers a loud and tearful protest at separation from its mother, so another stool is placed nearby, the other children are squished together on the floor of the bus, and the mother and baby are re-united.

The bus driver turns on the radio full blast as though we are not all confined to one small bus. I put in earplugs, which I have learned from experience to carry in noisy Asian cultures. And so, on my little stool, with a cold filling my nose, a facemask covering my mouth and nose, and earplugs clogging my ears, I stretch out one cramped leg into a tiny crevice and feel bearably comfortable. Thus I ponder the chicken with legs trussed that has managed to escape from the pouch of someone's bag. It is caught and ungently stuffed back into its little prison from which its head sticks out and it can eye the world for a short time before it will be on a plate. I experience a feeling of empathy with that chicken.

I try to remind myself not to forget how uncomfortable I have been on my many visits to China. But it doesn't help. I know the pain of the hardships will eventually recede like the cold and cough congealing in my head and throat. I can bear it again because I am bonded to my many young friends here, and to this intriguing country that fascinates me.

Feb. 12, 1994

Although I brought some fun games and toys for my granddaughters, it turns out that the best gift of all was a hot shower and bath. Elizabeth, her daughter, and a cousin came over to my hotel room where I have my own bathroom AND hot water. Squeals of laughter and the sounds of splashing water filled my room as my granddaughter and her little cousin played in the bathtub that they don't have at home. They emerged a long time later with shining, smiling red faces and dangling wet hair. The simple pleasure of hot running water brought them joy that they will most likely remember as a highlight of my visit.

My second little granddaughter had carefully practiced the phrase, "Grandma, play with me." And play we did. It is still easy to play with them at this age, but I worry about being a deaf, mute, illiterate grandmother as they get older and rely more on language than playing to relate to me. Their first language is not even Mandarin Chinese. It is the dialect that the grandmothers spoke who took care of them when they were infants and toddlers. As is still the custom, one grandmother moves in and cares for the baby for at least the first two years. When the child begins school, s/he learns the common Mandarin Chinese. But their Mandarin will immediately far surpass my puny supply of "survival" words and phrases.

It felt strange to visit Richard's family without him there. Another Hangzhou friend accompanied me to Richard's village where I was able to give the family some gifts and money from Richard. His mother had that worried look of all mothers whose children live far away. I took a lot of pictures of the family, especially his growing nephews and nieces, to give to Richard in Macau.

March 6, 1994

Returning to Macau, I have found a change in Richard. When he first came to Macau from China, he was keenly interested in observing everything new around him. He was also glad to be earning the equivalent of about $200 a month compared to the $50 a month he had been earning in China. But, as a mainland Chinese newcomer, he knew and felt that the rich Macau people looked down upon him. Compounding that was the inferior way he was viewed by his work colleagues from the big cities of Shanghai and Guangzhou. In turn, he looked down upon those from both Shanghai and Macau because they were generally less educated and much less fluent in English than he was. However, with me encouraging him to explore new territory, new foods, etc., he found an excitement in the newness around him. I introduced him to what was both western in Macau and what I appreciated about the Chinese and Portuguese cultures in Macau.

Then, there was a transition to a different stage. The colorful life he saw in Macau began to contrast starkly against the boredom of his dead-end, two-year job. He also found the delicate personal relationship balance, which is a reality of every Chinese workplace, a heavy burden. It was like always walking a tightrope and he was not adept at these relationships. He was also restricted by the Chinese government to working only at that hotel, so he had no options.

He had been a "model employee," but began to withdraw from his job, fulfilling only the basic requirements that were, after all, demanding time-wise (60 hours a week), but not brain-wise. He began to feel an emptiness, a going nowhere, a fear of losing more time (he was 26) of precious youth.

Now, I feel a shift to yet another stage. His basis of comparison has changed from China to the other people around him who get decent pay and much better living standards. He feels like someone who can only look at the displays in shop windows, but not touch. I can see that he is dipping into frustration, anger, and hopelessness. I don't know if there is some way to help him. I fear he is getting emotionally lost on the fringes of his culture.

April 2, 1994

I am not often aware of being an expatriate. In Asia, the troubles of South Africa are far away. Today I watched a movie about the South African struggle in the local theatre I've found that shows movies in English. The Chinese audience was small, but maybe the movie helped some Chinese to understand South Africa's pain.

Being an expatriate has made me feel each country's pain more acutely, perhaps because my view of the world is so much broader now, and much more personal. I am not a "typical expat" here. A large percentage of the foreign community in Macau has been brought in to head various projects such as the airport being built in Macau. They are brought in for a few years, paid very highly, and often enclose themselves in a world of expats much like themselves.

From my expat perspective, I can see parallels between South Africa and Macau, but I doubt they would be widely recognized. In 1999, Macau is becoming China once again; South Africa is unifying its population into one country equal for all its citizens. Both situations will entail substantial changes, adjustments, and reorientation. Another similarity is that the "coloreds" of South Africa are not too unlike the Macanese of Chinese and Portuguese mixture. The "coloreds" sought to be more white, and the Macanese sought to be more Portuguese. So, these minorities are hated by the majority that will now rule them.

The freeing of South Africa will have little impact on Macau residents, but I can rejoice about it because I have also seen the segregation in the U.S. I can remember Martin Luther King, Jr., Rosa Parks who wouldn't give up her seat on a bus to a white man, Malcolm X who came to my college in Boston to speak, the murders of idealistic white and black students who encouraged voter registration. I still have the slide of my husband standing at an ice cream counter marked "White Only" in the deep South during our honeymoon in 1964. I feel the freedom of South Africa more deeply because of the young black child I tutored in the Roxbury ghetto in the early 1960's when I was a college student, my son who was waiting to be adopted because he was a black/white mixture, the black girls in an after-school club I organized in a black section of Palo Alto, California, in the 1970's, and my black little sister in the Big Sister program. And, of course, black people always bring to mind the Ethiopian Jews I knew so well in Israel.

Just prior to the South African movie, "Sarafina," there were movie previews of coming attractions. "Schindler's List" will be showing soon. Born in 1943, I had watched countless World War II movies during my impressionable years. Later, living in Israel, the numbers on the arms of concentration camp victims seared my eyes. Once, a man in Tel Aviv ran toward me shouting wildly and lifting the sleeve of his shirt to expose the number that had changed his life and his mind forever. Here, in Macau one April night in 1994, I realized that, had Hitler come to Macau, out of the 600,000 people living here, he would have singled me out to die.

April 7, 1994

A chance conversation with another teacher at work tonight will give Richard the chance to teach as a substitute at the Baha'i international school while another teacher is away. There is even the chance for him to move into a permanent job with them for the fall semester since they expect to hire more Mandarin Chinese teachers in preparation for the 1999 handover to China. They can handle the necessary legal paperwork to keep him in Macau with a different job. I hope this will give him a happier view of future prospects here. He'll have equal treatment with all the other teachers at the school, including a much better salary than at the hotel. Life is looking up for him again!

May 10, 1994

Richard has been spending every spare moment with the Baha'i community. While he was a substitute teacher there, he met an American teacher about his own age whose mission it was as a Baha'i to convert him. It was easy. He was ripe for it. He flung himself into the international collection of foreigners who make up the Baha'i community in Macau. He is eagerly taking advantage of all aspects of the pre-packaged life they offer—instant attention, care, respect, social events, and a complete doctrine of what to believe in. His knowledge of Mandarin, Cantonese, and English fits in perfectly with the Baha'i attempts to convert the newer waves of mainlanders coming into Macau.

I miss him. We don't get together very often to eat or chat anymore.

June 1, 1994

Summer plans are beginning to shape up. Not only will Richard start teaching regularly at the Baha'i international school next fall, but he was able to recommend Max for a teaching job there too. Max is happy that he will be able to stay in Macau longer. And I am very happy that both Max and Richard will be roommates on the other side of the hallway from me in an apartment that will be vacant soon.

This summer, Richard will have his first visit back to China in a year. I'll escape most of Macau's simmering summer back in the U.S. with my parents. In the late summer, my American friend, Harriet, will join me in Macau and then into China for her to meet my Hangzhou friends. Then, we'll both go to Malaysia where we'll stay with Juliet and her new English husband. He's been sent there for work, so they've been given a spacious home to live in that can accommodate us. Finally, it's back to work for me at the adult evening school for the Canadian College of Macau. Lots to look forward to!

August 20, 1994

I've always loved walking down the ramp into the visitor's area of the Hong Kong airport. I've never been beautiful enough to be in a beauty pageant, but this is second best to the walk beauty contestants make with all eyes turned upon them. The wide ramp at the airport starts high as it continues down to the level of people waiting behind the barriers to greet new arrivals. All eyes expectantly scan everyone walking through the gates from the airport.

Harriet warned me that, after such a long flight from the U.S. to Hong Kong, she would be exhausted. Yet, I immediately spotted her energetically walking down the ramp while in an animated conversation with another new arrival. It turns out that this young man she met on the plane was Malaysian. He was on his way to Malaysia to get married. So, she arrived in Hong Kong with an invitation to his wedding that would take place just before she was scheduled to leave Malaysia! From that beginning, I knew she wouldn't be shy about meeting my friends in Macau and China.

Sept. 17, 1994

"I didn't quite understand what you meant when you said we'd be living in our sweat," Harriet said after another sweltering day in Asia. This trip has been hard for her, especially since she's used to the American mid-west's mild summers and cold winters. But she has been a willing traveling companion. I was surprised at how many pictures she took of just about everything. She explained that she doesn't retain a visual memory of people or places when she travels. Instead, her memories are sensual ones encompassing the "feeling" of the experience. I, on the other hand, hold visual details that I can re-play in my mind's eye.

Now that Harriet has flown home, I'm alone in Malaysia for a few more days. As hot and uncomfortable as it was for her, I was very glad to be able to share my world with her. We celebrated the Jewish New Year with Russell's family in the countryside, eating apples and honey for a sweet year. The children played a Jewish game she taught them, while I danced a Jewish dance with Russell's mom. Harriet found the constant gray skies of Hangzhou depressing. I understood because I, too, long for the blue skies of California when I'm in China. Even Macau, not so polluted and surrounded by sea, rarely has deep blue skies. My American and Australian students in the Macau high school used to say that the sky was too close and felt like it was smothering them.

We had a very good time with Juliet and her husband in Malaysia. She is glowing with being a newlywed and pregnant. Their home is large, cool, and beautiful. They took us to the picturesque mountains of Cameron Highlands where we got happily lost on the small roads in the hills among the tea farms. I had never been in a butterfly farm before and my camera went crazy with all the close-ups possible of multicolored butterflies. Eating a succulent steamed crab while looking out upon the Strait of Malacca and imagining all the trade that has passed through there was another memorable day together.

Harriet and I wandered together among the friendly, colorful people and flowers of Kuala Lumpur. In an extensive museum ringed by jungle vegetation, we learned more about the Malay, Indian, Chinese mixture of people that makes up largely Moslem Malaysia. One display that caught my eye was an "amok catcher," a tool for holding and restraining someone who was running amok. But the permanent haze of pollution blanketing the city, and the smell of clove cigarettes wherever men gathered told me that I would not like to live here.

Sept. 22, 1994

Penang attracts me more than other parts of Malaysia, partly because it seems so familiar. It's mainly Chinese and the buildings look remarkably similar to my own Taipa village in Macau, but with the addition of some velvety, sandy, wide beaches, friendlier people, and more night life.

There are also many relatives here of the mosquitoes and cockroaches of Taipa. And, I have made unhappy acquaintance with the "bedbug" of the rhyme, "Sleep tight and don't let the bedbugs bite." These merciless critters resist bug sprays and attack when and where one is most vulnerable—sleeping in bed. Their bite is distinguished from common mosquitoes by the size (more like welts), extreme itchiness that lasts for days, and the neat rows of bites, making me feel like a bedbug's cafeteria. Ugh!

The only mixed blessing of being tortured by bedbugs was that it got me out of bed at 6 a.m. to walk around the awakening city. In the sunrise, I discovered an amazing amount of activity at the Buddhist temple. The air was thick with the smoke of joss sticks, and people came and went in walking traffic jams. The next night, I splurged on a more expensive, and hopefully less bedbug-infested hotel.

Lantern Festival in Penang had its own special modern touch. There was a parade with a lantern of the AIDS virus and a warning. Knowing that Chinese prefer to hide such children from view, I felt touched by seeing several trishaws (large 3-wheel bikes) in the parade that held smiling, waving retarded children. Since Malaysia is multicultural, there was an integration of cultures all celebrating

Chinese Lantern Festival. I liked the feeling there and enjoyed a show of Indian dancing after the parade.

Oct. 10, 1994

Nothing seems to be going right with Richard. He has lost the euphoria of last spring's involvement with the Baha'i community. His teaching job seems to be okay, and he has moved in with Max across from my apartment. But, he rarely comes back there even to sleep. The small glimpses I have of him tell me he is feeling lonely. He's obviously hurting, but he won't talk to me about what's bothering him. Instead, he seems to be intentionally avoiding me.

Nov. 15, 1994

My heart has raged and seethed, twisted and tossed, broken into conflicting pieces, turned inside out and upside down. I still do not know why, but it's all too clear that Richard no longer wants me in his life. Our five-year relationship has shattered irretrievably, leaving sharp slivers and shards of pain scattered within me.

A sad ending to a close friendship doesn't take away all the fond memories of time and experiences shared. Goodbye, Richard. I wish you well.

Nov. 25, 1994

I remain somewhat mired in the muck of melancholy, but I've given notice at work that I'll leave Macau at the end of this semester. I'm making plans now to go to Munduk, a little village in Bali, where I'll teach the staff of a small hotel owned by the same man I met at the Bali Tourism School. Because of the visa restrictions, I'll have to leave there after two months, which works out perfectly for attending an international conference of SERVAS being held in Australia. I've always heard New Zealand is a magnificent country for nature-lovers, so I'll go see for myself and then to Fiji on my way back to the U.S. where my parents have moved to Dallas, Texas.

MEMORIAL TO AN ABANDONED HOUSE NO LONGER THERE

I look from my window across to the gaping hole where you used to be, and I wonder if anyone else misses you. I knew you were doomed when I saw two men, mobile phones in hand, looking at you and then down at a paper in their hands. Even though there is some kind of protection on paper for the remaining unique buildings in this remnant of an old Chinese village on Taipa island in Macau, I didn't hold out much hope that these men had preservation in mind. Dollar signs rule Macau now in the building boom frenzy leading up to the 1999 re-unification with China.

The banana tree leaves are fully visible now instead of the way they playfully waved at me from behind the old stone walls. I don't know how old you were, or just when your roof collapsed, but I found the way nature provided a flower and vine roof very attractive. The green stone lattice windows particularly appealed to me. I suppose you provided sanctuary for the hordes of mosquitoes that attack me daily, but you also attracted the swallows so that they chose the eaves of my house to nest in.

I was hoping to leave Macau before you were gone, but, alas, one Sunday evening two men came by and, with a few whacks of a hammer, crumbled some bricks. Then, bamboo scaffolding with red, white, and blue plastic was placed over the structure. Gutting commenced the next day. On the second day, the bulldozer tore down your walls and trucks took your parts away, most likely to be dumped into the sea for landfill.

Now, boards have been put up around where you used to be. For reasons I cannot understand, the boards around building sites here are then painted, sometimes quite decoratively. I don't know yet what kind of structure will stand in your place, but I know from seeing other buildings being put up so ugly and slapdash that it can never take your place.

Dec. 28, 1994

I've been saying my goodbyes to people and places in Macau. I am leaving with many fond memories, but I doubt I'll ever return to live here again because I like the way it was much more than what it is becoming.

My good friend Bobbie took me out to the western restaurant in the Hyatt Hotel for our goodbye. As she daintily tried out some western food she'd never eaten before, she leaned over to me and whispered, "Why is it so quiet in here?" I looked around at all the other patrons in the restaurant and realized how quiet it was to her compared to usually noisy Chinese restaurants.

Her simple question made me realize that I am able to easily flow from culture to culture, much like the multi-lingual people I've listened to who switch effortlessly and automatically from one language to another.

I'm ready to greet the New Year of the Pig in Bali!

16

BALI AUSTRALIA NEW ZEALAND FIJI 1995

Jan. 28, 1995

My plane ticket said Bali, but I've ended up in Heaven. This morning I awoke to an unusual sound—silence, except for the singing of the birds. I gasped involuntarily when I looked outside. There was space, precious green space with swaying coconut palms, blue, blue sky and distinct, puffy clouds. Up here in the cool mountains of Munduk village, the beauty of the panoramic views, the cleanliness, the friendliness and gentleness of the people envelop me in its spell.

I have traded a 100-year-old house in Macau for a 100-year-old renovated Dutch house on a mountaintop. When the cottages at Puri Lumbung aren't filled with tourists, I can spend a night now and then in a tourist cottage overlooking the rice paddies. My students are the staff of Puri Lumbung. And our classroom is a room with a roof but no walls in a colorful, fertile garden where the flowers can't wait to bloom and roosters walk through the classroom when they wish.

Jan. 30, 1995

Tonight is Chinese New Year's Eve. I am far away, yet my heart is there. I now know I am a whole person split in four parts—my personality is American, my homeland is Israel, my heart is in China, and my spirit is in Bali.

Someone once told me that nature is my god. There is proof of that in Bali where, every now and then when I look around, I exclaim spontaneously, "Oh, my god!" when I see particular views, light and shadows, and feel the incredible lightness and gentleness of the air.

As I walked through the village at night, I listened to the quiet around me and noticed that no blue lights of televisions and harsh noises came from the houses. Even my radio giving me the news of the world was intrusive, so I turned it off.

Only the music of the birds and the instrument called a *gamelan* sounds like it belongs here.

Feb. 10, 1995

It is now two weeks since I left Macau. I sit in one of the nicest homes I'll ever have in the most beautiful place I could imagine, in the safest surroundings of probably anywhere in the world. This is the rainy season, so it rains, sometimes pours, part of every day. Often, my amusement is watching and waiting for rain-clouds in the distance to make their way over the mountaintops to our village. The air is the purest I'll ever breathe. This place is filled with superlatives.

I have my work, my leisure, and I am well looked after by innumerable people. I talk to some of the international tourists who stay in Puri Lumbung. I feel so special when they ask how long I'll be here, and I can reply, "Two months." Near the end of my two months, I am looking forward to welcoming my friend, Virginia, from Taiwan, and a French couple I met in Macau as my guests. I have people of all ages, and nature of every smell and shape to be my friends and companions here. Only my stomach isn't happy here. I think it may be related to my extreme allergy to papaya. Even though I don't eat papaya, they may use it in spices. So, I've told the cooks to make me simple chicken soup and hard-boiled eggs. It's boring and much less tasty than the food on the hotel's menu, but doesn't upset my stomach.

LIFE IN MUNDUK VILLAGE

Magnificent sights, pleasant sounds, interesting smells, friendly smiles, sweetness, and the strength of Balinese tradition surround me in Munduk, perched on a mountaintop in northern Bali. I am working here for two months teaching English to the staff of the only hotel in the area. Puri Lumbung's tourist cottages are in the style of a barn used to store rice. They are furnished in the delicacy of all locally, handmade products—handmade hangers, carefully carved doors, and wooden furniture. The large bathroom has a full garden inside the room. A traditional "phone" made out of bamboo amplifies one's natural voice enough to be heard for a short distance.

Nature provides both the scenery and a cool mountain climate. The people of Munduk, and the astounding beauty of Munduk combine to delight every sense, especially the sixth sense that I call spiritual. Living right over the terraced rice paddies provides an all night symphony with the early morning disharmony of the resident roosters. I eat in a tree house restaurant perched over sweeping vistas of mountains and terraced rice paddies, coconut and clove plantations sloping

800 meters down to the sea. A local musician accompanies meals on a bamboo instrument called *gamelan*, blending in with the peace of the setting.

It was at Puri Lumbung that I first heard the term, "eco-tourism" which I distilled to mean making tourism more of a blessing than a curse. Is that really possible? Unfortunately, parts of Bali have sunk to the level of sad, bad examples of how tourism can completely change a local community. I was invited to come by the builder and owner of Puri Lumbung. Having traveled widely and lived in other countries, he is a native of Munduk and seeks to provide a place for local villagers and foreign guests to interact in ways that lead to mutual respect, enrichment, and understanding. Although locally made arts and crafts are available, they are never aggressively pushed at tourists by the high-pressure salesmen so prevalent in other parts of Bali.

Providing economic benefits for local people is another tenet of eco-tourism, which Mr. B. adheres to by hiring mostly local staff and using local skills. One purpose behind such hiring is to stem the tide of young adults leaving the village for the highly-touristed cities and towns.

Another way of giving dimension to the interaction between villagers and foreigners is to make everyday activities, rather than special ceremonies and holidays, the main attractions of Munduk. Hands-on opportunities include helping to cook a Balinese meal, working in the rice paddies, making a bamboo *gamelan*, learning to play the *gamelan*, weaving traditional baskets from bamboo, and making natural sugar from sugar palm trees.

In most of the world, the relationship of society to its environment is like that of a rapist to its victim, but in Munduk I watch people going about their daily lives in harmony and balance with nature. It is as refreshing as the air. I entertain myself for hours watching the clouds cover and uncover the mountains and valleys, the flowers that bloom in front of my eyes, the rice growing, the light and shadows playing, the sunset painting the sky one stroke at a time—all while breathing the lightest, purest air I've ever found. It is the most like heaven I can imagine.

Balinese culture surprises me in both its simplicity and its complexity. There are a large variety of ceremonies that mark a person's life from pregnancy until death and afterward. One day, I noticed the heightened activity at my neighbor's home in preparation for one such ceremony. The nimble fingers of the women fashioned intricate offerings from palm leaves and other products of nature. A large table was set up on the porch on which an impressive number of offerings were stored. Guests began to arrive from other areas of Bali and slept over the night before the ceremony. Although Balinese may move to other parts of Bali or beyond, they return to their family temples to perform ceremonies.

I learned that this ceremony was for a six-year-old girl who was considered to have a bad character—stubborn, hard to control, sometimes stealing and lying. She was symbolically purified in an elaborate ritual in which she was bathed in flowered holy water and had to break a few eggs and several coconuts, releasing the purifying coconut water. The village priest prayed in Sanskrit (which most Balinese cannot understand) while his wife translated for all to understand. Then, laden with offerings, we all went to a family temple to continue the request for purification. The father and mother were brought into the ceremony, with the hope (quietly confided to me), of purifying the father who had the unfortunate, but quite common, excessive love of gambling.

The little girl did all that was expected of her in exemplary fashion and was very proud of a string placed on her head, a leaf with flowers tied around her head, and braided yarn with ancient coins wound around her chest. Although she and I had no common language, she often came to visit me during the few days she was there. We played long and well together. Unlike her shy cousin just a little older who lived next door to me, the six-year-old's character was quite different. Her boldness and attraction to me, rather than fear of my strangeness, made me wonder if this was a case of independence being seen as contrariness.

The tooth filing ceremony is also one of purification that comes after puberty and before marriage. The teeth are actually filed down, especially the two canine teeth, to guard against specific bad behaviors. This gives the teeth of Balinese an unnatural evenness.

There are innumerable other ceremonies before and after planting and harvesting, a baby's first haircut, etc. No matter what the ceremony—family or holiday—the event takes precedence over jobs and employers routinely allow their employees to take the time off work.

The final ceremony in anyone's life is one of great importance. News of a death in the village spreads very quickly. Villagers come to visit the family, men traditionally bringing sugar to the men in the family and women bringing rice and other foods. Taking care of death, like life in the village, is a communal village responsibility. The neighbors try to cheer up the family and there is a lot of activity necessary to prepare the offerings for the funeral ceremony.

Thus, grief is purposely kept at a distance while the family has to properly receive many visitors, some of whom lay down on the floor to sleep together with the family at night. Since the family must make all the arrangements and decorations and offerings in a short time (rather than delegating the job to a funeral parlor as in the western cultures) they are kept in a rather constant state of activity until after the burial or cremation. It is usually after the funeral that grief sets in, but is muted by the belief in reincarnation.

And, it is quite likely that the loved one will be symbolically cremated again in a ceremony in combination with others, even many years later. Usually there is an all-village very elaborate cremation ceremony every ten years. I was told that the last one in Munduk had been held in grand style and celebration.

One of the last ceremonies a visitor to the west would choose to go to would be a funeral. And, in the western world, it would be unkind to intrude upon a family at such a time. However, in Bali, there is no reluctance to having a foreigner come to a funeral.

When I saw a large gathering of men near a house, I asked why and was told of the sudden, unexplained death of a young man in his late twenties. He was from Munduk village, but had been living as a *bemo*, small bus, driver in larger Singaraja. Without a moment's illness, he had died in his sleep.

Why? One person I spoke to said he might have died from stress because he was always working, hardly taking time out to eat. But, during the funeral, his cousin told me that he thought maybe black magic had killed him. However, with a sense of fair justice, he told me that the perpetrator could never be joined to God after such an act.

No one would ever know the reason because, after a couple of days of people visiting the family while the body was preserved in ice, they washed and prepared the young man for his cremation. He was then taken by procession to the village temple for a short ceremony and then on to the cemetery (always located at the end of a village) and cremated. A photographer from the *bemo* company documented the funeral.

I had read that funerals feel more like celebrations in Bali, but I knew there must be pain at death, especially of someone so young. I cannot say I saw happiness and celebration at this man's untimely death, but the anguish was quiet and repressed. The young wife fainted as the body was laid within the cement blocks for cremation. She was quietly carried off to the side. The dead man's co-workers had solemn, long faces as they carried the body, smoked, and finally put money in with the body before the fire was lit. A white canopy was held over the dead man's face as an old priest sang and sprinkled flowers. Some elaborate offerings were brought forward and laid on top of the body.

It is not so easy to burn a body, so two large gas-fed torches were inserted under the body, and pieces of metal placed on top. Three women sang as all was prepared for the cremation.

For the two hours it took for the body to burn, people sat around on the ground, some eating under a roofed structure and quietly talking. I saw only one woman sitting on the ground off to herself and crying quietly, but deeply. That was the young man's mother. In the western tradition, I would expect the father and mother to be consoling each other, but the father sat quite a distance away from the mother. No one attempted to console him either. He was left to his own thoughts, memories, and tears.

I learned that what was left after cremation would be taken in the afternoon to Lovina by the sea and put into the ocean. The spirit would then be taken back and ceremoniously placed in the village temple.

Not all bodies are cremated, depending upon specific religious beliefs or the high cost of cremation. During the cremation I watched, another funeral procession carried in the body of an old man. There was again a singer and a ceremony, and his body was lowered into the ground. He was covered over, the grave filled in, and a rather elaborate offering was placed on top of the grave.

In Bali, the death of the body is only another level of an ongoing life. The spirit lives on and is endlessly reincarnated, sometimes upward and sometimes downward depending upon the goodness of the person in the last life.

Unlike most of Indonesia, the Balinese are Hindus rather than Moslems. However, they have adapted Hinduism to their Balinese traditions so that it differs markedly from India's Hinduism. It is a monotheistic religion believing in one god and many manifestations of this god.

The two most impressive parts of Balinese Hinduism to me are its animism and the holistic way of life. Many cultures, both western and westernized lifestyles lead to a compartmentalization of life. We develop several mental spaces, and even sometimes personalities, for work, family, community, and social aspects of life. Nature is often not even included in our lives on a daily basis. But Balinese and nature cannot be divided. Nor can life be split up into convenient sections.

Everything is so alive in Bali, it is only natural to believe in animism. Each building, including the Puri Lumbung cottages, has an offering in it and pieces of cloth hanging from the roofs to recognize the cleansed spirit of the building before anyone can live in it. Respect for nature, spirits, and gods cannot be taken out of the culture.

Nature is both a part of the Balinese and apart from them. Graced with nature's beauty and bounty, Balinese never take nature for granted. You can watch them sitting and admiring a view or a sunset just like tourists do. Ask anyone in the village where the best view is to watch the full moon rise. Watching the fog rapidly rolling in over the mountains from two sides with the inevitable slow motion, silent collision, the restaurant staff and I all stopped our conversation to watch with the same appreciation.

Not only is there a personal appreciation of nature, but also a village responsibility to nature. One large-scale example of this is when the whole village goes on what is called a recycling procession. This involves many people, many days, to several areas. Due to the expense, it can't be done annually.

Put very simplistically, Balinese believe there is good and evil in the world. Both must be respected, and in the microcosm of oneself and the macrocosm of the world, kept in balance. White magic (for good), and black magic (for evil) also exist. Good can win over evil, but evil cannot be permanently vanquished. This was, to me, a refreshing departure from the Judeo-Christian concentration on sin.

Yet, there is a small, but growing Christian community in Munduk. Numbering perhaps 40, Balinese were attracted to Christianity often for economic reasons. Family ceremonies are expensive, and Christianity has very few ceremonies compared to Balinese Hinduism. Also, as confided to me, certain financial rewards and employment opportunities were offered to new converts.

A few people become outcasts from their villages. Like other societies based on social responsibility, there are clearly defined responsibilities to the village. Unlike some social cultures, the village gives much material support to each of its members. The one thing that cannot be forgiven is shirking one's social responsibilities. For that offense, there is ostracism and even expulsion from the village. However, excluding this part of life, there is in Bali an impressive tolerance for individualism in thought and choice. Whether converting to another religion, or marrying a non-Balinese, the main criterion for the acceptance of any differences is that the person be a "good" person.

THE RELIGION OF BALI

The most enjoyable and instructive way of understanding a culture is by meeting the people who are part of the culture. The priest, Made (pronounced Ma Day) D., is one of several priests in Munduk. A native of Munduk, Mr. D. spent 1952-1959 in Java and was educated there for three years in a Christian senior high school. Although he prayed with the Christians, he did not change his belief in Balinese Hinduism. As a matter of fact, he said that he could pray in any temple or church. He was at first a religious leader of his extended family's 150 couples in Munduk, but he now performs ceremonies for any families that invite him to do so. And many families invite him because of his deep knowledge of the religion. In 1987, he was selected to attend a one-month course in Denpasar, the capital of Bali, for intensive, in-depth training in Hinduism.

While most Balinese accept Hinduism with their hearts, Mr. D. also has the knowledge that goes with deep belief. In trying to explain Balinese Hinduism to me, he drew many arrows showing how the belief system is connected one to the other. The result is a Hinduism that can't separate god, man, nature, and the cultural traditions. All are interwoven and inseparable, which distinguishes Hinduism in Bali from what is practiced in other countries. It also accounts, I believe, for the strength and resilience of the culture. Rather than throwing away their traditions, Balinese integrate change into the traditions. In that way, they remain firmly rooted.

Hinduism is monotheistic with many manifestations of God who gave the holy book (*Weda*) through his voice (*Sruti*) over 6,000 years ago. There are five basic beliefs: belief in God; belief that every human, animal, tree (nature) has a spirit; belief in cause and effect (If I'm good, good will come from it.); belief in reincarnation (rebirth after the body dies); Nirvana (*Moksa*) is the destination and end to reincarnation. Nirvana may never be reached, but it is always important to leave behind something good for society.

All humans, animals, and nature must go through the immutable cycle of Birth, Life, and Death. When a person is born, his character is already divided into differing proportions of good, passive, and desires that result in aggression, ambition, etc. The balance of these three can be influenced and changed by one's deeds.

Putting their beliefs into practice is an arduous daily task. However, the work, energy, and money required is readily and joyously given by the Balinese whose lives are guided and spiritually enriched by it.

Actually achieving balance can be difficult, and is even trickier to maintain. A great deal of Balinese philosophy is based on the concept of balance in the world, and in one's life. In the Balinese view, evil must be respected too. The Nazi swastika was an inverted form of the symbol for balance. It can be seen on many carvings in Munduk.

You can see many dogs as you walk around the village. They will bark, but not usually bite unless you act aggressively toward them. Nor are they cute and lovable and ready to be petted. In Balinese society, dogs are neither loved nor hated. As one Balinese told me, "They are needed to complete the house." Their constant barking is a protection, but one wonders from what since crime is non-existent in Munduk.

Dogs have the run of wherever they want to go. And, although other animals are not wanted in the temples, a dog can go where it wishes because it was the only animal allowed to accompany its master into Nirvana, the highest possible heaven. Dogs also often eat the food offerings placed everywhere to placate the evil spirits. Since they are such unappealing dogs (and I'm usually a devout dog lover), it's easy to believe they are the incarnation of evil spirits.

MEET THE LOCALS OF MUNDUK

Cock fighting is a major preoccupation of Indonesia. Mr. Ketut M. is a pioneer in the cross-breeding of wild chickens and local chickens. Indonesians prize these chickens because they combine the best qualities of each. Wild chickens have bright, iridescent colors and a sound, which is shorter and sweeter to the Indonesian ear. The rooster's crown has no ridges. Being wild, it is difficult for humans to approach them, and they are resistant to breeding in captivity. A mixed rooster has an attractive body, a sweet sound, vague ridges on the crown, and is more tame toward humans.

While a local chicken might be worth $30 U.S., and a wild chicken worth $150, a mixed chicken can bring perhaps $1500 U.S. Buyers come to Mr. M. from as far away as Java as well as from Balinese villages. Training a wild chicken to get used to a local chicken requires patience and the natural skill Mr. M. possesses to calm the chickens so that they accept his handling them. He has devised a "family planning" technique of attaching a rubber shield over the hen's opening so that she cannot be impregnated by chance. In this way, he can carefully control the mating to produce the highest quality stock.

Along the main street, you can see women crocheting. Women like Made Y. are using skills taught by their mothers to earn extra money. Made's sister has a shop in the heavily-touristed Kuta area of Bali. Made and other village women provide a supply of pocketbooks, vests, and blouses for the shop. After mornings tending the rice paddies and clove trees, coffee beans and fruit trees, Made spends three to six hours sewing.

She is mother to three grown children, but when she was ten years old, she was trained as a dancer. Coming from a father who was a musician, she was asked to become a dancer for the village. Not only is this an honor since only the prettiest and healthiest are chosen, but it is also a social obligation to the village. Every Balinese village has a dance group and musicians, but Munduk in particular has a reputation for producing talented performers.

Both the music and the dance movements resemble nothing that can be compared to any western form I know. The movements, especially of the fingers, require years of practice from a young age. The dances often tell a story eloquently. Made performed such traditional dances and remembers it as an exciting time as well as a healthy time since dancing is such good exercise.

As with all aspects of Balinese life, the gods are a part of dancing. The dancers pray before dancing and draw energy and support to communicate with society through their dancing. In return, dancers and musicians are honored by the villagers.

Normally, the women stop performing when they marry. They then become instructors to those just learning. Made trained her eldest daughter, among other girls, to dance. Although she hasn't danced in many years now, she retains the grace and form of a dancer as she gardens, crochets, sews, and weaves floor rugs from bamboo.

I first met Mr. Nyoman B. in 1989 when he was the Director of the tourism school in Nusa Dua, Bali. We kept in touch annually and, when I was ready to leave Macau, he invited me to teach English to the staff of Puri Lumbung in Munduk, his own village. It was a relatively new venture, and was the first accommodation for tourists in Munduk. He could offer me no salary, but gave me free room and board for the two months allowed on a visa.

While in Munduk, I came to see the mixture that Mr. B. had become. While many of his boyhood friends were content to spend hours playing the *gamelan*, Mr. B.'s father forbade him to play and insisted on high education. By middle-age, Mr. B. had traveled a good portion of the world, and had lived in other countries. Did he still fit into the traditional, unsophisticated, non-technological village of Munduk, which did not even have phone service in 1995? Surprisingly, yes. Mr. B. still felt very much connected to his native village, as well as determined to improve it financially, environmentally, and spiritually. Because of his knowledge of how to get grant money to fund projects, he was constantly designing projects. Some included finding funding for the wild/local chicken breeding, planting vegetation that did not dry out the soil as did clove trees, building a local crafts center for Munduk. He had already brought selected artists to Munduk for one month to create new forms of art there such as a sculpture made from plastics and trash.

The villagers respect and admire him. To me, he personifies what the Balinese culture has been able to do by integrating traditional culture with new ideas and broader vision. On one particular day, Mr. B. inspected some new tourist cottages that had just been completed at Puri Lumbung. When he inspected the workmanship, he was disappointed. And yet, he felt great pride in the accomplishment. He explained it this way.

"I have a western eye and a Balinese eye. When I look at the cottages with my western eye, I can see all the imperfections and sloppiness. However, when I look with my Balinese eye, I marvel that these workmen can achieve what they have without ever having seen a modern bathroom, or a western structure."

And so, he is quite able to live in both worlds, feeling grounded in Balinese culture and being western in the breadth of his experiences.

A WALK IN THE VILLAGE

As you walk in the village, you notice sometimes new and sometimes decaying decorations of natural fronds, leaves, and flowers standing along the roadside. In many places, including Puri Lumbung, you will see small leaf baskets containing a few flowers and grains of rice. Such offerings are made daily to satisfy the needs of the many gods and spirits requiring attention and care.

For the most part, the villagers cannot speak English, but they smile widely and sincerely to greet you. If you try to capture these warm smiles in a photo, they turn quite serious-faced and stiff when a camera is aimed at them. After the click, the smile returns. Some may greet you with "Where you go?" which is not meant to be intrusive, but is a translation of the customary greeting they give each other. A smile in reply is fine. Many of the women will be gracefully carrying any variety of large loads on their heads. Can it really be so effortless?

Reminders of the Dutch occupation are in the architecture of some of the buildings, and the statues of soldiers along the road. You will pass several small stores selling simple supplies. From early morning until about 11 a.m., there is a food market just off the main road. And, of course, there are the *warungs*, small eating places, which are also gathering places as well as places to eat.

On your walk, you can stop in at the pool parlor to pit your skill against the locals. Continuing down the hill, you will see a large open meeting hall near the end of the village. This is the center of the all-important *banjar*, which is the lifeblood of the village that provides a structure to village life and takes care of most social welfare needs of the villagers.

Each man joins the *banjar* when he gets married. Therefore, membership totals just about the entire village since the families of the men are included in the membership. The community center never lacks volunteers because the social obligations are enforced by peer pressure. They give of their time, energy, and money. In return, they receive support, a sense of identity, and practical help when needed. It is a successful exchange.

If one of Mr. B.'s proposed projects receives funding, this meeting area for the village will provide a fuller community center offering a library, a place for local crafts to be sold, and a training center for youth to gain marketable skills.

The many temples you pass are family temples. The village temple, as in all Balinese villages, is at the end of the village. The very last end of the village is the cemetery, which offers another quite spectacular mountain view.

New Year in Bali comes every 210 days in the Balinese calendar. Munduk's observance is unique within Bali. After a day of strict fasting, the villagers all cook outside on the roadside in the middle of the night.

Although I spent a lot of time in the Puri Lumbung cottages, my home for two months was right in the village where there are two renovated Dutch buildings for guests. Nearby is the family of Made B., Mr. B.'s cousin. Tourists can also choose to live right within their home. He, his wife, and always smiling niece did everything they could to make me comfortable. Made, who knows some English, was born in Munduk and has spent most of his life in the village except for seven years in Java where he went to high school.

In 1966, Made B. became a teacher at the school you pass on your left on your way into the village from Puri Lumbung. In 1968, he became the principal of the school. His wife, Ketut P., also teaches at the school. She was once a dancer in the village and still teaches dance. She is a leader of the women in the village and teaches sewing. They have three children—the eldest daughter is in school in the main city in Bali called Denpasar, a son is studying in Java, and a teenage daughter is in high school in Singaraja, about 45 minutes away.

Afternoons, Made tends his gardens in which grow clove, coconut, banana, *selak*, *rambutan*, cocoa beans, and pineapple. He was happy to show me around the traditional style family home and his yard where the woodcarvings he has made are displayed. A very large number of Balinese are artists in carving or painting, playing *gamelan*, dancing, or simply doing everything in a visually pleasing, aesthetic way.

My one-room building in the family compound of Made B.'s extended family, had a wide, rain-protected porch. Sometimes I taught on that porch. At other times I just enjoyed sitting there absorbing the beauty around me. Every day, Mr. B.'s father, walking with the aid of a cane, came by, stared at me quizzically, and then went on his way. He was a healthy, still-smoking senior citizen born in 1900. His wife had died at 95 years old.

It is at first puzzling to meet so many people that have the same names. The similarity comes because children are often named number one, two, three, four, five—in order of their birth. Added confusion for the foreigner comes from the many names that one person has depending upon who's addressing him or her. The specific way you must address each person makes it very difficult for foreigners to learn the Balinese language. However, all Balinese understand the Indonesian language.

AROUND MUNDUK

I had never heard of palm sugar, but I was told that Jakeri sugar, mostly used in baking, is available throughout the world. The pleasant toffee taste brings high prices and comes only from a particular palm tree. I was able to see this sugar being made by Made K. in Perdawa village near Munduk. Accessible by road or a four kilometer walk from Munduk, this small village reveals an older, smaller, quieter lifestyle than Munduk.

The wild-growing palm trees around Perdawa are utilized in several ways. The hair from it is used in roofing, the sugar is taken from it, and the inside of the tree itself can be eaten. Getting the sap for the sugar involves climbing the tree, cutting a branch, and placing a gourd under it to collect what slowly drips out. After about 12 hours, the full gourd is collected, cleaned out by using melted sugar and replaced under the branch. The liquid is boiled for four hours. When placed on a banana leaf in a coconut shell, it hardens in five to ten minutes.

There is a fermentation process that occurs, making an intoxicating drink if the juice is drunk after about 12 hours. If the hardened sugar is wrapped in a special leaf and kept dry, it actually gets tastier over time and can last five to six years.

The sugar palm must be seven or eight years old before the liquid can be tapped. After the branch is cut, it will flow for three to four months with the strongest flow after dark. The flow from the tree stops mysteriously for one month, and then will continue to flow again. The tree can produce sap for more than ten years with each branch eventually dying after its flow permanently ceases.

What was even more fascinating to me than the palm sugar was the home where Made K. lives. It is a 100-year-old village home. More modern structures have replaced most of these practical, well-built homes. Consisting of one large room, there were two very large beds supported by sturdy wood from local trees. The floor was dirt, and the large oven had been built out of dirt. There was only one small window that looked out upon a simple bamboo family temple. But there was adequate ventilation because the walls of the house were not solid! The strips allowed a little light and air to flow through the smoke-darkened room.

There were shelves for cooking utensils and the family's belongings. Suspended baskets allowed food to be kept away from the ever-present dogs and cats.

Surprisingly, the darkness of the smoke-blackened room gave it a comfortable, cozy feeling. Certain hotels in Bali are actually going back to this old style in decorating the rooms. It made me, accustomed to plastic and bright colors, feel like a traveler to the primitive past.

If I conjured up in my imagination the most tranquil, serene lake I could, I would not even come close to the spectacular Lake Tamblingan. Tamblingan village is an intentionally small village, which lies between a forest and the sacred Lake Tamblingan. Considered Bali's center of prosperity in water, forest, and spirit, Tamblingan is a government-protected area that allows only 12 families to live in it. Each family is given a 250-meter area at no charge. In exchange, they protect the forest, lake, and the three important temples here. They fish three to four hours daily. Although there is yet no restaurant here, one can request a meal of one of the perhaps seven kinds of fish here. Although August to October are the best fishing months, some fish are available year round.

From the village, there is a two-hour walk to the cave called Nagaloka, which is indeed the center of Bali. The primeval forest (never planted) has the Cemare Pandak tree that only grows in that forest. In Tamblingan, Niluh S. is a small, but strong woman who takes passengers on the lake in a dugout canoe. There is a temple right in the middle of Lake Tamblingan. Although the lake looks inviting, it is not safe for swimming because of the weeds that can drag a person under.

These villagers welcome visitors. As a matter of fact, they told me that meeting travelers is one of the attractions of living there. They also enjoy fishing rather than being tied to crops like farmers must be.

What I remember most about Tamblingan was just sitting close to the lake in the late afternoon. There was the beauty and stillness to drink in, broken by the commotion of the fighting cocks lined up in their baskets all crowingly demanding their dinner before bedtime.

A waterfall a short walk from Puri Lumbung combines many elements that make Munduk so lovable a place. After negotiating the seemingly treacherous dogs and asking for permission to pass through someone's property, the gentle walk is made more interesting by observing the intricate and highly efficient waterways Bali is known for to irrigate the rice paddies. As I reached the sound of the waterfall, I also began to see some carvings placed along the trail. The carver was sometimes there, but often not. The waterfall enlarged or shrank depending upon the recent amount of rainfall. With the wonderful integration of nature and human culture that Balinese have achieved, there was a small wooden structure where one could sit and play a small bamboo *gamelan* to accompany the music of the waterfall.

The physical strength of the waterfall reflected the emotional strength of one of the tourists who once went to visit the waterfall with me. He was a young French musician, and his legs were terribly twisted from the polio that had attacked him as a baby. He used two crutches and pulled himself laboriously along the narrow trails. Many travelers I have met over the years have impressed me. Whenever I feel that traveling is a hard job, I remember him and his persistence to see the world.

THE IDEAL WOMAN

In my reading, I have found a description of the ideal woman's qualities to the Balinese. She has "teeth white as ivory, a glance like lightning, fingers straight as a *gancan* (a stick for winding thread), gums like a (bright red) *rijasa* flower, a waist like a handful of limp *gonad* (a long, thin, vegetable), calves like a *papah bui* (tapering banana stem), a body thin as a cigarette, hair that is all black, and a voice like a *sunari* (a bamboo wind chime) blown by the wind."

While I was teaching my students the words and uses for parts of the face, they shyly informed me that Balinese use their noses to kiss.

THE MEANING OF MUNDUK

On my flight into Bali, the man sitting next to me said nothing during the five-hour flight except that he could not speak English. As we neared the airport in Denpasar, he became visibly excited while straining to see out my window. He said with pride, and in perfect English, "Bali is my home." While at a Munduk dance performance for the villagers (rather than for tourists), the young Balinese man sitting next to me told me he had spent several happy years studying in an Indonesian city outside Bali. "But," he said pointing to his chest, "something inside me made me come back. I don't know why." I did.

I received a letter from my mother while I was in Bali letting me know that my good friend, Carolyn, had died. She had suffered too long with a respiratory illness that tried, but never fully succeeded, to take away her zest for life. I thought of the variety of our shared experiences over the years including standing together gathering signatures for petitions for non-smokers' rights, long, insightful conversations on many topics, her joy in eating hot fudge sundaes, her light, easy laughter, and her love for her pet cats. I wanted to bring Carolyn's spirit to me in the paradise of Munduk. One of my students prepared an appropriate offering and guided me through a little ceremony in my garden.

One night, just before it was my time to leave Munduk, a cat came onto my porch and looked me straight in the eyes. That started me floating in a stream of consciousness back in memory to people and times I hadn't thought of in years. I thought about the parts of my life in Munduk that I would have to do without—faces of my young and old students, people I had only been able to smile to, and those who had talked to me deeply. Then the stream of consciousness carried me past the magnificent views of the mountains, valleys, and terraces that echoed with thunder rolling in the limitless, infinite sky. I saw the flowers calling for my attention as they joyously burst into bloom. I again heard the peculiar sound of a certain bird that made a trilling sound as though it were playing an instrument. I felt all the things about Munduk that seemed so right to me—the indescribable beauty and peace of a life lived entwined with nature.

All this and more jumbled together in my mind, ran to my heart, and came down my face in a gush of tears. I felt so incredibly sad that I must leave Bali soon—perhaps for a while, perhaps for a long time, perhaps forever. Even if I returned, Bali may have changed. Munduk may have changed. When I thought my heart would truly break as panic took over, I intuited the invitation to walk out into the cool, star-filled night. As I calmed down in the embrace of nature surrounding me, I felt Carolyn's spirit slip her hand into mine. As her presence and I stood together in the garden, a very clear message enveloped me. It was a simple statement from Bali to me. "You can take with you everything you have learned and felt here."

I wrote a letter to Bali in that moonlight, declaring my gratitude, sincerest thank you, and deepest love. Then, I buried it in my garden. I had to leave Bali, but I carried the wisdom of Munduk inside me.

April 21, 1995

My stomach thankfully bounced back to health quickly "down under" in Australia. Staying with several SERVAS people has been a delight because they are so different, yet most quite easy to get along with. The SERVAS International Conference in Melbourne was inspiring. Due to the nature of people in an organization whose only focus is greeting tourists from all over the world, SERVAS people are open, warm, friendly, talkative, interesting, and often unusual. I was even able to get the names of a few hosts for my upcoming stay in New Zealand. In addition to SERVAS people, I've been able to re-connect with an Australian brother and sister I met when we all were *kibbutz* volunteers in Israel in 1982. We didn't think we'd ever see each other again, and certainly not in their homes in Australia. Some of my former students from the high school in Macau are now studying in the same university in Australia and came to see me. It's always gratifying for teachers to watch their students mature, especially when exposed to the challenges of life in a different culture.

It is fall now. The trees outside are red. The air is crisp, and the houses have that solid feeling required to withstand a cold winter. Although Australia is too vast for me to see much of it during my stay, I've found Sydney, Melbourne, and Canberra surprisingly beautiful. I wasn't going to take the tour on the Great Coast Road because I imagined it to be a runner-up to Route 1 along the California Coast. I was told by an Australian who had seen both not to miss it. It definitely offered its own gorgeous, dramatic ocean views. Looking out to sea in Australia, I have been able to see the distinct curvature of the horizon that's exciting visual proof that our planet Earth is round.

When I was in Bali, I had met an Australian man about my age who made me curious about Australians. His memories of the 1960's in Australia were identical to what I had experienced in the United States. That prepared me for a museum in Australia that portrayed those tumultuous times similarly in spite of so many thousands of miles separating us. My only other impression of Australian travelers I had met was that they usually traveled for many years once they left Australia.

After my limited time being a tourist in Australia, I wrote down some observations about Australians.

1. Australians put butter on their sandwiches regardless of the filling.

2. They walk down staircases the same way they drive—on the left.

3. They say "right" a lot.

4. They are now trying to find an identity further from Britain and closer to Asia.

5. They feel guilty about their prior treatment of aborigines, much like Americans toward the Indians.

6. They are generally friendly and tall.

7. They value individualism, but still provide socialized medicine and adequate pensions for all their citizens.

8. They have many touching monuments to their soldiers in the parks.

9. The men wear shorts in the winter and dress warmly only from the waist up.
10. They think Americans are quite egotistical, isolationist, stupidly patriotic, and more demanding of getting their money's worth.
11. No tipping in Australia!
12. They eat pasties instead of wearing them.
13. Young Australian males and females like to wear nose rings.
14. Their older buildings have a remarkably beautiful architecture for such a young country.
15. They have strong "no smoking" rules that make workers smoke outside on the sidewalks next to their office buildings.
16. Big cities have unsightly graffiti, scruffy-looking youth, and places to avoid after dark just like in the U.S.
17. All public restrooms and youth hostels in Australia have dispensers to dispose of needles after using drugs.

April 30, 1995

New Zealand is a place I never really expected I'd get to, but just a few days here have convinced me I'm glad I came. Fall is in the air, and the weather changes constantly within one day. Although I'm in a large city called Christchurch, there's the definite feeling of being in a less populated country.

Politically, the indigenous Maori people are demanding rights from the government. Although historically not as badly treated as the Australians treated the Aborigines, or America treated the Indians, the Maoris have suffered over the years and are making their cause known through books like Once Were Warriors by Alan Duff. The plight of the Maoris he describes is painfully reminiscent of what Eldridge Cleaver wrote in the 1960's about blacks in the U.S. I heard a particularly poignant comment today that white New Zealanders will feel like the Maoris as they watch the Asians, mainly Japanese and Taiwanese, buying up land and property in New Zealand. In fact, having tutored a Taiwanese family when I was in Taiwan that was planning to re-locate to New Zealand, I know that the New Zealand government makes immigration easy for wealthy Asians.

My visit to the Antarctic Experience in Christchurch had a profound effect on me as I watched the multi-media show at least four times. My mouth dropped open "experiencing" Antarctica as best I could in the museum and I decided to find a way to fly over similar terrain in New Zealand. I may get my chance on a trip through The Magic Bus. Guided by my trusty tour book, I have booked a mostly independent tour. I picked a route and have two months to complete it. A Magic Bus takes me to each destination, directly to a hotel or Youth Hostel of my choice, and leaves me there until I let them know I'm ready to go to the next stop.

May 1, 1995

New Zealand is an incredible place! Distances are not great, and the Magic Bus is an excellent and relatively inexpensive way of getting around from one extraordinary sight to another. Being let off and picked up right at the Youth Hostels means I don't have to lug my luggage very far. Many of the travelers are Japanese or Koreans who are studying English here. The Youth Hostel system in New Zealand has been voted the best in the world, and it's easy to see why. I wish I could take the Youth Hostels and the Magic Bus with me everywhere in the world.

No matter the weather, the bus drivers are typical New Zealand "blokes" who wear shorts and a t-shirt. Their New Zealand accents can be a bit difficult to understand, like "rise" for "rose," "sex" for "six." They aren't actually tour guides, but offer good information for the asking. I'm on my way to a place where the guide casually mentioned that this would be the best place to take a plane trip around Mt. Cook. It will most likely be the closest I'll ever get to Antarctica. I'm ready and willing, but will the weather cooperate?

May 2, 1995

I could feel the wonder of this place as I walked out under a canopy of zillions of stars. The might and mystery of Franz Josef Glacier and the Alps are all around me. The unlikely combination of semi-tropical rainforest, ocean, mountains and glaciers defies logic. I felt proud of a Jewish woman pictured in the little stone museum who was the first woman to climb Mt. Cook long before the days of lightweight ropes, high-tech climbing gear, and small cameras.

Today would have been perfect for flying in a four-seater plane up to an ice field where the pilot could land on snow skis and turn off the engine while we got out and walked around. Then, for the rest of the hour, we could have looked into the face of Mt. Cook and flown around it. But, I was the only one to sign up and the company requires three passengers. Fortunately, three of us are signed up to go tomorrow morning, weather permitting.

I keep waking up to go to the window to make sure I can still see the stars. I am as "keen as mustard," as they say around here to have my flight of a lifetime.

MESSAGE FROM A MOUNTAIN

Today I have taken back my solitude and privacy. I have once again hidden my huge self among the clouds and fog, showing nothing, inviting no one. Ah yes, but yesterday—yesterday I was in a different mood. I wanted blue skies and I wanted to see the sun and feel its warmth. And I wanted to meet you.

You were very anxious to see me too. I had tantalized you from your arrival the previous day in the little village that sits below me. I felt your keenness and then your disappointment when you could not find a plane to bring you close to me. You worried all through the night even though I let you see more stars at night than you'd ever seen before to tell you all would be clear the next day. You awoke early to scan the skies and each moment of the deepening dawn showed you I was getting ready to receive you.

You flew up to me with a tingling anticipation. And then your mouth dropped open and your eyes couldn't open wide enough to take it all in. I felt your exhilaration rising as the plane skied onto Davis Icefield on Franz Josef Glacier. What a pity he never saw his amazing namesake. The first words out of your mouth were "Oh, my god," as your feet touched the snow and your eyes looked while you tried to absorb what it was like to be where you could never walk to. Yes, you were on top of the world for ten ecstatic minutes. You knew you could never take in all the sights, pure silence, and the cleanest air, so you just "felt" it. I could sense you feeling absolutely wonderful and free—so free.

You looked, you clicked and clicked and then thought you must have taken enough pictures. But, "I must change to a new roll before we begin to fly again," you thought. And so you finished the roll with gay abandon, hoping for that once-in-a-lifetime photo to make you remember.

But you will remember those ten short minutes that are etched into your mind. The utter high you felt was a pure happiness. Little filled your mind except that you must soon leave, most likely never to come again. The snow was the deepest, cleanest white, and the sky the very bluest blue. The ocean was visible in the distance. Only shadows of the rocks towering above added other shades of color. Perhaps you will never again be so free or feel so good, so high in body and spirit. But perhaps experiencing this will make you open to such experiences elsewhere.

When you put one knee down on the many years' accumulation of deep ice, you felt my coldness and wetness. And when you tried to change the roll of film, your fingers were too numb to do it easily. I had shown you only my gentle side, but I wanted to remind you of the boundary between you and me. We are connected, but we are not one. I can destroy you utterly, or be benign. But today I was playful, like you.

As you rose once again into the air, I let you see my wrinkled and glacier-ridged face. You could not close your mouth as you went around 12,300 foot Mt. Cook. You only knew how to click madly, hopefully, as you felt only awe and my power emanating around you.

It was then that you lost your atheism. You were always spiritually attuned to nature, which easily spoke to you and you to it. In Bali, you understood that nature was your god. You had never felt any other god. It is not the god of Christians or Jews or Moslems, but the animistic god Balinese understand. I am not the god of love, or of people particularly. I am the majesty as I allowed you to see me and feel me and react to me on that Wednesday, the 3rd of May, 1995.

When you got off the plane, you tried to convey your gratitude to the pilot. Basically, and uncharacteristically for you, you were struck speechless and walked around quite dazed by the intensity of what you had felt in 60 minutes.

Exhausted, but also restless, you walked alone in the semi-tropical rainforest so unbelievably close to the glaciers. You watched the frolicking, but dangerous rapids of the glacial river and remembered a scene elsewhere—a memory of similar places in other countries you have visited. But never had you come so close to me before. There were no memories for that.

I showed you clearly how insignificant you are, but you had felt like an inconsequential grain of sand for many long years. That's why a god of love and caring and answering your prayers never made any impact upon you. But you are a part of nature by your being. That is your connectedness to all else, something else, outside yourself.

In the dying of the day, you came to look up at me again. The reflected rays of sunset turned me and the surrounding forested hills to a warm, golden hue. The light slowly moved across my face and I saluted you in farewell. You will not see me again, but you will remember. You are *mzima*, whole and well.

May 9, 1995

The days pass quickly, filled with remarkable sights and visual delights. The weather has sometimes obscured the extraordinary sights, but I feel lucky to have been in the right place in the right weather most of the time. The sun's rays in the

Southern Hemisphere have a different slant, exposing more shades of green than I ever could have imagined.

New Zealand gives me precious gifts each day. One day shows me dolphins leaping for joy as they follow our boat. Another day shows me "adventure travelers" who leap and dangle on bungy cords suspended over gorgeous canyon rivers, raft their way down raging rivers or tear around the rivers in boats at breakneck speeds. Yet another day offers a palette of colors and smells and boiling rivers that only a volcanic area like Rotorua can offer, followed by a massage under jets of warm water from under the earth. I met an Israeli young man at a real castle above the sea while we were climbing up a curving stairway made of the once-abundant kauri wood. That day at the castle, it rained and snowed and hailed and was sunny and warm, all just about simultaneously.

May 15, 1995

I thought the albatross of Coleridge was long extinct, but found out otherwise when I climbed a high hill on the chance of seeing one at a special reserve. I actually saw the long-reaching wingspan of two albatrosses and a chick with its fur flying in the wind as it waited patiently to be fed by one of its parents. They can only land and take off in very windy places, but are able to fly indefinitely over the seas without having to land often.

The white settlers of New Zealand have hurt their environment. They plowed up areas to plant crops and cleared land to make it look more like "back home." They exploited the huge, ageless trees like the kauri until most had been shipped off to wood-hungry countries. And, perhaps worst of all, they introduced animals that were not a part of the New Zealand ecology.

People with a passion for penguins are trying to right the balance once again. I stayed in a tourist accommodation in a reserve that was attempting to keep a yellow-eyed penguin colony alive. They had restored the vegetation and experimented to find a little house that the penguin couples would nest in. By trial and error, they discovered the penguins preferred an A-frame style home. Every night around sunset when the penguins returned, they kept watch over them and actually shot predators such as ferrets, which had been introduced into New Zealand and have devoured large penguin populations.

We could watch the penguins waddling to their nests through "hides," where we could see, but not be seen by the skittish penguins. One room in the reserve had the family trees of the colony drawn on the wall, including their given names. The baby chicks were worried over even more by their human protectors than by their parents.

May 24, 1995

In a state of wellbeing—that describes me surrounded constantly by magnificent beauty, or the comfort of serene peace in this land of gorgeous mountains, rivers, and seas. Unusual people pop into my life from time to time, like an elegant middle-aged Israeli originally from Romania who decided to travel around the world and stay at youth hostels to cure herself of being a snob. I stayed with a SERVAS family who live as caretakers on a 12 ½-acre island owned by the government. Over a yummy bowl of hot pumpkin soup, they spoke of their love for the land and their concerns about Asian money driving up the cost of land and house values in New Zealand.

I got back to Auckland in time for the ticker-tape parade to welcome home their winning Black Magic yachting crew. In a country of athletes and outdoor lovers, their win was a matter of national pride. What a colorful mess my first ticker-tape parade was! The day was glorious—in weather as well as spirit. The whole team walked on a very long red carpet made from glued-on red socks, which had been what every New Zealander was supposed to have worn to cheer their team on during the race. After the festivities, I joined the crowd pulling off the red socks for mementoes. "Good on ya, mate."

I haven't run out of spectacular places to visit in New Zealand yet, but it's getting on toward winter. With no central heating and only space heaters, I'm getting too cold. I've somewhat captured on film my exquisite visit to New Zealand. It's time to warm up in Fiji.

June 8, 1995

I am warm again and back in the third world among a cultural mélange of big, hairy, black Fijians, very dark East Indians, and some Chinese people. The Fijians and Indians communicate together only in English because they generally don't know each other's language. Fijians speak their own language, plus a village dialect, while the East Indians use Hindi among themselves.

I was curious as to why there are so many East Indians in Fiji. The British government once controlled Fiji and wanted to plant sugar cane as the major crop. In their colonial wisdom, they decided to import workers for the sugar cane fields from India and brought in large numbers of laborers. These laborers eventually multiplied and lost their connection to India. Born and raised in Fiji, they outgrew the sugar cane fields and became entrepreneurs. In the modern independence of Fiji, the business world is mostly led by the East Indians of Fiji who hire the native Fijians to work for them. This is a continuing predicament since the two groups remain distinct and separate; the East Indians becoming richer while the Fijians stay poor.

The Fijians are easy to get along with, and appear happy and relaxed. I've been told that the local drink, *kava*, helps to keep them calm. It is made from the root of the pepper tree and is always offered in social situations. During a tour, I was given *kava* to welcome me to a small village. Knowing that it can be intoxicating, I drank only a small bit, but it quickly numbed my lips. The East Indians also welcome tourists with the greeting, *bula*, but one senses the ulterior motive of selling something.

In New Zealand and Bali, a cloudy, rainy day could still be beautiful. But here in Suva, a blue sky makes a critical difference in how beautiful it is. In the sun, the ocean has the loveliest shades of blue-green.

June 12, 1995

Today this wandering Jew decided to pay respects to other wandering Jews. I went out to the cemetery I had read about in my guidebook and asked a uniformed man if he knew where the Jewish part of the cemetery was. Fijians adopted Christianity 180 years ago, and the cemetery was divided by religion.

The Jewish area was small but fenced in, keeping the Jews apart in death as they most likely were while living in Fiji. The most recent stone was for Zelda, buried in 1990. I took some photos, and then did what I tried not to do. I slipped in the mud, staining my skirt and mucking up my sandals. Luckily there was a faucet nearby where I washed my sandals and skirt as best I could.

A man was looking on from afar. There were actually quite a lot of men working in the cemetery. When I got to the path where the man was standing, he asked those inevitable questions, "Where do you come from? Are you alone?" He was holding a machete in his hand and asked me if I knew that all the men working in the cemetery were convicts. The uniformed man was their guard. He didn't say this in a particularly threatening way, nor did I act afraid. He smiled a big, white-toothed Fijian smile. Later on, I breathed a sigh of relief.

Later on, I coincidentally went to the same restaurant where Eceli worked. I had been told by Nyoman B. in Bali to look him up when I got to Fiji because he was a pastry chef who had visited Bali in 1989. It was good to talk about Bali together in Fiji.

June 14, 1995

I have flown over to Levuka, another island of Fiji, which was the old capital of Fiji. It is a "lost in time" little town. I'm staying in an old, rambling hotel, which at every turn evokes happy memories of a dilapidated hotel my grandparents used to own across from a beach in Massachusetts. There are very few restaurants in this town. In fact, there are few of everything here, but the food is surprisingly tasty. Impressive mountains rise as a backdrop just behind the town that occupies a rather narrow strip between sea and mountain.

It is Fijian-friendly to the extent that it is rare not to be greeted by passers-by. Strangely, they say "Good morning," regardless of the time of day, or "goodbye" instead of "hello" when you pass by. One unusual resident is a transvestite who works at a local restaurant. He seems to be accepted, but I can't help wondering what his life is like in this very small town.

Living in the peace of this place makes the rest of the world seem just plain crazy. I was ruminating today, as one's mind tends to in places like this, that I have lived in an age when travel has made it quite unlikely to be the "first one," anywhere, but yet I have been "the first foreigner" in many Chinese lives, which gives me a special kinship with the early explorers.

June 16, 1995

I have traveled by boat out to an island to enjoy the "out there even more" feeling of Robinson Crusoe, but with basic comforts. I am on a real gem of a remote island that takes only 30 minutes on foot to walk around slowly. It is small, self-contained, primitive, and magnificent. It has the greens, blues, and browns of an artist's palette. Here there are the sounds of silence and birds that only being out in nature can offer.

My "home" is a newly-constructed *bura*, made completely from natural vegetation on the island. Because I was the first resident of this new *bura*, the caretaker decorated one corner of my home with huge seashells. From a window without glass, I can lie on my bed and look out upon a slanting coconut palm tree that has a single coconut dangling precisely in the middle of my view. One footstep from the front cloth door opening is a soft, inviting, white sand beach that ends in an infinite blue-green sea.

It is like camping. The shared toilet and showers are not too far away. Very, very simple meals are served. The price, all-inclusive, is $15 a day! Four or us are sharing this island today—a happily married middle-aged Italian couple, and a woman from California who has the good luck to own a home near a beach that everyone wants to visit. She rents it out for a couple of months at a time, cash up front. Then, she takes the money and travels while it's rented.

This morning I was a true child at play. Being rather skittish about swimming over reefs, I opted to crawl and dogpaddle around most of the island at high tide.

I became part of a kinetic art piece as the light and colors played with me, and I with them. I wake up to the sound of waves and birds, and say goodnight to the lovely full moon that lights up the sand and water just outside my cloth door.

June 17, 1995

I had planned to spend only two days on the little island, but I went back to Levuka on the motorboat to change my ticket to Suva so that I can spend two more idyllic days as a total "beach bum." We sped through water that kept changing incredible colors—deep blue, aqua, aquamarine, turquoise, stunning green. I spent the afternoon back on the island in the tidepools, discovering creatures I've never seen before.

June 18, 1995

This tiny resort is owned and managed by the church of a village on another island. They invited us to come for Sunday service. Their church is still under construction. The children sat on mats on the floor, the women sat behind them, and the men sat in back. Believe me, sitting 1 ½ hours comfortably with crossed legs takes training from childhood!

The singing in the service was first-class, practiced and harmonized. The children sang a rather complicated piece. And then they asked us to sing. We were prepared for this beforehand. My singing repertoire is quite limited, so I had suggested to the others that we sing a rousing rendition of Jingle Bells since that had worked well for me in the Mongolian *yurt*. Our little choir consisted of Greg from Germany, Barbara from Slovenia, Tanya from England, Patty and me from the U.S.

I said the Hebrew word *shalom* to the Fijians gathered in that church. I explained that it meant, "hello," "goodbye," and "peace," which is what the Fijian soldiers in the United Nations are trying to bring to Israel. I remembered seeing Fijian United Nations soldiers when I lived in Israel, and had wondered then why they were willing to risk their lives for Israel. I felt grateful to all Fijians represented by those in that small island church surrounded by the sea. After the service, we shared a feast of many kinds of freshly caught fish superbly prepared.

This is my last night in my homemade *bura* next to the sea. I'm not adept at finding constellations, but the Southern Cross is gleaming brightly in the sky. When I need to remember what perfection in life means, I hope I can bring alive the velvety water, the warm breeze, the rustling palms, and the myriad colors.

June 21, 1995

I spent last evening with the Fijian mother of one of my international students in Macau. And today I rested in Raymond Burr's garden, so far away from Hollywood. He planted profusions of orchids, which so love this happy climate. Among the enormous banana leaves, the palms, the poinsettia trees, and the fountains, I leisurely thought about the spectacular five-month journey I've had since I left Macau—Bali, Australia, New Zealand, and Fiji. I have been so very lucky.

June 22, 1995

I saw my mother and father at the airport before they spotted me. The fleeting thought crossed my mind that, one day, they would not be there to welcome me home. I was temporarily overwhelmed by the premonition of the loneliness I will feel when that time comes.

17

CHINA KOREA EUROPE TURKEY 1997

Jan. 17, 1997

"Suellen, there's a call for you—from Korea," my father had said one late summer's night in 1996 with the lilt of surprise in his voice. I had pretty much given up hope that the ten letters I had sent out to universities in Korea in the spring of 1996 would get me a job. It was the first time I had dared look for work without first seeing the country or specific school, but I had been told by a Korean teacher at the community college in Dallas where I was teaching part time that Korea had good English teaching jobs at decent pay in small, less polluted cities.

The job offer was, for me, quite excellent. It not only offered the chance to see another culture in Asia, but had a better salary than I'd ever made, PLUS four months of paid vacation. The two large breaks, end of December to the beginning of March, and July through August, had short-term teaching programs with additional money, but I didn't have to participate in them. With Korea's proximity to China, I assumed I'd use the breaks to travel.

The university was located in a Korean city about a two-hour train ride from Seoul. They were hiring eight or nine native English teachers at one time to upgrade their program. I accepted on the spot and had several months to prepare.

That was before the mid-September night of the terrible, terrible phone call that told us my brother had died suddenly of a heart attack at the age of 46. I was the one who had traveled the world round and round. My brother had no yen to travel. He was content to stay in one area of the world that he loved and patiently meet me at the San Francisco Airport whenever my flight path allowed. Then, one sad day, without warning or a goodbye, he left and went too far to ever come back. It was a trip he had to take. We could not even say goodbye or wish him well. He is far, far away, and my parents and I can never be the same as before he went away.

My parents encouraged me to still take the job in Korea. They were more or less accustomed to their new home in Dallas, Texas, and had relatives close by. They said they'd be okay. So, after 1½ years in Dallas, I'm back in China before going on to Korea. Today I'm with Peter in Shenzhen. The frenzy of Shenzhen has calmed down somewhat, and a thin overlay of order prevails.

Peter is older and wiser, and somewhat the sadder for having been cheated badly in business. He feels he may not be well-suited for international trade, but likes the youthful energy of Shenzhen. Last night, I met with a Nanjing student who's now working in Hong Kong. His sensitivity and intelligence once again impressed me. I am growing old; they are growing up.

Jan. 24, 1997

As usual, my schedule is happily full in friendly, freezing Hangzhou. Russell and Bill met me at the airport, along with Russell's boss, a 73-year-old American who is a consultant for the joint venture highway construction company Russell now works for. Russell knew nothing about highway construction, but with his brother-in-law's *guanxi* and Russell's good English, he was hired as a translator. Russell's life is looking up in other ways, too. He will soon marry, which gives him the right to his own apartment from his work unit, and he will go on a two-month business trip to the U.S. He and my mother are still in contact, and he hopes they will be able to meet somewhere.

Bill took me out to his new home with his wife. It is comfortable, although they have to share a kitchen with another couple. I saw their brand new refrigerator. Since the street to his home was filled with vendors and markets to buy fresh food on the way home, I wondered what he had in the refrigerator. One lonely leftover dried up fish sat on one shelf, but Bill explained that he would store fruit in the refrigerator in summertime. Chinese people had told me they don't like frozen food and can always tell if meat has been frozen, so I asked Bill what he kept in the freezer section. He opened the freezer and said, "Ice cream bars. What else would you keep in a freezer?"

Jan. 27, 1997

Robert took me out to the resort hotel that has hired him as a trainer for the staff. Mountains and a lake made a pretty setting although the weather was cold and raw. Since the hotel had no other guests at the moment, I didn't have any heat or hot water in my room. Robert and his very pretty and English-speaking fiancée kept me warm with their hospitality and scrumptious crab meals—one of my favorites.

Robert credited me as his inspiration to go out on his own as a free-lance training instructor. He had had a regular job on the staff of a nice hotel in Hangzhou, but saw little future there. He went against the logic of the time that said you should stay in a government job until you retire. He had seen me go from job to job and decided he could do that too.

Thomas is struggling to do the same thing. Each time I come to Hangzhou, he has another office and is trying a different business. I don't know if he'll find his niche, but his determination to be his own boss only strengthens with time and disappointment.

Jan. 29, 1997

I'm sitting in a cement box with five stories of white tile and blue windows. It is the Chinese peasants' version of a palace and shows to all how rich they've become. This is what Pearl's parents have built just down the road from their old, but cozy and charming countryside home.

In their village outside Hangzhou, the men are semi-retired, making big money from their factories with little on their agenda. They've rented out their fields to others to farm. The wives, once overworked and overburdened, now gossip, eat sunflower seeds endlessly, and play mahjong all day.

This is a stark contrast to city factory workers whose factories have closed down and left them unemployed and desperate.

Yes, China is changing and growing, getting both richer and poorer, happier and sadder, filled with hope and despair. The gaps between rich and poor are widening, and purses are often stolen or slashed on buses. Amidst globalization and westernization, China is like a teenager trying out various behaviors to figure out who she is and what she wants to be.

COLORFUL CLOTHES, SINGING BIRDS, AND UPSIDE DOWN DUCKS ALL IN A TREE

A sunny day brightens dispositions all over the world, but none moreso than in the middle of winter in unheated China. Such was a day that brought me out of my hotel room in Hangzhou. The sky was unseasonably blue with gentle clouds floating in it.

I walked in the streets of a small neighborhood market and saw the smiles of people sitting outdoors playing cards, playing with grandchildren, chatting. Even a usually busy vendor who concentrates on making money with his goods had paused to turn his loaded cart into a table for playing cards.

I chanced upon a picturesque canal with small houses lining it on one side. The opposite side was already beginning to give way to the rather awkward, ungraceful, high-rise apartments springing up like unattractive weeds all over China. Each side of the street separated by the canal—one still filled with old, graceful one- and two-story homes, across from ungainly blue-windowed monsters—struck me as symbolic of the many fast-paced transitions of modern China.

I walked slowly along the grimy, although not trash-filled canal and took for granted the unusual cleanliness of the sidewalk and canal bank on this side. These were people who had a sense of the neighborhood that existed outside the walls of their homes. These were people who knew their neighbors and easily flowed between outside and inside. The people on the other side of the canal were apartment dwellers who had no sense of community outside their walls and who would live confined to their modern boxes with balconies from which to see the canal.

At times I regretted having left my camera behind, but in other ways was glad because I could blend in a bit better without the prying tourist's camera-eyed view of China. I took many mental pictures instead.

The cold chill that permeates unheated homes in winter had brought not only people outdoors, but also their clothes, bedding, and even whole beds that had been moved outside to air out. The puffy quilts made a gay sight. The tree branches were no longer bare, but happily bore birds in cages, and a variety of newly washed clothes excitedly waving and soaking up the wonderful fresh sunshine. Cooked ducks being preserved for the upcoming Chinese New Year were also sunbathing on the branches so they could develop the best taste possible.

China in the 1990's is a place of incredible transition, turmoil, and even chaos. The old and the new, whether with people or technology, often confront each other in discord. But on this day, in this place, there was only the warmth of sunshine and harmony.

Feb. 6, 1997

It seemed easy enough since I had done it once before in China. I had walked into an eyeglass frame shop, showed them my frame-less lenses, and they popped them into a perfect frame. I hoped to do it again since they had told me in the U.S. that they had no frames to fit those lenses.

Sam's sister, Pauline, came with me to translate. As I casually looked around, I saw the type of frame I might like. The middle-aged clerk was assuring my friend they could help me, but first I must take an on-site eye exam. Since I already had the lenses and wanted a frame so I'd have a spare pair of glasses, I protested. "No money," my young friend advised me.

A competent lady waiting there took me in hand and I had an eye test. Having just had an eye test in the U.S. and two new pair of glasses made, I had a twinge of curiosity and showed them my new glasses. "Not the same," I was told. Hard to know whom to trust—U.S. super technology and a $45 (including a discount) eye test, or this competent lady now joined by an interested colleague.

Pauline had trouble keeping up with what the clerk was saying. Of course they could sell me glasses with the correct frames. It would take one month to make them. Since I was only on a weekend stay in that town, it didn't sound too promising even though the price was tempting.

Well, they agreed that they could re-shape the lenses I had brought in with me to fit their existing frames. Having been told in the U.S. that it was impossible to re-shape lenses, I was skeptical.

My friend, looking perplexed at the barrage of salesmanship in Chinese, did her best to explain that yes, it is possible to re-shape the lenses if they have certain measurements. Upon measuring, yes, the distance was okay for re-shaping the lenses. "If not in the U.S., why in China?" I thought.

What was not possible in the U.S. was quite possible in record time in China for a total charge of $10, including the new frames.

Feb. 8, 1997

How special it is to celebrate the Chinese New Year at the Beijing home of Juliet and her husband and their two children! Harriet has flown in from Wisconsin too. Having been together once in Malaysia, we were together again. Juliet's husband now works for a company in Beijing that pays for their home in a very spacious, nicely laid out foreigners' complex.

It's cold for me, but Harriet is much more comfortable in China's winter than the summer when she visited before. We have plans to visit some Beijing sights together, sometimes with Juliet and her parents who are also visiting from Hangzhou, and sometimes with a former Nanjing student of mine from Beijing.

Feb. 13, 1997

It's been fun for me to show Harriet some places I've been before. One outstanding museum that was new to me was the Bell Museum where we happily wandered a long time. I had been to the Summer Palace before, but not in the winter. The lake around it was solidly frozen and men in ice skates pushed us across the ice in small chairs with runners. I loved it. Seeing the *hutong*, alleyways of Beijing, in a pedicab was more difficult since they are not meant for two large foreigners to ride in. Our skinny pedicab driver earned the respect of many of the other drivers who saw us that day. We invited him to eat with us in a restaurant as his well-earned tip.

Feb. 18, 1997

I've only been in Korea for a couple of days, but I've already faced some cultural quandaries. Do I sleep under or over what's covering the bed? Where do I put my camera and film so that the heated floors don't ruin them? How do I take a shower without a shower curtain and not get the floor all wet? Do I trust putting my clothes in a washing machine called Chaos? How can my SERVAS hostess who looks young enough to be my daughter but is two years my senior have gone through menopause without gaining an ounce? How can the supermarkets make enough money when the clerks encourage you to take a taste of everything you pass? How can anyone drink *ginseng* tea even though it's supposed to be so healthy?

I had a whirlwind tour of Seoul with my SERVAS hosts. Among the colorful temples and palaces were brides with goosebumps, freezing in their wedding gowns for picture-taking. They dotted the parks like spring flowers out of season. My accommodating host even took me to the train station to put me on the right train for my destination, Taejon.

"You have so many bags!" he exclaimed. I can't imagine that Koreans traveling for a year through different climates would travel with much less. Yet, apparently, carrying luggage disturbs Koreans as much as Chinese since I've been told this so many times. Connie, one of my Nanjing students who had recently come to see me in Hangzhou, had shed some light on this when she told me that Chinese adapt themselves to uncomfortable situations whereas we Americans like to be prepared for comfort in any eventuality. I have to admit I have envied American long-term travelers with very little luggage, but I've never been one of them.

MY HOME IN KOREA

My mind had been filled with best case and worst case scenarios as the train chugged into Taejon Station. Would my new home have a spacious view like the one I never tired of in Israel? Or would it have the charm of my 100-year-old home in an anachronistic remnant of a Chinese village on a small island connected to Macau? Perhaps it would have the roominess of my three-room apartment in Taiwan. Or, might there be the same leaden air around it where black soot from burning trash fell on my balcony in Taiwan? Would it be one tall building looking into the bedrooms of even taller buildings as was happening in Macau? Would it be as cold as my room in China where my sweet students lugged several thermos bottles at night so I could "bathe?" I had no hope it would share any resemblance to my one large room in Bali in a renovated Dutch building set amidst a garden with a sweeping panorama of mountains, valleys, and ocean.

I had been told I would have a two-room apartment in the dormitory on campus. But that plan had changed with the large number of foreign teachers coming. "It's very small," the department chairwoman began. "Does it have a view?" was my first concern. "No," she answered frankly. But perhaps I could chose which new apartment I wanted among those being prepared for the teachers who were due to arrive next week.

Relieved to see the pretty hillside at the edge of the city where the university nestles, I could choose among six almost ready apartments. "Oh, good," the chairwoman exclaimed, "some of the furniture has come." What indeed filled my view was an enormous (at least it looked so in the tiny room) double bed with footboard, sideboards, and a huge headboard. The room itself would be considered small under any conditions, but a huge closet (not built-in), the double bed, and a table with four chairs (two of which sat on top of the table for lack of space) filled it quite full.

Korean-style living is floor-oriented because the floor has water pipes running underneath. What covers one wall of the small balcony is a multi-pipe gadget with pipes extending under the floor and a long exhaust jutting outside the building like a rifle. I would much prefer to have no bed and use the Korean system of sleeping on pads on the floor. "There's no place to store the bed," the chairwoman responded rather sympathetically.

I picked the room with what I considered the best view. At the moment I saw it, some sunlight was nicely illuminating a portion of the table. The light and sun seemed adequate, and I liked looking out upon a field in front of the apartment where plastic greenhouses were erected for growing something or other. It reminded me fondly of the plastic tents housing strawberries I had looked over from my window in Kfar Saba, Israel.

Light and air is a puzzling aspect of Korean homes. My little efficiency has no less than 20 windows and doors. What amazes me is that, with all these, I can see only a miniscule portion of outdoors. I will try to explain. The balcony has four opaque windows. Only two of them can be open at one time. There are two sets of sliding glass doors from the balcony into the room. One set is transparent glass. The other set in front of them is opaque. Again, only one side can be seen through at any given time, thus halving the view at all times. Between the room and the kitchen, there is another opaque set of sliding doors.

The bathroom is off the kitchen. It has a door, shower, toilet, no sink, and a small double set of windows, which gives half a view into the corridor outside the apartment door. The kitchen window is also a double set that allows a sliver of a view when the corridor's windows to outside are also open. In the warm weather, I hope to be able to open the front door to let in more view and light and a cross breeze.

I went to bed that first night snuggled in a borrowed blanket of what I figured were Bambi and her mother and mentally reconfigured the room. When I had figured out how to dismantle the bed, store the boards on the balcony, and put the bookcase/headboard on the balcony to hold plants, I fell asleep.

I awoke to a sunny day and immediately opened up my balcony windows. The concerned landlady downstairs motioned to me to close them, saying "*munzi, munzi*" which, from her pantomime, must have meant "dusty." I reluctantly closed the windows on the outdoors and mumbled, "I'm a flower, not a mushroom." Having shocked her the first day by carrying my heavy suitcase into the room without first taking off my shoes, I didn't want to get another well-meaning lecture on "how to live properly in a Korean home."

I went out and bought a plant, which always means "home" to me. That day, and the next few days, I returned to find my little room shrinking. Still working on the assumption that westerners require certain items, the university did not skimp on providing us with a quite large refrigerator on top of which I've placed the thankfully small tv, an efficient, but bulky vacuum cleaner to clean up the small amount of exposed floor space, and a large washing machine adequate for a big family. The promised microwave hasn't arrived yet.

I did fairly well re-adjusting to each additional cramping of my space. But the part that truly tested my adjustability was the addition of a large air conditioner over the bed with big pipes extending out the balcony and around the walls, which are connected to a humongous exhaust fan mounted on a metal shelf right at the window level, thus reducing my already pitiful view. This fan also totally eliminated any hope of putting the headboard on the balcony.

Daunted and disappointed, I worked on the idea, "If you can't make it roomy, then make it womby." So, I added more plants to give the look and comfort of a greenhouse in the portion of the balcony not taken up by the pipes, exhaust fan and shelf, and the washing machine. These plants will test my light-green thumb to the maximum.

Comparisons with Alice in Wonderland who grew and shrunk in her environment have come to mind. Edward Albee's play of movers bringing furniture into an apartment until the owner disappears also took on new meaning. And then there is the touching story, A Patch of Blue, which seems to be what I must be content to see. But the most appropriate comparison is what it must be like to live in a dollhouse. Everything is easily at hand. Any speck of dirt can be seen and immediately picked up (which really gets annoying).

My little home is neat and clean, albeit crowded. This will definitely cut down on any natural propensity to accumulate "stuff." The warehouse/factory touch has advantages. For example, the white pipe going through the room conveying gas to the stove is convenient for hanging up clothes that are almost dry, or to air them out. The light from the bed can be easily removed over to the table when needed. My parents gave me a cheerful blue and yellow bird that activates when jiggled to let out a cheery chirp. He sits on my uneven table that easily wiggles and sets off his chirp.

It's always interesting to compare one's reactions to others. Upon seeing the tiny room, another teacher and her husband, both good-sized Americans, were pleased as punch not to have to share a kitchen and bathroom as they had been doing in their last job. Another couple thinks of it as "camping out" for a year. One teacher plans to put up many shelves for storage, and I can think only of minimal decorating and lots of plants.

Through perhaps a quirk of fate, or a performance in the theater of the absurd, one teacher has been given a dormitory apartment. It is enormous—and well furnished. We scratch our heads and wonder how it was decided to house us in shoeboxes over those spacious apartments.

My philosophy in going to other cultures to live has been to enjoy what is new and different instead of yearning for what "isn't" and what's "missing." And so I can enjoy the usual quietness of living in an alley with few cars, the short walk to the "downtown" of our neighborhood, bargaining in the marketplace, and taking the healthy, 20-minute walk on a small path through the waving rice up the hill to the university. Soon there will be my new students to enjoy teaching.

P.S. Later, I was able to get the bed removed, so I now sleep on the floor. This has opened up the room somewhat, making me more comfortable. However, just today they came and put a screen and bars (in this basically crime-free country) on my little kitchen window to the outside corridor. Alas, this final touch adds a prison look to my tiny view.

March 9, 1997

The students are in shock at having English teachers for the first time who do not speak Korean. Their level of English, especially spoken English, is extremely low even for the English language majors. Rather than the high motivation I was used to in China, these students don't really ever expect to learn English. The Korean government, however, has decided to emphasize English more than ever, even putting native speakers into primary schools. I also have some middle-aged men in my classes who have been sent back from their government jobs to learn English.

I don't think my greatest joy in Korea will be teaching. However, I'm enjoying the little neighborhood I live in, and get along well with middle-aged women. The other day I went to buy some groceries. A Korean lady came by, took me by the arm, and led me to a shortcut. I couldn't explain to her that I wanted as much walking exercise as possible, so I chatted in English and she in Korean as we walked arm in arm through the shortcut. Her good deed accomplished, she indicated goodbye and walked back the way we had come.

A troubling aspect to my finances is that Korea, and Asia in general, is starting to go through some kind of financial crisis. The value of the Korean currency I'm being paid is dropping every day. Well, at least I still have my long vacations.

March 23, 1997

I have found a spot for reflection in the hills surrounding my home. It is not spectacular wilderness, but gentle, often lovely hills. Up here, the noises of city life are muted, the birds twitter, and the wind—ah, yes, the wind speaks through the trees and the grass. There is an area enclosed by bright green pine trees, and an expansive, sunny view next to that. There are also mounds of dirt and stones that remind me of a cemetery. It is here that I come to sit and let the tears flow for my brother.

April 12, 1997

The young girl assigned by the school to "take care of us," took us to a Cherry Blossom Festival today. The delicate cherry blossoms fell on us and around us like gentle, warm snow. Koreans sat on the grass, and sometimes on mats, which they never walk on in shoes. Although the modern dress is quite drab, the traditional *hanbok* is often multicolored and bright. I delighted in the sun, but many Korean women used fashionable shiny parasols to shade themselves.

Although people were in a festive mood, their faces didn't show it. Even the children seemed subdued. However, watching traditional songs and dances often brought some of the old men to their feet in excitement. Some of the singing has an intense, haunting feeling to it. Young boys playing drums with lariats whirling from their hats according to their head movements defied normal equilibrium. Whole pigs were being roasted on large rotisseries along with some kind of worm that Koreans apparently love to eat.

The much-loved ginseng root was also for sale. Most interesting to me were the elaborate, natural ginseng sculptures that were on display and even painted as murals on some buildings.

Unfortunately, there is another image that stays in my mind. A crippled young man was lying on his stomach on a board that had little wheels. He propelled himself through the crowd pushing a radio playing music and a basket for donations. Our Korean guide said Korea is slowly changing from looking down on the handicapped.

PONDERING THE INSCRUTABLES

"I think they have music along the beach now," said my bus companion with a happy gleam in her eye. She wanted me to enjoy my first trip to a Korean beach. And yes, they had, in fact, piped music all along the beachfront in competition with one of nature's finest accomplishments—the sound of waves on a beach. Alas, 1984's Big Brother in control of the switches chased me to a little patch of sand at the end of the beach that had, thankfully, been spared a speaker.

Music was not the only unusual part of my first Korean beach experience. It was the sun and warmth of May—somewhat early for the traditional swimming of July and August. Visitors came in significant numbers, but not one had on a bathing suit. Some ventured, or were thrown, into the waves, but fully clothed! Most wore jeans instead of shorts. Strangely (to me), very few were barefoot in the sand. They entered the water or scampered near the edge in street shoes—those same Clarabelle-style shoes that middle-aged American Howdy Doody watchers can quickly recall. I felt sorriest for the little girls dressed in frilly Sunday dresses and shoes whose parents brought them to the beach and wouldn't let them get even the tiniest bit wet.

It was also on this beach that I saw in action what the Koreans call MT for Membership Training. In our university in Taejon, students were routinely and often excused from class when their departments sponsored an MT event. Held in faraway beauty spots like beaches and mountains, the students came in large numbers to "bond." Hundreds of little rooms with rolled up mats serve as hotels.

Their noisy all-night gatherings resembled to my eye a cross between an all-night campfire exuberance with college fraternity hazing. They stayed in defined groups singing and playing repetitive games to exhaustion, punctuated with throwing selected students into the cold waves. It is one of the favorite times for unlimited coed drinking, the strong alcohol having been brought by the sponsoring university or organization. It is during these MT gatherings that those who don't drink, or cannot hold their liquor, suffer the most as outcasts. One of my students had graphically and poignantly written about his own experience of being forced to sing endlessly and then having to sleep in the puke of his drunken classmates.

Although the activities I saw only looked childish and innocuous, in fact the purpose is extremely serious—reinforcing the established "groupiness" of Korean society. It also sets a lifetime pattern, especially of the men, of frequent drunken social gatherings among friends and associates. Why? The Confucian virtues upon which Korean society is based value repression of all strong emotions. In direct contrast, however, in true friendships Koreans value openness and honesty. I was told very sincerely that Koreans require the uninhibiting qualities of strong liquor in order to allow themselves to be open and honest. My students were never ashamed, or even defensive, of their own or others' drunkenness even when I saw them lying in the streets or vomiting along the road as I walked home from my late-night classes.

At first I was baffled by the strong reek of cigarette smoke in ladies' restrooms throughout Korea. Each toilet stall has an ashtray alongside the toilet paper. The ladies' room has become the smoking lounge for Korean women. Korean men smoke openly and voraciously from teenagers on up, but it is not acceptable for women to smoke. So, they do it in the ladies' rooms—perhaps out of modified rebellion, perhaps out of curiosity, and perhaps just because they enjoy this "forbidden fruit."

Once, while eating in a restaurant, I observed a group of six women who had come together without their husbands. They ate, and then took out cigarettes. What shocked me was the pace at which they smoked. They puffed and puffed, finishing their cigarettes in record time, probably due to the bathroom break mentality of women smokers.

What Koreans lack in the color and spiciness of their modern clothes, they make up for in their food. I have never seen more variety in vegetables, including many grasses. I was surprised more than once to find a haylike substance inside an otherwise ordinary-looking loaf of bread. My tastebuds never adjusted to nicely boiled potatoes with a sugary sauce covering, or ketchup on coleslaw. *Kimchee* pizza was beyond my curiosity.

When it comes to eating out, Koreans are consummate hosts. There are some scenes that must be seen rather than explained to be truly appreciated. I had been invited to a park by a Korean couple I had met because we both belonged to an international travel organization. They lived in Seoul, and I in Taejon. One Sunday, they came down to Taejon and invited me and a Taejon member of the same organization to go to a nearby national park.

We had a congenial meal. Since I hadn't had any of the wine to drink, I asked Mr. Park if they sold Coke at the restaurant. Mr. Park ordered me a Coke and then got up and walked toward the front of the restaurant. At the same time, the lady from Taejon got up, wallet in hand, and walked forward. Mr. Park's wife literally jumped up and ran after both of them. When I turned to look in bewilderment, both Mr. and Mrs. Park were physically pushing the other lady back. She was struggling. This struggle continued for several moments, accompanied by loud voices. I eventually realized that they were arguing over who would pay the whole bill. Asians, in general, never go dutch.

The Seoul couple finally won, but the Taejon lady said she should pay the bill because they were in her city of Taejon. I said she and I should pay for the other two because we were both from Taejon. The Seoul couple said they must pay the bill because they invited us. I said I thought I had caused the whole commotion by saying the simple word, "Coke." We all convulsed in hearty laughter, which was a fitting end to our meal since Koreans don't eat dessert.

There are, in each country, some things that cannot be understood, but only observed. For example, in Korea, grandfather clocks greet you in every large building, and in many restaurants too. What is this fascination with such a clock? Is it another form of ancestor worship or someone's idea of westernization that one rarely sees in the west?

And then there is the use of sidewalks to put posters about various events. It is the only country I've been in where you can learn a lot while looking down at your feet. From where to put a return address on an envelope, and which fingers to hold up for the number three, traveling and living in other countries teaches you that you can't take anything for granted.

A DIFFERENT VIEW OF NATURE

As is my nature, I gravitate to nature. But, here in Korea, I see how different my orientation to nature is from the Koreans'. They come *en masse*, not just to enjoy the beauty of nature, but to enjoy it primarily in the company of others. It is another form of "groupiness" that is a major theme in Korean culture.

Where does the need for groupiness come from? Perhaps in part it has some connection to Korea's sad history of having been conquered so often. They guard their culture jealously, with even a xenophobic overlay.

Kyeryongsan National Park, outside Taejon, has beautiful mountains much like many national parks around the world. But here they bring their groupiness with them into nature. To me, it is comparable to a carnival atmosphere complete with games, souvenir shops, and innumerable restaurants where they come in herds to eat—and of course to drink.

In nature, they do not bond to nature, but to each other within nature. And, it is a family affair. Toddlers just able to walk come. They are not put in carriers on their parents' backs, however. They must propel themselves over the mountains. Doubtless, such early training is the reason Koreans from young to very old scamper over trails like mountain goats. I plod along trying to figure out which stone to step on (their trails are paved with stones to retard erosion) while all gaily pass by me—of course in groups or family units. I am awed.

Their mountain attire is quite gay, riotously colorful, and even jaunty. From the cap to the multi-pocket safari jacket, to the argyle socks and hiking boots, they are ready for the mountains. A stylish telescoping walking stick sets off the hiker's ensemble. I, too, have a walking stick, but it is a necessary "third leg" for me.

The solitude and quiet of the mountains coexist with the sounds of people talking, eating, drinking, and praying at the monasteries and temples which can always be found in Korean mountains. It makes for a strange combination and can only partially assuage my yearning for the almost reverent peacefulness of the national parks and campgrounds in the U.S. Even the darkness of night is punctuated not with flashlights, but with well-positioned lights at short intervals so that one is always reminded that this park caters to people.

FOUR-HANDED RHYTHM

Korea generally gives me the impression of a sad country, but I get no clue of that in the public baths. Especially on a Saturday, women of all ages, along with their young children, gather and happily scrub themselves and each other. Even though all are undressed and there is no privacy, going to a public bath with a friend is considered an act of closeness. Scrubbing each other's backs strengthens the friendship.

Along with the cacophony of many conversations come the squeals and shrieks of the children as they throw water on each other, jump from the warm pool to the cold pool, and get scrubbed down—and I mean down a few layers—by their mothers.

For a small extra charge, I, too, was scrubbed about as far down as I could be. An energetic woman clad in underpants and bra motioned me to get on a table. For at least 30 minutes, she scrubbed me with something like a green Brillo pad. The goal was to get off the dry skin, which seems to be a vital part of proper grooming in Asia.

Top, bottom, and from top to bottom on each side, the scrubbing went. When she went off to a small table, I smelled the cool smell of yes, cucumbers, which were cut and put on my face. Ahh! If the second woman scrubber had no customer at the moment, she joined in and, in a definite rhythm and synchrony, without getting in the way of the other, four hands were busily moving up, down, and around. It can't be compared to a slow, soothing Esalen-style massage, but it definitely was refreshing.

An evening trip to the bath had a very different atmosphere. Then it was a women's night out—no shrieking children, only women pampering themselves with the baths, a scrubdown ending with a milkbath, a room for friends to dry and gently massage each other, and a warm room for lying down and even sleeping.

Yes, a public bath in Korea became my favorite weekly treat.

June 1, 1997

It's not unusual for me to have trouble falling asleep, but this morning at about 5 a.m., I still wasn't asleep, so I decided to take a walk. What I discovered was another world I'd never seen before. Many of my neighbors were gathering on the hillsides doing morning exercises. The pathways up the hills were filled with people walking, jogging, playing badminton, and even yelling out their joy at being alive another day. On my afternoon walks in the hills, I had noticed hula-hoops hanging in some trees. Now I saw them being used by the morning exercisers as they made their way up the hills.

I strongly doubted I would ever be a "morning person," but I was very glad to share their joy in the morning today. After my walk, I went home and quickly fell asleep.

June 8, 1997

I have great plans for my upcoming summer vacation. Among other friends I've made over the years who now live in Europe, I'm going to visit Benjamin at his school in The Hague, Holland, where he's working on a Master's in diplomacy.

He didn't know about the program until the school invited him to come. Then, I'll have the chance to see Jerry who is living in Frankfurt, Germany. He still works for a Hangzhou company, but his job is to develop the European market. Now that some of my Chinese friends are living in other countries, it's great to be able to visit them as I crisscross the world. And then on to Turkey, where the east and the west meet.

July 10, 1997

The Bosphorus is bluer than I had imagined. Here I sit in Istanbul overlooking the ruins of an old Turkish bath, and an active mosque and minaret located between me and the Sea of Marmara. I have spent most of the day inside because I have splurged just this one night on an expensive room with a wondrous view.

While watching the water and the large ships going by, I have had the leisure to think about my visits with Benjamin and Jerry. Benjamin seems to have adjusted quite quickly to his first home outside China. He introduced me to several of his friends in the same program for aspiring diplomats. The program has drawn young, intelligent people from all over the world. I saw him eating Dutch food with an appetite I never saw in China. Although he's doing well in the program, he has no great interest in being a diplomat. However, the international experience itself has been invaluable. He was an excellent host.

Jerry is lonely in Germany, far away from his wife and little son, as well as the Chinese culture. He can't say he really likes Germany, but he thinks this might be a good business opportunity for him. He shares his apartment with his office, so I got to see the kinds of crafts he is trying to sell in Europe. He hasn't learned to drive yet, so we did a lot of walking around town, and took the boat ride down the river that runs through Frankfurt. I am proud of both of them for spreading their wings outside the "known" of their own culture.

Within walking distance of my hotel, I have been to the Aya Sofia and the Blue Mosque several times. The inside and outside of both massive structures are endlessly fascinating. My camera and I have been very happy together snapping unsual angles and centuries of history.

What isn't so great are the touts and the louts who follow me around everywhere. Some of these men are somewhat comical in the manner of their approaches, such as the one who walked beside me trying out English, then French, then German to attract my attention. Another came running out of his shop with his hand outstretched saying, "Friendship, friendship, I believe in friendship. Don't you? Please come into my shop and sign my guestbook." Or, "You look like a person who buys carpets," said the carpet seller who walked a few blocks with me until he really believed I was a nomad with no floor on which to lay a carpet.

Scarier are the men who blatantly want sex, totally disregarding my age, my matronly body, and the wedding ring I bought for this occasion. A woman traveling alone in a Moslem country gets no respect in this male-dominated society.

July 16, 1997

I have come to the fairyland of Cappadocia. I am sitting at the end of a valley surrounded by cones of tufa, volcanic ash. Freud would be enthralled with the huge penile shapes loftily rising up from the ground, the green trees contrasting with the white-bright sun. Earlier, I had threaded my way through hallways made in the soft rock. Before that, I had explored an ingeniously designed old underground city.

I spent too much money last night to stay in an elegantly restored 200-year-old Ottoman house with Turkish carpets and an elaborate bath. The rich, delicious food so beautifully served gave me diarrhea. Tonight I have the same spectacular view for $8. I still have Turkish carpets on the wall and on the floor. It's simple, but has the most marvelous shared terrace overlooking the valley.

July 21, 1997

Tonight I sit in a place more wonderful than I could imagine, but at 5 a.m. two nights ago, I wasn't at all sure how it would end.

These all-night bus rides are as uncomfortable as they sound. They are non-smoking, except for the driver who is, of course, a typical chain smoker. The air-conditioning works, but only if turned on, which they generally aren't. And, since it is, in theory, an air-conditioned bus, the large windows are sealed shut.

I sat next to a French doctor-adventurer. He travels the world mostly by bike while his wife stays home. When he's with his wife, they go only to luxury hotels and fancy restaurants.

Just as I'd fall asleep for a few precious moments in the endless night, we would stop at one of the all-night circuses built expressly as bus stops. There, the men would emerge and drag on their cigarettes with the satisfaction of a baby sucking on a pacifier. While that night's road kill was washed off the windows, the other sleepy bus occupants would awaken for the toilets, and perhaps to eat. I had no appetite at 3 a.m.

Just as I sank into the bliss of sleep, the driver stopped and deposited a few of us in the 4 a.m. darkness where a garrulous man awaited with a dead van that he cajoled to life again to take us to the small town at the foot of Pamukkale. He dumped me at a dingy office when I said I wanted to go to the Palmiye Hotel where I had reservations and had already paid. Another younger version of the slick businessman wanted me to rent a room in his pension, but agreed to take me to the Palmiye where a sleepy clerk had answered the phone.

The sleepy clerk at the Palmiye, when confronted with my sleepy face and expectant eyes, told me there was no reservation for me. There being no other choice, I curled into the lobby couch and slept as best I could to await the manager who would, I hope, magically straighten it all out.

I awoke to the morning sound of doves. I finally drew out of the clerk what the problem was. Yes, they did have rooms available, and yes, they were the rooms with the nice view and private pools, but the travel agency I had paid in Urgup, Cappadocia, had never faxed my confirmation that was their agreement to pay the hotel. A phone call to Urgup produced only a ringing and no answer.

So, the voucher saying I had paid in Urgup held no guarantee that the Palmiye would ever get the money. Once they straightened it out, I would have to wait until check-out at noon. He asked what would help while we waited, and I said, too tired to be angry, "a place to sleep." He put me in the office in back where I was able to push two chairs together and lie down. The noise from the loud music at the pools outside the window mingled with the multi-lingual squeals of children jumping and swimming in the pools.

Somewhat refreshed, I emerged at 12:15 to claim my room and a "real" bed, but the clerk looked once again dour and said I'd have to wait for the manager to come back. I went for a brief lunch. Having had a little sleep and some food, I was beginning to get angry. I got the impression I wasn't being given the whole story.

As I wavered between patience and anger, the manager finally came back and gave me a key at last. I walked through to my room and noticed an extremely large swimming pool. When I entered the simple, but large room, my eyes widened again at seeing a private pool right out the back door of my room that appeared to go over the edge and into a very wide valley. My tiny peephole view in my apartment in Korea had given me a hunger for wide views. This view was definitely BIG. I briefly wondered why so many people were walking by on the edge of the cliff, and then, with joy in my heart, I fell blessedly asleep.

July 22, 1997

My place is even more idyllic than the guidebook had described it. Although the days are too hot, my little porch near the pool stays in the shade until late afternoon. The water is indeed special. It is untreated in any way and has a softness and gentleness that is unlike any water I've swum in. It is said to be medicinal and I can actually feel my blood pressure lower as soon as I enter its velvet touch.

Sun-drenched and waterlogged, the day tourists climb onto their tour buses and go away. When they leave, it becomes a more personal place. The evenings are cool and perfect for photography and walking around Hieropolis, the ancient city that has left its ruins all around. I often sit on my balcony, sipping delightful sour cherry juice.

Unfortunately, the natural travertine terraces no longer resemble their postcards. They, like so much of nature, have been overused and abused. The water is no longer allowed to fill the dainty pools among the terraces because the multitude of footsteps is destroying the travertine they are made of. The incredible water that was here even before Hieropolis was an actual city instead of ruins has somehow survived. From old pictures I've seen, Mammoth Terraces in New Zealand was probably much like this before the volcano took it away. While nature destroyed the terraces there, it is people who have destroyed these to the point that the government is closing this area to overnight tourists by next year. How lucky I am to be one of the last to sleep here.

July 23, 1997

Trouble again! Reception tried to throw me out saying that the agency only paid them for two nights and they have no rooms available tonight. As a tourist, I wonder if I have any rights. Are they trying to cheat me, or is it just poor organization? My blood pressure needs those soothing waters again.

It all turned out well. With the help of a local agency, someone came to my room that I was refusing to leave, apologized reasonably profusely, and said he had arranged for me to go to another hotel quite near. When I saw it, I wasn't reluctant to change. The room was uninspiring except for an incongruous print of people ice-skating in old Holland. But the pool, oh the pool! How can I possibly describe it?

Surely the biggest and most scenic pool I'd ever seen reached out seemingly endlessly over the cliff and into the valley beyond. Filled with that dreamy, gentle water that made me feel like I was swimming in a cloud, I luxuriated rather than swam in its deep, deep water. Swallows flew under the eaves to their nests. The hotel and the pool were unusually uncrowded.

I was able to appreciate the depth and beauty of the pool that night when they drained it and cleaned it out. They whitewashed the cement manmade portions. I could easily see without water that the largest huge cavern of the pool was a natural travertine terrace.

I awoke early the next morning intending to swim. The pool wasn't quite full yet, so I went to the pool at the Pamukkale Hotel with its unique Atlantis quality. For 45 magical minutes before the tour buses started rolling in, I had the pool all to myself. I glided over the real ruins of ancient columns and pieces of Hieropolis. I pinched my arm to reassure myself that I wasn't dreaming. It was too perfect.

Turkey has certainly been a place of unique sights where the east and the west come together.

Sept. 25, 1997

"Congratulations, you have another granddaughter," was the brief fax I received from Max. How wonderful! I now have four Chinese granddaughters. Pearl's daughter, born earlier this year, is my third granddaughter. When Pearl asked me to give their daughter an English name, it gave me some comfort to name her in memory of my brother.

Oct. 1, 1997

My students may not be enthusiastic about learning English, but they are very enthusiastic about taking me out to various scenic spots. One unusual visit was to a student's father who raises honeybees. He lives in a trailer and takes the bees to areas when certain plants bloom that attract the bees. They believe in the medicinal use of bee stings as healthy. That may be true, but I declined his offer to be stung.

Dec. 1, 1997

Some of my students are having little parties to say goodbye to me. I've received cards and embarrassingly expensive gifts. One artistic student drew and painted a picture for me of a traditionally dressed Korean girl playing the drums that I so enjoy hearing. Svetlana, who teaches Russian, took me to a very special teahouse for our goodbye. I'd never been in a place with an atmosphere quite like that. I could easily imagine that teahouses were places where people spoke gently and came up with great thoughts. We have become good friends over this last year, and she has invited me to come visit her at her home in Russia. Perhaps I'll get there.

I had been struggling over whether or not to renew my contract for 1998 when my father asked me not to remain so far away. Both my parents are nearing 80 years old. So, I'll return to Dallas where I can teach part time again at the community college. Instead of being the foreigner as I am in Korea, my students will be an international group of immigrants from all over the world.

But, never being one to go in a straight line, I'll return to China once again and then Vietnam before returning to the U.S. Korea has been good to me. I'm glad I came.

18

CHINA VIETNAM RUSSIA 1998

Jan. 10, 1998

Hong Kong has lost its vibrant personality. Becoming a part of China again in 1997, followed so closely by the Asian stock market collapse, has left this very special place quite depressed. The downtown business area has fewer international faces and more mainland Chinese in their ill-fitting suits.

I stopped in Shenzhen to see Peter. He's always a wonderful host, and I have come to love the variety of great food we can eat in Shenzhen. I think it's my favorite Chinese city to eat in. This was the first time he took me to a small restaurant where the waiter poured tea graciously from a teakettle with a very, very long spout while standing at quite a distance away. Not a drop spilled anywhere but right in the cup.

Shenzhen has been developing more tourist attractions. One has smaller than actual re-creations of famous buildings and sights around the world. It's very well done and we spent hours happily wandering from country to country. Although it wasn't a tourist site, he took me to a compound near Shenzhen where foreigners live. The single-family homes looked inviting, and the grounds were lush and well-kept. He said simply, "Why can't Chinese live like this?"

And then there was the tourist attraction I wish we had never gone to. It could not decide if it was a wild animal park, a zoo, a circus, or a freak show with real bears dressed in frilly dresses for tourists to stand next to and take pictures. One overused lion was first displayed as a dangerous wild animal, but was later put on a float in a grotesque animal circus parade. The grounds looked as close to death as the pitiful lion. Although the place was only two years old, everything had a decaying, rotting look to it. I suspect they had badly miscalculated how much money such a place would have to take in to maintain it properly. To salvage what they could, the place held dog races in the evening.

Peter still doesn't feel confident about the future of the company he's in. And he's still waiting to find a "good girl" to date.

This trip I was able to stay in Russell's first home with his new wife. I didn't know what to make of a large photo on the wall of Russell dressed as a bullfighter, and his wife as a Spanish dancer. He told me that it was one of his wedding photos. In fact, engaged couples in China spend a lot of money on a wedding album in which they wear different costumes on every page. I guess this is possible in China because they're almost all small and thin.

As they get married, my friends are buying apartments. Rather than being totally paid for by their work units as before, some get partially subsidized units. The newer places come only with the bare space. Each couple must decide how to decorate their apartment, which includes making a floor plan and putting in everything, including the walls. It's still the custom to pay for everything in cash, but Thomas thinks he might try getting a mortgage, which is slowly being introduced in China. It's a scary move for them.

Jan. 17, 1998

When I'd make the motion to put on my seatbelt in a taxi, my friends would assure me I didn't need it because the driver was skillful. I didn't agree that driving dangerously and then avoiding an accident could be classified as "skillful" driving. I had, in fact, witnessed a few accidents, although far fewer than I expected. I had seen an enclosed motorized bike cab roll over in slow motion after being hit by a taxi on a rainy Shanghai street. The silence and ominous stillness inside the enclosed bike as it lay on its side lingered in my mind. Each time I got into a taxi in China, I had a fleeting moment of wondering if we'd make it safely to our destination. I truly believed there were no rules for drivers, but last night I learned that there were, indeed, some unwritten rules.

Late last night, I had been initially suspicious when I got into a taxi with two people in the front. However, this was happening more and more as the taxi drivers feared being robbed, especially late at night. I wasn't sure what it meant when the driver suddenly stopped the taxi, jumped out, and the other man got out and switched into the driver's seat. It quickly became apparent when the new driver couldn't shift into gear that I was a paying participant in a driving lesson.

I have to admit some sympathy for the new driver. I thought back to how I learned to drive in high school with classroom lessons and then sitting in a car equipped with dual equipment. This man was driving a falling apart wreck of a car with one weak headlight and only one rear light, sitting next to a man yelling and berating his every move.

In a country where the best driver has ten near misses within a few minutes, and where drivers, bicyclists, pedicab drivers, and pedestrians are apt to do just about anything, I wondered just how anyone could learn to drive here. How can one prepare adequately for mayhem from all directions? And, if one managed to see the danger, how to react and avoid disaster seemed mere chance or luck.

One difference I saw between this new driver and experienced drivers was that he hesitated in dangerous circumstances, whereas experienced drivers seemed to respond with multi-directional antennae that provided warnings. Slowing down was rarely an option used by "real" drivers, but even they somehow knew when to give way. When the driver-in-training stopped less than one inch short of a bicyclist, the "teacher" let loose with a torrent of verbal abuse, as though the driver should have known this was a case where the taxi had to stop.

As he careened down the roads with his bright lights on, blinded by the bright lights of everyone else, I wished I could understand his "teacher's" advice. I'm sure it differed from the preventive, defensive driving my teacher had taught me. But I also knew that I would fail dismally as a driver in China.

I thanked my lucky star for getting us back to my hotel. I quickly got out of the dimly lit taxi—and left behind my wonderful raincoat that had faithfully accompanied me around the world several times.

To my sleepy surprise, a hotel attendant awakened me at 6:27 a.m. to give me back my raincoat.

Jan. 24. 1998

My timing was perfect this year to attend Robert's wedding. In fact, it was the first wedding of all my friends that I was able to attend. I traveled with them to the home of the bride's parents where I met other members of the family gathered for the wedding. One bedroom was gaily decorated. This room would forever be kept for the couple to come home to at any time.

On the day of the wedding, a rented car took us around. The first stop was a surprise to me. Certain family members had been invited to a small lunch at the local KFC! The bride, in her lovely long white gown, and the groom in his tuxedo, were warmly welcomed and seated in one area of the restaurant where tables were set and we were served the Colonel's best.

This small group eventually got back into cars and traveled to the hall that had been rented for the occasion. There is still no ceremony as we westerners are used to, but the crowd of invited guests celebrated with an abundance of energy. We all kept our coats on because the hall wasn't heated on this wintry day. The food was plentiful and good.

I was invited to go with the photographer and the bride and groom as they went to a few parks in the city to take pictures and make a video. The cold gave us all rosy complexions as he positioned the beautiful bride and handsome groom in various poses for the cameras. He took photographs of them at a park with a traditional sedan chair in which the bride used to be carried to the groom's home where she'd sometimes meet her husband for the very first time. My mind meandered back to those old days in China and I wondered what the traditional couple and this modern couple would have to say to each other.

Feb. 13, 1998

What can I see perched comfortably six stories above Ho Chi Minh city, more popularly called Saigon?

I can see an abnormally high number of Vietnamese flags—red cloth with one large yellow five-pointed star. I can also see a bright blue sky that belies the pollution of thousands of motorbikes on the streets below. The modern cranes that don't fly are busy, but the overall impression is of a low city rather than the crowded skyscrapers I have come to expect in Asia. Satellite dishes on the roof of the Rex Hotel adjoining the swimming pool insure the most up to date modern technology.

The swimmers are an odd assortment of foreigners from many countries. But the beauty of Saigon, besides the gingerbread leftovers from the French colonial time which are sometimes freshly painted and sometimes dilapidated and decaying quietly, are the people below who exhibit a fresh and innocent friendliness I didn't expect given their painful long term and short term history. Yes, there are those who want your money, those who will beg for it, and those who will outright steal it. But, compared to the cautiousness of Chinese and the Korean dislike and/or fear of foreigners, the Vietnamese are warm, sweet, gentle, and helpful.

At least, these have been my early impressions over the last three days. I have been "adopted" by a *cyclo*-driver/guide (the bike is in the back instead of China's front pedicab). Once he "claimed" me, the other *cyclo* drivers don't try for my business. I have even left a message for him with the other *cyclo* drivers, which he received quickly and reliably. He maneuvers this contraption with great skill through the chaotic masses of bikes, motorbikes, buses, and cars. The bikes and motorbikes convey a bride and groom on their way to a new life, trussed ducks hanging over a passenger seat, a woman passenger holding a live pig, boxes piled up even taller than the driver, and dainty young ladies holding one end of their attractive *ao dai* dresses with one hand on the handlebar. Equally elegant are the many ladies in shoulder-length silk gloves with frilly handkerchiefs covering their mouths.

The food is wonderful—fresh and fruity and tropical and French and Chinese and Vietnamese—and not too expensive. There are inexpensive hotels and an incredible tourism infrastructure designed for the poorer, independent tourists like me. I haven't traveled in any third-world countries that make it so easy and reasonably priced.

I finished off my lucky Friday the 13th with a French duck dinner for $4, lovely tropical fruits brought up to my room by the friendly family that runs the hotel, an International Herald Tribune to scan from front to back, and a good feeling about being here. However, it's already clear I wouldn't be able to teach in Saigon because it's too hot for me here.

Feb. 14, 1998

Thinking ahead when I was teaching Vietnamese students in Dallas, I kept the name of someone to contact in Saigon. He and a friend wanted to show me Saturday night in Saigon. It is a riotous affair. The usual chaotic traffic patterns around the rotary intersections swell to bursting with the New York Rockette style of bikes, etc. slipping through the ever-moving line of traffic with an amazing and perplexing confidence.

"Vietnam—wonderful," said my young Vietnamese companions with a look of joy on their faces. There is a hope, optimism, high-spirited, and fun-loving nature to these people who have gone through so much pain. Perhaps the insecurity of their lives makes them willingly, and even joyously "careless" as one of my new friends noted. They drive themselves in a good-natured frenzy of motorbikes, bicycles, and motorcycles. While old people were not too visible, children were everywhere, lining the sidewalks, parks, and islands in the middle of highways. Couples sat along curbsides looking for all the world like they were in privacy and solitude. I enjoyed the buoyancy and energy of it all from the seatbelt of my taxi.

Feb. 15, 1998

I had two big surprises today. While I was sitting in a ritzy hotel one evening sipping iced coffee and enjoying potato skins, my peripheral vision caught either a large mouse or a small rat leaping onto a nearby column and then into a large planter nearby. I felt somewhat sorry for it, and didn't report it.

As I was crossing the street on my way back to my hotel, I "sensed," rather than "felt" something. A thief on the back of a motorbike had snatched my bag slung over my head and across my chest. In the darkness, I could see my bag dangling from his hands as they sped away. It happened so quickly, and so gently, that I didn't react immediately. When I understood I'd been robbed, I started running after the thieves, but soon realized that was not only futile, but also dangerous on the dark road.

The staff at my hotel had convinced me to place valuables, such as my passport, in a box with them. As usual, the bulk of my money was in a pouch around my waist under my blouse, attached to my pants. There was some money in my purse, but I lost mostly items of no value to thieves and a nuisance to replace, such as my glasses. I preferred to dwell on the bright side—I was not dragged into the traffic when he tugged on my purse because the strap was hooked, not sewn, onto the bag. That made me aware that wearing a purse around my head with a securely sewn strap is potentially dangerous. I marveled at how skillful he had been in putting a finger under the purse on my chest and yanking it off without my really feeling it at all while speeding around the corner on the back of a motorbike. I was told that these motorbike thieves even steal cameras right out of the hands of picture-taking tourists.

The hotel sent a staff member with me to the police station. He also brought a gift of a carton of cigarettes for the police. My young friends who met me that night were very sympathetic. They took me to a modern fashion show with a Vietnamese flavor, which I particularly appreciated because it was for the local people, not tourists.

I asked my companions about the feelings of the southerners toward the northerners in Vietnam. One told me that the northerners still "punished" the southerners whose fathers had fought with the Americans against them. One way was to deny these children higher education and force them to into lower level jobs. Northerners were given the better jobs in Saigon. In this young man's opinion, the northerners were intelligent and hardworking, while southerners were kind, friendly, and a little lazy. When I asked him why people were so friendly to American tourists, he said they love being open again after years of enforced isolation.

Feb. 16, 1998

Before leaving Saigon, the *cyclo* driver who had taken me around for several days invited me to his home to meet his wife and children. I was aghast at how far he had to commute every day to the center of Saigon from his home. He explained in his street-learned English that his father had been a soldier, so he didn't have much choice of jobs. He pedaled on and on and on. Eventually, we reached an area of narrow alleyways with very small homes. To my surprise, it was a whole community of *cyclo* drivers. That's why they all knew each other so well.

His home was one small room with basically no furniture, and a ladder leading up to another room where, I believe, they slept. I met his wife and children. The 11-year-old boy left quickly for a friend's house, but his five-year-old son sat in my lap while we "read" a book together that I had brought. There was also a new baby.

After all the time and hard work of taking me there, he pedaled me all the way back to Saigon. I felt honored to have been invited to his home.

Feb. 18, 1998

I'm hard pressed to adequately describe my surroundings now. I can hear monkeys and look upward from my bed to see the stars through a skylight above my head. I'm in a cave-ish Gourd Room in the very top of a tree house in Dalat, Vietnam, in the central highlands between north and south Vietnam.

For a change, I'm not sweating because the weather is considerably cooler and less humid than Saigon. The people in Saigon described the weather here as winter, although it's spring to me.

This guesthouse was recommended in my tour book as "unique." And so it is. It is artist-inspired by a Vietnamese woman who studied architecture in Russia. It manages to be kitschy without being tacky. Each room has a different theme. The walls of my room actually undulate around the room, catching the changing light and shadow. I could be quite content here <u>except</u> that there is the clink, clunk of construction all around me yet again.

In general, my experiences in Vietnam have been unusual. In hot, steamy Saigon, I saw my first exhibition of huge ice sculptures in a tented enclosure where we donned warm down jackets and boots. I rode down the famous Mekong River, spoke at length to a South Vietnamese soldier who had worked with the Americans, watched a ritual in a temple whose religion does defy description, and saw a portion of the 200-kilometer network of tunnels that had survived literally under the noses of the American soldiers. It was chilling to go through a sparsely wooded area with trees all about the same size and realize that this spot was denuded with napalm during the war.

Feb. 20, 1998

The construction noise has driven me from the treehouse to a garden in Dalat. This guesthouse is not as creative, but I have a large and airy room through which

I can see multicolored flowers and terraced hills. Thunder is the main noisemaker here, along with the plops of raindrops.

Vietnam, along with this hotel, remains a curious mixture in transition. The government no longer seems as heavy handed with the tourists, who are genuinely welcomed as a positive influence to the economy. While some people will steal from you with quite amazing persistence and skill, other people warn you continually to protect your valuables. The spots of beauty are quite wonderful, but always accompanied by dirty, pathetic beggars with their hands out. It is difficult not to feel like a colonial master. The peaceful settings are marred by the imagination of what Rambo raids did to these people and places.

To my surprise, I am the only overnight guest in this large guesthouse. During the day, noisy children and others visit the gardens. They disappear with the sun and leave me to stroll through "my" gardens, eat wild boar, venison, crab, or the mundane at the local restaurant, and watch movies from India, which are all that my television has to offer. I was reminded of Richard telling me how much he appreciated movies from India, so China must get movies from India too. I had never seen one before. They're lively, colorful, romantic, and have a lot of pretty girls.

I became philosophical about photography while watching people taking pictures in the gardens. Photography, and even the poor man's ability to take photos with cheap cameras, has been a revolutionary change in our lives. The forever frozen image brings me a joy both in the taking and in the keeping. Perhaps it is like a visual book, both somehow deeper and more superficial than writing. There are relatively few things truly personal in today's plasticized, standardized society, but my pictures are, like my fingerprints, my very own regardless of how many similar and even better pictures have been taken of the same things. And yet, I met an American woman in Korea who doesn't own a camera anymore. She told me that she threw it away when she realized she was seeing everything through a camera lens, which, by definition, narrows what you see. Hmm.

Feb. 23, 1998

I went to the War Remnants Museum before leaving Vietnam. The name was poignantly appropriate. I expected it would sadden me by introducing the reality of the terrible war that in many ways seems to have been forgotten by the Vietnamese in preference to pursuing a better future. It was a rather straightforward remembrance of the war, not adorned with the aesthetic, artistic rendition of sorrow such as at the war museum in Israel. As a photographer, I wondered how anyone could take pictures while others writhe and bleed and die. And yet, because they did take them, we can "see" the horror instead of simply imagining it.

The museum made it easier to understand how "our boys" resorted to drugs, were haunted by nightmares, and never recovered from the war as depicted in numerous post-Vietnam War movies and books. While surrounded by horrifying photos, two stand forever before my eyes. One is the stark, undiluted terror on the face of a young girl surrounded by other women and children just an instant before she was massacred with all the rest. The other is of a bleeding very young child trying to put his body over his younger brother.

Being a child of the sixties tied me to Vietnam even before coming here. Being here has only made the tie stronger. If I had to sum up today's Vietnam in one word, it would be "energy."

August 13, 1998

I bought my first meal as a senior citizen tonight on my 55th birthday. It felt strange to be in the same category as my parents. What doesn't feel strange is that I'm packed up and on my way tomorrow to the other side of the world. That is my natural state.

Since the Korean currency had continued to drop, before leaving Korea I used my Korean currency rather than losing half its value by turning it into U.S. currency. I left with another around-the-world ticket in my pocket. The ticket is valid for one year, so, now I'm about to use it. I'll fly back to Korea, from Korea to Russia to visit Svetlana, then back to Asia and through Europe and Israel on my return to the U.S. in about four months.

I'll be visiting Russia for the very first time. Even though the former U.S.S.R. was the birthplace of all my grandparents, and most likely several generations before them, it wasn't a happy place for Jews. Even Jews born there for generations were never fully accepted. They had emigrated to the U.S. with their parents when they were children. The long ocean voyage over probably saved my grandmother's life. She was only two, and had been very sickly since birth. They didn't expect her to live, but the sea air apparently cured her.

My time in Dallas has had its high points, like getting to see one of my Nanjing students who's studying for her PhD in Dallas, but to me, living in the U.S. feels quite strange—like sleepwalking in cotton candy. However, when I return to the U.S., I will stay put to help out my aging parents.

MY ANCESTRAL PAST AND RUSSIA'S PRESENT

I was sure it would be easier for me to fly to Russia than it was for my grandparents to emigrate by ocean from the U.S.S.R. in the early 1900's. "Not all their planes crash," a friend commented helpfully when I said I had booked a seat to Moscow on the Russian airline, Aeroflot. Of course, he wouldn't dream of flying on an airline he was sure used bubblegum to repair its plane engines. My guidebook agreed with him. It warned, "Don't fly Aeroflot if you have any other choice. And, if you do, don't expect your checked baggage to reunite with you."

Although the Koreans boarding my flight in Seoul for Moscow had not read my guidebook, they refrained from checking baggage. Instead, they carried on multiple bags and distributed them wherever. The inside set-up of the Russian plane was different from any planes I'd seen before. The overhead compartment had an awkward slant that made it too small for most hand luggage. Nor did my bag fit comfortably under the seat in front of me.

The ten hours of the flight loomed before me. I pressed the button for the seat to recline. It didn't. I asked the attendant about it as he handed me a drink. He tried the button. "Broken," he said. He then reported it to the second attendant who also tried it. "Broken," he replied half-apologetically.

Tightly squeezed beside me was a good-looking Russian young man who spoke no English. However, he pointed out to me a newspaper article that said one U.S. dollar now equaled nine *rubles*. He was one of the few who didn't know we were landing in Russia the day after the *ruble* crashed.

It was a relatively small plane—six seats across with a tiny aisle in between. There were no headphones, music, or movies for diversion. The person next to my seat partner was a monk whose abilities to meditate I envied during the long ride. Accustomed to the meager meals offered now by all American airlines, I was pleasantly surprised by the nourishing and tasty meals that broke my solitude.

After landing and unfolding from my uncomfortable ten hours, I approached Immigration in the airport with the slight trepidation I always feel entering a third world country. The bags hadn't yet arrived. Would they? I awaited mine apprehensively. Eventually they appeared, and so did my Russian friend, Svetlana, with three beautiful roses and her husband.

Since I knew traveler's checks were not so easily exchanged in Russia, I suggested I exchange them at the airport. We tried, but no bank at that airport would take them that day because they didn't have an exchange rate. That was the first major clue that I had arrived in Russia in unusual and unpredictable times.

It takes a while for the depth of a crisis—whether personal or national—to sink in and overwhelm people's optimism and hope. I saw this balance shift in only two and a half weeks. I had the image of a sweater unraveling. The lines waiting at the banks grew longer as people massed to get their money out. Dollars were not available. Svetlana's husband had not been paid for three months.

The Russian news showed a young boy in a blue coat and blue hat sitting on the pavement in the rain. The camera zoomed in on a rapidly deteriorating cardboard box as the raindrops plopped in among the few *kopecks* scattered inside. "How's it going?" the television reporter asked the beggar boy. Shocked and shy in front of the camera and the attention directed at him, he simply said the Russian equivalent of "good."

The *ruble* had not fallen long ago enough to account for the droop of the weary faces I saw all around me. Their eyes held a weariness, regardless of age, that couldn't be cured by a few good nights of sleep. Even the young had pasty white skin and dark patches under their eyes. The profusion of brightly colored flowers turned pathetic when held out by work-roughened, arthritic hands under old and very desperate faces lining the subway stairs.

As the *ruble* sank lower and Yeltsin dismissed the present government, I picked berries at Svetlana's lovely *dacha*, country house, which was a pleasant walk from her apartment. As we plucked carrots and onions out of the ground, I unknowingly treaded on the lettuce for our salad. We had lovely homegrown meals in the *dacha*'s garden while the refrigerator in her apartment loomed larger and emptier.

The Dow Jones in the U.S. sank 358 points in a day and Clinton came to visit Yeltsin. My friend said, "It will be okay because the government is preparing to print more money," but Clinton advised, "Hang on and don't print more money." During a television interview with Yeltsin, Svetlana commented "He looks very sick," as Yeltsin mumbled incoherently. "That's all," Yeltsin said at the end of the interview, and the Russians believed that was definitely true of Yeltsin's ability and power to rule the country.

Worry lines on faces deepened as bank lines grew longer and butter and sugar disappeared from the shelves. Tempers flared and nerves frayed. "There's no butter because you people bought it all," snapped a clerk to a complaining customer. Svetlana whispered to me, "The store has probably taken it off the shelves and it will reappear at a higher price." It did.

A nasty vendor in a train station complained about me to my friend in Russian, "Why doesn't she learn to speak Russian if she comes here. We speak English when we go to her country." When I needed to go to the Aeroflot office, the unsmiling clerk said in Russian to my friend, "Phone number in Moscow." When Svetlana didn't reply, I translated, "She wants to know your phone number." We laughed at the absurdity of me, who didn't know Russian, translating for her. "I didn't answer her immediately because I'm wondering why it is that Russian clerks are so rude and unpleasant," Svetlana told me.

The tour guide at the Armoury Museum told us, "Now you can see why Russia had a revolution," as she pointed out the bejeweled blankets and saddles of the tzar's horses. The magnificence of the old Russia gleamed from many of the gold-topped buildings, but even the grandiose looked grim and grimy in the bleak rain and cold that set in for a solid week that August.

I knew the Russia that I was seeing wasn't the one Karl Marx had envisioned under communism. While something was terribly wrong when Ivan the Terrible and absurdly wealthy tzars dressed their horses in jewels while the people who paid for those jewels starved to death, something was going terribly wrong now too. I made several comparisons of Russia to China, but Svetlana looked at me quizzically saying that Russians never think of comparing themselves to China in spite of both being communist countries.

Economic chaos and instability have challenged the ingenuity of the Russian people to fix their own cars that regularly broke down and littered the streets. My friend's husband had devised a very clever lawn mower from a washing machine agitator, proving the adage, "Necessity is the mother of invention." When I looked at the fine architecture of Moscow's old buildings, or appreciated the stands of tall white birch trees and full forests, I felt the power of the past in contrast to the helplessness of Russia's people who float like flotsam and jetsam trying to keep breathing a little longer.

As in many countries, contradictions faced me every day. How did what went on above ground relate to the perfectly clean, painstakingly decorated subway stations with a precisely on time metro system far down in the depths of Moscow's underground? Why did it cost more to use a public toilet than to ride the metro? How could something be as grand and yet as whimsical as St. Basil's Cathedral in Red Square? How could a country produce such fantastic art museums and so much poor quality merchandise?

The place that came to symbolize Russia's contradictions to me was the Bolshoi Theatre. Who among ballet lovers does not want to see the Bolshoi perform? It was August and Giselle was scheduled on September 4th. The unmanned box office displayed a sign that said in Russian, "The box office will not open until October 1st." As we turned away disappointedly, a man quickly appeared with the good news that he could sell me tickets. The "system" is that scalpers buy all the tickets and then re-sell them—at ridiculously high rates, of course. Since I wanted four tickets, his price was prohibitive. Reluctant to miss my opportunity to see the Bolshoi Ballet in Moscow, we tried to buy the tickets in the corners of the metro stations. Two tickets were possible, three or four no. Eventually I bought two tickets from one vendor, one from another. "Hopefully they're not counterfeit," Svetlana sighed.

Delight and disappointment accompanied us to the theater. Although the three tickets cost me the same, two of the seats gave a thrilling view of the entire stage. The other one offered a view of only a tiny corner into which one could only hope a dancer or two would sometimes appear. In a true gesture of friendship, Svetlana took the single seat and commiserated with a distraught visitor from Texas who had paid $75 to sit in the seat beside her.

As I thrilled to the extremely high professional quality of the dancers, I was amazed to see that quite literally hundreds of spectators in the balconies were standing in order to see a decent amount of the stage. How could architects have designed such an expensive and elegant, yet useless and impractical auditorium?

Perhaps a certain degree of fatalism helps sustain people in countries in frequent crisis. I had observed that phenomenon in Israel. In Russia, I met a Russian Jew who was a long-time friend of Svetlana's. "I love Moscow. I'd never think of leaving it," she told me. Her parents had survived World War II by selling their extensive library, book by book. She took us to a small, dark restaurant one could only find by knowing where it was. It was here that Moscow's intelligentsia gathered to share ideas, thoughts, and music. What Moscow offers her is not fame and fortune, but mental stimulation and the knowledge that she's "home."

I left Russia a week earlier than I'd planned. "Now I can concentrate on the crisis," Svetlana said with forced gaiety. The absurdity that Russia had become followed me all the way through the airport. The lane at the airport for departures was unexplainably blocked. With the casualness Russians have developed toward inconvenience, we parked where it was blocked and rolled my heavy luggage up the long hill.

I wanted to buy a bottle of water to take with me. One vendor in the airport asked the *ruble* equivalent of $5. So, I went to the next vendor. She calmly asked the equivalent of $8! Svetlana and I could only laugh in response. We tried a third place only a few steps away and bought a bottle of water for $1.

I approached the Customs agent in front of the check-in counter. He took the form I had made out upon entering Russia. "No stamp. Serious problem. $500 fine," he said laconically. I had wondered why the customs agent who looked at my form as I entered Russia hadn't marked it in any way. Fortunately, Svetlana was still waiting to wave goodbye. I motioned her to come and see what the problem was. He mumbled something to her that did not seem to resemble what he had said to me in English. He backed down, and I hurriedly left when he abandoned this rather (from what I learned later) routine shakedown. I wondered what would have happened without a Russian friend along.

Checking in was very easy since the whole airport was perhaps one notch above abandoned. I waved goodbye to Svetlana and her husband with worry for their immediate future mired with my relief at getting closer to getting out of Russia.

Years of traveling have made me unsurprised at the inconvenience and inefficiency of third world countries. I tried reading in the waiting room under a 12-foot ceiling with tiny lightbulbs. It was eerie being in an almost-empty airport. I eavesdropped on a conversation between a man from Hong Kong and a Russian passenger, each one stumbling over the English. They spoke of economic disaster in their respective countries, punctuating their conversations with "tsk, tsks," head-shaking, and nervous laughter.

I thought in amazement of how much had happened in those two and a half weeks of my visit. I had filled in some of the gaps of understanding Svetlana better by living in her home and adjusting to the rhythm of her family's daily life. I thought of our joy at being together again and of her amusement at my glee in taking pictures of St. Basil's from every conceivable and inconceivable angle. Her father's grave was also in Red Square. Russia had lost a hero when she lost her father. He had been a cosmonaut who died tragically at the end of a mission. She showed me a letter to her from President Nixon that she treasured. Penned in his own handwriting, he sought to bring comfort to her, a now fatherless 12-year-old girl.

I thought of her large apartment high above a tall, thick forest, and the peacefulness of picking berries and pulling our salad out of the ground at the *dacha*. I walked the forest again with her daughter as we searched for mushrooms to cook with dinner. I saw once again the lacey shadows as the curtains of the *dacha* were imprinted on the wall by the waning sunset.

I marveled at how we had fit in so many happy moments in a time of crisis. On the day I was leaving, when I had suddenly remembered something I'd forgotten to pack, she told me to go the mirror and smile. When I wanted to dust off the shelves in the room where I'd been sleeping, she told me simply, "We never clean up the day a guest leaves." I once again pictured the Russian custom of saying goodbye to a guest. The four of us had sat silently in the living room with our shoes on, which was itself unusual in Russian homes. After the silence, we patted our knees and rose to go to the airport.

Before we parted, I gave Svetlana what was left of my *rubles*. The sum was equal to more than two months of her part time teacher's salary, about one half of a full time teacher's salary, or four small bottles of mineral water at the Moscow airport.

THE GLEAM, THE GLINT, AND THE TARNISH

The gleam of the September sun off the modern metal and glass skyscrapers is blinding. I'm back in Shenzhen, a city designated a Special Economic Zone in China. I first came here in 1990 when it was an idea rather than a reality. It was like an awkward puppy with huge paws to grow into. Dirt was everywhere and skeletons of buildings were rising from the dust. It was trying to be a Hong Kong look-alike and feel-alike. It succeeded only in being an uncomfortable mixture of east and west.

Amongst the gleam, there was also tarnish—cute Chinese girls who came with a dream and ended up as prostitutes, and enthusiastic, educated entrepreneurs-to-be who were seduced by corruption. Anything human or material could be bought and sold in Shenzhen. In the frenzied pace, I looked into young Chinese faces and, instead of two brown eyes, saw dollar signs clicking like a cash register.

It was disconcerting and even frightening. Unlike the rest of China in the early 1990's, crime was an element to beware of. Peter, a Nanjing student of mine, moved here to work and had witnessed two murders.

In the intervening years, Shenzhen has cleaned up its streets and gives at least an impression of more orderliness. Some of its showy skyscrapers are attractive. One can find Pizza Hut among TCBY's, KFC's, and McDonald's. A huge Wal-Mart is filled with "lots of things we never knew we needed," as Peter aptly pointed out. Attempts at westernization offer strangely oily cappuchino coffee, pretty fountains, long lines at the lottery office, pathetic beggars, and desperate-looking countryside faces streaming out of the train station.

I suppose it is the way all of China is going in its hurtling lunge into the westernization of our entire planet Earth. Peter tells me more and more people have guns. The guns come in, along with drugs, from Vietnam. Both direct and subtle forms of robbery are common. Beeps and even songs emanate from omnipresent hand phones held by just about everyone.

Shenzhen is now a gangly teenager growing in unsightly, disproportionate spurts in an energized state of becoming.

Sept. 20, 1998

The brand name on the shower is American Standard, but as so much else in China, it offers only a veneer of the west. It works poorly, with a pathetic coagulation that clogs most of its holes. But the water is hot all day, a welcome westernization in cheap hotels, even if you have to put the knob to the blue side to get hot water. Western toilets made it to China, but toilet technology didn't. The toilet flushes by pulling the handle up rather than the American Standard of down. It flushes eight times out of ten, but needs help to refill. Everyone must become a sort of toilet technician in China, so I always carry the strong pink ribbon that is used to fix just about everything in China. There is air one can turn on. It presumably blows hot in the winter and cool in the summer. If you want it to blow stronger, you use low instead of high on the dial.

But what do these quirks matter when one is deferentially cared for by willing attendants who smile when they see you? Such a welcome change from the dour look I was used to seeing on the faces of Chinese hotel staff.

I'm back in China, and best of all, in Hangzhou. My friends greet me as enthusiastically as ever, and, as usual, I quickly caught an icky cold. I hope I won't be sick long because I have far too many people and places to see while I'm here. In spite of my cold, I feel alive and rejuvenated.

Some of my friends are at a good point in their lives. Others are struggling, and some merely floating. Because there are more opportunities in China, there is also more pressure to be productive. Many of today's salaries are now based on the money you bring into the company, so there is more job stress if one wants to be promoted. How I long to live here again!

Sept. 23, 1998

The hammer goes tap, tap, tap. The whining drill drones on and on. Some kind of tool goes thump, thump, thump. And that's inside my hotel! Outside, the pile driver goes whump, whump, whump. Dust swirls and lands everywhere. China is renovating. China is building. And the noise is deafening.

A lady passed by. She was a new sight in China to my eyes. Her hair was in an elegant up-do, somewhat reminiscent of Marie Antoinette. Her blouse was bright red, and her brown shorts were very short indeed. Thick high heels all the rage in China these days were planted on the motorized small bike as it zoomed along the bike path paralleling the road. Her face was stylishly made-up, and to my surprise, quite middle-aged. "Perhaps she's a business woman," I thought.

A businessman dressed in a suit and holding a briefcase caught my eye as he walked down the street. He looked vaguely familiar. Suddenly, he smiled and waved to me. What a shock! I realized he was my former pedicab driver and FEC money-changer that had ridden me around Hangzhou for so many years. Wow, he was a definite sign of the changing times. I was happy for him, but a little sorry he wouldn't be taking me on any more pedicab rides.

THE PEDICAB TIME MACHINE

It was well worth the *yuan* equivalent of about $2 plus a 70-cent tip. During the one-hour pedicab ride, we rode through a maze of alleyways. We traversed the vastness of change and transition in Hangzhou in those narrow slices through several neighborhoods.

Open, smelly neighborhood toilets, old women knitting while seated outside on tiny children-sized stools, people eating while sitting on newspaper on the sidewalk, outside courtyards and rabbit warren-like dwellings of indeterminate age, new but old-looking multi-story apartment buildings with bars enclosing clothes drying from bamboo poles, small, dirty shops selling an incredible variety of goods, smart new boutiques with the latest fashions on glitzy mannequins with western faces, men with sledgehammers breaking rock on a recently demolished building looking like the chain gangs of old-time western movies, surprised faces staring at a foreigner, rarely if ever seen in their neighborhoods, babies and little children whose eyes stared at the foreigner while their faces puckered up to cry—all these sights and more blurred by on my journey.

Every now and then, the driver came to a main street. He became very alert as he proceeded to weave through the disorderly masses of bicycles, taxis, buses, and other pedicabs, using the evasive maneuvers that distinguish third world drivers from others. Luck was with us as we missed other vehicles by inches, and they barely missed us with nary a second look. The pedicab driver's calves, thick in comparison with his slight body, never quivered even though the effort to wheel my American-sized girth must have been considerable for such a long time.

When we finally arrived, he got off his bike with the look of pride in a job well done. He pointed out the building that one of my friends had written in Chinese on a piece of paper. After my appointment, I climbed into a taxi that sped along one long road as straight as an arrow, arriving quickly and costing about $1.25.

Sept. 27, 1998

I can forgive China many faults when I have a day as perfect as today. Thomas has brought me along on his business trip to Xiamen. Xiamen has a different, lighter feel than Hangzhou. We went to a tourist island nearby called Gulang Yu where all cars and even pedicabs are banned. Only electric carts ply tourists through the uncrowded, unhurried streets.

The beach was pretty, and the deep blue sky complemented the green of the palm trees. I swam a little, and then the warm sand and gentle breeze lulled me into a better sleep than I seem to have at night. The seafood was superb.

Sept. 29, 1998

As I boarded the plane from Xiamen to return to Hangzhou, I thought of how travel has filled my mind with sometimes helpful trivia. For example, I know that domestic Chinese airlines don't stop passengers from carrying on many small bags. I also know that Chinese passengers will get up and reach for their luggage just as the plane lands and is still moving on the runway. While many of the planes in China are relatively shiny and new, the food is strange, fitting neither eastern nor western tastes. The toilet is often minus soap and towels.

I also know to bring a gluestick with me to post offices in China because the glue at the post office used to seal envelopes is usually a sticky mess. Mailing several letters or packages can get confusing because the clerk hands you the stamps for everything and you must paste them on yourself. Since Chinese are usually better at math, it doesn't seem to confuse them as much as it confounds me. I often end up with not enough stamps, or some extras. Counting change is also a math puzzle for me. Chinese subtract the amount they gave to know if the change they've been given is correct. Clerks never count out your change to you. In fact, they often just throw it on the counter. Banks in different countries count money differently too. The prettiest was in Taiwan where they made a big fan out of the money and then counted it.

I have come to expect that bread in Asia as often as not will have some unexpected haylike stuff inside, and that yogurt comes in a bottle that must be drunk through a straw inserted through the top. It's just about impossible to get the top off in one piece.

There are many things I've adjusted to, but some I'll never adjust to. The traffic patterns are so erratic and terrifying, I'm always grateful for the arm of my Chinese friends who guide me like a child or little old lady across the street.

Oct. 7, 1998

Maybe it's just coincidence, but most of my friends live in apartments on the sixth or seventh floor. Since elevators are only in buildings of eight stories or more, I'm getting a work out going up and down. Very few of them have lights on the stairways, so I try to remember to bring a flashlight with me. The stairways and buildings are not very appealing-looking, but my friends have fixed up their apartments nicely. Generally, they don't have running hot water, but some have a solar water heater that gives at least some chance of a short hot shower.

Several years ago, I remember Richard telling me that his sister had bought a washing machine. Confused, I said, "But there's no running water in the house." He explained that they used to fill the washing machine with water from the well! Perhaps now, even in the countryside, most homes have running water and washing machines.

But what I don't know is where the kitchen god resides in today's countryside homes. Russell once told me the family tried never to argue near the old stoves because the kitchen god was listening. But now the old-style, hand-painted stoves have been left abandoned and fading while the family cooks on modern gas burners with fuel tanks.

Oct. 8, 1998

In 1988, I saw China when it was on the cusp of another revolution that would shake it to its deepest roots. In 1998, I see China stumbling, bumbling, hurtling, jerking, lunging, bungling, flinging, dragging, refusing, expecting, and denying change. Being in China now is like being in a time machine gone crazy that jerks constantly between time zones. One can never be in one era for long before being jolted into a future time zone, or an earlier one.

Another image is of dancers going forward, going backward, turning left, turning right, turning round and round until one gets quite dizzy even watching it.

Oct. 14, 1998

The call of nature has become a constant wild shriek that follows me day and night, and from place to place. It is an unwelcome memento from that lovely swim in Gulang Yu. Here in the countryside, Pearl's grandmother even went out to the hills to pick something local that she cooked into a soup. I have already tried a few doctors and their prescriptions that didn't work, so I had high hopes her grandma's home brew would end it.

I have the 5th floor of Pearl's family's home to myself. The first floor has the kitchen, an office for their business, and a large room that opens to the sidewalk where Pearl has a small store. The extended family sleeps basically on the 2nd and 3rd floor. The 4th floor is mostly unoccupied. The 5th floor has two small rooms, and one large, unfurnished room with floor to ceiling blue windows that was once planned to be a disco. In the middle of this immense room stands a desk that Pearl's husband and brother lugged up here for me to use for writing. If my mind weren't so preoccupied with the constant urge to pee, I could really enjoy writing in this unusual environment looking out the blue windows to the surrounding mountains.

We visited the large, quite charming old countryside home of others in her family. To Pearl's 80-year-old grandfather, I must have seemed to come from another planet. He asked how long the plane ride was from the U.S. When I told him, he said he could only imagine how many hours it would take by train. He has rarely gone to the nearest large city, one hour away by bus.

His eyes saw clearly without glasses, and his mind was quick to recall how he had had to run into the hills to escape the Japanese during the war. His large home sat prettily at the confluence of several small mountains, a few of which the family actually owned and where they once used to go to collect firewood before they switched to gas. No sound of cars interfered with the chirping of the birds. Some red-marked chickens wandered in the yard, and the dog barked for attention.

His garden next to the house was large and offered a profusion of vegetables. He pulled out some huge sweet potatoes and radishes, and plucked some tangerines from a tree for us to munch on. He was still an able gardener.

He accompanied Pearl and me on a walk past his home to a surprisingly dry reservoir considering that this had been a year of floods in China. The only other person around was a 71-year-old herdsman with his foraging goats. The grandfather walked easily with his large walking stick, belying his 65 plus years of smoking. I pointed out a multi-legged centipede-looking insect. I admired its perfect symmetry and the fluidity of its walk. Down came the walking stick to crush the delightful, perfect symmetry. "We don't think they're good," Pearl said. I silently apologized to the mangled little creature for calling attention to it.

It's understandably quite amazing to elderly Chinese that I, a middle-aged woman, travel the world alone. What seems to amaze Chinese even more is that my former husband and I are still friends. I've been told that's unheard of for the relatively few cases of divorce in China. As we chatted, the grandfather commented on a neighbor and his wife who had separate beds in the same house, and also cooked and washed clothes separately.

The grandfather became quite animated while we walked. Pearl translated that he could not imagine being cremated as required now by Chinese law. He was worried how his relatives could come to visit him on the annual *Ching Ming* Festival. He preferred a tomb in the hillsides like the ones we could see around us.

The phrase "romanticizing the primitive life," came to me as I sat in the grandparents' home, absorbing the beauty and peacefulness of the scene. I was aware that sanitary conditions were low. They had a western-style toilet, but it often ran out of water. I knew that winter days and nights were brutally cold without heat, and summer days stifling. But that seemed far away on a full stomach and a warm autumn day.

Oct. 17, 1998

Streams of relatives come and go daily on the small village street with the new multi-storied, blue-windowed homes. Since one large room is open to the street, it's a perpetual open house. Some come for a meal, a game of mahjong or poker, or just to companionably eat and spit seeds together. Perhaps the days seem long to the young who are unemployed in today's China. Getting rich quick is more appealing, so pyramid schemes of selling products are catching on.

The whole village is talking about the foreigner who has to pee all the time. A fair number of them came out to watch and laugh as I inexpertly planted mustard and green vegetables in the village garden, poured urine on them (which is why Chinese don't eat raw vegetables), and wished the little plants good luck.

Oct. 20, 1998

Walking along the riverbank in another friend's village, a peasant woman held up a trussed chicken by its bound legs and asked my friend to translate, "What is this called in English?" "Chicken," I replied with the guilt in my throat that arose from realizing the chicken was soon to be on a plate.

As my friend and I sat on a bench by the river's edge, curious peasants came by to stare at me. The woman holding the chicken was also holding a scissors. Trying not to think of what was soon to come, I answered questions about my age and where I came from. My mind stubbornly remained on the about-to-be executed as I was asked, "Do you like to eat chicken?" Replying truthfully that I did, I wanted to explain that I'm psychologically a vegetarian, but hypocritically continue to eat meat.

I steeled myself for the horrible squawking and screaming I expected as her husband stooped near the river holding the bird over the water. The fluttering of the wings was brief, and drowned out the snip of the scissors. As I tried to gaze into the river's distance, I saw the man's hands moving in a shaking motion.

He handed the victim back to his wife, who held it while the blood continued to drain out of the slash at its throat. Its legs moved uselessly. When its movements came to an end at long last, the woman came closer and asked wonderingly why we were the same age, but her hair was gray and mine wasn't. She pointed to her earrings and wondered why I didn't wear gold like rich Americans should. While she was wondering about me, I was wondering about the bleeding chicken and the heavy topic of death.

She continued to chat as she squatted and washed the chicken in the river. She disappeared briefly, and returned with the plucked chicken, which she once again cleaned in the dirty river. Of all the chicken I've eaten during my lifetime, this was the first time I had witnessed preparation from the earliest stages. I was glad I would not be eating this particular chicken.

Continuing to gaze over the river and discuss banalities, I silently pondered life and death.

Nov. 15, 1998

I have continued to see doctors along the way—China, Korea, Holland. Each one has given me a different drug that doesn't work. I even waited one week in China for a laboratory to culture what's growing in my urine, but that medicine didn't help either. Sleeping pills successfully put me to sleep for eight hours, but I never wake up feeling rested. A doctor in Korea decided the problem was in my head and prescribed an anti-depressant. A kind doctor in a clinic in Holland gave me some tests at a reduced rate because he had once been a world traveler on a low budget. His diagnosis is that the infection is no longer active, but my bladder is irritated. Instead of another antibiotic, he has given me medication that dulls the sensation of needing to urinate.

I am no longer a scintillating guest. I am an uncomfortable lump on a floor, couch, bed, afraid to go far from a toilet. The medication I'm taking fogs my brain and gives me headaches. The cold weather in Europe chills me inside and out.

I've been able to see many of my friends along the way. I'll have to give up the chance to see other friends in France, England, and Israel. There's no point in continuing this sojourn feeling sick and unhappy. I've decided to go back to the U.S. two months early and mend into my old self again.

Dec. 15, 1998

It took a long time of sleeping and resting to get back my health after more than six weeks of different antibiotics and sleeping pills. I'm back to myself again and am putting together a cute apartment not too far from my parents in Dallas. My life will be here for a while. I'm relying on frequent letter writing to keep in touch with my friends.

Dec. 28, 1998

Mom died unexpectedly tonight, two days before Dad's 80th birthday and about two years since my brother's death. After being thousands of miles away for so long, I'm glad I was here with my parents for what has unpredictably and ultimately been my mother's last month alive.

19

U.S. ICELAND "DOWN UNDER" ASIA 1999–2005

August 13, 1999

I almost never believe that people can improve on Mother Nature. However, in the case of the beaches along the city of Laguna Beach, the landscaped gardens along the bluffs right over the sea make the views even more stunning. After all these years and miles, I'm living back in California, albeit further south.

Dad and I moved in June to a large retirement community called Leisure World only six miles from the magnificent Pacific Ocean. Our small home is in a delightful park setting, complete with many wild bunny rabbits hopping around and eating everything they can find. I love the eternal spring weather and enjoy watching the sky linger in bright blue while the clouds turn very pink at sunset. There's even a nature preserve and babbling creek inside Leisure World just a short walk from our home. We live in a picture postcard perfect place.

This place is great for dad because there are many activities and literally thousands of old folks to meet. The internal bus system makes it possible for him to get around without driving. We've settled into an easy rhythm of living together although he misses mom a lot. I've begun to make friends with some of the "younger" people here. Inside the Leisure World gates, I'm young. But just outside the gates, I'm very aware that I turned 56 today.

Oct. 18, 2000

Dealing with death is debilitating physically, mentally, psychologically, philosophically—existentially. My dear father died on this date one year ago. It was ten months from mom's death and only four months after we came to Leisure World. As deaths go, it was a "good" death—not protracted and not painful. Intuition told me he would die earlier than his doctors did. There was time for me to say goodbye, express my love, and thank him for bringing me to Leisure

World. As I've heard is common in grief, I have replayed the death scene mentally over and over. A kind nurse and a technician were with me when he died. Seconds after my dad took his last breath, the technician asked if he could hug me. Even though we were strangers who had really never met, it was the best, most comforting hug I've ever had. He then asked my permission to sing me a song his grandfather taught him. It was an Irish tune. His strong voice musically expressed the sadness of losing someone you love.

"Slogging through a swamp," "wrapped in a fog"—there are many ways to poetically describe the disorientation of mourning. My state of being has ranged between sadness and numbness this past year. I have felt as vulnerable as an orphan. My mind has refused to focus for long. I sometimes wondered if I was going crazy.

I have recently begun to feel the numbness receding and life slowly seeping back into me. The future remains amorphous. Max has been a bright spot in my life. He came to the U.S. early in the year 2000 to see what life in the U.S. might hold for him. Unfortunately, his wife and daughter are still living back in Macau until he gets settled. We've been discovering this area together since it's new to me too. It's fun for me to be his guide to American life and hear his first reactions to America. For example, he's amazed at how car-oriented American society is, dedicating huge amounts of land to roads and making cars into our mini-homes.

I haven't been emotionally ready to think of my future. My feet are not itchy, but every now and then I sense a smidgen of restlessness—or perhaps it's a flicker of energy moving within me at last.

April 5, 2001

I'm back in China! The skies aren't so blue and it's not as orderly or convenient as Leisure World, but I immediately felt the draw on me of the shy faces smiling back and the laughs over the language difficulty. There is a magnetism to this place that has pulled me back about thirteen times so far.

Two and a half years was too long to be away from China. Luckily, I was able to get a leave of absence from my teaching job in California. I don't get any benefits with my part time job, but there is the availability of substitutes when I want an unpaid leave.

It was difficult to find gifts to bring my friends because nowadays everything in the U.S. says "Made in China." It used to be that items in the U.S. that were made in China were only for export and were not available for purchase in China. But, now it's hard to tell what you can buy in China. There is so much more of everything here than before. Sadly, those inexpensive but exquisitely handcrafted cutouts and painted wooden bookmarks I loved to buy are harder and harder to find.

After all the renovations of the airport in Hangzhou, I landed at a huge new airport built further away from the city. I thought of the American businessman I had met years before waiting in line at the old Hangzhou airport. He said he had a business in China. It wasn't making any money, but he felt he was contributing to China's development. I wondered what he would say about his business today.

It's great fun rediscovering my legs as a true mode of transportation rather than exercising at the fitness center like a hamster going round and round on a treadmill. I immediately noticed that the automobile traffic is much heavier. My friends are even talking about learning how to drive and eventually buying a car! The railway stations are overflowing with massive influxes of young people from the countryside areas of China looking for work in the wealthier eastern provinces. In fact, the railway stations are like squatters' villages. The bus stations are more orderly and spitting is now punishable by a fine. A very welcome surprise is that the long distance buses have a comfortable seat for everyone with no smoking allowed! Hooray, hooray!

April 6, 2001

"Do taxis in the U.S. drive with their windows open or shut?" my young friend translated the taxi driver's question.

"Sometimes up and sometimes down," I answered without realizing the real meaning of his question.

The taxi driver pointed to the closed windows in his taxi and the air conditioner going and said he wanted to keep the fumes of traffic out of our noses. "Thoughtful," I conceded and then noticed a rare touch in a taxi in Hangzhou—a plant along the back window and sparkling clean white seat covers. Here was a taxi driver who cared about his taxi and his customers. That was something one would not have found even a short time ago in rapidly changing China.

As much as I appreciated my considerate driver, I couldn't help thinking how sad it was that his seat belt sat unused and unwanted, hanging limply, while there was no access to seat belts in the back.

As in the taxi, the once drab and unnoticed in rapidly changing China is becoming a clean and colorful source of pride. The parks are getting nicer and cleaner. Like in Disneyland, numerous workers go around constantly picking up the trash. West Lake was always beautiful, but now it is much cleaner. While walking with a former student who had spent all night on a train from Nanjing to visit me in Hangzhou, we were both curious about a very attractive small building near the road. Since we both knew China in the days of finding the public toilets in back alleys by following the smell, we were shocked to discover that this immaculate building was a public toilet.

My days in China are like precious pearls strung one after the other.

April 8, 2001

I've finally seen the Qiantang River tide change. I had read about it, but never actually saw this very unusual phenomenon even though it's so close to Hangzhou. There is a different time of year when the tide is very high and more spectacular to watch, but, even so, I was definitely impressed by watching the moment on just an ordinary day when the sound changed and I could see the direction of the flow of water reverse. Elizabeth took me there. Her daughter, my first Chinese grandchild, is very bright, sensitive, sweet, and, unlike her American grandmother, mathematically inclined. And, to my surprise, they have a cute little dog in their apartment. Dogs as pampered pets is another change in China. As usual, there is always a lot of laughter when Elizabeth and I get together.

Life's moving along well for most of my friends—new apartments, growing children, and a beautiful new son for Robert and his wife. When he was born, I was once again honored by being asked to be his American grandmother. Thomas has a new office and seven people working for his company. I'm used to technology moving from the west to the east, but the quantity and cheapness of cell phones in the east surpasses the U.S. Everyone here carries a cell phone and has a home phone. Their salaries seem to allow for fancy meals at about $25 for three people compared to the $6 I used to spend for four of us. The hotels I stay in now for about $12 have hot showers all day, locks on the door from the inside, and 29 television stations in Chinese on a local cable. I now have to ask for a thermos of hot water because each room comes equipped with bottled water that is dispensed hot or cold. When I asked my friends how they know this water is safe to drink, they said they don't really know, but rely on the brand name. Alas, there is still cigarette smoke that lingers on the pillows and sheets, and overwhelms the restaurants.

April 17, 2001

The pollution of Beijing is even more apparent when flying through all the layers of guk coating the skies of the city. The gridlock of its traffic jams makes one of the major contributors to pollution very obvious. I was able to include time in Beijing to visit friends, including Benjamin who is working there. As a special treat, he took me to one of the many places where they do foot massage, but warned me that it could be painful. At first I thought he was joking. I said I insisted only on getting a gentle massage because I loved having my feet massaged. Four of us had a room to ourselves, complete with tea. Four people came in and massaged our feet for one whole glorious hour!

Supposedly, those with the knowledge of massage can feel problems throughout the body by only touching the feet. Deep massage can help. Interestingly, the one who did my feet told my friend that my wrist had a problem. In fact, one of my wrists was aching.

There were many signs that pointed out how many years I've been coming to China. The image that summed it up best was two glasses—Russell's mother's teeth sitting in a glass at night next to a glass holding some of mine.

April 23, 2001

As I stopped in Hong Kong on my way to Macau, I couldn't help but notice that Hong Kong is fading into a shadow of its former self since becoming part of China in 1997. Macau, on the other hand, is a boomtown since becoming China in 1999. There are new buildings everywhere, including where the sea used to be.

The plaza has been remodeled between the old bridge to Taipa and the playful-looking, but very serious Lisboa Casino. When I first came to Macau in the early 1990's and saw the statue of a Portuguese on horseback whipping Chinese people, I thought it was in bad taste. China had apparently felt the same way. Before the handover in 1999, Portugal had actually dismantled the offensive sculpture piece by piece and sent it back to Portugal.

In the dying days of Portuguese rule, Bobbie had been selected to study in Portugal for two years. Being on her own so far from isolated Macau has added a maturity and sophistication to her already bubbly personality.

It was strange to visit Max's wife and daughter without him there. We enjoyed our precious few days together as he continues his lonely way on the rocky and insecure path of being a new immigrant in the U.S.

Nov. 16, 2001

My son's days of living are over. His days of dying have begun. There is no hope of survival from his terminal illness. Will this be his last birthday?

Oct. 7, 2002

I have come back to visit China to feel the love of my friends here. No matter how much China has changed, the love and attentiveness of my friends remains steady and true. But China is changing before my eyes with a breathtaking, dizzying speed. It's a happier China all the way around.

"China is changing and it's changing fast," declares one TV channel in English and on the air 24 hours a day. I've been watching China change since 1988, but it has now speeded up like time-lapse photography. Some of the changes are only "cosmetic," as Debbie told me. Still, it was the first time I crossed the same long pedestrian overpass without encountering beggars with their hands out.

According to the news in English, the Chinese government is issuing 10,000 passports every day. Most of my friends now have passports and have traveled somewhere outside China. Some are living scattered around the world—Europe, the U.S., New Zealand.

Tucked away from the frenzy of change with Elizabeth and her daughter, I ate melon seeds and drank green tea while gazing across the water to "my bench." All felt peaceful and possible.

Oct. 12, 2002

It's hard to believe that we are actually all eating together in Jiaxin at a banquet hosted by Russell in a very special and elegant restaurant managed by Robert. Frank and his wife from Taiwan are on their first visit to China. Frank remembered Russell and Robert from the correspondence I set up between them when I taught in Taiwan in 1991. And they are finally getting to meet face to face. Surrounded by all of them in our private dining room, I felt very happy that they all became friends through me.

Oct. 15, 2002

How can you bomb heaven? "Bomb blast in Bali" can't be true. And yet it was. Two hundred are dead and 300 wounded. That beautiful land of happy, gentle people was treated so brutally. There is no compensation when perfection is defiled. My head already ached from the bad cold I caught. Now my heart aches also.

Oct. 18, 2002

My thoughts dart around my mind like a curious fly flitting from niche to niche, one dark recess to another. I experience it passively, letting it go at will against the background of cacophony so common in China—people yelling, street peddlers chanting what they're selling, cars, buses, and that ubiquitous ta-ta-ta-ta of the drill and chink-chink-chink of the hammer proclaiming construction of one sort or another. In this case, my hotel is erecting an advertising billboard on its roof.

There is another ominous background noise I can hear. Bush is beating the war drums to get support for toppling Saddam Hussein who popped up again like a sand-filled punching bag after the elder Bush stopped the storm in the desert ten years ago. Further distant is the blast of the suicide bombers in Israel and the sifting of the charred remains in Bali. No place is a peaceful paradise now if Bali can so tragically become a smaller Twin Tower.

The ocean has, I learned, a deeper current that can be opposite an upper current. And so my life seems now. In one current, I hear the funereal swoosh of the waves, bringing more and more pain. In the other current, I play and splash happily among loving friends in a country where I feel at home.

I don't know what chance China has to progress against the tide in the rest of the world. Perhaps, because it started slowly from so far behind, the energy has built up and is propelling the little engine that could. It's good, very good, to hear China laugh and play.

Oct. 20, 2002

Before leaving China, I had my first birthday party in advance of turning 60 in August of 2003. A jolly group of my friends took me out to lunch. The principal of the tourism school, now about 70, was part of our group. Over the years I've seen her, she has become more fluent in English than she was when I taught at the tourism school. I would be happy to age like she has. She has stayed physically and mentally healthy and is now studying computer.

August 13, 2003

Happy 60th birthday to me!! Fortunately, the present I gave myself—18 days in Iceland—drew me out of the depression that had built up over this momentous leap into "old age."

ICELAND—THE SCARRED BEAUTY

Every manner of nature's violence has created Iceland's beauty. Gashed, slashed, ripped, burned, scorched—Iceland's incredible beauty stands before the visitor's eyes and continues to change as we watch. Icebergs melt and new icebergs are calved, rivers change course and sometimes wreak havoc along the way, volcanoes erupt in violent spasms. Subdued and dominated by man in most of the world, nature reigns supreme in Iceland and people must deal with it.

Sitting almost at the top of the world, Iceland is overlooked by many tourists. Yet, 300,000 will stop by this year, equaling the 290,000 residents. Most will come in the summer when the 24-hour light, green grasses, and comfortable temperatures (50's and 60's) are the norm.

Hearty European hikers come like turtles, carrying their camping equipment on their backs. Wealthier tourists have a choice of many fine hotels and restaurants, while the poorer tourists of any age make do in a number of well-run hostels with cooking facilities. Areas are accessible by rental car, bus service, tours, and domestic flights to some destinations.

Even with what are bound to be many cloudy and sometimes rainy days, the often-staggering beauty of Iceland is intense. Waterfalls cascade, rivers, streams and brooks gush or meander, green crawls up the hills and mountains luxuriating in 24 hours a day of summer light. Fog lends atmosphere during walks along Vik's beach and the Iceberg Lagoon at Jokulsarlon.

For those fortunate enough to understand, Iceland is an open textbook on volcanoes, glaciers, tectonic plates, wildflowers and eighty varieties of nesting birds. Tortured landscapes, black sand, and vast lava fields show the power of nature. Much more of nature's power is hidden underground.

Iceland sits on the mid-Atlantic ridge. The spreading of the Atlantic is actually visible where the land is being literally ripped apart. Thingvellir is a remarkable example of the North American plate and the European plate pulling away from one another. In essence, you are standing on no-man's land in between those two plates. And, in another part of Iceland near Lake Myvatn, I trod where the astronauts came to practice walking on the moon.

Water conservation is necessary in a large part of our world, making a stark contrast to Iceland where water runs abundantly above ground, and underground. Not only is the air pure, but cool drinking water comes pristine-pure directly from the earth. Geothermally heated water is also nature's gift to Iceland, providing hot water for showers and home heating.

Rich in water, both salt and fresh, Iceland is also rich in the bounties that water brings. From abundant fishing, which is the financial mainstay of Iceland, to the uplifting beauty of its waterways, to the freshness and cleanliness water brings with it, to the simple entertainment of an evening listening to the waterfalls making their way to the sea, Iceland is indeed fortunate.

This seemingly endless supply of water has opened up a controversy in today's Iceland. Electricity is a valuable commodity. Being able to produce electricity cheaply, Iceland has taken the huge step of agreeing for the first time to sell electricity to a foreign country to fuel an aluminum smelter plant. Work has already begun on it in the sparsely populated eastern part of Iceland. This aluminum smelter plant will bring with it not only jobs, but also something Iceland is not used to—pollution. Some of the big money involved in this enterprise will go to preservation and conservation, but is it opening Pandora's box? Residents in the east definitely think so and don't want it built. People in other parts of Iceland vary in their response, but there is general concern that this is a worrying step toward making money in ways harmful to the natural environment.

Iceland is a colorful place. Especially in the summer, the various blues of the water, the fragile and courageous wildflowers, and the luscious greens of the vegetation stand out even though trees don't. All the trees, mostly low birch trees, were felled long ago by early settlers. There are attempts to re-forest, but it's a slow process. A very impressive exception is a true outdoor botanical garden in Akureyri. From a humble opening in 1912 by a local women's group, this amazing garden with mature trees and plants from around the world has flourished only miles from the Arctic Circle. Determination and careful tending still make it grow and bloom.

Among the vibrant summer wildflowers, Icelandic horses, sheep, and multicolored cows graze peacefully up and down the hillsides. During all seasons, vividly colored houses and farmhouses are a welcome sight. In the darker fall and winter, the aurora borealis thrills the eye as it splashes color across the sky.

Iceland has the feel of the countryside in its old-time friendliness, unspoiled air and water, lack of crime, and low population. However, Iceland is completely modern and high tech. Cell phones, computers, modern medicine, and imported goods from all over the world are the norm. Coming from a storytelling culture, Icelanders are rightfully proud of close to 100% literacy. Education is highly valued and available. Icelandic is the language of Iceland and most Icelanders are bilingual, learning English early in their school years. Many are multilingual in Scandinavian and European languages.

Icelanders work hard and pay high taxes, but receive a lot for their tax money. Poverty in recent times has not been a problem for the vast majority. However, it is being seen and felt very recently along with the new phenomenon of unemployment. Also new are the larger numbers of immigrants and refugees than Iceland has seen before. There are now Bosnians, Thais, Filipinos, Sri Lankans, etc. in their communities. Icelanders all know and are proud of their genealogy, which has, until recently, been rather pure and limited. Future Icelanders will not fit the blond, white-skinned image and will speak Icelandic in a variety of accents.

I left Iceland, but Iceland hasn't left me. Visions of beautifully blonde children, shaggy and sturdy Icelandic horses, sheep dotting unbelievable landscapes, basalt rock columns and lava-tossed fields, pink and delicious salmon, yummy breads and creamed soups, the colorful puffins, the 360 degree panoramas that no photo can capture—still dance in my head. I miss the alive, breathing nature, the places where torture and beauty are one. I'm so glad I celebrated my 60th birthday at almost the top of the world.

Jan. 5, 2004

"Is that wood?" the customs official in the New Zealand airport asked me as she pointed to my necklace with a branch my macramé owl was sitting on. "You can't bring wood into New Zealand," she added. I whisked the small twig from under the unsuspecting owl and gave it to her. I hoped the clever owl wouldn't unravel. Before I got through Customs, the hiking shoes in my luggage were removed and sent through a sanitizing process. New Zealand is very cautious about controlling what comes into their country.

Pauline and her husband eagerly greeted me at the Christchurch airport. I hadn't seen them since my visit to China in 2001, just after they were married and before they had left for New Zealand. When she had told me they had a dairy, I first imagined countryside and cows. However, a dairy in New Zealand is a small neighborhood store that sells small items like milk, bread, candy, newspapers, etc. Their home was connected to their dairy.

Taking advantage of her free time during winter break from the university she was attending, we three set out to start the new year right. They were crammed, but wonderful days in which I was once again bedazzled by New Zealand's deep blue skies, turquoise seas, and golden hills. We stayed in the Catlins, which I had not visited in 1995. The guidebook called the hostel "Hilltop," but I called it "Hostel Heaven" because it was possibly the best version of Heaven I could visualize with the sea sweeping the shore on one side, and multi-green high hillsides artistically dotted with sheep on other sides. The old house had been moved there and re-done very delicately and carefully. Each touch was deliberate and delicious—purple flowers ringing handmade driftwood seats. The fresh smells and sounds of birds added to the total sensual delight of the place.

On New Year's Eve, we went to a view called Nugget Point. From high cliffs, we looked down at seals and sea lions on the beaches only they could reach, a multitude of sea birds, and the turquoise sea with several huge rock "nuggets" jutting out of the sea. The sky treated us with a rainbow and about three different sunsets as the sun dipped between clouds. The colors of the land and sea competed with the colors of the sky for attention. The "nuggets" turned dark and then glowed once again. Dusk and sunset were exquisitely slow.

The coming of a new year had encouraged me to rent out my home for six months, disconnect the battery in my car, and buy a ticket that would take me to New Zealand, western Australia, Singapore, Macau, Taiwan, and China. My plan was to look for work in Taiwan and decide whether I wanted to live abroad again.

I was bringing my son with me in the only way possible. A small bottle of his ashes lay in my backpack, waiting for the "right" places to release him. He died of his illness in October of 2003, just shy of his 35th birthday. There are truly no words to express the feeling of a mother carrying her child's ashes.

Jan. 14, 2004

I never remotely imagined a "farmhouse" could be like this. Pauline had to return to her studies, so I decided to try the new experience of becoming a WOOFer. This absolutely wonderful organization matches "willing workers on organic farms," with farms where one works half a day in exchange for room and board. The organization is worldwide, and New Zealand has a very large number of farmers who want temporary workers. I got a WOOF directory and started calling around. Because it was the busy season with many young people visiting New Zealand during the summer "down under," I made many phone calls until I got a "Yes, please come for a week."

Having missed the "busy season" cutting a species of protea that this farm sells mostly to Asia, I am the only WOOFer in the home now. Since the time pressure is over for now, my days are spent leisurely pruning the next crop of flowers in a magnificently photogenic environment. The "farmhouse" is mostly windows perched on a cliff overlooking a turquoise bay. When I practice yoga on the balcony looking at the view, I can easily imagine I have found Nirvana.

Living with a New Zealand family is quite interesting too. Ironically, what the husband is hoping to accomplish with his 100 acres is to un-do the damage his farmer father did. During his father's time, the goal was to clear as much land as possible for farming. The natural balance of nature was disrupted. This farmer hopes to allow the natural vegetation to return. It's a slow process, requiring skill in protecting the natural vegetation that wants to return and restricting other plants that can take it over.

The income from selling the peonies and hardy protea flowers isn't enough to support the family. The wife commutes about three hours a day to and from her job as a veterinarian. There are two teenage sons who go away to a boarding school during the school year.

I feel like a slug compared to this middle-aged couple. The wife is in training for a competition that requires swimming, mountain biking, and running. She rises at 5 a.m. to have time to work out at a local swimming pool before going to work. During the lunch break, she runs and bikes. On the weekend I was there, they arose at 4 a.m. to take their boat out to do some spearfishing. They came back with large live lobsters, which were then cooked as part of an elegant meal served to some invited guests. During "tea," as New Zealanders refer to dinner, the adults talked about the cogs on their mountain bikes, the proper length of their skis, and the good places in Europe to ski during New Zealand's summer.

Before dinner, one overnight guest invited me for a "little wee walk," to give her old dog some exercise. The old, sick dog ambled easily as I struggled to follow through the hillside without paths and climbing over a barbed wire fence. The next day, they had picked fresh fruit from their trees and hiked four miles down to the little town before I woke up. Sunday's afternoon activities were equally vigorous.

Yes, this is definitely a different pace of life where healthy exercise is a daily way of life, unconnected to fitness centers and aerobics classes.

Jan. 31, 2004

I ended my stay in New Zealand in the idyllic village of Akaroa where I released some of my son's ashes to roam the turquoise sea. After hugging Pauline numerous times, I had a very long time getting to Perth, Australia, because of flight delays, long lines at customs, and having to change planes. A shower and 13 hours of sleep prepared me for exploring Perth on the "other" side of Australia.

Western Australia is wonderfully uncrowded with a variety of attractions, some of which are truly unique. In the very attractive city of Perth, the train station sounds like a concert hall with classical music playing. Friends of an Iceland friend took me out to an exciting aquarium and a couple of lovely parks. I was able to see the outdoor Oz Concert, which celebrated the diversity of the people of Australia, and view the 16,000 fireworks exploding on Australia Day. Knowing how the Australians love to drink to excess, I was at first apprehensive about being part of such a large crowd, but the authorities actually managed to keep it liquor-free. Frequent merry cries of "Aussie, Aussie, Aussie" found a ready response of "Oy, Oy, Oy" from the crowd.

In Fremantle, outside Perth, I was the one on the menu being bitten mercilessly by bedbugs and other "occupants" of the hostel I stayed in. A former prison guard at the Fremantle Prison made the old prison come alive with his sonorous voice and vivid memories. The prison had not been empty for so very long. It finally had to be abandoned because they couldn't find a way to put toilets and plumbing in those solid stone walls. I snorkeled with some fish above a large stingray in a clear turquoise sea near Carnac Island that a group of male Australian sea lions called "home." The glorious colors of the water are caused by the sun's reflection off the relatively shallow sandy bottom.

On a two-day and four-day tour, I admired the versatility of Australia's energetic tour guides who serve as drivers, cooks, local "experts," and entertainers in the evening (one did magic tricks and the other sang while accompanying himself on a guitar). One guide assured me that wiping soapy dishes without rinsing them off was the way they did it in Australia to save water. And so, I happily fed wild kangaroos, emus, and brilliantly colored wild parrots that came up to our cabin, climbed the winding staircase of a towering lighthouse that looked out toward Antarctica and a small island that was calibrated to be the furthest point of our earth, and saw more unusual beauty in a short time than many see in all their lifetime. The single most exciting sight I saw were the rocks where Australia and Antarctica tore apart millions of years ago when Gondwana broke apart. That thrilled me in some primordial way, such as when I have seen the exact place where two oceans come together.

Feb. 1, 2004

"When did you last have unsafe sex?" is the sign that greets me on the hostel Ladies Room door. A container for syringes is prominently displayed. The pharmacies give out clean, sterile needles to drug addicts. I don't know whether or not they get free drugs.

Although tucked "down under" the world, Australians seem as troubled as the rest of the world. There's quite a lot of violence, drugs, and unsavory behavior. Perhaps there will never be a good answer to the problem of race relations with the aborigines. While the government does more and more for the aborigines, some white Australians didn't mind telling me that they resent it. It doesn't sound too different from the New Zealand Maoris and Kiwis, or even American blacks and whites.

I find it difficult to be in a culture that considers liquor "medicine" that should be imbibed often and excessively. My next stop, squeaky clean and law-abiding Singapore, will be a nice contrast.

Feb. 5, 2004

The humidity and heat of Singapore wilts me, but produces lush, gorgeous vegetation everywhere. I came to Singapore expressly to see Benjamin and meet his wife who is a Singaporean Chinese. Unfortunately, I haven't spent much time with them because she's not feeling well and the demands of his job have been heavy while I'm here. Still, it's been good to see what his life is like now that he's permanently settled in Singapore. And, Singapore has some wonderful places I hadn't visited when I was here before. I spent an entire day enchanted in an immense bird park. And I loved the night safari at the zoo where you get to see nocturnal animals at their normally active hours. I no longer suffer from insomnia as I did in my pre-menopausal days, but like these animals, I feel at my peak during night hours and can't fall asleep until the middle of the night. The light of morning is my best sleeping time too.

Feb. 12, 2004

"My teacher, my teacher," greeted me at the Macau Airport where I stopped to visit Max's wife and daughter. A security guard came over excitedly and introduced me to his surprised co-workers. He warmly remembered me from the early 1990's when he studied in one of my evening classes. He said he would love to study with me again. Could I please come back to Macau to teach?

I may not be a movie star, but teachers, especially in the eyes of their Asian students, always remain a celebrity to them.

Feb. 19, 2004

Macau was much, much colder than usual. I left with the distinct feeling that I was coming down with a cold. It hit me in Taiwan, so my time here so far has mostly been spent coughing and blowing my nose.

But there's good news too. Rose accompanied me to Hualien to a friend of hers. Hualien is as lovely and unpolluted as I remembered it. The sidewalks in downtown are actually made of green marble! Hualien is known for its gorgeous stones. Many of the women walk around with a new accessory around their necks—their dainty cell phones are worn as necklaces. And, the laws have changed so that foreign English teachers are welcome to teach in the language schools that have sprung up with the increase in population. When I feel better, I'll figure out what to do during my two months in Hualien.

My bronchitis is being treated by an elderly English-speaking doctor that another foreign teacher introduced me too. He has a small neighborhood clinic with only a nurse and a pharmacist. He has returned to his birthplace after years of being a doctor in the U.S., England, Japan, and even spent two years in the Vatican in Rome. I enjoy talking to him. He says I have a viral infection and I like the fact that he's treating me with gentle medication. He charges me very,

very little. When I asked him why, he said that people in the U.S. were very nice to him.

March 24, 2004

I have no idea where the inspiration came from, but it was the key to my happy days in Hualien. Taking advantage of Rose's friend, I wrote up an ad for the local paper which he translated into Chinese. I wrote that I wanted to be a live-in English tutor. With his telephone number in the ad, he could talk to the twenty people or so who called in response. From that beginning, I found a place to live and a couple of unusual jobs to go along with private tutoring.

I have been living in a Taiwanese couple's immaculate home within walking distance of the center of the city. Communication has been the biggest challenge because the parents don't speak English, and the two daughters, aged 11 and 14, are just learning English. But the mother, always with a ready laugh and a smile, tries very hard to communicate with me. In fact, it's quite amazing how deep our conversations can get with the aid of two dictionaries—I find the word I want in the English-Chinese dictionary, and she replies by showing me a word in her Chinese-English dictionary.

Homestays are popular in Taiwan. It's a cheaper way to travel than going to hotels. It's not quite a bed and breakfast, since food is not included. The third floor of their home has two rooms for guests. They gave me the bigger room, which has six double bed mattresses on the floor. This room is usually for small tours that come to Hualien to sleep on their way to the famous Taroko Gorge, but the wife explained to me that it was just for me as long as I chose to stay. They brought in a little desk and lamp for my workspace.

I never quite understood what the husband's job was, but he was a magician in the kitchen. He came home at different times every day on his motorscooter with baskets overflowing with all sorts of vegetables and many fish that I'd never seen before. My friend had told him that I couldn't have much salt or MSG. That surprised him, but didn't stop him from turning out an absolutely delicious array of very tasty food. I certainly will never forget the barbecue on their front patio where he kept cooking and we kept eating delicacies for at least a couple of hours. As a matter of fact, he has prided himself on never serving me the same meal twice. My conversations with him are limited, but this is a busy election time in Taiwan and he is solidly for the party called DPP that looks more favorably upon independence from China. The DPP has become much more powerful since the early 1990's when I taught in Taichung, but Taiwan remains deeply divided politically.

Both the daughters were very shy with me at first because they had never met anyone who didn't speak Chinese, but the younger one took a sudden turn toward me recently. She likes taking me on walks to different spots in the neighborhood, and she has taken more interest in learning English. In spite of my baby Chinese and her limited English, we still manage to babble happily together. She has her mother's charming smile.

The best exercise I have found in Hualien is an energetic walk through the hills of a park about a mile away. Had I been there in the early morning as most Chinese believe is the best time to wake up, I would have seen many older people winding through the paths and stopping at certain exercising stations set up for that purpose. However, by the time I arrive in the afternoon, it is nicely uncrowded with no competition at the truly lovely views from the hills out across the sea. Many of my happiest hours in Hualien have been spent plodding those scenic hills.

Sometimes I go in another direction to get to the sea. There isn't much of a beach to walk on because cement boulders are placed on the sand to prevent erosion, but there's a path alongside to walk on. From there, I wave hello from Hualien across the Pacific Ocean to Laguna Beach. On one fun day, the younger girl and her mother and I walked and biked a long way following the sea.

In fact, the family has taken me on several trips to scenic areas. Hualien is a very beautiful part of Taiwan that I've come to appreciate even more with my friendly family. Rose has come up a few times. And Virginia, who's a member in Taipei, introduced me to the Toastmaster's Club in Hualien, which I've attended several times. Frank even traveled to Hualien with his wife and children. They treated me to a luxurious hotel in another scenic area near Hualien. I've had a busy social life here.

Also from the same newspaper ad, I was offered a couple of unusual jobs that are much more interesting than my job in California. In fact, I'm writing my first book—a children's story about Japanese immigrants who came to Taiwan. Gathering the necessary information has been an adventure in itself. My mentors have been two Chinese people, only one of whom speaks English, and a tri-lingual Japanese doctoral student who is doing research on the Japanese immigration to Taiwan. When we get together, three languages fly around the room. The Japanese scholar thinks aloud first in Japanese, then translates himself into Chinese, and then English. I catch what I can. The three of them don't always agree on the facts of the history and politely argue about it. These sessions have been mentally draining, stimulating, and quite hilarious at the same time.

I eventually pieced together that China gave Taiwan to Japan in 1895 after losing a war. In the early 1900's, Japanese immigrants came to Taiwan to set up small communities and establish farms. Generally, they went into mountainous areas of Taiwan with aborigine populations as well as Taiwanese. Socially and environmentally, life was very different from Japan, which made the beginning very difficult for these new and unwelcome immigrants. After years of hardships and perseverance, the Japanese had thriving farms where they intended to stay. However, all Japanese in Taiwan were forced to leave almost overnight in 1945 after they lost World War II. The younger generation had never even been to Japan before.

There had once been such a thriving Japanese settlement not far from Hualien. A rotting old Buddhist temple from those days had recently been beautifully restored as a tourist attraction and a community center. While that period of history had been a sad time for Taiwan, they wanted to acknowledge their history and teach children about it. One of the people who hired me had hope that the center would become an English learning center for the poorer children whose parents couldn't afford the private after-school English schools.

I developed the tale of a mythical Japanese family of immigrants and told the story from the perspective of the children in the family. Each week I go to a local sixth grade class to tell them one more chapter. Because their English level is so low, my partner is the principal of the school who translates the story into Chinese. I make a simple English lesson out of it and add a type of activity such as drawing or having the children enact what is going on in the story.

Another unusual job that came about through my newspaper ad has been assisting a professor at the Buddhist University in one of his upper level business classes. He lived in the U.S. for years and speaks English fluently. However, he wants his students to be forced to communicate with someone who can't speak or understand Chinese. He feels so strongly that the students need to overcome their fear of talking to a native English speaker that he is willing to pay me most of his hourly salary for the three hours a week that I come.

Through my host family's connections, I have several private students to tutor that range in age from high school down to elementary school. I particularly enjoy private tutoring because I always learn more about the culture through my students.

April 12, 2004

My time in Hualien is winding down to its end. I'll leave for China very soon. The time of saying goodbye is hard. As a treat before leaving, my hostess took me, together with two high-school-aged students I've been tutoring, to an incredible spa in a mountain town called Jiaosi. We spent the entire day dipping in hot springs that resembled an artist's palette—the brown of added coffee, the deep pink of rose petals, the bright yellow of sulphur, as well as other colors. In other pools, cleverly positioned jets and sprays squirted hot spring water, massaging our backs, chests, legs, and arms. There were steam rooms and saunas. And, when we were waterlogged, we dried out on wonderfully warm, relaxing stone floors. I left as wrinkled as a prune and wondering when I would ever be able to find such a fantastic watery playground again.

I bought some little gifts for my Hualien friends and host family and took them out to a good buffet as a small thank you for all they had done for me. My host family had insisted on weighing me when I first came to their home. Just before I left, I had to get on the scale again to see how much I'd gained from the father's great cooking. To his delight, I had gained three pounds. But, he had gained six!

The Hualien press was invited to the restored Japanese temple to observe my last lesson with my sixth grade students right inside the temple. The children's drawings of the story I had made up were hung around the temple compound. The children expressed their thanks to me with words and cards. One goal had been for these children to experience being close to a foreigner, and they showed how successfully that goal had been reached.

In many ways, my time in Hualien has surpassed anything I had expected. However, something happened to me while I was here that has never happened to me before—I was sometimes homesick for my little patch of paradise in California. That surprised me because I have always been able to enjoy what there is around me rather than missing what isn't there. Yet, thoughts of reading on my quiet patio surrounded by my plants, and the ocean view from Laguna Beach sometimes crowded out other thoughts. While I really enjoyed the variety of jobs I had in Hualien, and was even offered a chance to return next fall to a full time job at the Buddhist Technology School, the going rate of pay for native English teachers is lower than what I need on a long term basis if I am to keep my home in California. Also, some aspects of the living conditions, and certainly weather, cannot compare to what I've left behind. Such things didn't matter to me before. Why do they matter now? Physically I can still do it, but my energy level is definitely not the same. Is this long trip telling me I'm entering a new phase in my life cycle?

April 19, 2004

The changes I expected to see in Hangzhou began right away when I saw Thomas's welcoming face at the airport. He happily put me into his new car—a Honda with more electronic gadgets than I know how to use. On the ride into Hangzhou itself, it was clear that the wealthy Chinese peasants have taken the saying, "A man's home is his castle" to heart. We whizzed past ostentatious Disneyland-like castles, huge homes complete with numerous turrets, towers, and vast balconies.

Years of memories have been flooding in. Whereas being in China always did seem like being in a time warp, I feel I'm in ten time warps at the same time. Hangzhou has been flying into the new millennium. Yet, around the corner are still the rundown old shacks that seemed so charming during the 1980's and 1990's. New buildings have grown up, bringing in more people and much more traffic. A tunnel for cars now allows one side of West Lake for pedestrians only, and the road around the lake is partly closed for some work to "improve" West Lake.

My friends inhabit different time warps too. Several of them, including Debbie's husband, have begun their own businesses. All of their businesses are showing promise, and some are financially thriving. Smith has bought a new home that cost more than mine in California. It's in a beautiful apartment complex that has a private, park setting. As has become common in even cheaper apartment blocks, clever exercise equipment is scattered around outdoors. Their complex even has children's playground equipment. In general, my friends who took risks are doing much better financially than those who stuck to a more secure path.

The energy vibrates in China now, reminding me of the energy level I felt in Vietnam. Being in China now is like riding a fast moving escalator fueled by the sheer energy of the people. The sleeping giant, after awakening groggily, is fully awake now. I still know that I'm not in a western city in a million different ways, but it is nowhere near as oriental as it used to be.

The changes are not all good. My eyes still ache from the pollution. Elizabeth sadly told me she no longer enjoys teaching because the students of China today are too self-centered. The sweetness and purity of the respectful Chinese students I taught no longer exist. And students can buy their way into schools now rather than being assigned by their test scores. She and her husband also complained that rich "outsiders" from other parts of China as well as abroad have bought a lot of property in Hangzhou, forcing housing prices to rise higher than Hangzhou's local people can afford. They are feeling pushed out of their own city.

Elizabeth took me with her one day to the greatly enlarged tourism school now located not too far from the new airport. Whereas the old tourism school where I'd taught had had perhaps a few hundred students, this campus was planned for 3,000. The school grounds were spacious indeed, including a three-story library building! The old school hadn't even had a library. A lily pond with a curving bridge surrounded the new hotel where students would practice their skills. Had it only been 16 years ago when I taught on the small campus surrounded by fields in a suburb of Hangzhou? The city of Hangzhou had expanded and gobbled it up.

I went to visit "my bench" along West Lake, and, thankfully, found it still there. I can't be sure it's exactly the same bench, but the placement, the trees, the rocks, and the water are. I put some of my son's ashes into West Lake because it has been a place I've loved for so many years. I shared with him in death what I couldn't have shared in life. I sat on that bench a long time. I used to wonder how old people just sat for so long in parks, but now I, too, sat as if glued to the bench and only reluctantly finally left. I feel a shift in me from "doing" to "being."

I walked the short distance to "Have A Bite," to eat. Over the years I had seen that restaurant through several reincarnations and many laughter-filled meals with my friends. The food had never been particularly good, but my favorite incarnation was when they had live classical musicians and candles. Alas, it is no more. The building had been gutted in preparation for a totally different purpose.

The schedule for my days in China is filling up quickly and happily, and started with an elegant buffet Thomas wanted to treat me to because he remembered his very first buffet I had taken him to many years ago. This time, there would be a very important person he wanted me to meet—his fiancée.

This time it was difficult to decide what gifts to bring the children. Pearl's daughter had always looked forward eagerly to what I would bring her. But, last time I visited, Pearl told me to stop spending money on gifts for the children because, not only was everything available in China, but it was cheaper. And it's true that the children are well supplied with just about everything in today's China. I took a chance and bought some jewelry in New Zealand for the girls, but it didn't go over very well. To me, it was exotic and unusual. To the children, it was just strange.

April 22, 2004

Internet cafés are still difficult to find in China. They are always dingy, smoky holes-in-the-wall that conjure up images of back rooms where one has to whisper, "Joe sent me," to get in. The computers are filthy and are brands I've never heard of. At least I can now reach hotmail.com, which used to be blocked in China. Thankfully, prices to use the computer are quite cheap and it's been a good way for me to reach people while I'm away.

Prices aren't all cheap in Hangzhou, though. I wouldn't be able to afford much of a life in China nowadays.

April 25, 2004

The roads in Hangzhou are dedicated to cars now. The slow, lowly pedicab has been outlawed. I was glad to see that smaller cities like Jiaxin still have pedicabs for hire. When Russell was at work, his mother was my tour guide for a couple of days. Our lack of a common language was adequately compensated by the delight we took in being together again.

We are the same age, but she has embarked on a new career in a China that offers more opportunities to those who want to try. She has entered a new industry in China—selling insurance. Although she usually sells to other countryside peasants, I watched as she easily and eagerly started up conversations with strangers we met along our way. Eventually, out came her business card. Russell told me she has been given awards by her company for her success as an insurance agent.

The "old" Jiaxin has expanded into the "new" Jiaxin with shiny, newly built highrises. We visited some new tourist sites. At one, I felt my old anger rise at being charged twice the price of Russell's mother's ticket. I assumed it was because I was a foreigner even though the foreigner's currency, FEC, had long ago disappeared. When I mentioned it to Russell after we got home, he said that I wasn't being charged more because I was a foreigner. Now I was being charged more because I wasn't a resident of Jiaxin. Is that any fairer? Perhaps, because I remembered that Disneyland charges Orange County residents less than other visitors from outside the county.

As in the old days in Jiaxin, a *weiguo ren*, foreigner, was a spectacle, especially when accompanied by an old, most likely uneducated countryside peasant woman. When people stared at us quizzically, Russell's mother proudly announced "*laushr*," teacher, to explain me. Russell's mother later told him that many people had asked her if she spoke English well. No doubt with a twinkle in her eye, she had replied, "*mamahuhu,*" just so-so.

Russell took me to work with him one day. Years ago, he started out with a road construction company as a translator for an American boss. When translators were no longer needed, he struggled to find a place for himself within the company. Now that expressways are common in that area, he was helping to manage an expressway service area, combining a hotel, restaurant, stores, and a gas station. They can't begin to keep up with the demand for new service areas. Everything becomes obsolete even as it is being planned. It's a stressful job.

April 27, 2004

I hadn't seen Benjamin's brother for several years. I had visited him a few times before in the special economic zone area of Shanghai called Pudong. There had been great hopes for what Pudong would mature into. Some said Shenzhen had been a training ground to figure out all the rough spots so that Pudong would not repeat its mistakes. I found that both Benjamin's brother and Pudong had matured well together.

Pudong is now a very appealing, architecturally attractive, still less crowded area on the other side of the Huangpu River. I appreciated the blue skies and a huge newly constructed lake and park designed by a foreign company. I had a wonderful time there, including an excellent American sirloin steak and an hour-long foot massage. During the foot massage, the masseuse said something was "*bu hao,*" not good. I couldn't understand what was not good, so I asked her to write it down. Later, my friend translated that it was my arteries and veins that were "not good." High blood pressure? High cholesterol? My feet weren't lying. Oh, dear!

On the very crowded Shanghai side of the river, I remarked at how clear and blue the sky was. My friend said that Shanghai has been taking the polluting factories out of the city limits, allowing the skies to clear. It was during the weekend, and happy visitors were everywhere around us. I got the impression for the first time of the pre-Mao history of Shanghai when it was truly international, cosmopolitan, and multicultural.

When China was in its period of pain and agony, it suffered alone. In today's world, it has become the marketplace for the world—1.3 billion new consumers who need <u>everything</u>.

April 29, 2004

A friend took me to a restaurant last night, which much more resembled a trip to Alice's Wonderland. The décor was artistic, strange, unpredictable, and yet attractive and colorful. The food had recognizable names and ingredients, but was put together in equally artistic, strange, unpredictable, and yet attractive and colorful ways. It cost what once was more than one month of his salary.

My last day in Hangzhou, I walked down the street where I used to bicycle. Then, it was an unpaved, dusty, narrow road. Now it has not only been paved, but lined with streams, bridges, and beautiful trees. It is almost spotlessly clean. It is gorgeous, simply gorgeous. The negative parts of China's rapid development do exist, but so do these beauty spots that somehow help to balance the equation.

Amazing China!

April 30, 2004

My very last dinner before leaving Hangzhou was one of those experiences that still can happen in the newly sophisticated China. During my first days in Hangzhou this trip, I had walked into a modern coffee bar where one sits on couches at tables instead of chairs and drinks coffee that is as expensive as in the U.S. They sometimes also have a western-style food menu. Pretty girls stand at the door to greet customers. When they saw me, they hurried to bring out the chef himself, who was, it seems, the only one who felt comfortable speaking English.

As I drank my coffee, the chef said that he had been well trained in western cooking and invited me to call him in advance so he could make me a delicious lasagna. He gave me his phone number.

I enjoyed talking to him and arranged to return for his lasagna for my last dinner in Hangzhou before flying to Shenzhen. When I arrived, he personally greeted me, escorted me to a table, proudly brought out enough lasagna for three people, and sat down to accompany me and converse while I ate more than I wanted to.

May 8, 2004

She sat at a child-like height behind the desk. Her small face was almost totally obscured by a facemask. Her graying hair showed her to be an older doctor in one of Shenzhen's hospital clinics. Several people surrounded the desk. There were two chairs other than where the doctor sat—one for the patient now being seen, and one for the next person in line. Everyone listened to the conversation between patient and doctor. I could not understand the conversation, but it seemed to refer to a blood test and possibly other lab work. The doctor wrote out several different forms after getting some information from the patient.

Next, she turned her attention to me. My friend said in Chinese that I had a cough. She asked if I had a fever and took my word that I didn't. She listened to my chest through a stethoscope, proclaimed something my friend couldn't translate, and then proceeded to write out forms for me to have a blood test and a chest x-ray. When my friend translated to her that I didn't want to take a blood test, she continued to write out the forms and then turned her attention to the next waiting patient.

Since I wasn't willing to go through a blood test, but since she had apparently heard something wrong in my lungs, Peter then drove me to a small clinic. There was no wait to see an unmasked young male doctor sitting behind a computer. He listened to my chest and also found a problem, which he identified as in the middle of my left lung. He then typed on the computer and came up with a Chinese cough suppressant and a western antibiotic. I had many questions to ask the doctor, but Peter didn't want to ask them. I wondered how the doctor could prescribe for a bacterial infection without knowing for sure that it was bacterial. Three months ago, the doctor in Hualien had said I had a viral infection, which antibiotics would not help.

I had always spent my time in Shenzhen in a hotel, but this time Peter was anxious for me to stay in his new apartment. It's gorgeous. The apartment complex, designed by a French architect, is brand new and very large. The grounds are beautiful and immaculate; the swimming pool is enormous and beckoned invitingly to me even though I was sick. Peter's bedroom, which he let me use, looks out upon a high hill with walking trails around it. This place is far nicer than the foreigners' compound we had walked around in 1998.

Peter's parents and their adorable little dog live with him. Once again, I think about how the lives of my friends' parents have changed along with the lives of their modern, wealthy children. The age of retirement is earlier in China, so these parents are now enjoying a life of leisure and travel, without having to worry about money. They can finally relax from the hard years behind them. Yet, with a puzzled look, one friend had told me she didn't understand why her parents say that the old days, even with its hunger and severe poverty, were better days than now. I think I understand them.

My deep bronchitis hasn't made me very good company, but Peter hasn't been able to spend much time with me anyway because of an unexpected business trip. He still works for the same company, but has risen to being in charge of his department. His parents are taking care of me while he's gone.

I'm soon on my way to Hong Kong for a couple of days and then on to Taiwan again (those long promised direct flights between China and Taiwan are still in the future, if ever) where I need to get healthy again.

May 12, 2004

If I had had a fever accompanying my bronchitis, I would not have been able to get into Hong Kong. As I stood in line for immigration, my temperature flashed above my head. I'm not sure how they did that technologically, but since the terrible SARS of 2003, it is impossible to enter any Asian country without one's temperature being taken automatically as one passes through. Usually, I haven't been aware of it in the airports I've used, but I couldn't miss seeing it as I went into Hong Kong.

May 14, 2004

I've always liked Hong Kong. Even though I wasn't at my best, I managed to see an old friend and re-visit some of the sights I love. Hong Kong is a happier, more vibrant place than on my last visit. Some of her spirit is returning, although her glory days are most likely over.

I took the chance to see an English-speaking doctor. He prescribed even stronger antibiotics (without knowing that the infection was bacterial), plus a steroid to knock out the bronchitis. I felt it was like shooting a fly with a rifle. I thanked him, and paid, but I won't take such powerful drugs.

May 15, 2004

Her very, very long hair was plaited down her back with the thickness of a straw mat. She was a poet from New York on her sixth visit to Tibet. Now she was in Hong Kong on her way to trek into Tibet leading two other women. She called me a "baby" at 60, so her age exceeded mine. She spoke with a gleam in her eye about climbing a 16,000-foot mountain to reach an over 18,000-foot mountain. But she still wanted to get my bottom bunk when I left the hotel dormitory room that morning. I told her I admired her, but didn't envy her, as I coughed my way out the door.

May 21, 2004

I was glad to see Virginia's welcoming face when I got back to Taiwan. I desperately needed some time to do nothing, and she and her husband are graciously letting me stay in an apartment in Taipei that they are not using right now. They are living in a very small rented apartment to be closer to their son's school.

One of the first things I did was call my friendly doctor in Hualien and whined about getting sick again and the strong medicine that the Hong Kong doctor had prescribed. He reassured me that I didn't need to take those drugs because he could tell from my voice that my bronchitis was getting better. I calmed down. How I wish I could find a permanent doctor in the U.S. that I trust as much.

May 28, 2004

I'm getting healthy again after taking it very easy in the big apartment. I've taken advantage of this time to do very little but catch up with my sleep and my health. I was able to enjoy some day trips with Virginia and had a wonderful reunion with one of my former Taichung students who is expecting her second child.

I also had the chance to see Rose a few times. She always thinks of such enjoyable things to do. I went out to her university and caught up with some of the other teachers I knew when I was teaching there. We visited some exquisite lotus ponds in full bloom in the countryside not far from the school. We never quite found the trails in the mountains we were looking for in one of the big parks, but we had unusual experiences walking in the calla lily fields. The government is trying to help the farmers combine tourism and farming for better profits. The area was lovely with the backdrop of those beautifully wooded mountains.

Rose's ethnic roots led us to a very beautiful part of the park where very fresh and very Taiwanese (as compared to mainland Chinese) foods were sold by vendors in simple stalls. Old people—like us and older—sat under massive trees eating, chatting, sleeping, getting massages, or having the hair removed from their faces with rubber bands. Rose said her mother had lived many years in an inexpensive room there. Rose said she hadn't appreciated it then, but now she sees it as a fitting end for herself. So, now I have a mental image of old Rose eating sweet potato soup, or fish balls and baby bamboo shoots, walking, sitting, and enjoying that beautiful park every day.

Dec. 10, 2004

This afternoon was one of simple pleasures. There was enough sunshine and warmth to sit on my patio and read. I watched the tiny hummingbirds flitting back and forth like restless leaves. It was quiet enough to hear the swish of the leaves on the trees as they responded to silent breezes. There was also the joy of the vagaries of my mind, flitting around much like the hummingbirds. There was the warmth of season's greetings that have started to arrive from faraway friends, reminding me what an incredible life I've had.

I've been very glad to be back in my little patch of California paradise. As I drive to the sea, I love the anticipation of my first sight of the ocean, etched in shades of gray or blue as it meets the sky. I've spent hours at my favorite view over the ocean, happily entertaining myself with watching the variety of people who also come to see the sea, the wild sea lions on the rocks, the scuba divers practicing, the dolphins occasionally passing by, the gulls, cormorants, and pelicans. Close to sunset, with my binoculars, I distort the gleam of the sun on the ocean into thousands of moving cell-like creatures rejoicing in a dance over the water. The shining, shimmering path the sun makes across the water and all the way to the cliff where I'm standing connects me to the sea and the sun. Soon, the sun throws out flames of red and yellow across the blue sky as it sinks gracefully behind Catalina Island. I feel at home.

Dec. 12, 2004

My first American-born grandchild entered the world today. I can only ponder how different his life will be from his Chinese mother, his Korean father, and his American honorary grandmother who once was a hummingbird.

20

MEDLEYS

THROUGH THE CROOK OF MY ARM

Through the crook of my arm wondrous things happen. Although I learned to swim as a young camper, it was in adulthood that I became an avid swimmer. To some, swimming is a form of exercise. To me, it is the gentlest, cheapest form of therapy. I have found beauty, peace, inspiration, and emotional healing while swimming around the world over the years. I, like the seal and the dolphin, am heavy and ungainly out of the water. It is only in the water that I can feel graceful and the true lightness of being.

A sense of joy in the water follows me in creeks, lakes, oceans, and pools. I have swum in a lake in California, which was said to be a bottomless, extinct volcanic crater. I once swam three hours in a Washington state lake to celebrate my birthday. And I can recall the tingle of swimming in an ice-cold lake where the glacier that fed it could be seen at its edge.

Through the crook of my arm I have seen beautiful sights. In Israel, I splashed happily in fresh, cool water under tall date palms and a deep blue sky. When I lived in the picturesque city of Santa Barbara, California, which is sandwiched between mountains and the Pacific Ocean, I often swam in an outdoor pool where each stroke that brought my head out of the water revealed the mountains framed by the crook of my arm. On the other side of the world, an outdoor pool on the island of Coloane belonging to Macau gave me a similar vignette of the nearby high hills I often enjoyed walking through.

Swimming clears my brain. Without the normal distractions of daily life, my mind feels freer to wander, to meditate, and to create. It was in the water of the pool at my university where I studied for my Master's degree that I wrote my papers and prepared for exams. While swimming around a pool in odd patterns that puzzled my colleagues and students in Taiwan, I created an absolutely wonderful poem and came up with just the right name for my first Chinese grandchild.

However, it was in a pool in Macau that I found the spiritual "first aid" that I needed to help me get through an emotionally wrenching experience. I went to the pool in mental agony. As I stroked through the water, I imagined that my mental pain was leaving me and going out into the pool. Somehow, the thought of the water drawing the pain out of me did release some of my mental anguish. I have felt grateful ever after for the comfort the water offered me in my time of distress.

Some of my most magnificent views of China appeared through the crook of my arm. It was a cold November day when I first saw Thousand Islands Lake in Zhejiang Province. My first thought from the boat was how clean it was and how wonderful it would be to swim in. The second time I saw the lake was during the summer months, but, alas, it was unseasonably cool and rainy. The third time—aahh—it was just right. The soothing waters of this man-made lake offered views of mountaintops, now made into islands. Lake swimming is my favorite, and China's cleanest gem was my happy playground.

I have often been caught up by the wondrous cloud formations that one flies in and around in a plane, but I never expected to swim in a cloud. In Turkey, I did. Unlike other hot springs I've visited, the water at Pamukkale is a very comfortable body temperature and has no foul smelling sulphur. When I sank down into those silken waters, a total sense of well-being suffused my body. I have never felt anything quite like it before or since.

I didn't speak or read Korean, but how different could a swimming pool in Korea be? The first time I went swimming there, I did everything wrong. In the dressing room, I changed into my bathing suit and prepared to lightly shower before entering the pool. Wrong! A woman looked at me with concern and pantomimed to me to take off my suit. Not understanding, I continued to the showers. Before I reached them, another woman took my bathing suit straps off my shoulder. Then, an attendant working there pulled down my suit.

When I got to the showers, I understood. A naked scrubdown was required before putting on one's suit. In the shower room, women were gaily chatting, scrubbing each other's backs, sitting and even laying on the floor under the spray of the shower. What was expected here was to scrub off at least one layer of skin—and then to put on one's bathing suit.

It is difficult to pull on a wet bathing suit over a dripping body, especially my quite large dripping body. As I was inadequately tugging to pull the top of my suit up and the bottom part down, I felt another pair of hands helping me in a motherly fashion. Middle-aged Korean women were always doing such helpful things for me.

Since the pool was a place for socialization, very loud noise called music by some blared from the omnipresent speakers one finds everywhere in Korea. But the pool was cool and wide and I was grateful for the water that covered my ears and blocked out the music. Several swimming women smiled warmly and curiously at me, but lack of a common language limited communication to simple smiles and nods.

Koreans have very definite ideas about what stays clean and dry. Showers are wet; dressing rooms stay dry. But I had on my dripping suit while my locker in the dressing room held my towel and showering supplies. I had not put together the need to leave all my showering paraphernalia on a rack in the shower room. With an apologetic look at the attendant, I walked and dripped to my locker. She, with a look of disbelief at how uncultured I was, followed after me wiping up my every wet footprint. I tried to put on my face an expression that communicated, "I'll do better next time."

When I swim, I am never sure who will accompany me. For it is in my dream-like state that people from my past will appear. And so that is the time when my former mother-in-law sometimes comes to mind. Our relationship spanned many years. After my divorce, she no longer wanted contact with me. However, she was a regular, avid swimmer. When I swim, I know that somewhere she is also still swimming. It somehow fills in the gap between us.

It is in some of the most alive oceans where I have felt the most awed, and the least comfortable. In Hawaii, Key West, Jamaica, Tobago, the Indian Ocean, "down under" in Australia, and the blue-green waters of Fiji, I swam among the fish. It was truly fantastic to join a small part of an underwater society for a short time. The fish arrayed in outrageous colors and designs, the sea creatures, and the coral were truly another world. Although I was fascinated and amazed by the beauty, I sincerely regret that I could not shake off the feeling of being an unwanted intruder in a strange world. But I am forever grateful that I have at least peeked into this wondrous other world.

Swimming has given me countless hours of discovery and joy, and will, I hope, continue to be an adventure. Besides wading in memories of places I've swum, I can also look forward to exploring new depths I'll reach in other places and spaces I'll swim. Water, water, everywhere—and I'm very glad of it.

BEGGARS

Beggars confound me, confuse me, anger me, and immediately arouse my sympathy, and often my guilt. My guilt button presses oh, so easily—white toward black, have toward have nots, healthy toward the handicapped, American toward

Vietnamese, and doubtlessly many others. The anxiety of going out and having to run a gauntlet of beggars has sometimes made me a prisoner.

While some beggars are whiney and pathetic, others are demanding and insistent. But sometimes I have been impressed by the dignity and humanity of beggars I have encountered. In one instance, while waiting for a train in China, an old man and his wife came into the small waiting area. His wife was blind, but she sang for us and then they both walked around from person to person to collect what was offered. Since our train was late, my Chinese friend sat and talked to the man who explained he had been a soldier who fought for China, but had now been forgotten by his country.

There are beggars who want to sell you something you may or may not want. They make me feel I am their last hope in life, holding their fate within my hands. My backpack usually bulges with such items.

Some beggars stick with you like glue while walking down a street until you finally give them some money. There was such a beggar lady who finally got some money out of me. Then, noticing how much trouble I was having lugging my luggage, she smiled and good-naturedly shouldered a bag all the way to my hotel.

Often I have tried to lighten a child beggar's life by offering some money along with a balloon, or a gaily-colored postcard to connect with the little child that still might be within. More often than not, I see the light come on in their eyes and they briefly become a playful child again.

Over a one-week visit to Hangzhou, I walked along the SuDi near "my bench" several times. I was approached each time by an elderly man who only had one hand. I gave him money each time. He became my daily greeter with a little smile and nod of his head to say "thank you." One day I saw him at a later time of day. He was walking and talking with a friend. Miraculously, he now showed two hands protruding from the sleeves of his jacket. Apparently, I saw him after his "work day" had ended.

However, there are many beggars I see who were either intentionally or unintentionally maimed. Asia gives few options to their handicapped but to beg. I usually give to them and feel proud that the U.S. offers so many services to disabled people.

Con artists are more dishonest and sophisticated beggars. Once, when I was on my own in Hangzhou, a small, wizened, countryside lady half my height and weight was selling fruit in baskets that she carried on her shoulders. Some instinct told me she was going to cheat me, and yet my mind and my actions were not in synch. I had often watched my Chinese friends haggling endlessly when buying, insulting the quality of the items or insisting the hand-held scale was inaccurate. I didn't try that and just accepted her price. When I went to give her the money, she noticed a bill of a larger denomination in my wallet and indicated she would give me change for it. I had seen Richard refuse to accept money from a back alley moneychanger in Beijing because of the way he counted out the money. She palmed the money and counted it out in the same way. While my mind slowly grasped that she had shortchanged me, this magician/thief quickly disappeared in spite of her bulky burden of fruit.

It embarrasses my Chinese friends when beggars surround me. They ashamedly apologize for their countrymen and fumble in their own pockets or angrily send them off. It is uncomfortable for all of us. No matter in which country, in spite of my friends' warnings that begging is a "scam," I have come to the conclusion that I give because it makes me feel better than not giving. I can remember the dirty faces of begging children in Vietnam and China to whom I did not give—and I still feel sorry to this day that I didn't.

So, what does it really matter that the same dirt-encrusted little baby is passed around during the day from beggar woman to beggar woman? A little money goes a long way in terms of strengthening my image, my country's image, and that of my tourist kin in general. I am lucky to be healthy, to be able to travel, to live a life of my own choosing. Giving to beggars seems a small way of appreciating that I do not have to beg. And, quite to the contrary of the fakes my friends warned me about, I have read that some people do credit begging with actually getting them through hard times.

VARIATIONS ON A TOILET

It looked quite ordinary from the outside, standing under a tree along the roadside in Hokianga, New Zealand. Stepping inside, I pressed a button and the door closed. Classical music drifted into the immaculate little room with the very clean toilet. I pressed another button and the toilet paper rolled down. After washing at the sink, I reluctantly pressed another button that made the concert conclude and the door open. As I stepped outside, the door closed again and a loud, very unmusical noise commenced as the toilet dutifully scrubbed and sanitized itself.

The vast majority of toilets I have used around the world were definitely not as pleasant. Several in China might have been called downright traumatic because of the unsanitary conditions, lack of privacy, and the rather delicate balance required to squat. Chinese learn how to squat firmly from childhood, not only for elimination, but also for sitting comfortably anywhere they are without a chair. Anatomically, squatting over a toilet facilitates proper elimination. Chinese do it so naturally that I have seen shoeprints on western-style toilet seats in airplanes while traveling between Asia and the U.S.

Flushing has as many variations as the style of toilet—from none as in the trains in China where it all disappears down onto the tracks left behind, to the occasional sweep of water down a long trough in a public toilet, to the gentle but not always effective American swirl, and the New Zealand gush of water like a waterfall cleansing the bowl.

Toilet paper can be brown and rough in the Chinese countryside, or in tiny little packets of inefficient tissues that girls carry everywhere with them in China and Taiwan. Toilets, toilet accessories, and toilet culture are just another aspect of the fascinating and sometimes unpredictable similarities and differences found around the world.

THE PINNIPED AFFAIR

It's hard to believe there was a time I couldn't have even guessed the meaning of the word, "pinniped." Since 2001, I have spent most of my Sunday afternoons in the company of the creatures with that lofty appellation. I know I'm in love.

Although I can't claim it was love at first sight, there was a definite attraction I felt when I wandered into a marine mammal rescue center in Laguna Beach on my way to somewhere else. As the docent on duty explained facts about the animals I saw that day, she mentioned that she was a volunteer. I actually felt a thrill run through me when she said that. And I signed up. The duties of an animal care volunteer seemed just too energetic and risky given my slow reaction time and no health insurance. I thought I could perhaps handle being a docent.

Given the natural patterns of seal and seal lion rescue, the center's busiest time is usually in the spring and early summer. Slower months allow more time to read up on pinnipeds, ask questions of the staff, and just enjoy being in the sun and company of whichever pinniped patients we have at the time. Gracie, a beautiful, large, misnamed male Great Egret usually hangs out nearby waiting opportunistically for fish at feeding time.

I have gone from not having a clue as to the differences between seals and sea lions to telling people how to distinguish our three main groups of patients—sea lions, harbor seals, and elephant seals. I have gotten to know some of the staff, also mainly volunteers, and came to understand why they choose to spend their leisure hours cleaning out pens and risking being bitten by their ungrateful patients. I discovered a different group of people than I had known before. Being with people who, for the most part, enjoy being with animals more than people, made me suspect I was more in synch with them—and becoming moreso as time goes by.

The patients are named by the rescuers according to the seasons (Summer, Winter), holidays (Pumpkin Pie, Morticia, Vixen, Dasher, and Blixen), where they were rescued (Nuke from the area of the San Onofre nuclear power plant), movie heroes (Frodo and Gandalf), current events (Manhattan who arrived just after 9/11), size, (Little Tyke), and personalities (Vicious because he bit a volunteer). Sometimes we go through periods of naming them according to themes, such as different types of cheese, pasta, and fashion designers.

The names are not given to them so we can "talk" to the animals. As a matter of fact, the sign "Don't talk to the Animals" is for the staff as well as the visitors. These are wild creatures, and they will be returned to the wild when healthy again. Bonding to humans is not a goal and definitely not preferable for these animals to whom people usually mean trouble, pain, and even death.

But it is very hard for me not to talk to the animals. I understand and appreciate the rationale for the rule, so I abide by it. However, I sometimes stoop down to make contact with them in some small way. This must suffice for communication and, strangely, it does. After all, they don't know English anyway. We do not talk, touch, pet, or cuddle them. But we do "connect" with them on some human to pinniped level.

There have been a handful of exceptions to the "no touching, talking, cuddling" rule. These have been sea lion infants whose mothers died from a fearful disease, in part caused by humans. Domoic acid poisoning destroys the brains of pregnant sea lion mothers-to-be who feed on large numbers of anchovies and sardines in the springtime before giving birth in the summer. The normal algae blooms that the anchovies and sardines eat are abnormally fertilized, at least partly by the phosphates and nitrates that we add to the runoff from the land into the sea.

Since the sea lion mother normally has a close, intimate relationship with her baby for eight to twelve months, the infants simply die without deep bonding, much like a failure to thrive human baby. And so we have hand-raised, cuddled, bottle fed, and played with these infants. But, since we are not able to teach them how to survive in the wild, we raise them for about six months and then find a permanent zoo or wildlife park for the rest of their lives.

Over the years, I remember several animals as individual personalities. Summer was brought in looking exactly like the starving sea lion in one of our posters. Every rib poked out of her pathetic body. Parasites and worms had robbed her body of nutrition. Slowly she came back to life again and was returned to the wild looking like a poster sea lion for "happy and healthy."

Little Tyke was a harbor seal that lost her mom before she was taught how to fish. After being force-fed, she didn't seem interested in learning how to fish for herself. Patiently probing the child psychology of a pinniped's mind, one of the staff tried various ways of giving fishing lessons to Little Tyke. Eventually, Little Tyke got the hang of swallowing a fish, but had no interest in "catching" it. Since we feed them dead fish that don't move, the patient staff tied a string to the fish to make it wiggle in the water. Little Tyke became more interested, but was frightened to put her head deep into the water in the big pool. What to try next? A kiddie pool was the answer because Little Tyke eventually dared to put her head into the shallow water to scoop up the fish.

Because Little Tyke was so young when she came to us, she stayed a couple of months beyond the usual two or three. After five months, she was released with another buddy harbor seal. Her recollections of the open sea were few and long ago because she had only spent about two weeks in the wild. When she was brought close to the sea, and her kennel door was opened, she only tentatively came out. Overwhelmed, she stuck like glue to her buddy. With several looks back at us with confusion—and did I detect excitement?—she followed her bigger adopted brother. We hoped she'd be as happy, healthy, and well fed as she had been with us. I can't deny I had a little lump in my throat.

But the very first release I saw was the incarnation of pure joy. Three sea lions that had been together for a few months were brought "home" together. When their kennel doors were opened, they literally raced for the sea and kept going and going and going—out and out and out—and, most amazingly, porpoising in absolute synchrony all the way. "There they go," said a man watching them, "sharkfood."

The reality of the dangers we had sent them out into was a sobering thought. Not only could they be killed by storms and sharks, but also by the intentional and unintentional cruelty of humans. Such was the fate of two magnificent male sea lions that were shot within a month by a pellet gun. Although fishermen will sometimes club, gaff, or shoot sea lions competing for the same fish, these two seemed to be shot for sport. That humans can kill humans for fun boggles my mind, but a human who takes aim and shoots a non-threatening animal to make it suffer is beyond my comprehension. I watched helplessly as they died from man's inhumanity to animals.

Pinnipeds have taught me about humans. I watched Morticia, a three-year-old sea lion straining and groaning in constipation (which we eventually learned was due to tumors). A young friend of mine was going through a difficult time. When we got together, I watched the strain on his face as he attempted to tell me the pain he was feeling—but, like Morticia, couldn't get it out. Watching him was like watching Morticia. She taught me to be more patient with my friend and accept his struggle to give words to his feelings.

It is not only Walt Disney who anthropomorphizes animals into characters we can understand. And yet, watching the seals and sea lions, I can really see many of the same characteristics of humans. Some adjust easily to the unfamiliar surroundings and human caretakers. Some become aggressive. Some passive-aggressively refuse to eat in a show of resistance to their caretakers. Some are playful, curious, and cute. Others behave much like brats and bullies who gang up on weaker members of their own species.

Is it only my imagination when I see dignity and stoicism in the face of a dying animal? Their pain and suffering is universal. Do some know they are dying? Ask the caretaker who had a young sea lion crawl into her lap, put its head on her shoulder, sigh, and die. One might expect this of a trained animal who had bonded to a human trainer, but our animals are wild and unbonded. We are brought together by their medical needs. While there is no encouragement of bonding, there is definitely communication.

Humans agonize endlessly, politically, and morally, about euthanasia, but there is no need for Kevorkians to champion the cause in the veterinary world. It has long believed that putting animals to "sleep" is humane. At our center, after a sedative is administered, I have watched our staff of caretakers stand protectively around the animal, much like a deathbed vigil, while the solution that will stop its heart is given.

Death is an inescapable consequence of life, whether for a plant, an animal, or a human. This is a reality no one can change. Once a seal, sea lion, or dolphin dies in our care either naturally or by euthanasia, our vet performs a necropsy. I have found it interesting that some of the animal care workers will do anything to keep an animal alive, but once it's dead, they don't watch the necropsy. I feel sad that the animal has died, but I am keenly interested in watching the necropsy.

Since these are mammals, it's like seeing myself from the inside out—stomach, bladder, liver, lungs, heart, etc. "Just like us," the vet often comments as he cuts, slices, and probes. Some parts are very different from that of humans. I wasn't sure why one of the staff's mouths dropped open during a dolphin necropsy. Yes, the two extraordinarily long and full sausage-like testicles were indeed impressive. It is often during a necropsy that we can see all too clearly the cancer, the stomachs and intestines clogged with indigestible plastic bags and balloons, fishhooks and lines, and other indications of how humans are destructively changing the environment for all living creatures.

Getting to know the animals and their caretakers has enriched my life in many ways. The pinnipeds led me to study oceanography at our community college. During the oceanography course, I heard some enticing information about Iceland. I chose going to Iceland as my celebration for my 60th birthday. My desire to see whales in the wild strengthened and, in February, 2005, I spent an absolutely incredible afternoon surrounded by gray whales in Baja California, Mexico.

Now that I have mentally entered a complex watery world I never even imagined, I envy my pinniped friends who can close their nostrils, collapse their lungs, and almost stop breathing underwater. I envy their grace in the water and their comfort in a world that is so foreign, fascinating, and frightening to me.

A WHALE OF A TALE

I've made it once again to another place where I know there are whales. But I've never been able to actually see a whale in the wild. The day is beautiful—warm and sunny. The large lagoon is quite pretty with its fringe of white sand dunes. As the boat skips over the waves with the sea air and the wind in my face, I can enjoy just this. But I really do hope this will be my time to see a whale.

Can that be a whale? Yes, I see a mass in the water spouting its air through its two blowholes. One of the twelve passengers on our small boat shouts, "There's one." And another whale is lifting its huge head out of the water spyhopping just like in the picture I put over the bathroom sink and looked at every day for a year.

Yes, I'm seeing whales—for real—in the wild! They're so huge as they glide by silently without even the tiniest splash. I enjoy the way they are at one with the water. How I wish I could take in 360 degrees with my eyes. I hate to miss any chance to see them. I'm taking pictures even though I know I'm too far away to get a decent shot.

Is that—yes, it's a baby swimming beside its mother. A 1500-pound baby is so adorable! After the 5,000 mile migration from the Arctic to Baja California, Mexico, then delivering the big bundle of joy, how can the mother produce 50 gallons of milk a day for the baby? And she hasn't even eaten since she left the Arctic months ago. Nature's adaptations defy logic.

I think—yes, that baby has just fallen or intentionally tumbled off mom's back. The tail is so tiny and cute compared to mom's. Wish I had been fast enough to get a shot of that.

They said there were 1500 gray whales in this lagoon at the last count only a week ago. How wonderful to be hanging out on a sunny day in the company of these amazing creatures. I want my son to be a part of this. I took him along in the only way I could—in a film canister. I release this small amount of his ashes. "Be free, my son. Swim with the whales." The others on the boat comment on what looks like a spot of black scum on the water. They conjecture what it might be. Only I know it is my son coming to swim with the whales in the eternity he now inhabits.

My roll of film is finished. Oh, no! My finicky camera refuses to reload the next roll—at the worst possible time. Or is it such a catastrophe? I want to be more of a participant than an observer. And one of the people on the boat has been snapping constantly. Maybe she'll share her photos and I'll have a single focus on the whales without a camera lens between us.

With the boat's motor off, the silence is lovely, punctuated only by excited shouts of "There's one." But no, it's not really so silent. I've never heard such a sound in a sea before. I can actually hear the whales breathing all around me. I know it's the whales that are breathing, but I feel the water, the sea itself, is alive in a way I've never experienced it before.

We begin to distinguish the footprints of the whale—flat areas on the sea where they've gone down. I know that sometimes the whales will come very close to the boats. I'd like that, but if it doesn't happen, I feel content just being in the company of whales, inhabiting the same place on a warm, sunny day.

Oooooooh, my god! There's one right next to our boat. It seems to go on forever, like watching a freight train roll by. But it's going by so slowly, so intentionally. I am trying to digest what I've seen when someone says, "It's still down there." I can see the mottled barnacle-encrusted bulk, and its fins are distinct. It's going under the boat. I rush the short distance to the other side to watch it come up again and roll over ever so gently. Someone from the boat puts out her hand and touches it as it glides by.

Now everyone wants the chance to touch it. But this one stays tantalizingly just out of reach. "It's too close," exclaims the photographer who no longer needs a zoom lens.

Its eye! I want to see her eye! Now we know "it" is a "she" because of the two slits we saw when she went by on her back. She's much too big to be a baby, and we don't see a baby around her. She has come to play with us. It's true. She actually wants to be with us. Why else does she follow our boat?

She can hold her tail still in the air! I didn't know whales could do that. It looks like a huge flower growing out of the sea. With the backdrop of the blue sky, blue-green water, and the white sand dunes, it is a perfect picture. Hope the photographer got it. But I have it in my memory just in case. Her tail is very distinctive because there is a rather large half-moon bite out of it. Wonder what tail tales she could tell us.

How beautiful! She's a ballet dancer too. What an exquisite slow motion unfolding of her tail as she dives down a bit beneath the surface. Those are the same powerful flukes that they once used in self-defense when they were called "devil fish" in the sad days of whaling. We are in the same Scammon's Lagoon, named for the captain who turned the waters deadly red from the whales' blood.

What's she doing with her tail now? She's swirling the water. She's actually splashing us—not enough to hurt us, but just enough to hear us gaily laughing. How honored I feel that she wants to play with us mere mortals after all the terrible things we have done to her kin and their home, the ocean. One flip of her massive fluke could easily destroy our boat and us. But the furthest emotion from my mind is fear. I am thrilled, fascinated, reverent.

And now I really must see her eye. It's so hard to find among the barnacles. Even when her huge head comes out to spyhop so close to the boat, I still can't find the eye. And then she passes by—and I see her eye. She's not looking at me, but still I feel a jolt of pure joy go through me. It is magical. It is mystical. It is the most incredible single moment of my life!

I relax. I have seen a whale's eye. But I continue to dash from side to side of the boat. What's that? Someone is handing me a box lunch. I don't want to eat. I want to play some more with the two whales who have befriended us. Oh no! The boatman has started the engine. We're leaving this idyllic spot. When I look back, our whale is holding her tail with the half-moon bite up in the air. I'm sure she is saying goodbye, and I want to cry. I bid her "*namaste,*" and the boat picks up speed.

Now I have finally seen whales in the wild. But I have done something even better. I have played with whales and seen the eye of a whale. Many years ago, I re-named myself Zima—a word I adapted from the Swahili *mzima*, meaning "whole" or "well." I have never been more *mzima* than I am today.

20 chpts / 425 pgs

LAST WORDS

I am now old, and my young students are middle-aged. They have spread all over the world—England, Germany, France, Singapore, New Zealand, Canada and several parts of the United States. Most of them are married, and a couple of them have divorced. All are doing well financially, and more than a few of them have even become millionaires. The many letters between us that lovingly nurtured these relationships over so many years have now turned into shorter, less frequent, and less poetic e-mail messages. My next visit to China is planned for spring of 2007 when Max, who found his pot of gold at the end of the rainbow in Las Vegas where he's a poker dealer, and his wife want to arrange a big birthday party for me in Hangzhou, China, with as many friends as can come.

Since 1988, I have watched the rapid changes in China as though through the speed of time-lapse photography. China has once again become a world power. Some fear it will become a dangerous super power in international politics. SARS and the danger of an epidemic of Avian Flu loom threateningly in the future while the country vibrates in a frenzy of energy.

The long time connection between Jews and China has deepened. The city of Kaifeng was once known for its community of Chinese Jews. Later, Jews escaping Hitler gratefully accepted China's life-saving offer to shelter them from the Holocaust. Many of them settled in Shanghai to wait out World War II. In 2005, the woman who headed the same Israeli agency against child abuse where I'd been an intern in 1984 went to China in one of many exchange programs. It is now possible to attend weekly religious services with a rabbi at a Chabad House in Beijing. And December 2005 marked the first *Chanukah* celebration at the Great Wall of China with the rabbi lighting the candles.

I have read that the assimilation of Ethiopians in Israel has not been smooth. They remain mostly at the bottom rung in education and jobs. As with other waves of Jewish immigration, time will make the major difference. Israel continues to suffer through more long years of instability and danger. Many more cars have been bombed since mine, and suicide bombers have made daily life for the average Israeli much more tenuous. The major difference over the years has been a wider acceptance of an eventual separate Palestinian state next to Israel. People in many other countries have now come to understand much better what fear in

Israel is like because terrorism has spread worldwide, haunting subways, airplanes, office towers, buses, and entertainment venues.

Writing this book was itself a very different kind of journey than any I've taken before. Reliving these years through the details of the journals and letters made sights, faces, smells, tastes, and experiences return to me in a vibrant, overwhelming profusion. I started out wanting to write the book, but very quickly the Muse became my very demanding master. The feeling was like a movie I once saw in which one of the actors making a movie couldn't separate his real life from that of the characters in the movie. In similar fashion, my past and present blurred until daily chores and activities became burdensome, annoying distractions from writing. The present dimmed, my past took over, and the future went blank. Finishing the book became more and more important to me. My life couldn't move forward without going backward first.

Rather like an insistent playmate, the keyboard summoned me any time of day or night. Whether I was in a theatre watching a ballet, reading the newspaper, or even in the shower, I could hear the silent yet strident call to return to the keyboard. When the Muse dictated to me, I obeyed by scribbling words, phrases, ideas on scraps of paper that appeared everywhere around my home. I even pulled off the road into a parking lot to write down something that wouldn't stop niggling at my mind. Just the "right word," or the best turn of a phrase became my first thought upon awakening, and the last thought that kept me from sleeping. It was both exhilarating and exhausting.

The mind mellows memories and even eliminates some unpleasant ones. The journals and letters tell it like it happened. A book written with the 20/20 of hindsight would have been quite different. As the memories swarmed and buzzed around in my mind, I resisted writing with the knowledge of how it all turned out. Having the wisdom that hindsight gives, I understood some of what I had written better. But I purposely kept in some of my false impressions. I didn't want to make myself any smarter than I was at the time. I wanted the book to show some of the emotional and mental odyssey my long journey took me on.

I am proud of having traversed so many miles and cultures. I was a sculptor of sorts who could carve out niches for myself wherever I went. Learning another culture is like slowly peeling an onion, layer by layer, and cannot be hurried. And I took with me what I call, "the lesson of Kabuki." While watching Kabuki Theatre in Japan, I learned not to be judgmental about other cultures because there are so many things I am not able to appreciate or adequately understand.

No matter how eloquent they may be, how paltry words are to express experiences. They pale in comparison. A book, no matter the size, can only convey glimpses into the depth and breadth of what was seen, felt, done, thought. Like a camera's eye, it can convey only a limited portion of what can be seen. That said, writing as I traveled became the continuing thread through the years, connecting all the disjointed pieces of my life. The book has become the anchor for my drifting memories. It is my heart trying to write itself.

I have written this book because I never would have discovered Bali without that aging book on the dusty back of a library shelf that someone bothered to write. I wrote it for the people I know who have said, "I wish I could have traveled like you," as well as those who said, "I love to read about your travels because you do things I'd never do." And, I wrote it for myself. Not only does it remind me of why I'm unmarried and poor today, but it captures as best I can what, in many instances, can never be seen again, as well as the intangible value of the best years of my life.

Yet, all that I have accomplished through my travels is not what I consider to be the greatest achievement of my life. That honor goes to a hilltop in the city of Santa Barbara that I single-handedly saved from being destroyed by a housing development. Talking to those hills gave me the strength to fight for them. I convinced the city Planning Commission to turn down the developer's request. Many years later, other people pushed for the area to become a park forever.

In 1979, I renamed myself after giving up everything I had thought I wanted. Something very deep inside pushed me into the unknown. It was the most painful decision of my life. I knew there would always be a hole in me for leaving the husband I loved. I felt neither whole nor well. So, I fashioned a name for myself that had embedded in it my hopes for becoming whole and well. I used Swahili because Kenya was the last place my husband, son, and I visited as a family.

It was during the years, miles, and experiences contained within these pages that I traveled the path toward growing into the wholeness and wellness of my name, Zima. I am now ready at last to set Memoirs of a Middle-aged Hummingbird into flight. And I can begin the next journey into my future.

978-0-595-39460-9
0-595-39460-4

Printed in the United States
60088LVS00003B/79-102

9 780595 394609